THEY TOUCHED OUR HEROES FOR THE LAST TIME

Repatriation of Fallen POWs and Other Tales

TRUE STORIES OF LIFE AND DEATH

by Major John E. 'Jack' O'Connor USAF (RETIRED)

Independent Publisher
BROKEN ARROW, OKLAHOMA

ISBN: 978-1-7923-1201-4

Special thanks to Bradford E.L. Heath
Linda Hight
AircrewRemembered.com
Stefans & Kelvin Youngs
Susan Coman I Coman Creative I Tulsa

To order additional copies:
Contact: Major John Emmett O'Connor
OurHeroes12@gmail.com

This book could not have been written without the patience, understanding and encouragement of Kathleen Garringer

To Ron,
  Thanks for your service
  to our country.

[signature]
MAJOR, USAF, RETIRED
07/28/2019

DEDICATIONS

*A very special dedication to my lovely daughters
and their equally lovely mother, Bobbie*

Brenda, Patricia, Michelle, and Tina

This book is also dedicated to my comrades who died while performing their assigned flight duties and were killed or severely wounded in action:

AIRMEN OF THE 1009TH SPECIAL WEAPONS SQUADRON

TSgt Richard Brown, 30 August 1956
WB-50, Eielson AFB, Territory of Alaska
Crew Member on "Golden Heart"

TSgt Claude Burgess, Sept 1961
WB-50, Yokota AB, Japan

TSgt Charles Heckman, 21 April 1964
WB-47, Eielson AFB, Alaska

SSgt James Turk, 28 Dec 1956
WB-50, Yokota AB, Japan

AIRMEN OF THE 776TH TAS, 374TH TAW, CLARK AB, PHILIPPINES

Crew of Eight from 776th TAS, April 22, 1974
Clark AB, Philippines
Killed on take-off in C-130E from
Anderson AFB, Guam, USA

This book owns a special meaning for those men and women of the Military History Center who inspired, supported and encouraged me to write this book. Without them, it would not have happened.

Director: Brigadier General Thomas Mancino (RET)
Executive Assistant: JeanE Bailie
Administrative Assistant: Cathy Johnson
Lead Docent: Dennis Hoch
Honorary Lead Docent: Maggie Bond

Docents

Earl Laney	Brad Heath
Mitch Reed	Michael Tarman
Dennis Franchini	Janet Viel
Kenneth Collins	Jonathan Colburn
Oscar Nipps, Jr	Greg Baile
Cameron Howerton	Tim Decouq
John Jeffries	Dan Eiler
Howard Coy	Jim Reib

Volunteers

Kenneth Cook	Lindsey Donaldson
Claudia Price	Steve Olson
James Oestreich	Susan Virdel

Service Officers for DAV

Royce Caskey	Lou McGowan
Howard Coy	ITI Pete Collorafi
George Hedrick	

Flight Instructors

Earl Laney	Tim Collins

U.S. AIR FORCE

THEY TOUCHED OUR HEROES FOR THE LAST TIME

Repatriation of Fallen POWs and Other Tales

CONTENTS

Military pallbearers carry the remains of an American who died in North Vietnamese captivity from a U.S. Air Force transport plane at U Tapao AB in Thailand. (AP)

A Sad Journey to Thailand: Reds Return 12 Fallen POWs

U TAPAO AIR BASE, Thailand (AP) — The long, last trip home for 12 Americans who died in North Vietnamese captivity began here Wednesday.

Twelve silver-colored metal caskets draped with new American flags were carried one by one off a U.S. Air Force C130 transport that had brought them from Hanoi.

Only a handful of military spectators were on hand as the plane landed in the tropic dusk at this southern Thailand air base that had launched thousands of air strikes against North Vietnam.

Nearby a bare-chested airman worked on one drooping wing of a black-bellied B52 bomber, one of about 50 still based here waiting for the word to go back to war.

He snapped to attention as pallbearers, starched and shined, carried the caskets past four saluting escort officers and into a blue ambulance bus.

The remains of the 12 Americans are the first to be repatriated from Communist-held territory, over 13 months after the Vietnam cease-fire, which provided for recovery of remains. They were taken to the Army's nearby Central Identification Laboratory for positive identi-
(Continued on Back Page, Col. 1)

INTRODUCTION

Have you ever wondered what it would be like to survive a situation where a split second determined your life or death? Do you wonder what would go through your mind? How would you deal with several of these circumstances where your life could end in a heartbeat? Would you realize that all these experiences would lead you to more responsibility and, most of all, more honor?

Ask yourself what it would be like to be one of the crew members who find our heroes in twelve green boxes. They were in an open tent at the infamous Hanoi Hilton in Vietnam where our POWs who died in captivity were kept. Would you be as touched as I was by the honor, respect and love shown to these twelve heroes?

If you want the answers and the stories that go along with them, you must read *"They Touched Our Heroes for the Last Time."* Major John E. "Jack" O'Connor, USAF (retired) does an amazing job of making you feel as if you are actually on each of these memorable flights.

You will experience all the thoughts and feelings of one of our premier Navigators in the United States Air Force as he takes you on unforgettable and extraordinary missions. You will see why our military men and women are all considered to be our heroes. You will gain an understanding of what an Air Force Navigator's life is like and some of the experiences that, thankfully, Major John E. "Jack" O'Connor was able to survive.

Linda Hight, Author
HOW WE SERVED
HOW WE SERVED, VOLUME TWO

PREQUEL

It was with their typical arrogance that Hanoi Approach Control demanded that we return to our assigned altitude of eleven thousand feet. I had heard them twice before on previous trips.

We continued at seventy five hundred feet and stayed on this course in spite of the constant barrage of instructions which quickly deteriorated into the North Vietnamese language which, I would bet, had some profoundly nasty and profane instructions as to what we could do with various parts of our bodies.

It was Time!

"Ten seconds to turn. Five, four, three, two, begin turn to heading 022. Continue standard rate of descent until I tell you to break off the approach or until we break thru the cloud ceiling." No one else knew it, but I was not going to break off our decent! I had talked many planes down to touch down albeit in practice and clear weather, but I knew I could do it for real. WE WERE GOING TO LAND AND GET OUR HEROES! We were reaching minimums even for IFR conditions even though we were actually flying VFR in very bad weather. About thirty seconds later we broke out of the clouds at about four hundred feet, on centerline at Gia Lam. Our breakout was followed by a "Talley Ho" from the Recovery plane. The toughest part of our mission was over, or so we thought!

And so it began!

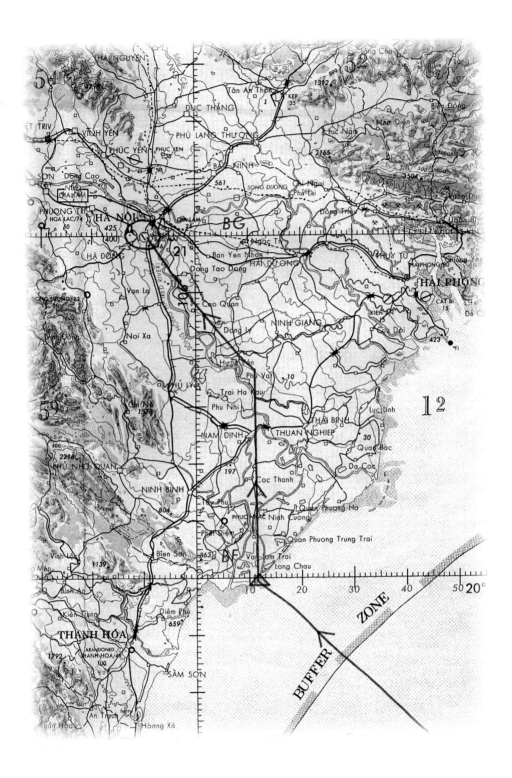

PERSONAL AUTOBIOGRAPHY

John Emmett O'Connor SSgt
USAF, Discharged
OFFICER CANDIDATE SCHOOL, 1960
Major, USAF, Retired

"There was nowhere to go but down..."

May 18, 1934 was an important day for me. I was delivered by a midwife in a humble private home in Salida, Colorado, the only child of seven not born in a hospital. I was raised on a ranch a mile south of Nathrop, CO Pop: 6-10, depending on day, month and/or year.

Two years in a one room school house (eight grades) with four older siblings fit my equally humble beginning. When the older kids started high school in Salida, 18 miles south of the ranch, I went along in the '28 Nash to grade school at St Joseph's Catholic School. I was taught by Benedictine Nuns, for 6 years. The three oldest boys, (that included me) had to go out around 5:30 AM in temperature sometimes down to thirty degrees below zero or colder to harness the mules so we could feed loose hay to about nine hundred head of sheep with pitch forks. We had the pitchforks, not the sheep. No bales yet!

View from the family ranch in Nathrop, Colorado.

On balmy mornings it was in the teens or 20's above zero! We also had to milk a couple cows, feed chickens, gather eggs and care for whatever others were in the menagerie that we happened to have at the time. All of this in the dark during the winter. When we came in from the cold, Dad would line us up and give us each a shot of Ten High whiskey to keep us from catching cold. Because I was over five years younger than my next older brother, I may have gotten only a half of a shot. I sincerely hope not. I was as cold as they were! Dad swore it kept us from catching cold. It worked. I do not remember ever catching a cold on the ranch. Summertime? No problem! After that there were four years of high School at The Abbey School: An all-boys college prep boarding school, at Holy Cross Monastery in Canon City, Colorado about 75 miles down the Arkansas River from the ranch. It was established by the Priests & Brothers of the Order of Saint Benedict in 1925 when the area was a hotbed of the KKK. They were fantastic instructors! It was my best education, by far! But it was also a boys only school, so my social development was/is sadly retarded. Afraid of girls, still? Oh, maybe not so much anymore.

Two incidents to show my sheer stupidity while at the Abbey:

1. We (Normally the same three: Don Jeffries, Ron Ryan and I) sometimes would go out east of Canon City and get into the many deep arroyos. They had small caves in the dirt sides that went way back in the walls, about 15 feet below solid dirt. We would crawl way back in there and find a coyote den, or whatever. I guess we were searching for treasure? Probably not! Just goofing around. Those tunnels could collapse any time and more than once we went back to a favorite that had done just that. It didn't make any difference. We'd just find another, not recognizing the risk. If one had collapsed on or between us and the opening of the tunnel, we would have been stuck. No one knew where we were.

I later often wondered if we had a cave-in deep in one of those tunnels that either fell on us or fell just behind us, how long it would take to find the suffocated bodies. The oxygen would have run out before we could dig out if the cave-in was of sufficient size. We could have easily died! We were young (and stupid) and didn't think of letting anyone know where we were going to be, not even which direction we would be going.

2. The three of us hiked up about a mile short of the Royal Gorge Bridge, nine miles west of and owned by Canon City, (Canon is pronounced as in Grand Canyon). It had that little deal above the 'n.' We decided to go back to the school, but didn't want to walk back thru the cactus sagebrush etc. So, we decided to climb down the gorge to the railroad tracks. It was about a mile east of the highest suspension bridge in the world at some 1,135 feet above the Arkansas River. In the middle of the bridge, there is a sign warning: "No Fishing From Bridge." Climbing down the canyon we found that the early going was fine, but soon, as the canyon walls got steeper, we were finding it harder to find good handholds to get us down. About half way down, I found myself in a position where I had no place to go. There was no way we'd ever make it back up. It was way too far and too steep. There was no way to go but down!

We were spotting for each other, pointing out places that looked like a good route. The other two found a better route than the one I chose and beat me down to the tracks. I saw a couple of outcroppings that I thought could lead to a better track down, but I had to take a little jump to get there. I jumped safely enough, but now realized that I REALLY had no place to go! I had to jump back to my previous untenable position. I think my defense mechanisms have taken over from there. That's all I remember about the descent. We were about half way down the approximately one thousand plus feet canyon wall, and I have no recollection of what happened after that except wandering down the railroad track, as if nothing unusual happened, back to the Abbey, about five miles away. We never did that again! None of the three got even a bruise (that I remember). It is a wonder that one or more of us didn't get killed on that soiree. It was mostly sheer cliffs and we just had our street shoes on. No gloves, either. It might be where I got my fear of heights, which I forced myself to get over years later, partially by forcing myself to walk across the Royal Gorge Bridge which had one-inch gaps be-

Col Emmett O'Connor (pointing at propeller) inspired Jack O'Connor to join the United States Air Force and become an aviator like his uncle.

tween the six-inch planks, through which I could see the Arkansas river and the Rio Grande Rail Road tracks far below. I could easily have been killed by a fall from the cliff. That doesn't count toward my number of ways I almost died.

Having survived my time at the Abbey School, it was time to move on: On to College after reluctantly turning down a Notre Dame partial scholarship to accept a full one at Regis College in North Denver. My rejection of my Notre Dame scholarship also helped obtain a better education for my two younger brothers. My childhood dream of going to Notre Dame University: Gone! But, now, as I am writing this autobiography, I'm thinking of going there for just one quarter. It would do no good except to cause my other dream to come to fruition. I'll ponder that one for a while.

After two years at Regis College, I took my first step to fulfill the second of my two dreams. I enlisted in the Air Force with the promise of pilot training after three months. Yeh, right! Typical recruiter BS! But, as it turned out, my timing was perfect. My selection to that Officer Electronics School at Lowry AFB in Denver set the stage for the rest of my career.

My Dad did not support my entry into the Air Force, and not only because he was losing a ranch hand. He just flat didn't want me to go, and he was not used to his kids not going along with what he wanted. Three and a half years later, I was a new E-5 (SSgt) home on leave, before he finally understood that I joined because I wanted to join, and not because I wanted to get away from him. We were just sitting on the front porch in Denver, which was unusual in itself, talking about a wide variety of things. After all, we hadn't seen each other for well over a year. I think my enthusiasm about being a SSgt in the Air Force and, the fact that, perhaps, I was on a career path like his brother had in the USAAF years earlier, tended to convince him that I wanted to wear a blue suit. It finally made him see the light. He finally realized that he was not the bad guy. And, it didn't hurt that he was really impressed by his brother and my favorite uncle, Emmett, my namesake. Talk about a mutual admiration society. Dad called Emmett "The Aviator," and Emmett called my Dad, "The Mountain Man." My Dad was an impressive sight at six foot two of muscle, especially when he was wearing his cowboy boots and tan cowboy hat, in a suit, coming down the steps of an airplane after arriving in Tampa, Florida. This fact was relayed to me by my uncle, himself. They were both quite successful in their chosen professions. We need more people like those two! My uncle and I corresponded extensively when I was on those long ten to fourteen-hour flights over the Pacific Ocean.

But now, I had just started to do what I had been dreaming of since I was about six years old. I was a "Flyer!" I was a member of the United States Air Force. How sweet it sounded! I was now in an outfit that actually flew in a variety of aircraft. After that front porch soul clearing session, Dad was very (too) proud of me and had a big board on a wall where he actually nailed my medals and ribbons each time I received a new one. I understand that he bragged on me a little bit too.

But I rush!

Basic Training was 17 weeks long then, so I left Lackland AFB with one stripe. It was a big deal to me. Then "IT" happened to me. "IT" was one of the most influential happenings of my career, and maybe my life. I received my first choice of assignments out of Basic Training! I was selected for electronics training at Lowry AFB in Denver. Then, things really turned my way. I was interviewed by a Captain that was full blown crazy. The electronics school was looking for a special type of airman. And it was not just any electronics school. After he interviewed me he said he would love to change places with me! He actually said that he would trade his captains bars with me for where I was going and what I was going to be able to do. And I had one stripe? Man, all I could think of is that this man's Air Force has some dumb ass officers! Could it be the reason that my new position would require a Top Secret clearance and his current one did not? It is still hard for me to believe that seven hundred plus airmen at Lowry AFB were interviewed, just seven selected and five were graduated.

Airmen in an officer electronics class? Separate from the officers, yes. But their course none-the-less. Yep, it happened. The course was so advanced that just before we graduated in May, 1955, they actually *showed* us a transistor. I do not believe that they let us actually touch it but, at least they gave us a glimpse of the future, though we did not understand the significance. At least I didn't, but the extent of my technological development with which I was familiar was a Farmall tractor, a side delivery rake and a tractor mower which clipped off the tip of one finger when I was six years old. It was my fault. After we moved to Denver, we eventually had a black & white TV with three channels which came on at 5:00 PM and went to test pattern at 11:00. I guess I should have known what to expect, but my mind went from current to perhaps being able to fly soon. That could be what the Captain wanted, as I did: Silver Wings! After having earned my second stripe on my twenty first birthday, May 18th, 1955, I was married three days later. All but one of my classmates came up to Buena Vista at the base of the Continental Divide for the wedding. Now it was onward to Mc-Clellan AFB, California to The Western Field Office (WFO) of the 1009th Special Weapons Squadron (SWS) with a new bride and a Top Secret clearance. Our first child was born nine months later! I always figured it was the overnight stop in Provo, Utah. After rapidly moving up the ranks of Delta Airlines, Brenda became a Flight Coordinator in only three and a half years. Yes, that number is correct. She had a brilliant future in front of her. That beautiful little girl went on to die of cancer at age 31. We all still miss her today as we do her mother!

The 1009th SWS, later named AFTAC, is a story in itself. We were charged with the detection of radioactivity from USSR nuclear debris. The first Long Rage Detection (LRD) of a nuclear explosion occurred in September of 1949. The first WB-29 aircraft detection of USSR nuclear activity occurred accidentally in 1953 on a Routine flight from Yokota AFB, Japan to Eielson AFB, Territory of Alaska. (You can Google AFTAC)

PROFESSIONAL AUTOBIOGRAPHY

STAFF SERGEANT
UNITED STATES AIR FORCE
HONORABLE DISCHARGE, 1960
OFFICER CANDIDATE SCHOOL
MAJOR, UNITED STATES AIR FORCE
RETIRED, 1978

I enlisted into the United States Air Force (USAF) on 7 Sept 1954 in Denver, Colorado after attending Regis College for two years. At that time, the USAF was only six years old.

After seventeen weeks of Basic Training at Lackland Air Force Base (AFB), San Antonio, Texas, I was selected to attend Electronics School at Lowry AFB, Denver Colorado. After graduating, I served for almost six years as a Special Equipment Operator (SEO) for the 1009th Special Weapons Squadron (SWS). First, with duty at Western Field Office (WFO), I was stationed at McClellan AFB, Sacramento, California, performing Top Secret duty flying in C-47, WB-29, WB-50 and RB-36 aircraft monitoring for foreign and U.S. nuclear radiation. This included many Temporary Duty assignments (TDYs) to Eielson AFB, Fairbanks, Territory of Alaska, and other Air Force bases around the Northern Hemisphere. Then, after

1963 Honolulu, Hawaii
1st Lt John E. "Jack" O'Connor

three years, I assumed similar duties at Hickam AFB, Territory of Hawaii, mostly processing and monitoring for radioactive material collected by WB-50's flying in from McClellan AFB. My flying was curtailed and done mostly where I began, in a tail dragging C-47 (DC-3). Because of the drawdown of forces after the Korean "Police Action," promotion to E-6 was frozen. Ergo, I opted to attend Officer Candidate School (OCS) from which I graduated as a Second Lieutenant on 18 October 1960.

MILITARY AND CIVILIAN EDUCATION: I successfully completed Squadron Officer School, Command and Staff College and Industrial College of the Armed Forces by correspondence rather than taking time from flying the line to attend the schools at Maxwell AFB, Alabama and Washington DC. During this time, I was also attending night school at University of Hawaii to gain enough undergraduate hours to apply for and be accepted into "Project Bootstrap."

I was given permission to participate in this fine program and graduated from Weber State College in Ogden, Utah with a Bachelor of Science degree. During this time, while being consistently on the Dean's list, including straight A's in my first semester, I flew missions into Vietnam each chance I had from Hill AFB where I continued to be stationed.

ASSIGNMENT HIGHLIGHTS: After OCS, I attended Basic Navigator School, Navigator/Bombardier School and Survival School before returning to the State of Hawaii for duty as a First Lieutenant Line Navigator with the 48th Military Air Transport Service (MATS) flying in C-118B (DC-6B) aircraft. Our planes normally transported personnel from Travis AFB, California to and from Tachikawa Air Base (AB) in north Tokyo, Japan with refueling stops at Hickam AFB, Hawaii and Wake Island. When the Squadron closed in June of 1965, I requested and received a transfer to the 28th Logistics Command Squadron at Hill AFB, Ogden, Utah for duty flying in

C-124 (Globemaster II) Aircraft primarily into South Vietnam and various Southeast Asia countries with additional duty at Hill AFB as Squadron Administrative Officer.

With the closure of the 28th MAS, now Military Airlift Command (MAC) Squadron, My Permanent Change of Station (PCS) orders for flying in C-141 aircraft from Norton AFB, San Bernardino, CA to Southeast Asia (SEA) and the Far East were changed, much to my chagrin, by Base Closure Personnel Officers from MAC HQ to Directorate of Personnel, MAC HQ, itself. I

*Jack O'Connor
in Rome, Italy, 1971*

was chosen for assignment to the Directorate of Personnel at MAC Headquarters, Scott AFB, Illinois, proving that old axiom that no good deed (job) goes unpunished. I had evidently received attention from the HQ Crew for my handling of the Top Secret briefing on the Squadron closing. I received permission to tape the briefing because it was no longer top secret. Now, I could respond to questions by playing back the briefing officers' actual words. I rapidly closed the door on many complaints and misunderstandings. After nine months hating my time as Chief of Morale Welfare and Recreation (MWR), I eventually began enjoying serving in Officer Assignments Control, a much more responsible job, which I was initially promised. Every Officer assignment had to be OK'd by me or my boss, Lt Col Bob Downs. After two and a half years, I was invited by the new commander, Lt Col Bill Hoskings, of the 57th Aerospace Rescue and Recovery Squadron (ARRS) at Lajes Field, the Azores, Portugal to accompany him as one of his line navigators and as the Ground Safety Officer in the summer of 1971.

There were occasions when I would grab my clipboard and the Ground Safety NCO for some no-notice inspections of the local watering holes. We did this primarily to make sure that their locally brewed Cuca beer was still safe to drink. One bottle or two would normally meet the minimal requirements for a safety check.

We took our job seriously. If we weren't absolutely sure, we would have another to be safe. We always made sure that the bar stools were safe for our GI's. Somehow, those inspection reports were never placed in the official Safety Inspection Report File. The Base Golf Club Bar up on the hill was probably the most closely examined. We also did perform the other duties of the office.

I did rotational turns for a week at a time every six weeks to Keflavik Naval Air Station, Iceland. I participated in rescues of lost aircraft or foundering boats as well as dropping Para Rescue Jumpers to help ships of several different nations with medical emergencies. As with the 48th Military Airlift Transport Service (MATS) and the 28th renamed MAC Squadron, the 57th ARRS was unexpectedly closed. Instead of extending my tour for a year, the entire squadron was curtailed by six months and I was assigned an unaccompanied tour to the 776th Tactical Airlift Squadron (TAS) at Ching Chuan Kang (CCK) (AB) in Taichung, Taiwan. My orders also directed me to go to C-130 Tactical Air Drop School and Water Survival Training while enroute.

Upon arrival at the 776th TAS, at CCK, I requested and was selected to be the Squadron Executive Officer. I served in this capacity for my entire year-long tour at CCK and after the squadron and 374th Tactical Airlift Wing was moved to Clark AB, Philippines at the request of Chairman Mao of China and the direction of President Nixon.

It was during this tour of duty that I was selected to fly three missions to Hanoi, North Vietnam. The first two missions on successive Wednesdays, were to take the Peace negotiators for their talks of accommodation between the United States and North Vietnam. All crewmen were ordered to wear civilian clothing and to be nice to our North Vietnam hosts. We all swallowed hard and said: Yes Sir." My third and last mission was special and is related in detail later in this book. In fact, that mission was the genesis of a well-received speech and the origin of this book.

My last duty station was at Birmingham International Airport, Alabama test flying C-130 models from A thru H, one of which came on active duty before I did. I also flew test flights in RB-57 and KC-97 aircraft. I retired on 30 June, 1978 after a satisfying and very unique twenty-four year career.

AWARDS AND DECORATIONS AND SCHOOLS

BRONZE STAR with "V" device
MERITORIOUS SERVICE MEDAL
AIR MEDAL WITH ONE OAK LEAF CLUSTER (OLC)
JOINT SERVICES COMMENDATION MEDAL
AIR FORCE COMMENDATION MEDAL WITH ONE OLC
AIR FORCE OUTSTANDING UNIT AWARD W/1 SILVER 1
   BRONZE OLC
COMBAT READINESS MEDAL
AIR FORCE GOOD CONDUCT MEDAL
GOOD CONDUCT MEDAL WITH TWO KNOT ROPE
NATIONAL DEFENSE SERVICE MEDAL WITH ONE OLC
ARMED FORCES EXPEDITIONART MEDAL W/1 BRONZE STAR
VIETNAM SERVICE MEDAL WITH 1 SILVER 3 BRONZE OLC
ARMED FORCES. RESERVE MEDAL
AIR FORCE LONGEVITY SERVICE AWARD WITH FOUR OLC
SMALL ARMS EXPERT MARKSMANSHIP RIBBON
REPUBLIC OF VIETNAM CAMPAIGN MEDAL WITH BANNER

BADGES

ENLISTED AIRCREW WINGS
MASTER NAVIGATOR WINGS

SCHOOLS AND AWARDS

BASIC NAVIGATOR TRAINING
NAVIGATOR/BOMBARDIER TRAINING
SURVIVAL TRAINING COURSE
WATER SURVIVAL TRAINING
C-130 TACTICAL FLYING TRAINING COURSE
JUNGLE SURVIVAL COURSE
SQUADRON OFFICERS SCHOOL (ECI)

AIR COMMAND AND STAFF SCHOOL (ECI)
INDUSTRIAL COLLEGE OF ARMED FORCES (ECI)

AIRMAN OF THE MONTH FOR MCCLELLAN AFB, CA
    DECEMBER, 1957
OUTSTANDING NAVIGATOR, 62ND AIRLIFT WING, 4TH
    QUARTER, 1968

AIRCRAFT IN WHICH I WAS A CREWMEMBER

C-47	**T-29 (Navigator Trainer)
WB-29	**U-3, Blue Canoe
WB-50	**C-9
RB-36	**C-141
RB-57	*T-33*
C-118 (DC-6)	*T-28*
C-124	*B-25*
C-130	*B-26*

* *One flight only*
** *Several to many flights as ACM just to log time*

Maj (Ret) John O'Connor's Flight Jacket

Lt John "Jack" O'Connor –
Harlingen AFB, May 1961

Eugene Timothy
O'Connor and
Antoinette Ann
Eussen O'Connor

Parents to John E.
O'Connor
Salida, Colorado

NOW I UNDERSTAND WHAT THEY MEAN BY LITERALLY STANDING ON DEATH'S DOOR.

"I was there"

The day they thought I was going to die

I had been admitted to Penrose Main Hospital in Colorado Springs on March 27, 2015. I had developed a very bad case of pneumonia. The following is how I remember an unusual phenomenon during the next few days. Some of these days seem mixed up, but as I said, this is how I remember them.

I was in a strange, yet wonderful world. That world was spinning all around me in multi-colored triangle shaped papers while I stood still. The strange thing was that the papers were in bright gold, yellow, and, yes, even bright brown. It was strange because none of those rank very high on my list of favorite colors. I'm really more of a spring/summer guy, not fall.

The wonderful thing was that the colors were spinning very rapidly all around me. The best way I could describe them at the time was like the type of paper you would use to make a paper Mache bowl, but they were moving fast as in in a supersonic wind tunnel. Yeh, it was really kind of strange.

Then I was standing near an open door. The eerie thing about this was that I couldn't quite see through the opening. It was dark, a soft dark, on the other side, but I knew I could walk through it, if I chose, and be gone forever!

There were two little white circles below me that seemed to represent things I needed to do before I crossed over the threshold. I forget now what those things even were. I looked at them and decided they were not important enough to stop me from going to the other side. I decided to go on through that door.

My eyes had been closed. It was dark. Then, I opened my eyes briefly and saw my daughter Tina's face. For some reason, her face was strangely round and it was the only thing not spinning. Her face was still, but I could see her lips moving. I knew not what she was saying. Those same colored things were spinning even more rapidly and not five inches from me was a perfectly round-faced Tina. She was the only thing not spinning! I remember saying: "What in the hell are you doing here?" I'm sorry that I do not recall her response, but I decided immediately not to go through the door. Suddenly, the door with all the other symbols disappeared! They just plain old disappeared!

Then another phenomenon happened, continuing this strange odyssey. I witnessed two multi-colored ribbons of gold and orange, the same colors as before, but with some blue, rust and reddish stripes also. They came from somewhere, went straight from right to left and a little beyond me. Both ribbons fell downward side by side. They made a smooth right turn, straightened out and went straight away from me. The one on the left continued forward and disappeared in the distance. The other one, which I think represented me, turned right very smoothly and it also faded away to the right. As it disappeared, I found myself sitting, facing to the right, in a white room with a piece of something like a white, small diameter triangle forward and left of me. It appeared to be a white metal tube angling at about forty-five degrees upward at my left side from bottom left to stop at about the height of my head. The same type of tube continued straight down as if supporting the rising portion. I don't know what that represented.

I was sitting on the floor with my legs drawn about half-way up in a completely white room. I was even dressed in white. It was a white like a new sheet only brighter. It was not a brilliant white, but white like I've never seen before or since. That's all I remember about that episode.

I have other memories of that day or night or whenever it was. It seems I was fussing at the staff because I was very thirsty and they wouldn't give me any more water. This was even after I explained to them that an elephant had sat down and knocked my water over. I ended up getting some applesauce which gave me some of the moisture I needed or at least some of the moisture I wanted. I vaguely remember visits from Ben and Judy DeVries, my brother Jerry, daughter Pat and a priest I didn't like. I argued with the priest. I understand he gave me "Last Rites" anyway. Others were there, too, whom I vaguely remember like my nephew Tim and nieces Maureen and Cathy.

On 1 April, they said I was going to die. They had given up and decided they couldn't save me even after moving me to a room with forty liters, yes forty, of oxygen for a long period of time. The doctors didn't think so at the time, but that much extra oxygen must have helped. They had called my kids in to see their daddy for the last time. Tina arrived first. Pat came second. Kathleen said that immediately after I saw Tina, I started getting better. They didn't know about my "near death" experience yet. Nor did I. The doctors eventually knew I would recover and estimated that I could leave the hospital for rehab on April 9. I left on April 5th!

Rehab was supposed to take from two to three weeks. I left in ten days after I had proven to them that I could cook a ham and cheese sandwich. Rehab?

I learned later that I had a bad case (I wonder if there is a good case) of Acute Respiratory Distress Syndrome (ARDS) which is a lung disease that is considered quite rare. Come to find out later, I had also been afflicted with congestive heart failure and some other malady as well as pneumonia.

ARDS is fatal to 80% of my age group and those who survive take a very long time to fully recover. Normally, there are long-lasting complications and maladies. Not only did I live, I was back to "normal" within about five days after I left the hospital even though I really was weaker than I thought.

After I was home for five days, I felt as good as I did the week before I went in. I guess God didn't need me yet, but I still have not figured out why and for what reason. Hopefully, someday I will. But I'm in no rush!

I did wonder for a while how it would have been for everyone if I had stepped through that door.

NOTE: This was written shortly after I was comfortably back in my home in Colorado Springs.

I didn't know at the time but, He may have been saving me, so I would move to Broken Arrow, Oklahoma to meet all those wonderful folks at the Military History Center who eventually gave me cause to write this book.

Perhaps. However, if He saved me to put my experiences down on paper, I guess we will just have to see what happens after the book is finished.

Will I be finished, too?

PROLOGUE

"Just a Lookin' for a Home"

It was hot! It was humid! It was Oklahoma! I was miserable, I was frustrated and I was grouchy! I needed a break in the worst way! I had been fighting the heat and humidity ever since I had arrived from my beloved Colorado in mid-May 2017. It was now early June and I was working my way through another three T-shirt day. That is how I had decided to time the amount of work to do in the process of emptying our garage so we could get our cars inside. Three T-shirts! As soon as the third T-shirt was so saturated with sweat that it was virtually impossible to wear, which normally happened at about noon-time, I would quit emptying boxes in a garage that seemed to reach a few hundred degrees when in actuality the thermometer was only reading 94 degrees. It Lied!

I decided I might need to buy a new thermometer. Surely the one I brought from Colorado wasn't working at this lower altitude. I had just finished saturating my third T-shirt and was looking for some relief, and it was telling me it was only ninety-four degrees. Baloney! or as I would normally say:

Toro PooPoo!

Actually, our move from 6,380 feet and 20% humidity in Colorado Springs, Colorado to 777 feet and 85% humidity in Broken Arrow, Oklahoma which is a southeast (I think) suburb of Tulsa, was proving to be a challenge. The transition was difficult at best. The gyro in my head was caged ninety degrees out of phase. The streets all ran the wrong direction, and every street had several names, and/or numbers as well as a few N, W, S or E's thrown in. I was a Navigator and was completely lost when trying to find anything. There was no Pikes Peak to keep me oriented. Siri became my steady girlfriend, boy did I ever need her now. If she could cook I'd marry her. I had last thought of doing something like that in SEA. Different time, different circumstance.

The way they pronounced "Miami" was like "Miama" and they would let you know about it. It seemed to be one of their most important idiotsyncacies. Ooops! I Guess I should correct that to idiosyncrasies? Nah! I'm being too easy on them now. OK, I'll continue with this strange saga. They have a working oil well on the grounds of the State Capitol which makes them the only state to have such a thing. I've heard that it is right up under the Governor's chair. They have the longest amount of shoreline of any state in America. Go measure if you don't believe me.

In Broken Arrow, they have a religious organization that keeps popping up unexpectedly every time I drive down (or up) 71st Street, Avenue or Kenosha, or whatever else it may be called. I know the street runs north and south. However, the locals insist it runs east and west. Now, who are you going to believe? The State Bird is the scissor tail flycatcher whose long tail splits and moves like a long pair of scissors when it is airborne. I'm not sure which end catches the flies. But, one dropped by one of the first days I sat on the lanai (patio?) overlooking a nice pond like it was bidding me, "Welcome!" Haven't seen one since! They have a town up north called Nowata. Way south of here just off of I-40 they have a road called Lottawatta and somewhere in between, is there a town called "Sumwata?" Someday I expect to find a town named "Empty Bucket"! And we live in a town with a Broken Arrow. In fact, my old flying buddy, Tom Kuhns, asked if we were near "Spent Bullet." I really wouldn't doubt it, but I have been afraid to ask. Yep! Of course, Bugtussle and Ixl (Pronounced 'I Excel') are nearby. Adair is pronounced differently depending upon where you are and upon if you are referring to the town, the area or the family. Yep, this was going to be a difficult transition.

To add to my confusion, even the Red Bud trees of which they are so proud, are PURPLE! And, the locally famous Pink House restaurant was in a white house. It has recently moved into a red Brick Mansion, but is still "The Pink House!" No wonder I'm going nuts! To top things off, there are no Redbud trees in Redbud Park! The move had been made because one of those know-it-all doctors in Colorado Springs told me that there was more oxygen at seven hundred plus feet than at the elevations in my "Colorful Colorado." He didn't tell me that instead of oxygen, there was more "crazy" floating around. I may have been better prepared if he had. Nah, nothing could prepare me for this place.

I was born and raised in Colorado on a ranch at almost eight thousand feet elevation and had returned to Colorado Springs at about sixty six hundred feet after my retirement from a very unique Air Force career. Believe me, I knew all about the relationship of elevation to oxygen. I had been through enough schools and altitude chambers where they would simulate running the elevation up to thirty-five thousand feet, take off your oxygen mask and as a buddy watched, you would have to write things. I had always thought I was doing well, having been from the mountains and everything, but as time without my mask went on and I was feeling great, they pointed out that my fingernails had turned blue, as had my lips, and it was time for my buddy to put my oxygen mask back on my face. After a few breaths of 100% oxygen, everything changed. I now saw that the writing I thought was so perfect started each sentence with large letters and ended with letters so small that I couldn't even read them. There were even some mis-spellings which was really unusual for me. I was a believer. Yep, I knew the relationship between air and elevation and that's why I yielded. I had promised myself years ago that I would never walk around Colorado Springs with a hose stuck up my nose emanating from a small but heavy oxygen tank. So, a lower elevation it was. I had considered Texas but ended up in Broken Arrow because I liked the name, although in Air Force parlance, it meant a nuclear accident! Those I didn't like!

At this point, I couldn't have cared less about oxygen, career or elevation, or even Redbuds and nuclear accidents. Right then, I was hot, tired, dirty and thinking about looking for relief from all. I had saturated my third T-shirt and was ready for an air-conditioned break. I couldn't stand to cool off in the house because it was as big of an overstuffed mess as was the garage. I needed something new, fresh and INDOORS! I knew just the place to kill a few cool minutes.

A few days earlier, we had seen a military museum while looking over our new main street. And what a main street it was! There were maybe six blocks of one and two story buildings accented with almost every restaurant in one eclectic block. I decided to see what this little military museum place looked like after I took a cool shower. I threw on a dry (not sure if it was clean and didn't care!) T-shirt and went "downtown." I wasn't expecting anything special and the one or two old ladies who normally manage such a place probably wouldn't have too much to offer so they wouldn't be expecting too much from a visitor either.

With a bucolic looking exterior, and in a typical semi-backward (I thought) small southern town, I wasn't expecting much and then I fell in love. I fell in love with a museum! In love with a town! In love with my New Home! In love with my New Home Town! In love with Broken Arrow, Oklahoma!

The Military History Center at 112 South (OOPS, I told ya) North Main Street became my nice cool home away from home, probably much to the chagrin of the resident Docents who looked at me with jaundiced eyes when I first walked in. I was not really dressed as well as I should have been when I first encountered these men with whom I would soon create a bond, the likes of which I had not had since my remote tour in Southeast Asia. But when I walked in wearing my Vietnam Veteran hat, I was immediately and automatically accepted. I grew a great big smile when I saw about four similar hats looking back at me and wandering around in the front entryway. Funny how a war or two can create such an automatic rapport. In fact, after several visits, I felt at times like I was back with my buddies in the Air Force and Southeast Asia. These guys made me think, especially about my last mission to North Vietnam, and my run in a C-130E up the Red River to Hanoi.

I had been anticipating the normal museum where you pay a nominal entry fee and then just saunter around for a little while trying to figure out just what they had to offer. Usually, in the many military museums I had wandered through in many locations throughout these United States, there would be some Civil war relics and a few things from other conflicts, the likeness of which you'd find in any military museum in the country.

WOW! This was entirely different. It was like no other museum I had ever seen. It was neat, it was tight, and set in chronological order from the Revolutionary war through Afghanistan. Instead of the fifteen minutes I had expected, it took me a couple hours and I had barely scratched the surface. It was soon to become an almost demanding daily visit. If it is possible to become addicted to an inanimate place, I became addicted to the Oklahoma Military History Center.

Each one of these men who greeted me was a Docent, defined as, "A person knowledgeable enough to act as a guide, typically on a volunteer basis, in a museum, art gallery or zoo." (Yeah, I had to look it up).

Though not an official member, I was accepted as such. I was there virtually every day to be able to converse and swap old military stories with different folks. The anchor of this extremely knowledgeable group is Dennis Hoch. He is there all day, every day from 10:00 AM until 4:00 PM which is the normal closing time. He is always early and often stays late to finish a fully-guided tour of the museum for a late arrival.

I was invited to become a docent, but with the vast amount of history in this small, but tightly arranged military display, I knew I just wouldn't be able to become as proficient as those Docents who had "earned their stripes" along with the right to be called a full-fledged Docent, who is ready to explain any aspect of the museum. They really know this place. The feeling of "belongingness" of these veterans who volunteer much of their time was palpable. You could actually feel that they loved and honored this repository of military history.

Another thing that set this History Center apart from others was the fact that there was always at least one Docent available to give a guided tour of the entire museum. If the visitor wants a self-guided tour, each item has an object label on the wall which not only explains the artifact, but also lists the donor's name. These many object labels were written by the boss himself, Retired Army Brigadier General Thomas Mancino. Many of the artifacts are his and many throughout the museum are one of a kind, including some of his.

I just looked back on the definition of a Docent and it fits all of these men to a "T!" The Military History Center is officially a museum, it has lots of art and if the guys, or docents if you will, are in the right mood, it really becomes a zoo!

I compare this organization to an onion. I continue to peel back one segment after another and find something new on each layer. This gathering of gentlemen is a unique group. They have one individual who has a Masters' Degree in music and has played lead guitar for many musical groups, including for several world-renowned tele-evangelists. One of these gentlemen had his own band for years. His Oklahoma Playboys played at the famous Cain's Ballroom every Saturday night for the enjoyment of Tulsans and visitors alike. This, after having had his own band in Las Vegas where he would regularly join Tex Ritter, Jim Reeves, Homer & Jethroe and others for late night jam sessions. He was the best of friends with many of my western singing heroes including the great Hank Thompson.

Another of the docents was sent by the U. S. Air Force to Yale University (Yes, that Yale!) for ten months of intense language training. He can speak and write Mandarin Chinese fluently. These talents were of great value during the Vietnam War as he flew off shore in a C-130 and eavesdropped on Chinese "advisors" in North

Vietnam. A couple of the docents even had and have the guts to be school teachers! There was a manager of a restaurant and of a retirement home. Another was awarded the Purple Heart for wounds received doing battle in northern South Vietnam. One of the Docents was writing extensive computer programs in such a manner that only his customer and not even he would know how to operate it. One worked for the U.S. Postal Department and one is the local Chief of the Order of the Purple Heart. There is a master machinist who knows more about wrenches and tooling than most people including me could ever know nor understand in a lifetime.

To instill discipline, we have a couple of First Sergeants, one who had a career with the Tulsa Police Department. According to some observations, I am the only one who really needs to be disciplined, though not that badly. Those First Sergeants are invaluable to any organization, especially to the Executive Officer or, in this case the one-star boss!

That singer I mentioned is also a pilot who has his own flight simulator and gives flight lessons. He can take off from Tulsa International Airport and land in Hong Kong less than ten minutes after takeoff from Tulsa. I think I'll have him fly me to Melbourne rather than taking the normal seventeen-hour flight on Qantas Airlines! And now, that he is going to need a little R & R while the docs patch up at least one of his landing gear, enter Tim Collins to pinch hit. Here is a man with over twenty thousand flight hours, in Crop-Duster aircraft! That's getting those flight hours the hard way!

Several of these folks were long haul truckers for the likes of Wal-Mart and J B Hunt, both headquartered in northwest Arkansas where some also probably did some trucking for Tyson Chicken as well. One even drove hanging beef which swung at every turn for Monfort Meat, Headquartered in Greely, Colorado. I love to hear them tell stories of how they dearly loved driving those mountain passes in Colorado. It must have been real fun in the winter snows. I know those passes well and understood the trials of trucking "Through the Rockies, not Around Them." That's an old

Rio Grande Rail Road slogan. But, they all smartened up and quit driving, though one is still in the trucking business. He rents out trucks now and lets the other fool do the driving!

One of the Docents puts out the Official Newsletter while another resigned his Docent position in order to have the time to take care of many necessary chores around the Center including maintaining the Brick Honor Walk. He does everything including having moved the monument honoring those soldiers from Broken Arrow High School who sacrificed their lives in Vietnam to a Place of Honor next to the Brick Honor Walk. He also designed and built a cement and chain sitting area with a couple beautiful benches where I have seen folks sit and seem to meditate over these lost lives. He also reclaimed a rocking chair from the trash bin behind The Cracker Barrel restaurant, refurbish it, imbedded a USAF emblem, painted it AF Blue and presented it to an old, and some say, eccentric retired member of the Air Force. He, in turn, donated it to be used by all in the entry office in the front of the History Center. It is widely used by many. This talented gentleman is also an accomplished musician and vocalist who ramrods and makes sure that our celebrations run smoothly. He is also a Master cement czar. One of the Docents had a long career with American Airlines right here in the Tulsa Airport and one brave soul worked for Ross Perot, the founder of EDS and many more businesses. Several are in the Reserves of various Armed Services. What a group! Talented and drenched with quiet professional reserve. Except for me. But I still consider myself to be the stabilizing influence on these guys. I kind of doubt you'll get anyone to agree, but they don't understand how I keep them calm and settled down!

There is also a phantom whose identity has remained a mystery to me. I've seen him come in with his Army Officer Wheel hat, do good things around the Center and sort of fade away without a word. He just flat out disappears! I have recently discovered another Docent who has had a full career in law-enforcement. A thirty-year career in the Oklahoma Bureau of Investigation! Unfortunately, I haven't been there long enough to find out about everyone and I apologize for that. They are all unique unto themselves.

There are individuals in residence from every war since World War II, which is represented by Oscar Nipps, Jr. who is called "Junior" by everyone. He came ashore on the Island of Leyte in the initial invasion of the Philippines alongside General MacArthur as he fulfilled his famous "I Shall Return" promise. While liberating thirty-seven hundred civilian Prisoners of War at Saint Thomas in Manila, MacArthur tripped on some barbed wire that was used to imprison these civilians. Junior was there to keep him from falling when he caught his toe and tripped on that barbed wired while entering this hotel/prison. Junior didn't even get a thank you, but he was granted a rare smile. He was also on the ship next to the USS Missouri where he personally witnessed the surrender papers being signed by Emperor Hirohito, General Wainwright and others, including MacArthur himself.

An original native of Broken Arrow, Junior has been here so long that they say he may be the one who "Broke the Arrow!" We all affectionately call him our living artifact. He nods his head and smiles at this honorable title. Still sharp at 93? You bet your sweet ass he is! Not only is he sharp, but he is quite the character and beloved by all. Once in a while, he looks like he is sleeping in "his" chair. I explain to the rest of the Docents that, same as an aviator (which he wasn't), he is just pre-flighting his eyelids for pinholes. He has never told me if he found any! They are quite small and Junior is quiet and keeps a lot of things to himself.

He is well known in the Broken Arrow/Tulsa area having received many awards and honors, including a one-mile stretch of street where he has always lived being renamed: "Oscar Nipps, Junior Blvd" by the City of Broken Arrow in his honor at special ceremonies at the Military History Center and on the street where he lives. He even has a section on one of the walls of the Military History Center dedicated just to him!

Our second hero from World War II is Corporal Frank Riesinger who still looks sharp and ready to go to war in his World War II Army uniform. He doesn't walk into our midst out front. He just appears! A walking encyclopedia, you do not want to get in an argument with Frank. You can have a discussion, yes, but an argument, no! He comes into the Military History Center so fast that it seems like he just, well, he's there!

Frank has single-handedly initiated a Memorial Service to celebrate Victory over Japan (VJ Day) here in Broken Arrow. That is the day, August 14th in the United States and August 15th west of the International Date Line, when Imperial Japan surrendered in World War II which brought World War II to an end. It is dedicated to those military men and women who made VJ Day happen. It has become a well-attended ceremony which is heading well into its fifth year and Frank remains the central figure. When I grow up, I want to be just like these two!

If you haven't caught on yet, I am in awe of each and every one of our troops.

I need to make special mention of the more gentle gender, who keeps everything humming. Without them, the whole operation would come to a screeching halt. First is "My Fair Lady," JeanE (the spelling is correct) Bailie, Executive Assistant to the boss, friend of all and the only paid person in the Center.

Then there are the vital full-time volunteers. There's the constantly smiling dynamo Claudia Price, a "do everything" woman. We also enjoy the equally fast-moving Susan Virdell who is the only women I have ever known who seems to have memorized the entire four thousand plus volumes of books in the library. This well-kept library is used by many students and others for military research purposes.

There are also several other vital part-time volunteers who make sure things keep running smoothly including Lindsey Donaldson who is many things, including the unofficial photographer of the Center.

And let's not overlook our Special Honorary Head Docent, Miss Maggie Bond. Miss Tulsa, Miss University of Oklahoma City and currently, Miss Broken Arrow. She is our Miss Everything who mesmerizes us with her operatic voice, rendering the National Anthem and other patriotic songs whenever Dennis so requests which is frequently. We all love "our" Maggie! We love her even more when she slips into the songs of the Greatest Generation. Fantastic! "I'll Be Seeing You" is dying to be sung!

Maggie Bond with Jack O'Connor

If you are ever in or near Broken Arrow, do yourself a favor and trundle on down to 112 North Main Street and enjoy one of the finest, if not *the* finest, small military museums in the country. As I have mentioned, these daily gatherings of several Docents upon which I intrude, normally turn into plain old BS sessions as the war stories as well as stories of all aspects of life fly high and wide. And I am fortunate. By spending a little time down there almost every day, I have five distinct and disparate gatherings of veterans with whom to visit. The BS flows easily and ranges from hearty laughter to almost tears. I have had as have others, an occasional tearful twinkle in the corner of the eye.

But, when it comes to war stories, well, what do they say? "The first liar hasn't got a chance." Another way you can always tell which is which, A Fairy Tale always begins with: "Once upon a time." A war story always begins with: "Listen man, this ain't no shit!"

There is great enjoyment with all of these guys and, with that enjoyment, many memories that had been buried come flooding back to the forefront, some of which I wish had stayed buried. Like

I now remember well how the bad guys "trick or treat" at Tan Son Nhut Airdrome right outside of Saigon in South Vietnam and why my third mission to Hanoi was so different from the first two. And the reputed biggest explosion in the Vietnam war? One of our guys was there and was blown quite a ways from the explosion which killed many, including very young children. He picked himself up and, though he was temporarily deaf, disoriented and still hurting from the intensity of the explosion, he selflessly and immediately turned to assist in cleaning up the chaos, casualties and the carnage caused by the explosion. As you have probably noticed, most of the stories are from the Vietnam era, with a few tossed in by Junior and everyone who had a relative in WW II. We all hope that more younger veterans from the Mideast wars will continue to join this group.

We all have almost unbelievable stories to tell, and there is no doubt in my mind that these adventures are all true, and *not* BS. There is a feeling of warmth and great enjoyment with these guys and with that, the deep-rooted scars of some of the traumatic incidences get lessened, just because they have finally been put into words. Words that were heard by another who has shared similar difficult episodes. Many memories that have been buried for years come flooding back to each one, some wanted, some which we wish hadn't come back to our consciousness. Each and every one of us can recount a time when it was either divine intervention or plain dumb assed luck that we didn't get ourselves killed. Man, some of those were close! Later, we referred to them as "interesting."

These BS sessions we enjoy while being together down at the Military History Center (MCH) are a lot more than just plain Bull Shit! Without realizing it, they are really quite therapeutic. I have heard things and said things that I would have never heard nor said had it not been for this group. Dennis Hoch and Junior are there every day. As pointed out, the other Docents rotate each day so I get a different group of veterans and thus a different perspective each time I join them. And I try to go there for a little while every day. With each mix of veterans, we share different thoughts and experiences that we could never share with someone who had never experienced the nearness of death. That sensation leaves a residual feeling like no other thing.

Damn! I'm so blessed, or whatever, that I happened upon this unique group and that they accepted me as one of them, even though I am not qualified to be a Docent. Perhaps these Docents and this place was the reason that I was kept alive through so many of my close encounters with death. It took Dennis to point out to me the therapeutic value of these BS sessions. It was he who made me understand that I was benefitting mentally and psychologically from being with this group as much as they are, even though I was not realizing it. I just hope I have contributed a little and not just received.

We laugh a lot and give each other a hard time, normally about nothing. The laughs, while good within themselves, are also good for the depth of that particular subject to someone. We also just plain enjoy being with each other. What a great bunch of individuals! Yep, we are good for each other and I have yet to hear an angry word among any of us in two years of almost daily attendance. I recently mentioned that though I still cannot comprehend why our entire crew didn't die that night in Vietnam on the Tan Son Nhut ramp I had not thought about it for many years.

Neither can I come to grips with why we all didn't die going into Kwajalein Atoll from Midway Island or why all of my friends died in that crash at Guam. I still worry over whether I could have saved them, or if I would have died too.

Also, it is now clear to me why my third and much more special flight to Hanoi, North Vietnam was monitored very closely, not only by the North Vietnamese and I even know now why I was there. But, as with many things, these adventures had their genesis outside of Vietnam and are explained within.

With this group, many old memories re-enter our lives, some of which we didn't want to come back. However, eventually these memories become like dragons. They must be faced and slain. I am doing that with this book.

The Docents themselves are an eclectic group of individuals. Each one has his own personal and electrifying story. They are all worthy of their own book.

This is mine.

LOWRY AIR FORCE BASE, DENVER, COLORADO
NOVEMBER 1954 – MAY 1955

"This Man's Air Force has Some Pretty Dumbassed Officers"

After many air-stops along the way from San Antonio, I finally returned to Denver, my place of enlistment. This time, as an Airman Third Class, I was ordered to report to the 3400th Technical Training Squadron, bypassing the 3405th Student Group at the 3400th Student Wing Headquarters at Lowry Air Force Base.

I had expected a hero's welcome, being a uniformed warrior and all. I had really expected my entire family to be there to celebrate my return as they had my brother Bill when he came back on leave from the Navy in WW II. Realistically, I guess coming home from basic training was a little different from a guy who came back after damned nearly being killed by Kamikaze's in the Pacific Theater of WW II.

Instead of the hero's welcome I had anticipated, my mom told me over the phone the proper bus lines to catch to get me all the way over to northwest Denver where we lived. I even had to walk the four blocks from the bus stop to home. So much for a dynamic entrance to the Air Force life. Hell, I was ready to go back to Lowry and they'd not miss me anyway.

As normal for a new airman at Lowry AFB, I was placed in a huge World War II era wooden barracks, just a number among the masses in green one-piece ill-fitting fatigues. I was bored as hell, just laying on my bunk most of the time. There was absolutely nothing to do except watch the craps (dice) games which got old fast. The only other thing I remember is getting with a few faceless airmen at the snack areas to tell jokes and compare backgrounds which were quickly forgotten.

After seventeen weeks of basic training, which my defense mechanisms have successfully closed down in my memory, I was on my way to my first choice of career fields. I would be learning electronics at Lowry Field, or more properly, AFB now, in East Denver. I had taken the train down to Lackland Air Force Base in San Antonio, Texas a few months earlier on a twenty-four hour sit up ride. For this trip to Denver, I actually got to do my first flying. It was only on a DC-3, but it was flying! I thoroughly enjoyed seeing the landscape creep slowly under the wings of my first airplane ride!

Then, things took a really unexpected turn. I was reclining, as usual, in my bunk in the open bay-barracks which was comprised of seventy-eight strangers in one big open room, double bunked. I was approached by a "runner" advising me that I was to report to a certain building in an hour. This took place during my second week in the barracks.

I cleaned up, put on a new uniform and proceeded as ordered. After reporting properly, I was interviewed by a Captain. He said that I was one of seven airmen selected out of well over seven hundred interviewees who will have been accepted to attend a new, special, classified Officer Electronics Course.

For some reason, I remember specifically what the captain said and it set the course for my career. He told me, "I'd trade my Captain bars to go where you are going to be able to go." I had one stripe (Airman 3rd Class) and I wasn't too proud of it, but he sounded pretty impressed with where I was going. I had no idea, but it must be pretty good! I also thought that if he would trade those shiny Captain bars, for one cloth stripe, this man's Air Force had some pretty dumbass officers! But I was thoroughly intimidated so I said, "Yes sir." and followed another one stripe Airman who took me from Lowry #1 on the west side of the runway to Lowry #2 on the east side of the base. This type of move was normally made after about two or more months of training (spell marching and KP). Of course, I didn't know any better. I thought that was normal.

I thought of that Captain eleven years later when I was actually pinning on my own Captain's bars. And, no, I would not trade ranks with a one-strip airman, no matter where in hell he was going or whatever in hell he was doing!

The seven of us moved to a different building that housed less than half as many Airmen and didn't have double bunks. We had our own little area at the far end from the door. The others in the barracks couldn't quite understand how we got to this side of the base so quickly and were irritated because we were exempt from Kitchen Police (KP) duty. KP was short for having to do the dirtiest jobs in a kitchen that served many hundreds of meals per day and some other less than lovely duties. They didn't realize it was because we had to study way more than they did! They also couldn't quite understand or quite believe that we were going to a school normally attended only by officers. Plus, they didn't comprehend why the few of us that looked like them, same clothing, etc. were probably going to get a Top Secret clearance. Some of them were even interviewed and were asked about our current state of mind. I'm not sure they even understood what a Top Secret clearance was. Actually, I'm not sure I did either!

The seven of us were the only ones in this class. They didn't mix officers with lowly one stripe airmen. We just knew that something different was going on, but we didn't know what. We had a great instructor: (I can still visualize him but can't remember his name). Great guy! But we soon found out that Electronics School was tough. After about six weeks of school, because of some stupid personal actions, we were down to six students. One of the airmen in our class was busted for trying to sell an electric razor to a guy about three bunks toward the front from ours. The only problem I could see was that the dipshit tried to sell it to the same guy from whom he had stolen it a few weeks earlier. He stole it when the original owner was in Sick Bay (hospital). Out of the thousands on the base, he tried to make the deal with the guy from whose foot-locker it was taken? Really? I began to wonder about their selection

(Back Row L-R) Jack O'Connor, Jim Turk, Evans (Front Row L-R) John Griffiths, Joel Sroaka

process. Maybe we weren't really that special after all?

Then a tall student who had two stripes came along and joined us. Judging by his drawl, he was from Texas. He had been in a previous class but had lost enough time from school after having been hospitalized that he was held back. He joined us at about the same juncture as he was when he had been forced to withdraw. He was sharp and well liked so we "original" guys didn't mind him taking over our group as the ranking man. Naturally, we called him "Tex."

Though we did not have to get involved in KP duties, we were required to "volunteer" for different additional duties to keep avoiding said KP. I think it was Jim Turk who joined me in stoking the furnaces of several buildings with big, heavy roughly eighteen inch cube chunks of coal every three hours during the sometimes very cold Colorado winter nights. It was cold and dirty, but not nearly as bad as KP at which I had toiled only once. Once was enough!

I also remember seeing across an open field the first class of United States Air Force Academy students, some doing calisthenics and others marching in formation. I learned that Lowry AFB was the temporary home of the new Air Force Academy cadets while they were awaiting their permanent establishment just north of Colorado Springs. I couldn't quite get my mind around the fact that we were living on the same base that had just "welcomed" its first cadets at the beginning of the month in which we would be leaving Lowry. Or that this group was the first to establish an Academy which would be the equal of the well-established West Point and Annapolis. I stared at them more in fascination than envy. I just couldn't get over the fact that I was looking at the very first class.

Another more common sight was Airman "No Stripe Electric Razor Thief/Seller" waving at us as we marched past the Brig which is the military jail. I'll never forget him. He always seemed to be happy. He constantly had a big smile on his face as he waved at his former classmates. Of course, since we were in a formation, we couldn't acknowledge his warm greetings. All of us, though on occasion, would sneak a little wave at this well-liked idiot.

In mid-May, after graduation, I just turned age twenty-one which was a few years older than the normal airman at that stage of his career. I married my long-time girlfriend from Buena Vista, Colorado. All but one of my classmates attended the wedding. I still have the big fork out of the set of Cutco Cutlery that they bought us for a wedding present. The airman that was absent from the ceremony was the two striper who had just been removed from our class under mysterious circumstances. I remember some of the rumors of

Jim Turk & I 1955, Skivies & Mop. Note three piece fatigues.

the reason for his dismissal, but I never knew exactly the reason for his dismissal and see nothing to gain by speculating.

The Air Force was now almost eight years old. It was just under seven years old when I enlisted so we had a real mix of uniforms. I was lucky, but now that I think of it, all of our "huge" six-man class had complete USAF regulation uniforms. Flashing through my mind, though, is a picture of John Griffiths trying to make his brown shoes black. It never did really come out right, but he surely worked on it. I'll have to check with him on that. There were yellow Army Corporal and Buck Sergeant stripes which clashed terribly with the Air Force Blue uniforms. We still had the "Ike" jacket but mine was blue. It remains to be the best uniform piece I have ever worn, designed by Five Star General Dwight Eisenhower. Later, after my commissioning, I wore "Silver Tans" which would rival the "Ike" jacket. Most uniforms were a mixture of the new Air Force and the Army Air Corps which was the uniform that my Uncle Emmett wore so proudly.

Cornelius Emmett O'Connor. My uncle. My idol! One of what was supposed to be the class of '18, but instead were graduated from West Point in three years and were being rushed over to Europe to end the war. There never was a class of '18. Their promotion to Second Lieutenant early caused no end of problems.

Aviator and personal fiend of "Hap" Arnold, the "Father of the Air Force," more of my uncles exploits can be found on an exceptional website: www.aircrewremembered.com (Note that aircrew is singular). Click on personal and then USAAF/USAF and scroll down a little ways. Irlene Mandrell sings a great patriotic song: "Thanks to You." Click on her picture with a flag in the background. I look a little worn.

Strangely enough, I was kind of the opposite of my uncle. He was involved in quite a few crashes and though I came close enough several times, I was never involved in a crash of aircraft nor automobile after over fifteen thousand flying hours and who knows how many road miles?

I like to tell jumpers about Lt Col Peter Plank who has, and still does, escort many World War II veterans to Normandy. His counter-parts make memorial jumps in Normandy. I tell him that several times I also jumped out of a C-47 like they use. He was curious as to the highest altitude from which I had jumped? I had to tell him it was about two and a half feet. (The C-47 was still on the ground)! He may have felt like it, but he didn't kill me!

While Uncle Emmett or "Pat" was visiting us on our ranch in Colorado in the summer of 1954, looking for uranium like everyone else, his flying stories enamored me even more with the thoughts of glory and of flying airplanes with the fledgling United States Air Force.

Colonel Cornelius Emmett O'Connor, my uncle, my idol! One of the class of '18 that graduated from West Point a year early, in three years and were being rushed over to Europe to end the war. Well, the war ended while they were on the high seas on their way to The battle fields of Europe, but the war ended without them. The Secretary of War said they would go to European battle fields, and even though the war had ended he said a promise is a promise and sent them on to Europe to tour the battle fields as 2nd Lieutenants. Much to their chagrin they had to go back to the 'Point and finish their fourth year as officers. Ergo, there never was a class of '18. That mess didn't get straightened out for many years. The class of '18 is a phantom class. There is no class of '18. I'm not sure it is straightened out yet.

Uncle Emmett was who I thought of each time I saw a flight of planes going overhead at the ranch, probably headed for the west coast and on to the war. At the same time, I saw a movie starring June Allison with the song "Thou Fair, Thou Witty." The song doesn't matter, but I had discovered looking at June Allison in all her loveliness, something that fascinated me as much, or even more, and gave me a greater tickle tummy than did those high-flying machines. "Hmm," I muttered, "There may be something out there as good or, it feels, even better than airplanes." Sadly, I recognized that for now, both were way out of reach. I eventually got to both at about the same time. The Air Force just a bit earlier. At that point, my decision was made. In spite of my parents' misgivings, I enlisted in the United States Air Force on September 7th, 1954.

Now, almost nine months later, our ground training had come to an end. It was time to do what I was meant to do in the newly minted Air Force: FLY!

One more note on Lowry AFB that haunts me still. I was driving up to Buena Vista to see my girlfriend, when they announced over radio station KOSI that they were having a retirement parade for some Major. Though only a one stripe airman, for some reason I thought: "That poor guy, retiring as only a Major." Prescience?

MCCLELLAN AFB, CALIFORNIA

"June 1955, New Wife, New Life"

"And the tale of the "Honey Bucket"

It was May 21st, 1955 and just three days after my twenty first birthday. I had started my two new careers which were beginning a family and becoming an aviator. I signed in for duty as a married man sporting my second stripe (Airman 2nd Class) at McClellan AFB in California. I had also received my Top Secret clearance after much consternation caused by FBI agents asking family, friends and friends of friends all about me for several months. Many of these folks asked me what kind of trouble I was in now? When I told them that I was going to be flying, they looked at me incredulously. I never knew if those looks were doubt or that they were looking at a crazy man. Way up in the mountains the type of population there just would not even give flying a second thought. It was just something that no one would even consider. Yet, here I was! Then, after I learned that I was going to be flying with a very special outfit, wow! I didn't bother telling them that. They would never believe me nor understand, especially if they knew I would get an extra fifty dollars per month hazardous duty pay for flying. Once again, I wasn't sure that I understood. I figured that I should be paying them! It was also here where I learned that it is hard to exist with a wife and a child while making a paltry one hundred and eighty seven dollars per month. (I think that may have been before we started drawing the hazardous duty pay). Our entertainment for the month was often when we would shake out the cushions on the couch and find enough dropped visitor money to buy a six pack of cokes. I still have a W-2 Form where I made a little over twelve hundred seventy dollars for the year! Years later, the military started trying to catch up with the outside world to get their troops equivalent pay for similar work. They were catching up pretty well about the time I entered OCS. After that, my pay scale was a little different, especially after I earned my wings. Dollars be damned! Civilians would never get the satisfaction nor the sensation of having their office at forty five thousand feet above sea level!

I was assigned to the Western Field Office (WFO) of the 1009th Special Weapons Squadron (SWS) of Headquarters Command, HEADCOMUSAF. Most squadrons are commanded by Majors or more likely, Lieutenant Colonels. Our Commanders were two star, Major Generals! Major General Hooks by name during most of my time. Major General Rohdenhouser commanded during my last days there. The 1009th got whatever they wanted, even personnel and airplanes, from Strategic Air Command (SAC) and General Curtis LeMay. We had the number one priority in all of the Air Force because were charged with gathering radio-active nuclear debris from USSR atomic and later hydrogen bomb tests so that the debris could be analyzed. This analysis would let us know what the Soviets were using in their bombs and just how far along they were in developing a bomb that could match ours.

WFO had a Full Colonel Commander and three full Colonel physicists. There were more back at Headquarters in Virginia, as well as a full complement of officers and enlisted men to support them. Some of these folks had gone through Lowry AFB also. We were to join a few other airmen and NCO's already flying for them. It was a grave responsibility we were taking on and we accepted it gladly! If only we had known the hazards, beyond flying in propeller driven machines left over from World War II which had been over for just under ten years! We also gathered debris from our own, the Brits and French tests in the Pacific. Some debris was gathered with and some without their permission.

After a few months of ground school where I learned about radiation and nuclear weapons, I was finally going to fly! Much to my chagrin, my first experience was in a C-47, tail #263. This C-47 was set up with all of the equipment that we would be using and an instrument with instructor who simulated a radioactive air mass. We were to learn the techniques needed for searching and finding radioactive air masses of any intensity. They were teaching us how to maneuver in said airmass to maintain contact with such a cloud. It was as real and as tense as the real thing. Of course, that was the idea. Get us used to the pressure. This C-47 was the military version of the DC-3 which was my first airplane ride from San Antonio to Denver. I really wanted to get into an aircraft with more than two engines and with a tail that wasn't on the ground. It would happen soon. My first experience was in the rear compartment of a giant World War II WB-29 Super Fortress with four engines and a nose gear. It would take me at ten thousand pressurized feet altitude over The Bering Sea to the end of the Aleutian chain or to the North Pole and return at eighteen thousand feet, normally without incident. What more could I ask for?

After several training missions, I was checked out and almost on my own. What was tried and true, we would be required to learn from the experienced Special Equipment Operators (SEOs) before we could go out on our own. We knew that our mission was to search and gather nuclear debris sent into the atmosphere by super-secret Soviet Union Atomic Bomb tests. We also knew there were normal techniques, and some things we would make up on the spot. Some would be just gut feel and instinct. Now it was up to us! A main requirement to become an SEO was the ability to think for ourselves and adjust as needed. We would not rely on just what we were being taught. It was a huge responsibility. Our country's existence literally depended upon it! And, we would be up there on our own! I also had to be ready to depart home with just a thirty-minute warning for thirty days. Needless to say, it was tough on my newly pregnant wife because I could not tell her what I was doing. The calls always came at about 3:AM which, happens to be about mid-day in the USSR. This was my life for a full year and then I got the answer to my earlier question of, "what more could I ask for?"

It was my job as a two-stripe airman (Airman Second Class) to seek, find and collect radioactive debris on an oil impregnated cloth which had been extended into the air stream in a special device designed by 1009th SWS personnel. It could be utilized continually by exchanging impregnated cloths with new ones. We often took in the cloths while we were eating, handling the highly contaminated filters in between bites of sandwich or chicken. More on that later. I don't really know how much radiation I ate during those flights, but it was a considerable amount. At least one of my fellow Special Equipment Operators died of lymphatic cancer. From his flight activities? How could you tell? So far, I've been lucky. Eighty-five years old on the 18th of May 2019 and still going strong or at least still going! I do act a little strange sometimes, but I continue to amaze the doctors with all of my physical conditions "in the green." It could be the martinis! Or Scotch and water? They never buy that. Probably my Gin and Tonic.

We flew most of our missions with the Air Weather Service (AWS). Their aircraft were all modified for our purposes. After a couple years in WB-29s, the Weather Service "upgraded" to WB-50s. They were similar in appearance to the WB-29s, but the mechanics and electronics were different, and not friendly to their crews.

Tech Sergeant Brown and crew took off from Eielson Air Force Base as most of our serious flights did. Eielson Air Force Base is about thirty miles south southeast of Fairbanks, Alaska. They had leveled at ten thousand feet in their Pride of Fairbanks WB-50 christened "The Golden Heart," and had settled in for a modified track to the end of the Aleutian Chain when, without warning, the aircraft took a notion to go straight down into a river north of Talkeetna. This is the town upon which the TV series Northern Exposure was based. No survivors and no cause ever determined. Autopilot malfunction was considered probable cause. Nothing final was ever determined, as far as I know. Strangely, from ten thousand feet, there were no distress signals or calls, the damned thing just augured in nose first. There were others!

This may be a good place to explain the rear pressurized compartment of the WB-29 which is like the WB-50 with two exceptions which I will explain along the way. WB-29's were also stationed at McClellan AFB, but as the 57th Air Weather Squadron. We flew with the 57th when there was no action "Up North." The SEO would be the eleventh man on the crew. We had no crew position available, so we sat on the floor in the rear compartment with our back against the bomb bay bulkhead between the two scanners with no seatbelts. After hanging on for dear life during takeoff, the SEO would take over the right scanner position where our equipment had been pre-positioned and tied down. Looking back upon it, we were the only thing not tied down. We didn't know any better and we had a job to do on that aircraft, so we didn't worry about it.

Let's take a tour starting with the right scanner. They were called scanners, because that's what they did: Scan. They started scanning when they began turning the engine. They looked to make certain there was no fire coming out of the engine nor excessive smoking/fire after engine ignition. The engine start sequence always began with number three because that is where most of the power came from to power up the aircraft equipment. It should be noted that there was always a fireguard who stood slightly front and to one side of each engine at startup. They used to manually turn the engine six times before start-up because all of the oil had settled to the bottom cylinders when the plane sat idle. They turn them now with the starter. The engines always put out a bunch of smoke at start-up because of that oil. Start sequence of both planes is number three followed in order by four, two and one. The scanners also verify flap settings and engine condition. Only two B-29's are now flying. They are called Fifi and Doc. Doc just came on board.

I'll start the tour of the B-29 with the right scanner position because it is the position the SEO occupied after takeoff, though we normally did not take occupation until the aircraft leveled at cruising altitude assigned for this mission. The SEO's equipment is positioned and tied down here. The B-199 sits in a rackmount built into the front of the scanner position. The Esterline Angus, an instrument which copies activity by using a needle that leaves a redline at all times of operation. It sits in a rack mounted on the floor next to the equipment rack. All of the controls which operate the SEOs equipment is mounted in front of the right scanner position. These would include the doors for the E-1 Shoebox, the heaters for same and the power switches for all of this equipment. The Geiger-Muller tube is placed in the "Shoebox" directly behind the filter. All these equipment pieces are tied into the B-199 which is considered a classified instruments so only the SEO can handle it, even getting it in and out of the aircraft. Practically, the scanner normally lent a hand. It determines whether there is radio-active materiel in the air.

Behind the Right Scanner is the Radio Operator. He really has his work cut out for him. When the aircraft is way out over the Aleutian Islands or the far north Arctic Ocean radio reception is spotty or non-existent. I have witnessed a frustrated Radio Operator pounding the radio equipment with a crash axe trying to get the balky thing to talk to him. The antenna reels out of the tail section of the aircraft for hundreds of feet with a lead weight (mouse) which just has to be reeled in before landing or else the lead weight will end up bouncing on past the slowing airplane possibly doing damage to tail, wing or fuselage as it bounces past the plane. He probably has the most frustrating position on the aircraft! He also buys the beer if he forgets to reel in the antenna, though sometimes it gets stuck. Then, all bets are off!

Aft of him is some equipment storage, spare radio parts and then, the far aft unpressurized compartment with the entrance and exit hatch, The tail gunner position was last. Coming forward on the port side of the plane are more equipment racks, storage for the parachutes, the "Honey Bucket" and that large open space which is filled with a big cardboard box which holds all the crew lunches for the flight, normally thirty-three (three for each crewmember). There is a small tunnel above the bomb bay through which a man could squeeze but which, on the WB's just had a small wooden shallow box on wheels attached to a cable, track and reel system by which they could send items fore and aft. This is how the forward crew compartment was able to receive their box lunches from the rear. Next forward was a Dropsonde chute. Perhaps it should be dropsonde "shoot" because it is here that the dropsonde instrument package is propelled by the differential pressure in the aircraft. This is normally the left scanner duty. The dropsonde instruments are shot out of the chute and a parachute is deployed to stabilize the dropsonde decent rate. The dropsonde is an instrument which radios back information while it is falling into the ocean. Some of the more important information relayed back to the Radio Operator is temperature, pressure and altitude. This, folks, used to be the only way you got the weather forecast before satellites were a common thing.

Forward of that is the Left Scanner position. The SEO sat in between the scanners with his back up against the rear bomb bay hanging onto the floorboard for takeoff and landing. When the WB-50 arrived, they added a seatbelt. That was a most important improvement. They also added a relief tube which was almost as important as the seatbelts. On a Routine Loon Echo Mission on which I was the SEO, we were cruising at ten thousand feet passing over Bethel, Alaska getting close to the coast of the Bering Sea and soon to pass over the Pribilof Islands on a beautiful spring like day. We had been delayed for about an hour and a half because when they started to open the hangar door to have the WB-29 pulled out for engine start, there was a cow moose and her new calf right outside of the big sliding door opening! And she was not about to move and no one with any brains was about to challenge her. We all deplaned and went to the ready room and the snack machine and, of course, more coffee. After we finally got going, there was a steady stream of guys using the "Honey Bucket."

We were nearing the coast of the Bering Sea when out of no-where came a short but strong downdraft. It could have come from a single thunderhead building about a mile to the left of our flight path. Anyway, we were hit by that strong downdraft. It lifted me off of the floor and then slammed me back down. No injuries to anything but my pride. Of import is that in the WB-29's, we only had that "honey bucket" I mentioned earlier which was situated about four feet aft of the left scanner position to hold waste. All human excretions from the current flight went into that bucket. You can imagine, though you may not want to, just how bad that thing was smelling after we all had been drinking coffee for a while in briefings and preflight duties without being able to avail ourselves of the scant facilities in the hangar. The beloved "honey bucket" was used soon and often. Directly between the honey bucket and the left scanner position was the space where we put the box containing all of our lunches, three per crewmember. Thirty three box lunches. We had no heated lunches back in those days. We didn't have a means to heat them.

Then the depth of the shock and damage from the downdraft began to creep into our consciousness.

The rear compartment crew all just sat there stunned, and not so much from the jolt of the downdraft. We were stunned alright. All we could do was stare at the bucket, yes, the honey bucket, sitting upside down on our lunches. Would this be a good time to say: "Oh Holy Crap!" One of the brave crewman, not me, gabbed the bucket and returned it to its proper location, but the damage had been done! The lunches were covered with whatever was in the bucket, and after all that extra coffee we drank while waiting for the moose to move? Well, the bucket was now empty. Now, some of the boxes may have been left unscathed and even some, perhaps a lot, of those directly affected probably had dry food inside. It was just that no one, and I mean, no one wanted to handle the top boxes to find out. Damn it got hungry that flight. We shared whatever candy, etc that any crewmember had carried aboard. Scant rations indeed for a long flight!

NORTH POLE - THREE ENGINES OUT

WB-50 Ptarmigan Flight (Modified-Special)
North Pole (Geographic)

"When you Run out of Airspeed Altitude and Ideas all at the Same Time!"

The telephone's shrill ring startled us awake. The time was 0300 hours (3:00 AM) as usual. Another emergency Temporary Duty (TDY) from the 1009th Special Weapons Squadron at McClellan AFB to Eielson AFB, Territory of Alaska.

The caller informed me that a staff car would be by to pick me up in thirty minutes. Others going with me would already be in the car when they stopped for me. They told us thirty days, but could be more. They wouldn't say where we were going, but since there was no extra equipment in the car, I knew it would probably be Eielson AFB to fly with the WB-29's and later the WB-50's of the 58th Air Weather Service (AWS) "Pole Vaulters." We were whisked to San Francisco International Airport (SFO). Our families had no idea where we were going and the destination was so classified that, even if we knew, we couldn't tell them. My wife didn't know for over fifteen years (until after it was partially de-classified) a little bit of what I did. At least she didn't let me know that she did. Our squadron's Top Secret Mission was the #1 priority in the USAF at the time. The mission was of sufficient import that we always carried first class tickets in case there was no room in coach, which in those days was up front.

I was an Airman Second Class (A/2C) Special Equipment Operator (SEO) at the time of this particular action. It was going to be a Modified Special "Ptarmigan" mission flying a track to the North Pole and return unless we hit an unusual air mass. We hit none. Had we detected something, I would have taken control of the aircraft. It seemed strange to everyone, especially the Aircraft Commander (AC), when an A/2C or some other enlisted guy would take control of the aircraft and began telling a Lieutenant Colonel or Major what to do with his airplane, how and where, including altitude changes. When we ran across a radio-active air mass, the airplane belonged to the SEO until he was through with it. The Aircraft Commanders didn't like strangers in their aircraft anyway, but once they were briefed on the importance of the situation, they mellowed out a bit. And besides, they had no choice. One AC objected, didn't follow my instructions and found out what happens. But that's another story in an RB-36.

Nothing had reached us yet from farther west, so we were just out hunting. This mission would be an up and back, departing over Point Barrow and re-turning over the same point, many hours later.

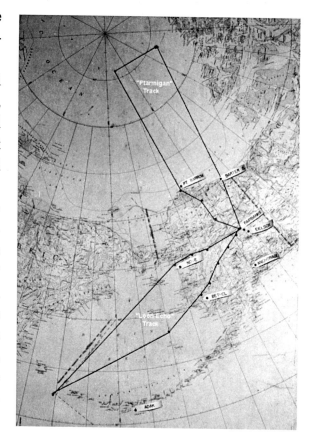

I have explained our equipment earlier, but not the physical location of the biggest piece of specialized equipment.

This most conspicuous piece of equipment, the "Shoe Box" or "Bug Catcher" was a contraption which stuck out of the WB-29 and later the WB-50 from what was originally the top rear gun turret. On the RB-36, it replaced the blister bubble left and aft of the forward crew compartment. On all planes, it stuck out into the air stream around four and a half feet and had electrical vertically moveable doors which could be opened and closed to maintain pressurization while we were changing the filters used for airborne debris collection. Prior to the electric doors, we would have to pull the filter frame out of the airstream, fighting the pressurization of the aircraft and try to plug the hole with a metal insert to stop pressure leakage while we were doing the filter exchange. No matter how quick the effort to plug the hole, both taking out and then replacing the filter, the sudden loss of pressure was hard on the ears of the whole crew. The doors were modified to be heated to avoid freezing up during flight, thanks to Jim Davis in 1955. The filter itself was an oily paper like sturdy, thin cloth that was exposed to the airflow of the aircraft when the doors were open. Thus, any debris which was being carried in the unseen air-mass could be collected on the oily surface of the filter as the air went through the filter.

Though we had attended the Officer Electronics School at Low-ry AFB in Denver, we had not been briefed about the effect of the debris (or fallout) from a nuclear explosion on the human body. Upon our arrival at WFO, we had sessions with movies depicting the effects of the radioactive debris and how damage from an atom-ic explosion really happened. None of it really prepared us for all of the exposure we received. I think they had no answers for the ef-fects. It was just something that had to be done. We were constantly exposing ourselves to the danger of radioactive poisoning as well as long-term effects of cancer and other maladies. Not to mention the inherent physical danger involved in flying in the old bombers.

We were especially vulnerable when we found a "hot spot" with an intense amount of debris in the air mass that coincided with eating our lunch while orbiting in the debris "cloud." Though called a cloud, we actually were searching for an unseen air mass which may be in "the clear" or embedded in actual visible clouds. We searched for and found these air masses at all altitudes and in all kinds of weather. If it was a "good" cloud, we might stay in it for hours. On one mission, a cloud that another operator found was really hot and he was staying in it as long as he could. Unfortunately, he found it when his time in the air was becoming limited due to the amount of fuel remaining. A WB-50 crew was on alert for us. They were "scrambled" to go right away, and I was chosen to be the SEO on the flight. To be "scrambled" meant that we launched as rapidly as possible. We arrived on scene just as they hit "Bingo" fuel and absolutely had to go home. We pulled up alongside the other WB-50 and after I told him I had solid reading, they peeled off and headed back to Eielson. What a beautiful sight to see that big old WB-50 aircraft turning away from us so gracefully. I'll never forget the marvelous feeling I had while watching that plane turning away. There should have been music!

We maintained an orbit in that cloud for a short time until we were advised we had enough of that one and that I should search for another radioactive cloud that they suspected was from a secondary explosion that might be of more significance. In digging deeper into their seismic information, it appeared that two explosions occurred close enough in space and time as to try to fool our detection equipment. We had so many ways to cross reference the findings that they couldn't do much without us knowing about it. This was one of those times.

It didn't take long until we found the other "hot" air-mass. It was following the first cloud by about fifty miles and, naturally, west of the first one. This one was even hotter than the first. I got lucky and flew into the edge of what I thought may be the "hidden" one. I had to turn the plane a few times in different orbital directions until I decided I had found the area with the most radiation. This cloud was truly a hot one!

Later on, they found that this new air mass had debris that our lab folks had never seen before. No wonder the USSR tried to hide it. But we found it and later discovered that they had made a giant leap in their nuclear weapon development. Our lab folks anticipated that it was important enough that they had our Operations people launch another WB-50 to join me and eventually replace me when we went Bingo on fuel and had to return to base (RTB) which was very shortly after they arrived. I don't know what was in that new debris, but I doubt that it did me much good health-wise. It really was a busy and important day and another beautiful scene as the new WB-50 that was taking our place flew on and it was our plane that banked away this time.

Often, I would be eating a sandwich or piece of chicken from our box lunches when the B-199 indicated it had hit its maximum level of detection. The filter had to be changed immediately! And sometimes, if I had found a great hot spot, it would take only ten to fifteen minutes or less of orbiting to max out the filter when the B-199 hit toward the high side of scale ten, the highest scale on the Geiger Counter-like instrument. In this type situation, it wasn't unusual to start the counter on the fifth scale where it would peg almost immediately. When we were onto a great one, we really only used the scales of eight through ten. During this time, I would put down my cold chicken, for instance, for a few minutes, take the exposed filter out of the frame, and fold it several times, all the while handling it with bare hands. Then, I would insert a clean, new filter. After folding the dirty (exposed and debris laden) filter paper several times, inserting it in a paper envelope, writing pertinent information like time, location, intensity, etc. on the envelope, it would be placed in a briefcase right beside us because it was now, though unmarked, ipso facto, also classified. During this period, the exposure would be intense and my hands would be completely covered with an exceptional amount of radioactivity which I would promptly eat. On rare occasions, we would change the hottest filters two or three times during one sandwich. As a result of eating my food after handling the oily filter and then sitting next to several exposed "hot" filters for the rest of the flight, I always joke that, "I probably ate and was exposed to more radiation than was released on Three Mile Island." In fact, I feel certain that all of the SEO's were.

Of course, there were times when we were chasing radio activity which only registered on the top of the lower scales. That's when you earned your money. It was a lot of work to maintain contact with that light contact. Then, when it was time to go home, you might hit a very hot return form that same cloud. Tango Sierra (TS). Nothing you could do about it.

Let me tell you about a kinda strange mission. I set up a saw-tooth pattern in which the plane was to zig-zag back and forth searching while drifting, purposely, in a chosen direction. On this particular mission, I was over the Bering Sea and set up an east to west sawtooth pattern while drifting a little farther west and north on each zig or zag as we searched. We started at early morn and went west until it was very dark and then turned east and greeted the sun only to turn back west again after a short run into the sun, and run out of daylight again We repeated that pattern for hours. I think we saw something like eight sun rises and sun sets on that flight. We did not catch any debris that flight, but we caught a lot of sunrises for one day. My pilots hated me for causing them to face so many bright and unyielding sunrises. Man they really get your eyes!

But, back to the mission.

We were to track north leaving the Territory of Alaska coast over Point Barrow. We normally would come back over Barter Island near the barren northern ANWAR to reach the mainland again, but this time we would be retracing our steps so we would be flying in a new air mass which would have moved to the east and into our path while we were traveling north. Everything was routine and getting boring as hell. We were level at ten thousand feet altitude, cruising at about two hundred forty knots True Air Speed (TAS) up to the geographic North Pole where (since we would be light enough because of burnt off fuel), we would climb to eighteen thousand feet for our return to Eielson AFB. By the way: At the

North Pole, the Navigators' job is easy. Head South!! As we left the coast, I took the right scanner position which had been modified to accommodate our equipment, so it was mine when in flight. Unfortunately, as previously stated, on takeoff and landing, we sat on the floor of the aircraft with our back to the bomb bay bulkhead. At least, unlike the WB-29, they had added a seatbelt in the WB-50. "How sweet of them," I thought. Better, though!

As we cruised along and finally left the frigid waters and were now over the ice pack, I gazed down at the huge pressure ridges. "Damn," I thought. "That would not be a pleasant place to have to crash land. I wonder how many polar bears are down there." As I searched for them, I pondered an earlier briefing: "Polar bears are the only creature that will actually stalk a human being." I searched and found a few shadows that could have been of their creation, but it was probably my overactive imagination? Then I told myself, "Maybe not. Oh crap, get your mind back on the mission. Everything will be fine."

With a noticeable increase of engine power, we began climbing. "Must be at the Pole," I mused. We had leveled at eighteen thousand feet and had been at altitude for probably all of an hour when the first hint that this definitely was not going to be a routine mission occurred, and it wasn't radioactivity.

I was unaware of any problem until I heard the aircraft commander order the Flight Engineer to shut down Number two engine (inboard engine on the left side). Well, I thought, "I don't particularly care for that since we were over the North Pole area, about 1200 miles away from home, over mainly hostile Arctic Territory," but being a non-rated crewman, I wasn't too sure just what that meant except we would be flying over the Arctic ice pack with only three engines working. It wouldn't be my first time one engine was shut down on a WB-29, but, as far as I had heard, it was not as normal on a WB-50, but it still happened. I had also heard that the WB-50 had plenty of troubles, so who knows? I just knew that when they told me to fly, I needed a WB-50 or hopefully, a WB-29 in order to do it. We were assured that, though we wouldn't be able to maintain eighteen thousand feet, we would start a slow descent until we hit an altitude that three engines could maintain until we got home, roughly thirteen thousand feet, no sweat!! In spite of my denials, I kept thinking while looking down at the seemingly endless ice pack out of the blister (the concave window out of which the gunners aimed on the bombers), "How many bears are really down there. I don't like this situation!" But things were going smoothly even on only three engines. Again, "No sweat!" A favored confidence-laden term of the day.

After some hours of uneventful three engine flight, the Navigator's voice came over the intercom to inform the crew that we were over land now, making landfall back over Barter Island, so no more worry about going down on the Arctic ice pack with its pressure ridges or in the Arctic Ocean which was clear of ice, but looked rough if we had to ditch. We were now west of ANWAR's northern barren landscape so I knew that the only thing that now stood between us and safety was the Brooks Range.

The Brooks Range is an unusual formation in so far that it is the only mountain range in the world completely above the Arctic Circle. It is part of the Rocky Mountains and runs east to west in Northern Alaska about one hundred and seventy-five miles north of Eielson AFB. We were holding level at just a tad higher than twelve thousand feet so the long mound of rocks and trees was not going to be a factor in completing a semi-routine flight. The tallest peak was just a few feet less than nine thousand, but was way to the east of us. But, we were continuing to lose altitude!

About thirty minutes after crossing the coastline, I heard that old familiar, "Oh, shit!" from the AC. With that, he really cussed and said: "Feathering number four." I really didn't like the sound of that. That engine was the outboard engine on the right side. A second engine was caged. Now, still north of the Brooks Range, we were down to two engines. I don't know if you've ever gazed out to see two engines feathered and standing at attention when they were supposed to be turning and churning. It most definitely is not a comforting sight! These aircraft were not designed to fly on two engines but at least it was one engine on each side. So, once again, not liking it one bit, we began the slowest descent the aircraft could maintain without falling out of the sky. The increased workload on the two remaining engines did not bode well for their longevity.

We now found ourselves in basically uncharted territory or air if you will. We began descending more rapidly now. I had no idea of what two engines could do to maintain an altitude a little greater than the Brooks Range before us. The Flight Engineer probably hit the books to find out, but they never let us know in the rear compartment. They just told the Navigator to find the lowest way through the range. All we could do was prepare for the worst and hope for the best! It looked like the worst was coming and, as a young airman, I was not real happy when we received the next bit of news. The Navigator said: "The mountain range was considerably lower farther east of our planned flight track. About a hundred miles further it rose up to the highest elevation, Mt Isto. But if we flew about sixty miles farther east of our filed flight plan, we should be able to find a lower area and be able to find a pass and get through, if not over, the mountain range." The AC opined: "This bird should be able to maintain a minimum of six thousand feet, but I'm not going to plan on it. The lowest point in the Range was a little above forty-six hundred feet, Atigan Pass. I'd think we can possibly maintain closer to eight thousand feet, but that may not be possible. I'd like to have at least seven hundred feet above ground level (AGL), if we have to bail. There are several passes through the range but few less than fifty-five hundred feet." This ingenious plan, of course, would take us off of our programmed flight plan route and make it considerably more difficult to be found if we did have to bail out or crash land. And the farther we went, the lower we flew and the longer the flight. Damned if we do, double damned if we don't. Someone said that before me. This lower flight altitude with the current eight-thousand foot range between us and home was making radio contact virtually impossible, so, knowing our position would be a WAG (Wild Assed Guess) at best. This was a real mixture of good and bad news. The good news was that we would have a better chance of clearing the Brooks Range. The bad news: If we did have to go down, search and Rescue would no longer really know where to look for us except farther east of where we should be. "Hells' Bells!" One of my mom's favorite crisis phrases came to mind. "Oh Crap" was a milder version of what I was thinking!

"How would this work out?" I found out in short order. The Aircraft Commander gave the order to suit up just to be safe and ready. "OK, crew, prepare for bailout!" His order was followed by three surprisingly very loud and shrill rings on the emergency bell that you could actually feel. Those three rings did nothing to console me, but it did make it official that we may have to leave this airship. I could have gone my entire career and would have enjoyed not ever hearing those bells. Everyone knew for sure now that we were in a life threatening situation. And if there was anything in the area which I didn't want threatened, it was my life. Three shrill bells was supposed to get you ready for an emergency. They just scared the living shit out of me! If I had been standing I probably would have been running in tight circles in the narrow space between the scanner positions. I was going to have to give up the right seat for the rest of the flight. Hopefully, until we land. As it was, I was fortunate I was sitting on the aircraft floor. If I hadn't been, I'm not sure where I would have ended up. Emergency bailout in arctic temperatures over remote unpopulated terrain is a terrifying ordeal to contemplate, especially for an airman who was untrained in survival techniques. That command is always a chilling thought (literally) to me and most sane aviators. We were still over very hostile terrain and headed for worse. As we neared the Brooks Range, I could hear the crew up front on the intercom, discussing our options, which were few.

A decision had to be made! Try a crash landing in terrain about which we knew nothing or bail out. And, as we could see, the area below was wall to wall, or rather limb to limb with trees which would tear this plane apart if we tried to crash-land. We had two choices the way I could see it: Bail or find a hole in the mountain range. Not real good options, but they were options! Our best option, in my mind, which didn't weigh anything in this situation, was attempt to look for a low point in the mountain range or limp through a valley we didn't know was there. My vivid imagination imagined, "It was like choosing whether you wanted to be hung or shot!" One hell of a choice!

Finally, I heard the Navigator say that he thought he found a pass on his radar that he thought was the Atigan Pass. If so, we could squeeze through at our current rate of descent, but it would be close. This was the chosen option with the proviso that we all be ready to jump if it became clear that we would not be able to make it through and over the narrow break in the mountains. "I hope this Topo (topographical) chart is accurate. If it is, we'll clear the pass the with about fifteen hundred feet to spare," It was the only real choice. The Aircraft Commander ordered everyone to be ready. The sudden sound of the extremely loud and shrill bell ringing three times again, (prepare for bail-out) was not comforting. Once again it about made me piss in my arctic flight suit. It was a real attention getter! That was also the signal for everyone to tighten their parachutes and get into position to take a leap of faith. Scared? You bet your ass I was, and probably not the only one!

I'd never had this much problem putting on a 'chute before. Why in hell did I take it off when we were still in a bail-out situation? Now I was having a hell of a time trying to get the son-of-a-bitch back on. I had to re-loosen the straps to fit them over my arctic gear. Then, I found myself fumbling with the straps. Fear will do that to you when you are rushing so much that not a damned thing worked right. I don't know how the crew up front prepared, but in the rear it was dis-organized chaos.

In the aft of the aircraft, our jump point was the rear ingress/egress hatch located on the starboard side of the aircraft. The front compartment crew would go out through the open wheel well door. The Aircraft Commander had already depressurized the airplane and we were at only about sixty-five hundred feet and slowly sinking as we approached the mountain range.

Finally, with my chute on so tight I could barely walk, I left the two scanners and waddled past the radio operator on my left. They each gave me a good luck pat on my butt. Just like playing football, I thought! I managed to make it through the hatch that opened to the rear unpressurized compartment and tail gunner position without throwing up, but I now knew what dry mouth and bile from raw fear felt like. With a feeling of foreboding, I pulled in the rear exit hatch door and tossed it toward the unmanned tail gunner position. What a shock! The wind rushing by was loud and cold. I used to want to have to bail out. Today, I changed my mind with a feeling so strong, it would last throughout my flying career or forever, whichever came last. I just flat ass no longer wanted to bail out! I was too frightened looking out our open hatch watching the trees go by to even think about anything or anyone else!! I felt about as numb as my fingers, which were out in the slip stream, did from grabbing the sides of the door so hard. Just moments ago, we were snug in a metal cocoon. Now our safe cocoon had a couple holes in it and I was standing so close to one hole that I definitely no longer felt safe. I also knew that dropping the nose gear for egress up front was going to cause more interruption of airflow which wouldn't help at all. Lowering the front landing gear and hatch door would cause more drag and make our sink rate increase, I just didn't know how much. I didn't know anything nor feel anything. "Well, shit," I thought, "What in hell kind of a mess did I get myself into this time? I might have to reconsider my life's vocation if we get through this."

The SEO, being an Additional Aircrew Member (ACM) would be the first to jump. I never did like to lead the pack and I could think of no worse time to experience that feeling than right now! I had my gloved hands on each side of the open hatch, ready to propel myself out and down when the "GO" signal came. We had already been alerted by the very loud three rings of the "prepare to bail out" signal so the three other crewmembers in the rear of the aircraft were lined up behind me at the rear hatch preparing for the single prolonged "GO" signal ring which would mean that the Aircraft Commander had flipped the toggle switch to the "On Steady" position and had left his seat. I knew that I If didn't go immediately, I would be pushed out and have no control over my egress, so I was committed. Right at that time, I saw a road below us. Possibly near hysteria, my mind wondered (I wonder a lot in tight situations about things that have nothing to do with the tight situation), if there may be an eighteen wheeler going against our direction. I wondered what he would be thinking when he saw this giant airplane coming straight at him at tree top level doing about a hundred and fifty very noisy Miles Per Hour! I wondered if he would have swerved off the road! I wondered if he had a change of shorts! I wondered if I did! I wondered if we would make it. I wondered if I would make it. I wondered why I wondered! Stupid thoughts at the scariest times! Defense mechanism? I'd bet it would scare the crap out of him too! That would make one more scared soul in this area.

We felt the plane banking several times as the Radar Operator feverishly worked to find a way through the Atigan Pass. The Pilot merely tried to follow his instincts and the brown dirt road of the Atigan or whatever pass it was below him and take advice from the radar Nav. The dirt road should be taking the lowest route. The Nav had his eyes on the absolute altimeter which measures the distance from the ground directly below you to the belly of the plane. Obviously, it was changing too fast to be of much use at this time, but the last reading was a solid sixteen hundred eighty feet. Finally, the aircraft stabilized and the "all clear" call came. We had made it through the pass!

With the greatest feeling of relief I had ever felt and a return to normal breathing, we returned to our crew positions. I didn't even bother closing the egress door. The warmth of the aircraft interior with closed compartment hatch was a welcome respite compared to what we almost had to do. I assumed that everyone still had dry pants (though we left our Arctic gear on, just in case of another engine failure) and another potential to still bail out. I admitted to myself, "I know damned good and well I would have pissed my pants if I had been forced to bail out. And, if we do have to go, I'm sure I will." We were getting back to normal, if you can call flying on only half of your engines normal.

As fate would have it, not too long after clearing that low, narrow pass in the center part of the Brooks Range, but a little closer to Eielson AFB, number three engine decided to quit. "Now," I thought, "I might end up pissing my pants anyway!" We were basically a power-assisted glider with only number one engine engaged. Fortunately, we still had about six thousand feet in altitude and the elevation at Eielson was only at about 550 ft or so. Plus there were no more obstacles of any import between us and the extra-long three mile plus Eielson AFB Runway. And, if we had to crash land now, we would at least be on the right side of those damned mountains, have only semi short aspen trees instead of tall fir and spruce to crash through and be closer to the rescue choppers, which were standing airborne alert at both Eielson AFB and Fairbanks Airport. But, the worst part about number three quitting is that most systems on the plane relied on power from that engine. Now, elevator, aileron and many other hydraulic and electrical controls would be more difficult to work. Damn, those trees and bushes were really close now and I could not see any sign of a runway from where I was sitting. A shut down number three engine was in the way. The AC had not rung another bell, so I guess things were OK. Not for me. I was still logging some real pucker time. I would give anything to be standing on the Eielson flight line tarmac now watching this little drama from down there. Hell, anywhere would work as long as I was standing on the ground. Instead, I was sitting on the floor of a wounded airplane with my ass cheeks trying to grab hold of the floor where I sat cross legged! With both pilots working together exerting energy to work the flight controls, we rode a long, low and slow descent to final approach and a smooth landing. I barely felt the bump on landing. Good pilots! The fourth engine quit on roll out after touchdown. I never knew why. I didn't want to know. Because number three was out and braking was so difficult, the pilot just let it roll out. Later, I found out that we had barely made it to the runway. Or, at least, that is what I was told.

Amid the eerie silence of our wounded bird, we quickly exited the aircraft and left it sitting on the runway for the ground crew to handle. We didn't want any more to do with it! I do not know to this day exactly why the fourth engine quit. I also do not know why any of them had to be shut down along the way. I suspect fuel contamination, but here again, not being part of the 58th Air Weather Squadron nor cockpit crew, I never did find out nor did I care. We were on the ground safely, thoroughly traumatized, but on the ground safely! No one said much.

After it was over, it just seemed like a wild adventure to tell stories about to other members of our Team TDY personnel. As with all emergencies, it was hard to believe that it had happened, after it was over. Besides, I had another mission to fly.

An aside: Back in the old days, a lot of folks described flying as hours and hours of boredom punctuated by moments of stark terror. Well, those were my minutes of stark terror. On some missions, as with the F-4 Phantoms, it would be split seconds, or a micro second. And, as you will read later, it could be hours long, but still moments. Unfortunately, SEO's were never sent to any type of survival school, so we knew absolutely NOTHING about surviving aircraft emergencies and accidents except to go upwind if you made it out of a burning aircraft. The rest of the crew had been through at least some survival schools and certainly Arctic Survival School or Arctic Exercises. I was a neophyte and scared shitless. I had no Arctic training and no idea of what to expect.

As I learned years later in the longest damned three week Official USAF Survival School, the worst thing to face is the fear of the unknown. This was facing both stark terror and the fear of the unknown through an open hatch, preparing to bail out into the Alaskan wilderness and into the extremely hazardous terrain. I remember thinking, "That 'chute better open fast because I could see the individual trees swishing by below me." I knew that I had to pull the ripcord handle fast, but not before I had pushed myself out and down after I had completely exited the aircraft or I could easily get tangled on the horizontal stabilizer. I remember that the air rushing by was loud and cold, but I had my arctic uniform gloved hands on either side of the hatch, cold but ready to propel myself into the unknown. Fortunately, there was still light during the long summer. This could easily have been my last minutes of facing stark terror and the unknown, a potentially deadly combination. Add in dark of night and it would have been even devastating! All in all, it was a day in the life of a crewman in the reciprocal engine days! Little did I know, I would have worse and more frightening days on down the road.

Although there were more than several other frightening occasions during my fifteen thousand plus flying hours, I still feel that I lived in the Golden Age of Flying as well as Sports, Music and Automobiles but, especially flying and that sweet danceable music. For some reason I always thought of close dancing to those old songs as a sweet, enjoyable navel engagement. One of the only battles to be enjoyed. Among those golden things, I feel that the most important part of my fifteen thousand plus hours of flying was with the Aviators of the 1009th Special Weapons Squadron (SWS). They are so different, but I feel those flights rank right up there with my flight to Gia Lam Airport in North Vietnam. From almost each flight for the 1009th SWS, we brought back something VERY important to the United States. Radioactive debris from USSR nuclear tests so our physicists could analyze our progress against theirs. The USSR was definitely our enemy!

There would be more flights of WB-29 and WB-50's out of Eielson, including the tragically interrupted flight of The Golden Heart. We had a Special Equipment Operator (SEO) on board. Tech Sergeant Richard "Brownie" Brown, arguably our best SEO, was flying a special mission. The WFO Commander, his Executive Officer (XO) and I went to Alaska the next day. I replaced Tech Sergeant Brown and filled the rest of his Temporary Duty and flying schedule. We had lost one of our most competent and admired Special Equipment Operators as well as one hell of an NCO.

Two more of my close friends were in horrific accidents while flying WB-50's from Yokota Air Base just north of Tokyo, Japan. On one flight, the entire crew perished when they ran into a mountain on approach to landing. The other accident claimed all of the nine man crew except for our Special Equipment Operator and the Radio Operator. Both were alive with severe life-altering burns from the crash. That crash was the catalyst for changing from leather gloves to Nomex (fire retardant) flight gloves which was a great adjustment.

One notable crash happened when one of our SEO's was on a WB-47 six jet medium bomber. It's possible that the crew was inexperienced with the local runway. The jet crashed on takeoff at the notorious "ski jump" which was a small, but dangerous lift of the runway just short of the location of normal takeoff speed. It lifted the bomber into the air before it had achieved enough airspeed to maintain flight. A few feet either way, and our guy might still be alive.

We lost several other crews in non-WB aircraft. We lost the whole crew in a YC-121 turboprop. It was a high flying, speedy, non-conventional three tailed Constellation "Connie" which kept ground radar continually seeking answers, especially when it set a trans-continental record for prop driven aircraft, making it from McClellan AFB to Langley Field in four hours and fifty-five minutes! In those days an aircraft was required to check in frequently when they were handed off to traffic controllers of different air sectors. Each time they called: "C-121, Lockheed Constellation, flight level thirty-two thousand feet, air speed four hundred fifty knots and ground speed an estimated five hundred forty knots," the response was always: "Say again type of aircraft." They couldn't quite believe it. There were only four "Connies" converted to turbo prop. Two went to the Navy and two went to the Air Force. As I said earlier, we had some clout. Our squadron was given one for its Western Field Office Operation. This crash was a tremendous blow to the 1009th Special Operations Squadron. Here again, we lost some very good men to what it was surmised to be an auto pilot that locked onto ground level and could not be overridden. We later also lost a C-118 North of Sacramento to supposedly the same problem, with the same tragic loss of life.

Even though we had lost several of our aircraft and best men, the search for that important radio-active debris continued.

RB-36, THE EQUATOR

"Six Churning and Four Burning"

At one time earlier I asked: "Could I ask for anything more?" I received my answer not too long after. I guess the bosses felt I needed some flying time with approximately zero chance of running across something worthwhile. They wanted, I guess, to let me fly a non-contact mission in the RB-36 in order to get over the awesome feeling of being inside this 'beast'. And I was ready. What a thrill to be able to fly in the largest production airplane ever built (still to this day). It boasted six of the largest piston driven engines ever made for flight. They were, in this case, pusher prop engines, meaning they were facing the rear and mounted on the back side of the wings. It also had four jet engines, in pods of two, slung under the outer wing tips. They faced forward! The wings were seven feet thick, so the engineer could access the piston engines in flight. If there was a problem with the main landing gear, they also could be worked on in flight. The two Flight Engineers would keep those six engines churning for as long as possible, working on them as necessary. Of course, the plane had to be unpressurized to do this maintenance. The two jets on the outer and under part of the wing were not accessible in flight, but they were so reliable that they were almost always burning though normally not used in level flight. The landing gear could also be worked on in flight, though it was rarely necessary. The six engines were so complex and the panel so large that it took two men to man the thing! Originally, the engineers were Technical Sergeants, but when General LeMay realized how complex was their job,, hey were immediately upgraded to Captain. Now, that is one hell of a spot promotion!

Obviously, it was quite a thrill to hear all ten of those engines roaring at almost full power while the pilot kept the brakes on and the plane was rocking and shaking like a stallion ready to come out of the starting chute while the two engineers made final checks. The noise made by these ten engines at power level Maximum Except For Take

Off (METO Power) was deafening. My body throbbed in response to the violent vibrations of this much horsepower and thrust. If I had tried to make conversation it would be impossible. Even trying to think was difficult. Forget all the thrill rides in any amusement park. They couldn't begin to measure up to the thrill of sitting in an aluminum tube with this much power (about twenty-five thousand horsepower from the six piston engines and twenty thousand pounds of thrust from the jets shaking the plane in all directions), while sitting, strapped and confined, to such a small area. Then, the two engineers, at their huge panels, took the engines to full power and waited for a few seconds before the Aircraft Commander released the brakes. When the brakes were released and maximum power was applied to this monster, we were physically thrown back into our seats as we began thundering down the runway. We couldn't have moved if we had wanted to. If you happened to live within, hell, I don't even know how many miles, of a B-36 base, there was never any doubt when one of these babies was taking off, especially when they started their takeoff roll. Oh, that beautiful sound!

This may be a good time to explain the importance and capability of the B-36. It was called the "Peacemaker" because it never fired a shot in anger, though I will later tell you how close it came to not maintaining that reputation. It was an essential machine to the U.S. Air Force and our country as a whole. It is now my intent to describe the specifications of this aircraft in a narrative so it doesn't

sound too much like a Tech Manual. It is written in a manner intended to interest you and let you understand just how this aircraft protected our country for years after WWII without ever firing a shot.

One of its most important characteristics which kept the enemy at bay was its massive bomb carrying capacity of 89,000 pounds of nuclear weapons at an altitude of forty-five thousand feet (It could cruise at up to fifty thousand feet and a little over, though fifty was the max allowable) for a distance of over 10,000 miles. This put any target on earth within its striking range. Yep, these statistics are pretty impressive! At this altitude, it flew above any anti-aircraft weapons available and it was also above the effective range of the radars of the day. The combination of those two things made it the most formidable weapon system of the late 1950's and into the 1960's until the B-52 replaced it. Some might argue that the six jet engine B-47 was the real replacement. Not true! The B-47, a magnificent machine in itself, merely supplemented the B-36 until the B-52 arrived on the scene. It did not replace it.

Of course, because the B-36 could not be refueled in mid-air, most of the missions they would fly if called upon, were one-way missions. This meant you could reach your target and deliver your bombs, but you couldn't get home. Hopefully, you would have reached friendly forces awaiting your arrival in enemy territory or, better yet, just reach friendly territory! They were not truly suicide missions, as they were normally called, because you would have been ordered to go and survival was always a real possibility, though sometimes a long shot.

The B-36 was truly a monster. Imagine, if you can, an aircraft larger than the Air Force's C-5 which in turn is larger than a commercial 747. The wingspan of the B-36, 230 feet, was longer than the distance of the Wright Brothers first flight! The closer you lived to the base, the more your dishes in the cabinet would rattle.

Each R-4360 pusher engine had four curved rows of seven cylinders earning it the nickname, "the corncob." Each cylinder had two sparkplugs. Doing the math gives a total of fifty-two sparkplugs per engine and an astounding three hundred thirty-six sparkplugs powering each aircraft. Maintenance people hated it when a bad engine start easily fouled all the plugs and the entire block of fifty-two plugs had to be swapped out. It was safer to not even be around when they had to change all three hundred thirty-six of them. Maintenance on the R-4360 piston driven engine could be a real pain in the ass! It was the largest piston propelled engine ever used for flight with a propeller that measured nineteen feet in diameter, which was geared down, so the prop tips wouldn't break the sound barrier, causing it to lose efficiency. The R-4360 was used not only on the largest airplane ever mass-produced, but on C-119, B-50 and C-97 aircraft. Additionally, it was used on the KB-50 and KC-97 aircraft. The K stands for refueling, but I never knew why. The extreme loaded weight of both aircraft loaded with fuel caused the reject speed to be quite low because of the time it took to get the heavy refuelers rolling. I have been told by "tankers" that the reject speed was about thirty-five knots because it took a fully overloaded plane so long to gain speed that it was so far down the runway, that by the time it reached thirty-five knots, it could no longer stop safely, again determined by the weight. This was considered the speed at which the decision had to be made to either "go or no go." Many times, the way these overloaded refuelers got airborne was simply because they ran out of runway! If they couldn't "GO," they had to get off of the active runway immediately because there well could be another KC or KB coming fifteen seconds behind it.

There was no such problem with the RB-36. Once that behemoth got rolling, it picked up speed rapidly and we were airborne in just a few moments. Once off the ground, the lighter RB model climbed like a homesick angel. I once watched thirty-six of these wonders of flight take off at minimum intervals at Eielson AFB outside of Fairbanks.

After takeoff, they formed up southeast of the base and then made a low-level pass in formation above the three-mile plus long runway. I was where I could see them and hear them for a longer time after the flyby. About ten or fifteen minutes after their fly over, the noise faded. They went out of sight several minutes before. As soon as I heard the rumble of their impending return the next morning, I made it out to the ramp in plenty of time to see them fly over again, back in formation, but with more than several engines trailing smoke or standing at attention, feathered or if you will, just plain stopped. "Shut down because of oil light on steady would be my guess," I thought. It seemed like it took them forever to land. The spacing was always longer for landing than the fast-paced takeoff. Thirty-six B-36's could take off in eighteen minutes at fifteen second intervals. It took almost an hour for all of them to get on the ground.

Having been designed to carry nuclear weapons that weighed as much as eighty-nine thousand pounds of individual or combined weight, the Reconnaissance model was much lighter than the straight bomber version. It has been said that flying this thing was similar to driving your house from a small front porch. It could still climb like crazy and though it maneuvered like a battle ship, the massive size of its wings gave it a pretty good maneuverability at high attitude which as you will see later, could come in handy at times.

It wasn't an uncommon sight to see a full Squadron of B-36's flying together on some Strategic Air Command (SAC) exercise. Six cells of three of these huge aircraft for a total of eighteen planes was a beautiful sight! Some B-36 airbases had squadrons of fifteen and some even twelve. As far as I know, three squadrons of any size made up a wing. Though it didn't happen often, a full SAC Wing of these aircraft would be launched and joined up for a formation flight of these monsters flying overhead. It seemed they blotted out the sun. It was called the "Aluminum Overcast" for a reason. As you may be able to discern, I loved this plane. Where else could you call Squadron or Wing Operations and say: "Three engines out, no emergency!" You would still have seven engines working.

It would be time to go home and you weren't going to fly at 45,000 feet, but you could still fly with no problem.

And the sound! It was like no other! It was a medium pitched drone. Absolutely unforgettable! If you can find it, you should watch the movie "Strategic Air Command" with Jimmy Stewart and June Allyson. It is worth the hour plus it takes to watch it. You can get a snippet of takeoff by googling "SAC," Strategic Air Command or B-36. They have a great replication of the sound of a B-36 taking off and in flight at cruise power. The geared down nineteen foot propellers gave a very low pulse at ground level and also betrayed its approach from miles away. There are several websites on Google with this feature.

As described earlier, The RB-36, the Reconnaissance (Recon) model, was lighter than the standard B-36 because it carried no bombs or associated equipment. As the Recon model was set up, the bomb bays were loaded with men and equipment. It was outfitted primarily for photo, communication and detection stuff including an in-flight dark room for finishing photos in flight. It carried one camera so powerful that it could focus on a golf ball from forty thousand feet. Now, why you would want to focus on a golf ball from forty thousand feet, I truly don't know. But, if you did, it could! All models also had on the port side a long tunnel. It was the length of the bomb bays with a trolley on two rails and an overhead pulley and rope system so men, equipment and food could be transported back and forth between the rear and forward compartments. It was easy going to the rear compartment. In fact, the trolley had to be restrained when going from forward to aft. However, it was a little tougher pulling yourself along that long tube to get to the forward crew compartment which I had to do early on many missions. A parachute was always worn when going thru the tunnel. We were always warned not to hit the outside of the tunnel with the parachute hardware for fear of a rupture. It was about negative sixty degrees at altitude. This tube was closed off upon reaching thirty thousand feet elevation. Because the aircraft was pressurized, if a rapid decompression occurred, the person in the tube would be shot in the direction of the decompression area like a cannon ball out of a long-barreled cannon. This was not ever considered to be a good thing, so I had to be sure to be in the proper end, normally the front, before the hatches were sealed. If I had nothing to do at the time, I would often sit on one of the steps leading from the Radio/Radar compartment to the flight deck. I'd swear, you could almost count the revolutions of those gigantic prop blades as we cruised along at forty-five thousand feet.

Whenever an aircraft left on a mission, it always had an alternate airfield assigned in case home base was unable to take them back in because of fog, high crosswinds or, perhaps, an accident on the runway. I was thinking about that on this particular flight. We were flying out of Travis AFB, California in one of the RB-36's. After the briefing, I was dreaming, "Acapulco!" That was our alternate airfield. All we had to do was shut down (or lose) several engines, declare an emergency and I would finally see a city that I had heard so much about. I was dreaming of those warm, white sand beaches, exotic flowers, enticing seafood and all the other wonderful things offered in the movies and in printed commercials. We were headed for the Equator on this mission, planned for twenty-seven hours. From all my previous flights on this monster, I knew we would lose at least one and up to four engines. Wow! My chance to see Acapulco! Of course, I had about two bucks in my flight suit pockets. Surely the officers would help out a little airman like me! Actually, I'm not sure why I was on this mission except to get experience. We most definitely did not expect to find anything going south out of Travis AFB, but I changed filters hourly as required on a normal mission. Well, it happened before we reached the equator. "Shut down number two. The low oil light just switched from flashing to steady." I thought, "OK, one engine out, a long way from home, and still headed away. Just a couple more and it would be several days in Acapulco, paid for by Uncle Sam." But, it was not to be. We hit the equator and flew west along the dividing latitude (zero degrees) of the earth for about an hour and a half, cutting the mission a little short during which time, after clearing with the radar navigator that there were no fishing or other sea craft in the area, the AC told the tail gunner to lock, load and fire about two hundred rounds from his dual 20 millimeter (mm) guns. I was shocked! The noise and the shaking of the aircraft from several short, quick volleys surprised me. It lasted for a short moment, but in that time it had disrupted some electronics by shaking the vacuum tubes sufficiently that they became loose in their sockets. Fortunately, the electronics affected were easily accessible as was everything else and it was all quickly fixed. Because it had happened many times before, they were pretty sure which ones to check first. It also occurred to me that, "It was a hell of a long way to go just to fire a few rounds of ammunition!"

I couldn't help but wonder what happened when they still had their full complement of weapons if they fired their double twin 20 mm's from the six retractable turrets and the forward and aft weapons all at once. These retractable turrets rose out of the aircraft from hidden spaces imbedded right behind the flight crew compartment and one more just forward of the vertical stabilizer plus four others. That really must have shaken up an intercept aircraft pilot. I know one of those pilots who was shaken up by such a thing when he was stationed at Roosevelt "Rosie" Rhodes NAS in Puerto Rico. Gene Ockuly never forgot seeing those twin 20 mm's rising out of the top turret of the B-36, locking on him and knowing that he had been had! He could see that those twin weapons were not pointed at him, but they were leading him just right so his aircraft and the bullets from the 22 mm's would arrive at the same airspace at the same time. One Marine A-4 fighter/interceptor splashed! He said that it was the most incredible feeling in the world. Incredible and most eerie! He lived next door to me in Kailua, Hawaii, stationed at MCAS Kaneohe when he recounted that to me.

From my experience of hearing and feeling just one set of twin 22 mm's fire a few short bursts, it seems to me that firing them all at once in a heated battle would shake the aircraft so severely that it could do real damage. I'm just speculating here, but I really doubt that they ever fired them all at once in practice just to avoid such damage. The shaking of the entire aircraft from the tail stingers alone would actually be scary until you got used to it. Then it would be only worrisome! It also must have been disconcerting and have been something to behold. Making a run at a huge aircraft with no discernible defense except a nose and a tail gun position, when suddenly, where there had been no defensive equipment, these twin agents of death rose out of the aircraft as menacing as anything ever seen! Shortly after turning back north toward the United States Mainland, the panel engineers were told to shut down number six engine. Two engines shut down and still no emergency. I was thinking, "Each of these Pratt and Whitney 4360 engines carries about 100 gallons of oil. Wow! That's just about enough to float a boat and they would still run low after twelve hours or so." It makes a person appreciate the efficiency of an automobile.

I suffered such disappointment because I realized there would be no diversion into Acapulco this trip. I told myself, "I'll make it someday." Years later, after I retired from the Air Force, I did get to visit there several times. The sand is brown!

After we landed and taxied in, the marshals directed us to the appropriate spot on the tarmac. The ground crew scurried to set the blocks in front and in back of each landing gear. "Good Lord," I silently prayed, "Thank You for letting me fly instead of being on a ground crew or some inside desk job." Really, when you get right down to it, I guess, it is all about the flight wings. There's not a very large percentage that get to wear them. That is especially true of the enlisted ranks. The military is only about two percent of the population and the Air Force is just about twenty percent of that. Only approximately five percent of the Air Force personnel are authorized to wear wings and only a minute number are authorized to wear both Enlisted Crewman and Rated Navigator wings. I am among those fortunate few!

Upon deplaning, I became aware of something that rocked my sensibilities. The ground crew was just getting ready to go to lunch when we launched, debating where they should go for lunch. Now, here was that same ground crew chewing on toothpicks and discussing what a great lunch they had just eaten. "This is unreal," I thought. "I have either lost my mind and we have only been gone for an hour or I have just lost twenty-five hours to eternity!" A surreal experience for sure!

CHRISTMAS, 1956

"I Hear It Coming. Hear It? Sounds Better than Santa."

It was almost Christmas. In fact, it was 22 December 1956. We had just finished up another operation at Eielson AFB, Territory of Alaska, and we wanted to get back home to Sacramento in time for Christmas. We had just completed a very long but successful ten day session of gathering nuclear debris from USSR nuclear tests. Now it was time to go home!

Right now, it was looking a little dicey. There were three of us. I'm not certain of all their names, but there was a Staff Sergeant, an Airman First Class and an Airman Second Class. I was the Airman Second Class. We were stuck in Alaska which was a long ways from home.

We had lost time trying to wend our way down from Eielson AFB where we had been hunting the debris. The hottest it got during those ten days was a minus forty four degrees and it got down to a minus fifty five. They were expecting a cold snap when we left! We had reached Elmendorf AFB and were now dead in the water. We finally caught a C-124 out of Anchorage to McChord AFB, Washington. Now we were stuck between the new Seattle-Tacoma International Airport (SEATAC) and McChord AFB. Naturally, we tried getting a ride from McChord AFB to McClellan AFB in Sacramento, California first, but there was nothing active and nothing scheduled which would get us home in time. In fact, McChord was virtually closed down until after Christmas. We weren't really too concerned though since we had commercial tickets, including First Class, which we always carried with us. So, off we went in a jolly mood because we thought we might be able to get tickets into Sacramento Airport or, if not that, at least to San Francisco International (SFO). We had decided to just go ahead and use the First Class tickets as a nice "thank you" from our outfit, the 1009th

Special Weapons Squadron for a job well done in extreme weather. No sweat, right? Wrong!

We arrived at the great new airport and with broad smiles, wandered up to the ticket counter and plunked our blanket tickets on the counter, explaining our preference, but ready to accept the alternative. We could get home by either flying to Sacramento or to San Francisco International Airport. The 1009th would send a staff car to pick us up at SFO, which we would prefer because they would drop each of us in front of our homes.

The jolly atmosphere turned a little sour when we were told there were no seats in coach. Fine, we were going to go First Class anyway! They looked a little askance at these enlisted guys asking about First Class. Their attitude changed when we showed them our open passes. Nope, no space there either. Well, crapola! Here we were, world travelers with the most important mission in the Air Force, and we appeared to be grounded. No problem, we could take a later flight. SEATAC was a nice new airport with shops and eating places with nice comfortable chairs. We could cool our heels a little bit and then be on our merry way. Back to the jolly mood again!

Nope, no later flights available either. That's when near panic set in. As we had all learned through our Air Force and Flight training,

it did no good to panic. We just had to discuss things and something would fall in place. We decided we had better call "mother," a term for our home office at the 1009th. The home office then called McChord AFB and was told that a flight was coming down from Elmendorf AFB. It would be stopping at McChord for refueling before going on to Travis AFB, between Sacramento and San Francisco. There, a staff car would be waiting for us. Just let them know what time. Off to McChord we went on the Air Force shuttle bus which ran from SEATAC to McChord AFB and then on to the Army's Fort Lewis, just south of Tacoma. The Air Force Base and the Fort were separated by a ten foot chain link fence. Yea! We were going home. Well, to this day, I don't know what in the world happened to that big old C-124 that was supposed stop at McChord and take us on to Travis AFB. Evidently, they decided they had enough fuel to overfly McChord or they never got out of Elmendorf or just whatever. Bottom line: It never showed.

The good folks at SEATAC had told us that we could sit on standby and hope that someone would not show for their flight and we could have their seat. That started the serious talking. What if only one or maybe two seats opened up? Who goes? By protocol, the ranking man or men would go first, but these were great guys. They said that since I had a family and they didn't, that I, the lowest ranking man, should go first. In this outfit, we didn't depend on protocol. We just did what we saw as best for the overall well-being of the unit. I tried to talk them into a lottery type drawing or some other means of deciding. They would not hear of it. They also decided that only one would not stay behind. It would be one or three seats. Two seats would not work, except to get me on my way!

Well, we were getting nowhere fast, but at least if we went back to McChord AFB, we could check in with Base Operations again and Passenger Service and see if anything had changed. At least, we could grab some free eats at the Chow Hall. So, we gathered our bags once more and got on the old blue Air Force Shuttle. I wondered, "When will it stop running? When it did stop, what would happen if we were caught at the wrong place?" We must be careful, so we checked and kept checking the schedule. We would be OK for now. But, it quit running at nine o'clock. It was six o'clock and Passenger Service had closed for the day and nothing was going on at Base Ops. They didn't know what happened to the C-124 either. There are two more fully-booked flights to SFO over at SEATAC, so away we went again. We stood near the gate as we watched one, then the other depart without us. It was now eight-thirty and closing in on the nine o'clock shut off time for the shuttle. Time to catch that last shuttle to McChord. We had been keeping our own Flight Ops up to speed with what was happening. Captains Martin and Copeland felt our pain! Didn't help!

Same story at McChord, so I figured, "We need to put this and us to bed and get up early for the first shuttle to SEATAC, after checking with Base Ops, of course. First, catch a late dinner at the Dining Hall."

The next day, we ate an early breakfast at the Chow Hall and then jumped on the first shuttle to SEATAC. Damn it! We got the same old story, except many fewer flights this day, which really cut down on our odds of making it home. Still, we had to sit and hope. Again, the futile shuttles back and forth. We were waiting for the most recent and next to the last plane to leave for San Francisco. No room! I wondered aloud, "Is this how Joseph felt? No room at the inn?" We were not anywhere in the same league as Joseph, but we were looking for a ride, just not on a donkey. We'd take almost anything that was flying south. Then, one of the guys alerted the others to pay attention and listen. Then all three of us heard it, even though it was not very loud and a tad garbled.

We almost missed it! And, we still weren't sure. "Did you hear what I heard?" a puzzled Staff Sergeant said to no one in particular. "Yep" I said, "It sounded like someone is paging you. Where is a white phone?"

I stressed again, "It sounded like you are supposed to pick up the white telephone. I haven't seen one, have you guys?" I heard two "Nopes!" The now settled down Staff Sergeant again looked serious as he said, "Well, let's get busy and find one. Let's spread out and don't wait for me to pick up the phone. Go ahead and pick it up and see who is calling me and why." That said, we all took off on a scavenger hunt. As luck would have it, the ranking man of our little contingent found one and answered. By the time the others picked one up, it didn't even have a tone. It was dead! My heart, which had been hopeful when I heard the intercom call, just hit bottom. "Well, I hope one of the others got to it." I wondered what it had been about.

Suddenly, almost flying around the corner was the happiest Staff Sergeant I had ever seen. The big ol' grin almost broke the corners of his mouth as he said, "Guys, we have to get back to Mc-Chord. That was Lt Col Koeschner and he said that we needed to be at McChord in two hours. WFO was sending a plane up to get us." Damn, that was hard to believe. They were making a special flight from Sacramento just to pick up a couple stranded enlisted guys. "Man, I'll never cuss out an officer behind his back again! Well, at least, not without cause." It turned out that our HQ at WFO had been calling the Enlisted Quarters, Base Ops and the Terminal and couldn't find us. The page we finally heard was the third page they had tried here. What luck that the crowd thinned out when that plane left without us and we finally heard the page! We had to catch one of the shuttles back to McChord ASAP! They were running less often now because of the holidays. But, we finally caught one and it would get us to Base Operations in time. We all wondered who would be flying up here on December 23rd to get us home in time for Christmas? EXCITEMENT REIGNED SUPREME!

After we were finally inside Base Operations, we found nothing but empty seats. We had the place to ourselves! We took our seats and began a long nervous wait. The Estimated Time of Arrival (ETA) was still over an hour and a half away, but soon, we were straining our ears to hear the sound of our faithful training plane, the Gooney Bird we so loved, Tail Number 263. Then it dawned on us exactly what was playing out before our eyes. Well not actually before our eyes, but in our minds and understanding. We asked Base Ops who was flying the plane up here to greet us and what type of plane. We actually were pretty sure from the long-awaited ETA to get us. As soon as he told us, we understood. Two of the finest officers in the organization!

There was a Captain and a Major from our organization who were giving up their day before Christmas Eve to fly all day long to salvage the Christmas holiday for a couple of Airmen and a Staff Sergeant. But we were THEIR Airmen and Sergeant! What a sacrifice on their part. If I ever write a book, they will definitely be a part of it and a VERY IMPORTANT part of it!

Captain Copeland and Major Davidson are flying up from McClellan AFB in old "263." It was just a C-47, but it was our C-47 and, I'll say it again. It was similar to the DC-3 in which I had thrilled to my first flight in a real airplane from San Antonio to Denver. I was thrilled with the DC-3 then and I would be thrilled with the C-47 now. That now seemed so long ago! Captain Copeland and I became very close, lifelong friends, and not just because of this incident!

I hollered at the other two, "I hear it coming! Hear it?" The Airman First Class said, "That was a motorcycle, dummy!" I guess I was straining so hard that any sound seemed like the little C-47 coming in on final approach for landing. We decided to stop trying to hear the plane and discuss exactly what these two rated officers were giving up for us little guys.

We figured out that they would have to give up their whole day because the Gooney Bird, aka C-47, could travel at only about one hundred thirty-five knots. The distance between McClellan AFB and McChord AFB is about six hundred statute miles or about five hundred twenty-five nautical miles. It would take about four hours flying time including approach, landing, taxi, time, etc. Ground time for refueling, re-filing flight plan and checking out the old bird would be another hour or so. That gave these valiant and selfless pilots just enough time to quickly wolf down a quick lunch. They had given up over ten hours of valuable time from their own Christmas preparations so we could make some of our own. If you count their pre-flight and other times mentioned above in preparation for the first leg of the flight from McClellan, we are talking upwards of thirteen hours that they gave up for their men. That, folks, really counts in my mind! Is it any wonder that we would do anything for them?

Several times we thought we may have heard that two engine beauty, and strained our eyes looking south to see if we could spot it coming in from California. It was time. No dice! Then we heard a little sputtering sound and looked over to see it coming off the runway onto the taxiway. It had landed from the north! Dumb shits! If any of us had half a brain working, we would have noticed that there was a south wind, and they would always land into the prevailing wind. As aviators, we knew this, but in our excitement and anticipation, just flat forgot about it. Feeling foolish and elated at the same time, elation rapidly took over the stupid!

We all made it home on the eve of Christmas Eve!

OPERATION PLUMBBOB

"Don't Trust Anything with Wings That Go in Circles"

Summertime! Hot and dry with HOT being the operative word. Nonetheless, it was still summer in a little US Airbase about forty miles as the crow flies north of Las Vegas.

Frenchman Flat and Yucca Flat were farther north, just south of the Yucca Mountains. Frenchman Flat was used as the continental nuclear test site and there is a nearly six square mile dry lake bed that used to be Frenchman Lake. This was used as a 1950's airstrip before it was chosen after the start of the Korean War for the Nevada Proving Grounds. The name was changed in 1955 to the Nevada Testing Site. It is considered to be one of the most significant nuclear weapons test sites that existed in the United States. I read that somewhere, but I'll be damned if I can think of many other sites of nuclear explosions outside of Nevada except for digging a hole in a mountain in New Mexico and, of course, Trinity Site in New Mexico where the first nuclear explosion occurred. Farther from home, a harbor in The Territory of Alaska didn't work too well. Digging a trench in Alaska with nuclear explosions didn't work out either nor trying to dig a parallel to the Panama Canal. All things were thought to be possible with nuclear power. It is still best for just blowing things up! One thing we were taught at WFO that I think is worth sharing: The initial force of the blast is not what causes the most destruction. That outgoing rush of air, weakens the building or anything in its path. But, it is the force of the expelled air rushing back to fill the vacuum caused by the explosion that really does the flattening of the buildings. It just happens so fast it appears that the initial explosion wipes out everything.

Yucca Flat was one of four major nuclear test regions within the Nevada Test Site. It is located about ten miles from Frenchman Flat and sixty-five miles from Las Vegas. Yucca Flat served as the testing site for seven hundred thirty-nine nuclear tests.

Operation Plumbbob is one example of the thermonuclear tests that were conducted at the Nevada Testing Site. It was also the biggest, longest and most controversial test series to ever take place in the continental United States and included twenty-nine nuclear tests. A series of twenty-nine atomic bombs were detonated to allow the study of the effects that nuclear explosions had on structures, people and animals. After this operation was declassified, it was noted that about three thousand servicemen were also exposed to high levels of radiation during the testing.

For those at the gambling tables, it was "business as usual" for the chandeliers and lights over the tables to start swaying. That was a sign that yet another nuclear blast had just been detonated and if you looked north of the city, you would be able to watch a mushroom-shaped cloud rising quickly at first and then getting slower as the top of the mushroom flattened out. Fortunately, the crows were not flying today.

However, there was a lone RB-57 Canberra which was flying right into the middle of that rising cloud. Though shaken terribly by the intense turbulence within the roiling cloud, the light bomber came back into view and headed south, intent on making a quick and unobstructed landing at Indian Springs Air Force Base.

The B-57! What a plane! The batwing aircraft was a British born airplane which I would later learn to hate as a crewmember after it had been modified by us smart Americans, but not because of it. The cockpit was now tandem instead of side by side as shown. The wide winged plane had two jet engines imbedded about ten feet on either side of the fuselage.

The wide wing made it very maneuverable. On this occasion, the two-seat crew compartment was occupied by a shaken up, but steady-handed pilot, looking to get out of the immediate area and that doubly hot plane. He was more than ready to get back to an air-conditioned de-briefing room where he would be grilled on his

opinion of just what he had seen, heard, felt and any other affront to his sensibilities that he could remember clearly while going through the rising cloud. He had come out of it at a higher altitude than he went in though he fought to keep it level. They could see that from the instrumentation they had on the ground which was a safe distance from that nightmare cloud he had just penetrated.

The B-57 was also hot! Very hot! But not only desert hot from the oppressive heat of the desert sun. It was very hot from nuclear radiation that covered every inch of the low slung aircraft. It had just been driven by a test pilot through a radio-active nuclear cloud which was the result of the explosion.

The sequence to cause a nuclear explosion required a certain finesse. First, there was a small amount of TNT strategically placed so it would cause intense and precise inward pressure for less than a micro second on the radioactive core of the bomb. This caused the equivalent of seventeen kilotons of TNT (seventeen thousand tons, or a full 34,000,000 pounds of TNT) to explode. The size of this nuclear explosion was that of the "Fat Boy" bomb dropped on Hiroshima. You know how that turned out! That's why this bomb was detonated so far outside the city and population centers in the middle of the desert where it was barren of any sign of life of any kind!

A hefty gambler glanced up at the swinging lights as he picked up his dice and from around his cigar-filled mouth growled, "Yeah, Baby!" as he rolled a seven. Life went on without a break in the gambler's game. Another explosion of lesser magnitude would rock things later in the month, but they knew that was it for this day.

Back at Indian Springs, we were not concerned about the gambler, his cigar or his natural seven. A cherry picker was standing by to lift the pilot out of the aircraft so the he could avoid touching the side of the plane, thus avoiding coming in contact with some very intense radiation. That was nice of them, but why didn't they have a little bit of the same consideration for us little guys? Instead of getting away, we had to go toward the nuclear hotness. We were in the middle of a nuclear nightmare, though we or they couldn't see it. They didn't have that much consideration for their little airmen. Actually, that could be wrong thinking. They still did not understand the unforeseen consequences of the intense radiation. One would think that the after effects of the radiation and resultant suffering of the Hiroshima and Nagasaki weapon explosions should have given them a clue. In their defense, the difference in intensity cannot be overstated and the time element must be considered. So many of the maladies of such tests were not realized until years later.

At this time, in retrospect, I guess we were expendable, but not on purpose. They meant us no harm, but they did not care to join us either! More likely, even the "Powers That Be" did not yet understand the full extent of the dangers involved. Giving them the benefit of the doubt, I think they did not know just how bad this exposure could be or else they wouldn't have given us that pathetic protection which they issued. Of course, my simple mind wondered if we might be a continuation of their test on the human body as was the nuclear shot exploded with about six thousand troops nearby and another one with a few brave (or crazy) folks directly under it with no protective clothing. I just do not know how either test turned out and if those souls suffered as a consequence.

As for the preparation for our participation in the B-57 combined experiment, our intrepid and ever-so-concerned leaders issued us one-piece fatigues on a temporary basis. They were covered with a spray painted rubber coating and we were given meat-cutter gloves sprayed with the same protection. I guess that after World War II, they figured that rubbers protected everything. Not always! The spray painted rubber coating on our fatigues and the meat-cutter gloves were hardly the protection needed to provide a real barrier against new and highly radio-active nuclear debris. They would however stop Alpha particles.

Oh! They also issued dosimeters which measure the radio activity level near you. They are normally worn on your uniform. The first one they gave me pegged at maximum exposure while I was looking at it before I put it on my "uniform." The issuer said, "Hmmm, must be a bad one. Here's another brand new one." It pegged at maximum before I could even get it on my uniform. "Well, shit," he sighed. "This must be a bad batch of dosimeters. Let's try a different kind." Pegged! Finally, he told us, "Well, their effectiveness is questionable anyway so go on without them." Being still fairly young Airmen First Class (A1C), we couldn't very well argue with these "experts." This is when I discovered the honest to God truth: An "ex" is a "has been" and a "spert" is a "drip under pressure." I wasn't buying that "Expert" part.

Now it all made sense. We'd have to go it alone with no one really taking care of us. Bill Drake and I ventured forward after the B-57 taxied into its dedicated spot. After the pilot opened his canopy, the "Cherry Picker" picked him clear of the plane. So much for him, he is safe, but he also is a pilot and an officer. Actually, he was a Major which made him much more valuable than a couple of three stripers! Doubtful in retrospect, having been both.

But we sallied forth with the specially designed poles, which had never before been used to remove filters. They didn't work! You would think they would have tried it once on the B-57 sitting on the ramp before it flew through the cloud. We found out later that it hadn't worked in practice either. They had tried it on mock-ups of B-57 tip tanks. I guess they assumed us "experts" in the field would, just by being "experts," instinctively know how to work a pole contraption which we had never seen before. Their logic was fatally flawed from the git-go! Bill and I took the poles anyway to give them a try. We looked like quite the pair in ill-fitting, blue rubber covered suits out looking for windmills to tilt!

The poles wouldn't work so Bill walked up to one tip tank and I walked up to the other with the spray rubber painted meat-cutter gloves. We discovered the fingers wouldn't bend enough to allow us to hold on to the filter. We had to discard those worthless gloves and did the only thing that made sense since we couldn't just disappear.

We couldn't run away (First Choice), so we went in barehanded, throwing the meat-cutter gloves aside. Our bare hands had about the same amount of protection the meat-cutter gloves offered so we grabbed the filters with no protection at all. The only advantage was the speed with which we could act. The shorter amount of time at the B-57 meant less exposure. Even barehanded, we had problems getting the filters loose from the filter frame. They had been designed to withstand the 450 knot speed the B-57 reached going through the cloud. They were not designed for easy removal! It was no wonder that the pole contraptions were ineffective in removing the filters.

While handling these contaminated filters for way too long, we were being bombarded by Alpha and Beta particles as well as Gama rays. All are microscopic types of radiation. At least the Gamma rays would go on through our bodies, although excessive amounts would do harm to the recipient of the bombardment of these rays. Alpha particles were of sufficient size that they would only cause harm if they entered the body through a sore, abrasion or, by *breathing*. Beta particles were of such minute microscopic size that they could easily penetrate skin and soft tissue where they can cause burns of body cells with sufficient exposure. Normally, though we are surrounded by of all of these particles, they are of insufficient quantities to cause harm. A nuclear detonation is "another kettle of fish," as my father would say. Excessive amounts of any of these can cause extreme damage to body cells, normally resulting in cancer. I've been very fortunate. So far, no scare. My buddy Bill, not so much!

After a struggle, we both finally got the filters removed and, out of habit, folded them neatly before beginning the short trek to some special boxes. We carried them from the B-57 tip tanks to where the transport boxes were situated, a prudent distance away from the "hot spot, and deposited them into those pretty wooden cases in which they would be transported to the lab for analysis. Those pretty boxes were lead-lined! The lead was at least two inches thick all the way around. I guess they wanted to protect someone! "Damn," I thought. "Look at the lead in those boxes. They must have thought this stuff was really hot! They were right! And they knew it! From that point forward, anyone around these cases would be well protected.

They called Bill and me over to a cement slab where a high-power water washer hose was located and subjected us to a hurricane force spray as we were told to turn with our arms in the air to cleanse us of the contamination. "Too little, too late" was my thought! About fifty years later, Bill died of lymphatic cancer. No connection was ever established as far as I am aware.

While still in Nevada, Bill and I discussed the situation while broiling in the incredible heat of the sun-drenched Quonset huts. We were searching our minds trying to resolve just what negative things could happen to us because the mission didn't go as programmed.

How were we protected? We certainly weren't protected by two inches of lead. We were protected from a courts martial because we had followed legitimate, if misguided orders. However, I'm not too sure these would be considered legitimate orders. But we followed our orders so we were protected there. Bill offered another but. "But we were in this Top Secret outfit so perhaps no one would ever know because we couldn't speak out without violating our clearance agreement and really getting into trouble." I chimed in: "I'm upset because they just treated us like they would damned guinea pigs. In fact, we weren't even treated like real guinea pigs. They are used to test new things." As far as I knew, the dosimeter fiasco was never revealed beyond our mentioning the problems to our immediate superiors. That is, I felt sure, as far as it went. A couple of young airmen might have just been sacrificed.

The scientists and other real experts knew enough to stay a prudent distance from the ultra-hot B-57. They told us since we were military and from the 1009th Special Weapons Squadron, we should be able to handle the job more efficiently than they could. "What a pile of horse shit! But worrying about abstract potentials would get us nowhere." Bill agreed.

At that moment, Captain Coppage, an Officer Candidate School (OCS) graduate himself, walked in unannounced and asked us if we would like to see Las Vegas from a helicopter. Upon hearing this invitation, we both answered "Yes, Sir." It was an almost simultaneous response. Neither of us had ever ridden in a "chopper" before and it immediately made us quit mulling over the negatives of the trip. Perhaps this unexpected treat was designed to do exactly that? Captain Coppage said, "I have a buddy here who is an H-21 pilot and he said he would give us a guided tour from about five hundred feet if we could go right now." Bill and I jumped up, grabbed our hats and damned near ran over the good Captain as we exited that hot Quonset.

He had a jeep waiting right outside of our door so we were off to the flight line in a flash. Waiting for us was the H-21 which is a banana-shaped double rotor, double ugly machine. I began to have my doubts. My Uncle Emmett had warned me not to get into anything where the wings go in circles. But a tour from the air of Las Vegas was enough to override his admonition. With a great roar, the helicopter jerked itself into the air. Bill and I were both strapped in, so we could sit at the edge of the open sliding door. What a thrill! But, I have to admit that a tickle tummy bit of fear ran through me. Years later, I figured it was just a shot of adrenalin from the excitement! I was airborne in a machine that I had never been in before and that I would likely never ride in again. That thought about the shot of adrenalin was pretty damned close, as was proven in later years, but at that age and rank, I couldn't see the future very clearly. For some unknown reason, I still can't!

Oh yeh. The ride! It didn't take that long to cover the forty some miles from Indian Springs AFB flight line to downtown Las Vegas, but it was one heck of a ride for a couple of young airmen who were used to flying in C-47, B-29, B-50 and B-36's. In retrospect, it seems strange that we were excited to be flying in a helicopter which was actually comparatively small. However, for its day, it was considered a large helicopter, if not the biggest. Nonetheless, we had already flown in the biggest production aircraft in the world. It was just so different with those two wings rotating around while the chopper was doing whatever the pilot wanted it to do. We stared at downtown Las Vegas as the pilot gave us a guided tour. He pointed out the Mint Hotel and the Golden Nugget. Those two and a couple more like the Horseshoe and Moulin Rouge were the biggest gambling casinos at the time. The Golden Nugget reportedly had one million dollars-worth of twenty dollar gold pieces in its window. I couldn't fathom that at all. Then we flew on to Henderson, Boulder City and beyond to Boulder Dam. What a tour! On the main street south of the downtown area was a place called the Saddle Club where an aspiring young star with "an Eastwood smile and Robert Redford hair" was performing nightly and then getting together with the likes of Tex Ritter, Jim Reeves, Hank Thompson and other future and current Stars after his own show for an after-hours jam session at the Showboat. Years later, he became a flight instructor at the Military History Center at 112 North Main.

We were just beginning to tour the relatively new Las Vegas Strip which, at the time, consisted of only about ten smallish hotels, some of which were still under construction. The pilot mentioned that Bugsy Siegel who was famous for operating the Flamingo Hotel and gambling operation was murdered in June of that year, just in the last month! Evidently one mobster killed another mobster. They all had great influence in Vegas at that time. His killer was never "found."

Suddenly, the H-21 swerved and headed back toward the base. It had been called out on a rescue mission in the Lake Meade area which was its purpose for being stationed at Indian Springs. We were unceremoniously dumped on the Air Base ramp while he whirled off. That's what helicopters do. They "whirl off." Hopefully, it "whirled off" (I like that term) to a successful mission.

After two weeks in the hot sun and several nuclear shots, none other in which we were involved, we were going to go home. The only reason we were there that long was just waiting for our shot to go off.

Now, it was back to McClellan AFB to get our radiation the old fashioned way: Eating it! Yep, eating it on our lunches during cloud chasing missions!

And so it went!

EIELSON AFB RB-36

"Nav, Where in Hell are We?"

The cause of one of my next deployments was that Moscow had set off an air shot which would carry the debris much higher than a tower explosion. This time, two of the four modified high-flying RB-36's were dispatched on short notice to Eielson AFB. Where the bomber version (B-36) carried a normal crew of fifteen men, the RB-36, because of all of its cameras, dark room and other reconnaissance equipment carried a crew of twenty-two. The Special Equipment Operator (SEO) from the 1009th (us) would be the twenty-third crew member. I was designated to be the SEO on the first mission. I had flown in this magnificent flying machine earlier on a familiarization twenty-five hour flight during which I had plenty of time to study this beauty. Living up to its great nickname, "The Peacekeeper," it never fired a shot in anger during the long "Cold War!"

But it almost did!

This would not be the first RB-36 of which I was in control, but it was the first one to get airborne for this rather unusual shot by the USSR. I was selected to go up in the big plane, the first aircraft to go after this shot. WB-50's would go up a little later because, the thought was, that the lower heights of the debris field would travel more slowly than the winds that should be in the fast-moving higher altitudes. (They hadn't started calling them jet steams because there were no jets flying up there yet). The WB's also didn't have the range or endurance of the RB-36. I had found a fairly productive air mass a few hours after leaving the frozen tundra and the east coast of the Bering Sea. My instruments as well as my instincts told me we had run into the leading edge of a much larger cloud of USSR nuclear debris. It wasn't real hot, but as I had the navigator elongate the orbit toward the west, it kept getting hotter and my Geiger-Mueller meter kept going up to a higher scale. I kept changing filters as required. I finally told the AC to go on heading 255 degrees for about ten minutes and see what we would see. What I saw was the readings increase in intensity until I felt it was fading a bit. I requested and received an orbit that I felt was completely within this hot air mass. I requested a racetrack orbit in an east to west elongated orbit. Then, all hell broke loose!

The Radar Navigator said over the intercom, "Hey, Aircraft Commander, I have a fast-moving target coming up toward us from a peninsula just south of our location. He is closing fairly fast. It must be one of those new jets."

The AC shouted, "Nav, where in hell are we?" Silence for a few seconds and then, "OH, SHIT! We're over Siberia! There must have been a wind shift 'cause we're now over USSR territory!" The AC shouted over the headset, "We're doing a 180 degree turn and getting our asses out of here, NOW!" Engineers, give me METO power. The Navigator came on and said that a heading east, north east would get us clear of the land mass quickest and we'd be going away from that damned jet. "Go to heading 075 degrees!"

All engines went very close to max power and the beast started shaking from all the power being applied so suddenly. The tail gunner came on the intercom and said softly, "I have him on radar and he is closing fairly fast. What do you want me to do?" The AC said, "We don't have much choice. He is going to try to shoot us down! Lock and load and when he gets within two thousand yards, let him have it!" He was still closing pretty fast, going over four hundred and fifty knots. Our airspeed was up to two hundred ninety and the gunner was keeping the AC apprised of the situation. The gunner said, "Six thousand yards and closing!" An intense silence took over the intercom. Everyone was holding their collective breaths. Everyone, including me, was wondering. We were wondering what it would feel like to get shot down. We didn't know how much time we would have to get out of a fatally crippled aircraft. We couldn't help wondering if our flight would end up with all of us floating slowly to the ground or crash landing on the partially frozen Bering

Sea? Our thoughts were suddenly interrupted by three very shrill rings on the alarm bell! Scared the living shit out of everyone. Damnit! Couldn't he at least give us a little warning? Three bells told the entire crew to get ready to bail out.

We all immediately went for our parachutes. I was getting tired of this drill! After fumbling a little bit because of nerves, my 'chute was fastened as tightly as I could get it on this skinny body. If we get shot down, each of us would try to get out of the crippled or destroyed aircraft. There were several egress positions throughout the plane. I had no idea of the fire-power of whatever it was that was chasing us. Ultimately, we were all wondering if we would die. I was wishing I could get into the tunnel and go back to the rear of the aircraft where it would be easier to egress. The gunner again reported, "Five thousand yards and closing." The sudden, rather loud and shrill voice that harshly broke the silence startled me, "Shit, man. I really didn't need that!" "He's still gaining" came the words from the gunner as he broke the silence again, but I was listening for him this time. Then I heard him again, "I have a visual on him at about forty-five hundred yards and closing pretty fast. I am locked on to him with my weapons' radar. He's going to be dead meat if he keeps on closing." The AC ordered the tail gunner to continue counting down in five hundred-yard increments. The AC had been around a long time and had heard stories about a maneuver which could be used against these fighters though it had never been tried before as far as he knew in an actual combat situation. He had nothing to lose by trying it. The gunner reported, "He's at four thousand yards and closing."

Man, it was getting tense in here. We all started logging pucker time. "Oh crap!" We could all end up dying while over Soviet territory. I doubted they would ever return the bodies, but, that might be preferable to ending up in a Gulag which were getting a lot of publicity lately.

I wondered what my last thoughts would be. Would they be about my wife and child or of God? Maybe it would be about Mom as they always cry out in the movies. I decided it really wouldn't matter. I'll find out what everyone wonders about. What in hell is really on the other side after you "buy the farm." The gunner stated, "Thirty-five hundred yards." Scared me again! His voice was higher pitched and a lot louder this time. It really caught me off guard again! I knew I should pay attention, but there was nothing I could do but wait and see what fate had in store.

"OK, crew. This is the AC speaking." I jumped again! He warned us, "First of all, we're going to have to pull back on the throttles before we shake this plane apart. Then it wouldn't matter what that fighter does! In the meantime, at three thousand yards, I'm going to put this plane into a hard bank to the right. You will be experiencing up to three G's so get buckled in if you aren't already. We have to go south around Saint Lawrence Island anyway, so we might as well start now. The "Ruskies" shot down one of our unarmed Navy planes that was flying overhead there about three weeks ago. I understand we lost thirteen good men. I'd just about as soon shoot this bastard down to get even, but that would cause a whole lot of trouble. We just cannot over-fly St Lawrence anymore. But the reason for the tight turn is that I have heard that a MIG 15 or possibly, even the new MIG 17, can't stay with us at this altitude in a tight turn. I want to make it before he has a chance to get off a shot or before we have to shoot him." "OK, AC." I jumped again. Talk about tense! Again, we heard from the gunner, "He will be at three thousand yards in about ten seconds." I was buckled in tight in the canvas seats, but I grabbed the seat supports for good measure, not that it would do any good! "Holy Crap, let's get this over with! I have to take a leak now, but with much more of this, I won't have to worry about it!"

The AC shouted over the intercom, "Hang on folks, we're going for a little ride and see if that boy can keep up with this grand old lady!" Man, he stood that big ol' plane on its wing tip or so it seemed. He held it that way for about thirty seconds until the "G" force began to dissipate. He leveled off after a turn of about ninety degrees. Man, it felt good to be flying level in this monster again, even being chased down by enemy aircraft. It crossed my mind that flying level was a strange thought in this situation! We heard from the gunner, "Still closing at about twenty-eight hundred yards." "What?! It didn't work. Now what in hell do we do?" I had barely gotten that thought out when the tail gunner said quietly, "He's starting to make his turn after us. You can see him out the right side view ports." I got up and immediately ran to one of the narrow windows. The gunner was right! I could see him. He was a small dot with stubby wings. I wondered if this would count as combat action if we ended up shooting him down or if he gets us. Another one of my wild, wondering thoughts!

"He's slowing down," was the almost scream I heard in my headset. This time I was ready for it. All senses were tingling! I heard the gunner reporting, "He's fading. The yardage distance is getting larger! We are getting separation now! Wow, it looks like he's quit. Oh, oh, it looks like he is falling out of the sky. AC, tail gunner here. I think we've lost him. My guess is that he flamed out." Our leader then reassuringly replied, "I think you're right Gunner. Now let's get our asses out of here before they send up a better one. Nav, give me a good heading for going around the south side of St Lawrence Island, and then we'll go back north and try to intercept that debris field again but hopefully over neutral or US territory. Better yet, just take us over Saint Matthew Island and overfly Nome. That way you'll have a definite starting point for your grid navigation. I know it is a real pain in the ass to do, so that will give you a decent start. Then we can turn northwest and be pretty safe. We still have about thirteen hours of gas left for this mission, so let's settle in and relax for the remainder of our little jaunt. And, Nav. Don't screw it up this time!" Yep, over the open water of the Bering Sea and Arctic Ocean sounds pretty good right now. I'm glad the AC made the decision to go do some more cloud hunting so I didn't have to ask him. After what just happened, I'm not sure how he would have taken it. But, if we went home early, he would have a hard time explaining it. Now, he can just say that we went looking for better returns. "Attention all crewmembers. You can loosen your chutes now but keep them on for a little while longer. This little trespass may have pissed them off and they could launch out of St Lawrence Island. I had heard the theory about that last maneuver and that those MIGS couldn't hang with us at this altitude. Now it has been proven, Theory no more, but I'm glad we weren't at thirty-five thousand feet. That could have been a different story entirely."

The AC told the tail gunner to secure his weapon and quietly observed that: "No airplane in the world could keep up with us in a turn at forty-five thousand feet.

They may get one shot off, but that is all. And not even that if the turn is done correctly. He didn't get that close, fortunately for him!" Then I heard, "Hey, AC. Radar Nav here." I thought, "Uh, Oh. Now what?" Radar said, "There is a small slow-moving target going toward where we had last seen the MIG. Looks like they are sending a rescue chopper for the pilot." The AC said, "Let's get on with the mission and say nothing about this. Got that Mr. Weather Control? (The name of our crew position when we were in control of the aircraft) I humbly mumbled, "Yes sir. I know nothing," and this was before Schultz!! "I realize that this is a Top Secret mission." One of the crew of twenty-three said, "About what?" That's the last I ever heard of the incident and this will be the first that anyone other than the involved crew and a few they talked to will hear of it!

It was beginning to get dark when we hit the cloud again even farther north west. This cloud must be huge! We set up a productive orbit again and I was getting some great high-level returns. Our operations folks figured I had found part of the same debris cloud so they told us to come on home. That finished off a very productive mission when we were called and directed to Return to Base (RTB) early because they were anxious to start analyzing this stuff and we had enough already. The WB's would probably get more anyway since our position was given with each message I had the

Radio Operator send back to "Mother." In fact, they said they had a WB-50 in the air already heading toward our last position of contact to intercept the lower stuff.. But, we were all ready to call it a day. The Radio Operator relayed the message from my people that I could just do routine hourly filter changes from now on. "Hunting season is over. Nice job!"

The return to Nome and home was quite routine after we were once again over our side of the Bering Sea and were back in US territory. At least, it was routine until we landed back at Eielson AFB. As soon as we had taxied into our parking spot on the ramp, the airplane was surrounded by flashing red lights. "Oh, crap!" I thought, "They know we violated Soviet airspace and it was because of me. I'm really in big trouble!" The AC came on over the intercom, "Well, crew, it looks like we are having a little reception of some sort. Weather Control, do you know anything about this in your Top Secret World?" "Don't even know what it is, sir. But it may be because I led you astray?" "Not about the mission. They just told me after we shut down. We're going to have a "No Notice" trip into the Alaskan winter wilderness I hope everyone brought their A-3 survival bag with them and that it is not stuffed with newspaper." That was a common way to make an arctic survival bag look like it is full of heavy gear when it is only full of paper. Those who did that and were caught in this situation immediately regretted trying to get by without following the rules. You would be in for a rough week, mostly trying to sponge survival things off of other disgruntled crewmembers. That crewmember would not be very popular because he had caused the crew to be downgraded as a result of his indifference to the rules. In Strategic Air Command (SAC), rules are sacrosanct.

This did not look good! "Damn, where do I hide?" I didn't know what to do. Here I was an A/1C from a different unit, knowing nothing about what was happening except that I didn't like it. The aircrew was being herded directly from the B-36 into two blue Air Force buses. After I climbed down from the big plane with my B-199 in hand, I weakly tried to voice a protest, pointing at my equipment and telling the Non Commissioned Officer (NCO) in charge of this new survival situation that I wasn't one of them. He really didn't believe me, but I told him I was scheduled for a WB-50 flight in two days and that my outfit needed me to be there. He thought I was nuts! He called a Major over who was the overseer of the entire survival school. The Major asked me, "Do you mean that after this mission on an B-36, you are going to go fly in a measly B-50? I think you're either crazy or lying. Where is your arctic gear?" I replied, "I have none. I just have the Mukluks and this parka that I am wearing. I'm with a Top Secret team here on Eielson AFB. They don't issue survival gear to any of us. Perhaps they should, but they don't. See, here is my Classified equipment." He said, "Yeh, right. Top Secret, huh? If you are, you are the only Top Secret airman I have ever had the displeasure of meeting. What is the equipment for?" "I'm sorry, sir. I'm not allowed to tell you." This got him steamed. He still didn't believe me, and I didn't think he liked me and he said, "I think you are lying and I also think you are in a heap of trouble if you are not ready for a little trip into the frozen unknown. Now get on that second bus! Also, I want you in my office within one hour of your return from this exercise." Being scared halfway shitless, I finally shouted, "I am not a member of SAC!" It was actually more of a plea. "I'm from Headquarters Command and you'll have to check with my Team commander here on base for verification." The AC wandered over and explained my unique situation to the frustrated Major. He had been watching the exchange from a short distance away and enjoyed seeing an airman who had taken over his aircraft and had almost gotten him killed, getting his ass chewed out. After explaining the situation to the Major, he said, "Major, you have just met an airman who indeed has a Top Secret clearance and is doing a pretty important job. I think you best listen to any airman who claims to have a Top Secret clearance, especially on this base. There are things that are more important than running a damned survival school. Now, let's get this exercise underway. It's dark and cold already and it will be fun enough getting set up in a base camp after we all try to get back together after they drop us off scattered across the wilderness."

That got me away from a miserable week or so in the Alaskan wilderness simulating survival after a bail out. I thought, "I am certain that I definitely do not need an Arctic Survival experience." Then, I thought, "Maybe, and probably, I do, but I do not want one!"

BURTONWOOD AB, UK & KEFLAVIK NAS, ICELAND

"We expect our crewmen to be exceptional"

"That's why we hand selected them"

This time, it was not the 3:00 AM phone call which I would normally get to alert me to get my skinny ass up to Alaska. (I still only weighed about a hundred and thirty- five pounds) It was mid-morning at McClellan AFB, when we heard a commotion outside of our normally tranquil "A" Section. The "A" was the designator for the flying part of the 1009th SWS. I guess we were the original "A" Team? Suddenly, the door to our tranquility burst open, completely upsetting my chess game! And, I was winning and about to lay a checkmate on my chess nemesis, Gary Moles. An unusual happening indeed.

Captain Copeland was the doing the "bursting." "Damn it, guys, we missed it, and this may be the one we were waiting for!" About ten of our Flight Ops team had been lying in wait, in Alaska like buzzards for this special Soviet air mass. They had gone out early in their WB-29, WB-50 and RB-36s. And they were even deploying the U-2 for ultra-high altitude. By this time the 58th AWS (Air Weather Service) "Pole Vaulters" were receiving their first bunch of WB-50's and had used them to maintain between 22 and 25 thousand feet elevation. The WB-29 was flying lower between ten and eighteen thousand feet while the two RB-36's, one at thirty five thousand feet and the other at forty five thousand feet, were flying long range twenty five hour missions, all in a futile attempt to intercept this airmass that evidently was from a pretty special USSR nuclear detonation, That was pretty damned good coverage, but "it" had slipped by them." "Buck" Copeland eyed the group of his men who had gathered to hear about the problem.

"Thompson & O'Connor, get on home and be ready to go in an hour. The staff car will pick you up as usual and by now you know the rest of the drill." Well, holy crap! I thought I was going to sit this one out." I had only been home for about six days, and hadn't caught up yet. I figured on not being deployed for another few weeks. "Well double crap," I was irritated enough that I almost missed Captain Copeland saying, "TSgt Thompson and Airman O'Connor, before you go, meet me in my office in five minutes." We were there in about two minutes damned nearly beating him back to his own office, where I also worked part time. "I'm sorry guys, I know this is quite unexpected, but I need my best operators on this one. Most of the rest of the guys are already flying their asses off in Alaska and Sgt Moles just got home. Captain Coover will be going with you, but he will not be flying SEO missions. He is not SEO qualified anyway. He will be there to "grease the skids" and take care of any problems. Don't mention this to anyone outside of this room, but this time you will not be going to Alaska. You already have first class tickets to London. Try to come back in coach, but if you need them, the first class tickets will be available to you. The 56th AWS will pick you up at Heathrow Airport and fly you to Burtonwood Air Base near Warrington, UK on the west coast. You will get further instructions from the OPS people at Burtonwood. This is a most important mission. See if you can 'bring home the bacon' for us." My focus returned just as he was telling us that; "We are sending lab people and a weather man from Langley AFB to support you. We need anything from this one that you can find. Expect the returns to be slight, but orbit and gather what you can. Now, get on your way, and, Good Hunting! Oh, take some warm clothes!" "Damn," I thought, "he must know every cliché in the book. Oh well, it's your job, so get with it, and besides, a First Class ticket to London beats the hell out of an ol' chess game, any day!"

And, so it was. We began an odyssey that would rival a lot of other things I have done. It was September of 1957, and we thought this USSR test could be a big step for them. We also thought it was way earlier than anyone had anticipated! Although I was not aware of it our Big Boys in Virginia were pretty sure it was an H-bomb because our seismic detectors had picked it up and it was BIG. They figured it was about one and a half megaton. That figures out to be about one point five million tons of TNT. One million, five hundred thousand pounds of TNT! I couldn't wrap my mind around them having one that big even though I knew we had even bigger ones up to fifty megaton. This was more than BIG! That's *REALLY BIG!* And, thus the urgency to try to catch up with the debris field to find out what they used to create such a massive detonation.

We would also be carrying one set of five boxes of backup equipment along with two sets of our operational equipment. After unloading them at SFO (San Francisco International Airport), I watched as one of the porters eyeballed the cases. This would be interesting! There were two small cases, one medium sized and two large cases. He quickly opted for the two small ones while the others picked up the larger ones. I thought his eyes were going to pop out of their sockets when he grabbed the handles of those small cases. He damned nearly fell on his face when he tried to pick them up! Hemorrhoid Heaven! They were lined with over two inches of lead. Man, they were seriously heavy. Our bosses were deadly serious about this trip. Early thinking was that Technical Sergeant George Thompson and I will be in the air at the same time, hunting the elusive cloud going in different directions. "Yep, this must be a good one if we are putting out all this effort and we could possibly come up empty." I figured at best, we'd probably find just a little bit of the remnants of a days old nuclear blast from the USSR." So, off we go again "into the wild blue yonder." Only this time, after San Francisco (SFO), then Seattle, Tacoma International Airport (SEAT-AC), we would be going "over the pole" after refueling at Frobisher Bay, Baffin Island, Canada. And, so the flight went on, receiving the typical, I supposed, First Class treatment. After a fantastic meal and more adult beverages, it was getting late. A stewardess came through sauntering, or more like slinking, down the aisle. "May I make up your beds?" All kinds of visions flew through my mind, with all of them being impossible. The three of us looked at each other in a state of confusion. What, exactly did she mean. None of us had experienced this situation before. Do we undress, do we wander up and down the aisle dressed only in our skivies? As in our shorts and T shirts? How do we prepare for such a luxury? Rather than take a chance on being embarrassed, we stupidly declined her kind offer. Even after she had fixed the beds for several others, we were still too naive to let her fix them for us. If I remember correctly, every four seats converted into two bunk type beds. Having a sleep-mate bothered all of us. She offered one more time. Tempting, but idiotically, still no. Maybe it was the uniforms, but I always wondered about the disappointed look on her face. She probably understood that we were not very sophisticated and were not used to such amenities. We got what little sleep we could in First Class Luxury. We sat up in First Class Seats all night instead of lying in some sort of a Pullman like bed as we traversed near the North Pole and went on into London's Heathrow International Airport.

As forecast, our transport to Burtonwood AB was waiting for us. We arrived and were immediately whisked to one WB-29 and one WB-50. TSgt Thompson had first choice because of his rank, and I was stuck with the WB-29 with the old "Shoebox" design. After I got on board, I was relieved to see that at least it had the model of shoebox that had electric doors and heated tracks which prevent the filter from being frozen in the shoe box. All the newer ones had the Jim Davis heated electric doors which would close tightly. They maintained the integrity of the aircraft pressure and thus cause no loss of pressure. And I didn't have to warn the crew each time I changed filters. That was so much nicer!

Thompson had the longest route toward the northeast while I was to cover the area northwest toward Iceland and perhaps beyond, heading toward the magnetic north pole which was located about six hundred miles southeast of the geographic north pole.

Many years later, I found the magnetic pole myself, in a C-130E using grid navigation, which finally gave me the transit of four different North Poles. I must admit that one was an amusement center just west into the mountains out of Colorado Springs, and another a town between Fairbanks and Eielson AFB. But the other two were a little harder to reach.

TSgt Thompson took off on his mission as soon as he could get his equipment set up. It had been decided that he would go first and the "Powers that Be" (I guess they could also see the big picture), decided that I should go into a quasi-crew rest. We didn't really have any crew rest rules. We just flew as required to fulfill the mission. The importance of our responsibilities was such that a crewmember may have to put in sixty-five plus hours (two flights and working the desk for fifteen hours in between) or more consecutively as I have done in order to get the job done.

I would be taking off when Thompson would be coming back in. They wanted at least one plane in the air at all times and wanted to hold my flight back in case George hit upon something significant enough for me to pursue. We would maintain that schedule. Though Thompson didn't get anything but background radiation, he did hit a little blip on the way back in. They didn't have enough fuel to pursue it, and they wouldn't know if was "good" until the lab folks analyzed the filter. It would be a fools game to try to track down that little blip. I told my Aircraft Commander to head toward Iceland and "see what we would see" or "find what we would find." "Man, I swear I have to give up these clichés!" We were airborne about three hours before the other plane got back down, so for now we were doing as ordered.

Off into the wild blue we go again and this time, we would be flying over the North Atlantic Ocean and possibly the Norwegian Sea instead of the Arctic Ocean or Bering Sea as was normal. "Nice for a change," I mused as we hit our assigned altitude of fourteen thousand feet. "This was an unusual altitude, but this was an unusual mission and I guess that after more than one and a half times around the world, the airmass may have settled to a lower altitude. "Made sense to me!" Still, I had the feeling that this mission was going to get even more unusual." I tried to shake the feeling, but it just stayed with me. It was that tingle of instinct you get when you are anticipating something, but not sure what. That "gut" feeling. I didn't like it! I couldn't let that feeling affect the mission, so I tucked it into a nice little compartment in the back of my mind. With that thought neatly hidden from sight, we flew on our assigned track as I changed filters for the third time, one per hour. Each time, however, the filter became more difficult to get into the aircraft. I was keeping an eye on the Esterline Angus (EA). Then, I noticed a little quiver and then a bigger one. Something was out there and I had to try to get better returns. It was like a fish hitting your line. Then it decreased. I called the Aircraft Commander over the intercom and asked for a 180 degree turn to the right to see if I could find that air mass again. While he was turning the plane around, I decided to take a gamble and change to a new filter so I could get the most pure sample possible. I hit the switch to close the electric doors on the shoe box. As soon as they indicated that they were closed, I moved to extract the filter. STUCK! The filter was completely stuck this time. That unusual feeling was suddenly front and center. "Now what?" No answer! "How was I going to get the damned thing out? This mission was essential, and here I was unable to retrieve the little bit of debris I believed was there." I asked the Navigator if he could orbit and stay with this air mass, he replied "Roger that." He told the Aircraft Commander that I wanted an orbit, so we began going in a wide circle.

The AC kept telling me we were going back to Burtonwood AB since the foil was stuck, but I overruled his every attempt. Even though he was a Lt Col and I was a three stripe Airman, I could override his complaints. It was very unusual, but our squadron commander was a Major (two-star) General. And we were the number one priority in the Air Force. Some pilots didn't like it, because when we were on board, we had the authority to direct their aircraft, and the pilots had to follow our directions. This Aircraft Commander was especially obnoxious with more than a small touch of arrogance. I was told that he was the OPS Officer and soon to be the commander of the Squadron. Also, they were not used to having an SEO on board. In fact, this was a first for them, and as of now this AC didn't care one bit for this arrangement. I got tired of having to stop trying to fix the foil to argue with him, so I suggested he have his Command Post get in touch with Captain Coover who was in his Operations Office back on Burtonwood AB. I don't know for sure, but I heard later that this dispute reached the Department of Defense level, and as I knew I would, I won. He finally went silent. I guess his higher authority received their instructions when they talked directly with the Secretary of Defense. That will get the attention of most folks. The only time that I am aware of an Aircraft Commander deciding to ignore our instructions, an RB-36 pilot failed to follow the profile I gave him. He was a co-pilot the next day! And probably not too happy about it, but it also alerted everyone that we had some power behind us.

It took me over an hour of pounding and prying before I broke the filter frame loose, but over the protestations of the pilot, I overcame his misgivings and saved the mission.

Re-inserting a new filter into the shoe box, I was very relieved that the readings were slightly higher. "Good work Nav, you kept us in the debris field." Now, AC, could we extend the orbit to the west? No answer, but the plane straightened out for a little bit and then resumed orbit. The readings lessened so I asked him to take a two-minute run east and then start a moving orbit, gliding to the north. Still no answer, but I could tell he was doing as I requested. Bingo! We hit a hot spot which would give us enough samples to make the mission a success. I advised the AC that we were in a good airmass. I finally got a response, "It's a damned good thing!" He sounded pissed, but I was happy! I requested the AC set up a standard orbit in the present air mass. We gathered debris in this "cloud" for about 45 minutes. It wasn't a cloud in the everyday sense of the word. You couldn't see anything out there, but our equipment could sense it. Then, I decided to take a chance. Since I had changed filters several times, we had enough of a sample for this one cloud and my instincts told me there was better hunting somewhere else. I requested the AC to head northwest toward and on past Iceland if necessary. "WHAT?" came the reply over the intercom. "I don't want to take this aircraft past Iceland." Well, I wanted the debris that the Alaska teams missed. My gut kept telling me it was north of our location. I was betting it was closer to the North Pole. I requested again that we continue. We just had to. A chastened more subdued voice said, "Roger, Wilco." And comply he did. Roger Wilco is an old aviator phrase meaning "message received and will comply."

We flew a couple more hours and now were above the Arctic Circle. Nothing! I was beginning to doubt my instincts which all good SEOs trusted, second only to the weather man, and sometimes more than him. Suddenly, my E.A. needle began quivering. I alerted the crew. Then, BINGO! The needle started going nuts. My hunch paid off! If this was the right one. They had said it was big enough to be a Hydrogen Bomb. If it was, it would be a new type, and a sign that their technology was catching up with ours. I said a quick prayer and requested he put the plane in an orbit. As I switched the dial on my B-199 sensing equipment, I switched it up to level five. A pretty good hit, but I sensed there was more. Now, after two more orbits which maintained the same level of intensity, I told the pilot to start expanding the orbit to the north, I changed filters to maintain the purity of this filter. I had left the same filter in since we hit the mass. Holy nuclear bombs! The intensity started to increase, big time!

Just as we hit what I figured was the "big cloud," the Aircraft Commander called on the intercom and said we had to go home because of fuel, or rather, lack thereof. After an OH CRAP! I thought, "Just as we found the big one and we have to go?" Then, the proverbial light bulb came on. I looked up and it said Iceland. It had

Keflavic Naval Air Station flashing inside that bulb, and we might have a small lab there. "Hey Nav, Weather Control (Our inflight name) here. What is the distance to Keflavic NAS in hours and how much more time can we orbit if we keep flying and refuel there." The Aircraft Commander exploded over the intercom! "Weather Control or whoever in hell you are. This is my airplane and I will still make the decisions." "Yes sir," I said. "I apologize. I was just trying to figure how to get the most out of this flight and refueling in Iceland to get back to Burtonwood would do it." "Well, I am the AC and I make the decisions, and we're going home." "Yes sir, but I want to maintain the orbit and it is getting hotter as we extend the orbit. With all due respect, you are commanding an augmented crew (an extra pilot, navigator and engineer). Sir, I'm requesting we change the flight plan and requesting you contact your Command Post again and explain my request. I'll abide by their decision. I only need a couple more hours."

We kept expanding the orbit while the AC was contacting "Mother," a derisive term for those who make the decision while on the ground. A few moments later, I heard a subdued intercom call. "Hey Nav, continue the orbit and figure bingo fuel to Keflavic." I tried not to smile. My general has the authority of the chief of staff and the President. We normally got our way. "This is not the time for gloating. I have to prove my decision was worth the extra time." The further we expanded the orbit northward, the hotter it got. Eventually, we were pegging out on scale 10, the highest reading that I could record, almost every ten minutes. I told the AC to just stay in the airmass where we were. We immediately went into a standard orbit. I think that I was the only one who was having fun.

I was also trying to eat my second lunch. It was a cold chicken leg and a sandwich. I didn't think of it at the time, but I was also eating radiation. Radiation that was most likely from a Russian hydrogen bomb. Only God knows how much radio-active debris I ate over the years, and He may not be sure. We maintained the orbit and I was changing filters often now. It was taking only a few minutes for the scales to hit the top level. After I had what I considered to be the hottest flight ever in our organization, I called the AC and told him we could go home. I received a very sarcastic "Thank you." "Nav, get me a heading to Keflavic. Copilot, call Kevlavic Ops and tell them we need a quick turn around by order of Secretary of Defense. We had been ordered by Sec Def to get these filter papers back to Burtonwood AB, ASAP." After receiving my coded information, 1009th HQ at Langley AFB was eager to see what we had, and we had quite a lot. If what I thought we collected was real, we were making history. If this debris really was from a new type Russian H-Bomb we will have been the first to intercept and collect the debris.

After we were back in the air after a very quick (we didn't even get out of the aircraft) refueling stop at Keflavic NAS, the Aircraft Commander came on over the intercom and got everyone's attention. He thanked the crew for the long crew duty day, but it was worth it. It was considered a very successful flight. And, the main thing was, we had caught up with the cloud that had eluded them twice in Alaska. Stuff that they needed!

The rest of the mission was uneventful. I was through cloud hunting for this trip. That even seemed to make the Aircraft Commander mellow out a bit. Now it was time for us to go home, back to the states.

NOTE: I was put in for a Commendation Medal for saving the mission. It was rejected because, "We expect our airmen to do the exceptional. That's why they were hand selected."

BURTONWOOD AB WARRINGTON, UK

"At Least the Trains Ran on Time"

After wrapping up a successful mission, we were already cleared to spend two free days in London, but suddenly, Sergeant George Thompson came down with a serious case of the Asian flu. Great timing!

I ended up going to see a football game on the base field and trying out my newly purchased 35 mm camera. It was getting to be past time for me as far as spending too much time on base. I thought, "No sense in my hanging around the base by myself. I might as well go into town!"

Off I went by myself to do what George and I had planned to do together. I had no idea where Captain Coover was and couldn't care less. I hit a pub in downtown Warrington and ordered a pint. As I pulled out my wallet, I heard this deep voice over my shoulder, "You can't do that here, pal. Put that wallet away. You can't buy a beer in this pub!" Whoa! I thought I was in friendly Limey Country. Are they still ticked off that we broke away from them and formed the colonies? Shit! They should be grateful. We pulled their "fat out of the fire" twice now." While I was thinking about how to avoid getting in an argument, a big paw with a wad of pounds came over my shoulder and let the money fall to the bar top with the comment, "Yanks drink free when I'm around. We are still very grateful that you came across the pond to help us kick some kraut ass. You will drink free tonight." With that, another Yank/Brit relationship was formed. My new friend, still celebrating our joint defeat of Germany, was treating me like a long-lost cousin, even buying me "Bangers and Mash" for our evening meal. We drank until closing which for some reason unknown to me was 8:00 PM. I remember thinking that we had enjoyed only a few beers at that point. I couldn't see myself going back to the base at 8:00.

He eased my anxiety by suggesting we should go to a private club to which he belonged. These clubs were everywhere and everyone had a membership to at least one. The fee was minimal. What a great (?) idea! After we arrived at the upstairs drink and dance club, it appeared that everyone in Warrington had a club membership! The place was absolutely crowded. We couldn't even get to the bar, but waitresses were wandering through with steins of beer for the taking. Somehow, they kept track of what he and I drank. A guest was not allowed to purchase anything in a private club, so it was a full free ride!

I danced the night away with a sweet young thing and ended up sitting on her lap between dances because there weren't enough chairs to go around, and for some reason she insisted I sit on her lap instead of what I would consider to be the normal arrangement. "Her" chair was always available when we sat one out. I didn't understand how they did that either. Brit logic? Then I almost choked when my dance partner suggested we take the train to Liverpool to see the "Illuminations" and spend the night. I demurred, but she stayed at the club with me anyway. They closed at midnight, but by now we both had a pretty good load on. My dance partner asked me to walk her home so being the gentleman that I am, I politely agreed. The gentleman who befriended me had disappeared and I hadn't even thanked him. The sweetie I walked home asked me in for a little bit, but though tipsy, I didn't lose sight of my wedding ring. She acted quite disappointed, so I gently turned her head toward me and tenderly kissed her goodbye. I turned my back to her and walked away. I heard what sounded like muffled sobs, but I didn't take that turn.

Speaking of turns, I had no idea which one to take. Yogi Berra once famously said that, "If you came to a fork in the road, take it!" The fog was of the consistency of the infamous "Pea Soup." I had no idea of where I was (kinda like I am in Broken Arrow now) and really had no idea which way to go (same). I literally had no idea which fork to take. I just started walking down a slight decline on the sidewalk, hoping to find something or someone. I did not know what else to do. I was lost in a British city, at midnight, possibly even going in circles as Dick Ward and I had done in Alaska.

On top of this, I could feel a temperature coming on. I was feeling weak, cold and miserable, worse by the minute. It was cold and it was dark. These strange streets were illuminated only slightly by fog enshrouded, very dim street lights. It was eerie and becoming scary. Then, as if on cue, a Bobby came out of the fog, scaring the living stew out of me again. This ghostly, formless shadow appeared out of nowhere! That was enough to get me pleasantly excited if I hadn't had to watch him pound his open and opposite palm with his night stick. I definitely didn't want to get clobbered by this guy, so I approached him slowly and quietly explained my situation. He was as gentle as he could be, considering my condition or maybe because of it. He pointed me toward the base and said it was only a few blocks. I don't know where he got his idea of a "few." It probably was just a few, but in my condition, it seemed like forever. Just as I was beginning to think that he had pulled a fast one on me and sent me in the opposite direction, the lights of the main gate began to come slowly into view through the thick fog. I probably would have run to them if I had been able to run, but I managed to get there without crawling which by now I considered an admirable feat!

I can't remember how I got to the hospital, but when I came to, I was in the same ward as George. Open bay sick bay. Aptly named! I was again in open bay barracks with single bunks this time. I noticed the lack of privacy again, but this time, I really didn't care. Good Lord, were we sick! I don't think I have felt so downright bad in my life. Thompson felt the same way. We were both definitely getting rid of toxins and everything else very quickly. It was horrible! I will advise you right now. Always get your flu shots!

Meanwhile, we later discovered that Captain Coover was "bright eyed and bushy tailed" running around enjoying the country side. George and I discussed our plight as we were getting better. How in hell do you catch the Asian flu in jolly old England? We were almost half way around the world from Asia. Just not fair!

Several days later, George and I were released at the same time. Captain Coover picked us up out front. He was grinning from ear to ear. I didn't blame him. George and I were looking pretty sad and he was riding high. "Hey, guys!" he greeted us. He followed up with, "The deal still stands. We can still take two days to see the sights." I looked at George looking at me. Almost as if we rehearsed it, we both blurted out: "Oh, Hell No! We've had enough of England." Still feeling weak, we had both decided we'd rather go home. The Captain said he had seen enough and he was ready, too. So, he turned in the staff car and had our hosts take us to the rail station for the trip down to London. We were more than ready to get out of "Jolly Old."

While waiting for the train, we decided to check to make sure we were all squared away to leave England and return home.

Passports:	Check
Shot Records:	Check
Tickets arranged for:	Check

Everything was in order, but when we settled down for a fairly long wait, I started flipping through my shot record which I often did to kill time. Something was bugging me about mine. In the back of my mind, I vaguely remembered that there was "something" I was going to do before we left McClellan so quickly. Actually, we only had time to go home, take care of a few essential things, and grab our bags. Then it dawned on me. SMALLPOX! So, I started looking a little closer at mine. Holy shit in a bucket! My shot record is out of date! I'm overdue a smallpox shot by four flipping days!

They suddenly they became interested in their own shot records.

Shot Record:	Smallpox
Out of Date:	Check
Out of Date:	Check

I can't even put in print what my thoughts were after looking
at that shot record! I figured there was no way we would be able
to leave England with out-of-date smallpox inoculations. Captain
Coover was going nuts! He began to tell us that we had to go back to
the base immediately, get inoculated and hope they would let us go
even without the ten to fourteen-day incubation period. We knew
Captain Coover had to be living in some sort of a dream to think
the authorities would actually overlook the incubation period. No
way! Not a chance! If we hadn't had the flu, we would have made
it OK, barely.

While he and George were fussing with each other, I went over
to the Station Master and asked if I could borrow his date stamp.
There were no other trains due out before ours in about an hour, so
he acquiesced. Wrong move on his part! I took the stamp, turned
the date back about a month, stamped my shot record and forged
the name of Doctor Fuller, our family doctor back in Salida, Colorado. I took my up-to-date shot record over to show Thompson and
Coover. They just stared at the shot record and then, with mouths
agape, they stared at me.

I said, "I'm going home." Captain Coover, being the straight
shooter, said, "You can't do that!" I said, "Do what?" He sputtered,
"Do that! That is illegal! It just isn't right!" George was just standing
there speechless with his mouth still hanging open. I responded,
"Like I said, my shot record is current and I'm legal to leave this
lovely island which I will miss like a bleeding case of the piles!" I
continued, "You guys can stay here for a ten or so day vacation, but
I'd rather be home in Sacramento. Now, if you want to join me on a

First Class flight home, give me your shot records, turn your backs and we'll all be on our way. If something happens, you'll be able to truthfully say that you don't know what happened. The health guys at the airport will never know the difference if we just act normal. Now, give me your records and go get a drink of water, and everything will be wonderful." They left and I altered the dates somewhat and used the same doctor's name. Voila! Their shot records were up to date. I took the date stamp back to the station master, thanked him graciously and by the time I got back to our seats, the boys were back. They took their shot records and, without looking at them, put them in their travel folders. Everything was wonderful, and the train arrived right on time.

Toward the end of World War II, when everything else was falling apart in Italy, Benito Mussolini supposedly made a famous quote still used today. It remains to be about the only bright spot in any bad situation. Mussolini, aka Il Duce, had been taking credit for great improvement in the country when, in fact, there was precious little improvement anywhere except in the decrepit rail system that had been virtually destroyed by World War I: "The War to end ALL Wars." From that decidedly desperate time, came the oft-quoted or misquoted saying, purportedly spoken by IL Duce, "At least, the trains run on time!" In fact, these minor improvements to the train system, especially that supposed quote, is perhaps more memorable than the sight which greeted American troops. One last and lasting impression of IL Duce is the sight of Mussolini and his mistress hanging upside down from a girder over a service station in Milan. They were shot dead, then beaten, even with hammers and shot some more as they hung there in the town square of Milan as Italy fell to the United States Armed Forces. His fellow countrymen had taken matters into their own hands and got their revenge!

That is one thing England learned from this failed ruler. "To keep folks happy, make sure the trains run on time." When things were falling apart for us in Warrington, they did!

After we had boarded our train and were clickety-clacking our way from the east coast of England to Heathrow International Airport outside of London, we finally relaxed and took a satisfyingly deep breath, knowing we were going home! That little nugget of a fact made me smile until it hit me that I had forgotten to turn the date stamp back to the current date! Holy crap! I wondered how many train tickets sold that day had the wrong date on it, thus rendering them worthless. If any, I'd bet not very many got turned down before enough of the locals complained sufficiently to get the Station Masters' attention. Well, it was out of my control now, and we were going home. With a stupid smile and a feeling of self-imposed guilt, I told the others. Sgt Thompson laughed and Captain Coover turned white. That probably bothered him until his dying day, even though HE didn't do anything wrong. "Well, nothing I can do to change things." I relaxed and closed my eyes. I was tired!

I couldn't help but wonder how much trouble our out-of-date shot records caused the citizens of Warrington trying to get on any train with expired tickets. I just felt guilty until I smiled and put all of that in the back of my mind with all of the other little tidbits from this trip. Except for the unbelievable bout with the flu which kept George and me from seeing the English countryside, it had been a pretty satisfying and successful trip. We got more than we came for and, although I could have had more, there were no regrets. I had suffered enough in England from the Asian flu! No sense in adding guiltless guilt to it!

The rest of the trip was unremarkable. We flew back to San Francisco. I remember checking into First Class without even checking for space in coach. By now, the other two were following my lead because they were enjoying the results and were doing nothing wrong. We talked ourselves into believing that after everything we had been through along with the results of a super successful mission, we deserved it. Unbelievably, we always flew coach when we could until now and here we were enjoying First Class and, if Captain Coover kept his yap closed, no one would ever know that there was room in coach. The good Captain was enjoying the spoils of riding with the upper echelon enough that I was quite sure he would never tell. Either way, we were almost home after a very long flight and touchdown at San Francisco International Airport. A staff car was standing by to pick us up with orders to drop us off at our various residences. I was glad that mine was first in Del Paso Heights. Captain Coover had called Lt Col Koerschner requesting transport to home. He got it and just like the trains in England, it ran on time, but with no date stamp.

One last thing about our flight home. On the way back to the good ole' USA, I showed an amazing naiveté and lack of sophistication as well as an equal lack of experience. We were flying in our well-deserved First Class seats in a triple tailed "Connie," Lockheed Super Constellation. First Class was in the rear of the plane back in the day. We were between SEATAC and SFO. After she had given us more free drinks, our stewardess made her way back to me with a tray of hors d'oeuvres, which I had always called appetizers. Being a good old country boy from the mountains of Colorado, I picked up a nice-looking piece of toast with a pile of blackberries on it. The other stuff on the tray looked funny to me. A bad funny. I took that toast and took it in all at once. "Oh holy shit, and I do mean shit! What did I do?" I felt like throwing up. It tasted like fish, but very rotten fish! It tasted like shit! Evidently, I had tasted caviar for the first time and it didn't go over very well. Who in hell eats raw fish eggs. We used them for bait in Colorado! I just knew I was going to be sick. I also knew I couldn't sit there holding the stinking stuff stuck in my mouth for the rest of the trip. I knew there was only one of two things I could do and they both were bad choices. Really bad choices. I could either throw up in a barf bag, which I had never done. Or worse, I could get rid of it the old-fashioned way. I could just grit my teeth, hold my nose, swallow it and hope I didn't either die or throw up. At that point, I couldn't have cared less which one! I chose the latter way of disposing of that stinking rotten crap and thought I was going to get sick all over again. My mind was screaming: "Let me off this f'ing plane! Let me off this f'ing planet!"

I learned a quick lesson. "Never put something in your mouth unless you know where in hell it came from and what the hell it is!"

Strangely enough, I would eventually learn to love caviar. That first overwhelming bite was the genesis of a love affair with those tiny black fish eggs. Roe, I guess they called them. Now, if I could only afford it! When Oliver W. The "Owl" Lewis, made his first star as Chief of Personnel at Military Airlift Command (MAC) Head-quarters, he threw a self-celebratory reception at the Scott AFB Of-ficer's Club. For one of the niceties and, you might say a bit of an over-extravagance, he had arranged for the tables to be situated to resemble a great big star. Each of the five tips of the giant star was graced with a huge bowl of caviar with toast points on the side. I ate too much! But not so much as to get that sickening feeling again. And I thought of a First Class flight in a Triple Tail "Connie" Lock-heed Constellation long ago! I remember it well enough that I even remember that I was seated in the next to the last row, aisle seat on the port side of the" Connie." Memories of traumatic events leave a lasting impression. That experience with the "blackberries" on a toast point was one of them.

Now we were back at McClellan AFB, facing a barrage of questions from the troops as to what our trip was like. And we got a stream of questions from a lot of them because they were in a line for a shot in the arm with a big needle which was a little unusual. George and I joined the lineup. Then we found out what it was about. We quickly got back out of the line! They were giving shots for the Asian flu! I don't know where Captain Coover was, but in those days shots hurt for days. We got to the nurse and told her our story. She said: "You can't catch Asian flu in England." We agreed with her in principle, but there are al-ways exceptions to every rule. She asked how we felt during the flu. Where was Capt Coover when we needed him? Both of us answered with, "High temperature and regurgitation of everything except our stomach lining, along with other things we'd rather not mention." I finally told her that it felt like someone was twisting a stick in my lower intestines. With that statement, she readily agreed that we indeed had endured the flu. The things we do to keep this country safe!

Footnote: After we left England, the Asian flu turned into a national as well as worldwide Pandemic. I have often wondered if my tiny kiss gave the flu to that innocent young woman. Two out of three in England suffered from the flu and many thousands died. I wonder.

It had been a great trip except for the little inconvenience of getting the flu and the unusual flight experiences. In retrospect, I guess it had been a great trip for collecting missing air masses. After they had given us a week off, we were ready to go again. They knew how to handle us! We were ready for any flights anywhere any time, but after that wild ride, they would be relatively calm for me, so I thought. Being relatively new to flying, that was my mindset, and the only way a flyer could continue flying. We always felt that the last scare would actually be the last one. After the surprises of that last trip, I should have known better.

Here, my life started to take a different direction. Captain Copeland and Captain Martin asked me if I would move upstairs permanently into the Operations Section and help them with general duties in the Operations areas. I started by designing several wall charts to making it an easier task to keep track of flying time for each of our SEOs. After a period of time, I was doing much more. They asked if I would take over the scheduling of C-47 #263. It was used not only by pilots in our squadron but also the rest of the Air Base. I told them I would do whatever they wanted me to do. It was fun, but turned into a mess every so often as when I lost the airplane. Tail # 263 was missing!

Oh Crap! Now what? I checked with Base Operations who actually performed the action of assigning the pilots according to my scheduling. I had not scheduled anyone for about a week ahead of current date. That's where the breakdown came.

Now, I wouldn't accuse a superior officer of skullduggery, but two of our own (WFO) pilots just happened to wander into Base Ops when there was a brand new Base Ops Officer on duty. They checked out #263 without advising the new guy of their ultimate intentions nor of their ultimate destination. They were off and running, or flying if you will, with MY airplane! Now, I was up to my eyeballs in deep Kimchi. In real trouble! Captain Copeland said, "Sgt O'Connor, 263 is your airplane, it is missing and we need it here right now. I think you had better get on the job of finding it, wherever it may be, and getting it back to home base."

First, I had to track down who the pilots were, and then where they went. They had let no one know where they were headed. I even had to get their names from Base Ops. When I told Captain Copeland who they were, he exploded in a minor fit of rage or laughter, I didn't know which, probably half and half. I know I didn't like it. I had the Base Ops officer chase down the flight plan they filed when they left here some days ago. I forget now where the destination was planned. But I knew where they should have been after their first refueling stop. Then it was just a matter of calling the place they were flight planning for their next stop. This went on hop-scotching across the country for a little while until I caught up with them through a phone number they had left with Base Ops at the last leg they had flown. It was somewhere in South Carolina, just about as far away from

McClellan AFB as they could get. Now to find them in their current local area and get them to come home. I knew I had the power of our Full Colonel Western Field Office Commander behind me if I needed it. I didn't! They laughed and said they would hurry home with no more delays, in about three days. I told them that though they may be laughing, I would be in trouble until they got home.

They promised to fly long crew duty days. Copeland just laughed and said, "Good Work!" Three days later, #263 was no longer missing. Checking out an airplane was a normal pastime and way to log flight hours back in those days. They also finished off all of their cross-country requirements. That was the last time I lost a whole aircraft!

TERRITORY OF HAWAII, 1958

"Really, a Hardship Tour! Oh, yeh"

In 1958, I made a Permanent Change of Station (PCS) to another highly classified unit at Hickam Air Force Base, Hawaii which was considered an overseas tour. It was within the same organization and my flying was limited, but I continued to handle radioactive debris brought in by WB-50 crews coming in from Alaska or California.

Our unit consisted of one Captain and four Staff Sergeants. We still had the highest priority in the Air Force. Our messages containing the results of my analysis were to be sent Operations Immediate (Ops Immediate) which is one of the highest priorities of transmission to be sent to our Field Office in California and our Headquarters in Washington, DC. Early one morning I was refused. The guy inside the "Cage" was a newly minted Tech Sergeant. He refused because in his judgment, it was not of sufficient importance to be sent as anything but Routine which could take hours before it was even sent. Ops Immediate meant just that — Immediate! It would also cause him a little more effort. I argued with him for a few minutes, but it was about 4:30 in the morning and I had been working for a while getting this message ready. As I had been briefed by my boss when I arrived on station, I finally told him too check his access list and to send the message via FLASH and not to argue with me anymore! FLASH is the classification used almost exclusively for declaration of war. He got a little pale, swallowed hard and said, "Yes Sir!" He sent it OPS IMMEDIATE as originally requested. We didn't have any trouble with those Communications folks after that. I guess the word had spread that we meant business!

But there were many enjoyable minutes and hours in our tropical heaven in a three bedroom one bath home overlooking Pearl Harbor. It was a typical stilted home on about a one half acre lot.

I had taken an early out and reenlistment in order to get a down payment for the home. It was a fifteen hundred dollar re-up bonus. The home cost Fifteen Thousand Dollars. Yes, $15,000! We sold it for eighteen thousand five hundred dollars when we left for the Mainland and OCS twenty months later.

While in Hawaii, my parents came for a visit, and a good one it was. I'm not sure we planned it this way or if it was just by chance, but they were there when the NCO Club held a good old-fashioned Luau. They even had a Polynesian band being pulled back and forth across the NCO Club swimming pool filled with floating orchid petals. I have great photos of my folks deeply enjoying their Mai Tais. Bobbie and I were right there with them. Great time! Before they went back to the ranch along the Continental Divide in Colorado, we had traveled each way around Oahu, strolled the sidewalks of Waikiki and took in several shows. We took them to two of our favorite haunts on Waikiki. Alfred Apaca and Hilo Hati were performing in the main room and Authur Lyman was performing in the famous Shell Bar of Henry Kaisers' new Hawaiian Village Hotel. This was during the time before Hawaii had become a state. There were only five buildings over four stories tall on Waikiki, two of them being the Moana Hotel and the Royal Hawaiian. Genoa Keave was entertaining and knew us well enough from our many previous visits that she invited both parents up on stage. Dad enjoyed photos with several of the Hula dancers and mom posed with the twirling fire sword dancer. He had several band aides over his naked upper torso. Mom didn't seem to mind!

We also managed to take them to Kilauea Military Camp, on the Big Island which is perched across the street from the Volcano House Hotel and Restaurant which in turn hangs on the rim of Halemaumau Caldera who's ultra-hot magma normally rests six hundred feet deep, but because of pressure from the molten core will slowly rise and fall hundreds of feet within its confines. Quite a sight! Three quarters of a mile across. We showed them many sights on the leeward side and the volcano parks area including the black sands beach which is now part of a great lava field. By the way, Kilauea Military Camp is there for us poor souls stationed in the islands so we could go there and relieve the stress of having to live in Paradise.

Moana Loa volcano at thirteen thousand six hundred and seventy seven feet is the largest volcano in the world. Its dome is seventy five miles long and sixty four miles wide Moku'aweoweo, normally called Halemaumau, has an area of nearly six square miles and has a depth of six hundred feet. Moana Loa decided to birth a new fissure on its flank for the first time in many years. She started acting up one night while my folks were visiting us.

Little known fact for a few: Both Moana Loa and Moana Kea, at thirteen thousand eight hundred and two feet above sea level are tall enough to have snow. Moana Kea is high enough so that they have a snow ski complex there among an array of the most important and famous telescopes in the world. It is the only place I know of where you can be snow skiing at almost fourteen thousand feet and see your friends surfing on the Pacific Ocean down below. Now for the little known fact for a few more of you. These two Island mountains are the tallest in the world. They are considerably taller than Mt Everest.

Oh, I was talking about Moana Loa birthing a new fissure on her flanks for the first time in many years. Mom and Dad were within days of leaving when at about ten thirty or so, I get a phone call from my boss, Captain Copeland. He is really excited and more than a little tipsy as was I. Lyn, his wife, had her parents visiting them at the same time and both parties were enjoying the pleasant evening before bed time with several adult beverages. He literally shouted (not sure he need a telephone): John, Kilauea has just erupted and is putting on a show. Want to go see it? Talk about catnip to a lonely pussy, I jumped at it. He told me he would pick me up in ten minute. I lived fifteen away! He was there in ten!

As he was straightening the curves to get to Hicham AFB, he said he had contacted his normal co-pilot who had also been partying. Did I mention that it was a Friday night? No Sweat! We passed through the Hickam AFB Gate properly and after returning a salute to the guard on duty, sped off to Base Operations and, in spite of his condition, of which I had taken note on the way to the base, (he scared hell out of me) they would let him check out a C-47 (DC-3) only if it was for official business. He told them in no uncertain terms that it damned well was official business. "I am a Captain in this mans' Air Force and I want to go see a new volcano erupt." Not good enough! After losing a good argument, he was pondering how we could make it an official flight. I suggested a base photographer. Great thought, John. (Lyn and Buck always called me John instead of Jack for about forty years), Buck (Captain Copeland) began to track down the on duty base photographer. Damn, they couldn't find him at his emergency number, but one of the others remembered it was his birthday. Now, if you were living on base celebrating your birthday, where would you go? Ya Damned right! The NCO Club. Bingo! He was having a big party, but it didn't take much to enable Buck to lure him out for an evening of airborne excitement. I think he just didn't know any better. Actually, in his condition, I wasn't sure he was having any thoughts!

We picked him up and toddled of to Base Ops again. We left the photographer sitting outside. The co-pilot was there, and I thought, "Oh Oh, this is going to be interesting." I knew the photographer was probably the drunkest because we noticed after we tied him in that he had no camera. "Oh to hell with it. Dumb requirement anyway." With that, Buck and the other pilot climbed into the C-47 cockpit and started our mighty steed. A C-47 is a steed? Nonetheless, we were on our way taxiing out to the active runway which in 1958 wasn't very active. I was a little concerned because though on headset, I don't recall them ever going through a checklist, and there were several you should accomplish before you ever get airborne. I wasn't sure, because in my condition I could have missed it and these guys had plenty time in this airplane, so I didn't know if they really needed one. Well, hell yes! All pilots have checklists, and only a crazy one would skip them. Well, I think that was a fit description of our two Captains this lovely evening! We taxied onto the main runway 04. I wondered why not 08? It was closer and about twice as long, but maybe it was closed for the night? It mattered not. 08 was a better runway and banked your plane more easily away from the Nuuanu Pali Valley. It didn't matter, we were on 04. They went to max power and we went trundling down the runway (the Air force trundles quite a bit) on takeoff roll at max power. Hell, I thought the purpose of max power and all that good stuff was in order to get off the ground. It wasn't happening. I began to worry about the end of the runway. We were getting there fast. The tail was in the air for about a half an hour now. (actually, it was probably a thousand feet. It just seemed longer). Finally, I heard one of the pilots asking the other why it wasn't getting off the ground, the co-pilot said, "I've been holding it down for you until you were ready to go." "Well, shit! I was holding it forward for you. Well, one of them said in what I thought was a too slow reaction: "We better get this thing off the ground. We are almost at the end of the runway." Note: We were also damned nearly at cruising speed! The plane was actually bumping down the runway. It was ready to fly even if the pilots weren't

Buck said, "I got it!" He pulled back on the yoke and I would swear we jumped over eight hundred feet into the air. We were flat airborne and turning to go over Waikiki way closer than normal. Good night view anyway! Even back then! I'm not even sure the photographer thought there was anything unusual with him dangling out of a speeding "Gooney Bird." I was damned glad we were airborne surprising myself that I was that aware. Now, on to the Big island and Volcanic History to be recorded by our photographer without his camera. Not to worry, we could give vivid recollections, if anyone was sober enough to recollect.

Well, it would be awhile getting down to the site because this little dual motor could only cruise at one hundred thirty-five knots, which was about our takeoff speed for this night and we were about two hundred and forty miles from the action. I wondered if anyone had calculated that. I figured that like everything else, they thought the other had taken care of it. Hope we have gas!

Anyway, by the time we arrived in the eruption zone it had been a couple hours since anyone had a drink and we started to wake up, especially when we started to see fireworks out of the cockpit window. Oh, hell yeh! Looking good! Somehow, I assume Buck received permission from the Hilo Control Tower to go VFR into the holding pattern while we swung around the volcano taking our own personal pictures. He set up a standard left hand orbit with the photographer hanging over the erupting miles long rift in the side of Kilauea volcano. They would call it Kilauea Iki or "Little Kilauea." We were enjoying the beginning of our scenic tour when I looked up and saw a passenger plane going the other direction. Oh Shit! I could see the faces in the F-27 aircraft windows. Hmmmm, not a bad looking honey in about the middle of the plane. Copeland immediately got on the horn to the Hilo Tower. "Hilo. You have some idiot out here going the wrong way in the pattern. All standard orbit patterns go left. Get him out of our way before we have a great big mix-up." "Roger Hickam 69. I will contact him and have him leave the area and return in a left turn pattern." "Thanks Tower, it just almost got a little messy in my pants on that last flyby! I could have shaken the pilots hand, and I noticed a good looking chick in about the middle of that high winged plane." Buck and I were a lot alike on things like that. We enjoyed the finer things in life. We even kept our Beefeaters in the freezer so it was like a thin syrup. What little vermouth we used was kept in the refrigerator as were the olives.

NOTE: The F-27 was a high winged Fairchild turbo prop with big windows. Great for sightseeing. That was why owner Ruddy Tongg bought them. They were a huge success until they started having problems with the wing box. They were retired in June 1967, so Aloha Airlines could go with pure jets. A new era had begun in Hawaii since that day in 1959 when I watched the first Pan American 707 arrive. I knew it would never work! My typical view on any successful venture. Always on the wrong side. But I received a pretty damned good return on my one hundred share of Aloha Airlines stock that I bought for about a quarter per share. Many years later I sold them for around three and a half dollars. Probably the only time I ever made money!

I took many still shots and movies from my friends eight mm camera. And, Lo and behold! (I do a lot of Lo and Beholding) the photographer had his camera after all. He had clutched it to his chest while we were strapping him in. We overlooked a lot of things that night, but I still remember the faces, especially that one that Buck had noticed, in the F-27. I had another close miss like that one other time going into Lihue Airport on Kauai. Didn't see any honeys in that plane. It was another F-27, in daylight! Well, we made it back to Honolulu and Hickam AFB after about an hour watching new growth of an island. They shared runways. I had a great time relating the nights experiences to my wife and parents after Buck dropped me off at my place on Keaka Drive. By the way: We lived one block from the corner of Pikini and Lakini streets. Damned near as confusing as the streets in Broken Arrow.

After a few years of basking in lovely Hawaii, I discovered that the promotion to the next higher grade which would be Technical Sergeant (E-6) was frozen for an indefinite period for the drawdown of airmen from the Korean War. We didn't need that many folks in the Air Force any more so they decided to do it humanely through attrition rather than just throwing people out into the cold. My boss decided that since I wouldn't be promoted for several years, I should apply for Officer Candidate School (OCS) again. Since I had been accepted before and declined the appointment, I decided to try it again and go thru with it if I was accepted.

I was!

Oh yeh! I mentioned that Moana Loa and Moana Kea were the two tallest mountains in the world. That may have caused a little consternation among a few of you and there could even be some non-believers. You see, and as you may know, mountains are measured in an unbroken slope from its base to the top. The base of these two mountains are in an unbroken line from about twenty miles beneath the surface of the ocean, so they both are over thirty three thousand feet tall! Perhaps a little known fact which could win you a free beer some-day.

Reluctantly, and with a new child, we left the "Loveliest Chain of Islands Anchored in any Ocean:" Mark Twain. We would be leaving the new State of Hawaii where one of my children, Michelle, was born while it was still a Territory, which caused her no end of problems later on, especially in getting her TSA pre-Select Pass. Brenda, Pat and Tina were all born in Sacramento while I was stationed at the two different Air Force Bases there.

My wife and oldest children actually cried half the way to California. A new venture was about to begin! Actually, a new life was about to begin!

MILITARY FLYING SCHOOLS

"I was Assured of My Return to My Islands"

For the sake of a little, (damned little as it turned out) brevity, I will quickly cover OCS at Lackland AFB, Navigator School at Harlingen AFB, Harlingen, Texas and Navigator/Bombardier School at Mather AFB on the south side opposite McClellan AFB in south eastern Sacramento, California and some of the results thereof. They were all tough with Harlingen being the easiest and, well, I'd rather not talk about the other two. As far as classroom instruction, Nav/Bomb school was by far the toughest school I had ever attended, bar none. And, It may have benefitted me most during my flying career. Of course, getting a commission through OCS was necessary to be able to get to any flight school. A college degree would not be required for commissioning for exactly three more years from the October of my graduation. There were still some folks who realized that there is a difference between intelligence and education. OCS had a 96% retention rate, far higher than the next highest: US Air Force Academy: 55%.

I must attempt to show further, the design for my life by a Higher Authority. For the previous five years that I am aware of, every student officer who graduated from Nav/Bomb School (one class every two weeks) went to Strategic Air Command in either B-47 or B-52 bombers. Our time to graduate finally arrived. I thought it never would! Along with the usual bomber assignments, there came a requirement for fifteen of the thirty graduates of our class to PCS to Hickam AFB, Hawaii. Twelve were needed in the 48th MATS to assume duties in C-118 (DC-6) aircraft and three were needed in the 50th MATS flying giant C-124's (no civilian equivalent). My class standing was in the top half of the of the class, and since the students were able to pick their assignments by class ranking, I was assured of my return to my beloved Islands. **An aside here:** Going home for lunch that day, excited to share the news of my assignment with my lovely wife, I rushed in the front door only to find her standing in the middle of the living room with a huge smile on her face. I don't know who blurted first, but behind her back, she was holding a check for fifteen plus hundred dollars, just received as final payment for our original home in Hawaii. That did it! We both shared our fantastic news and began anew, dreaming of returning to the exotic Hawaiian Islands. Fifteen hundred dollars seemed to be the magic number regarding homes in the Islands.

Back to assignments: The top graduate, Chuck Wittmaak opted to return to SAC from whence he came as a reformed tail gunner. Similar to my navigator friend Tom Kuhns losing his mind and going to pilot school, Chuck went back to SAC. After flying with SAC in the RB-36's, I wanted no part of that over disciplined bunch. Their philosophy was so different from other commands, but it worked for them. They flew dedicated crews meaning that you flew with the same crewmates at all times. You stood alert, went on vacation at the same time and basically did everything as a unit. Military Air Transport Service, later named more appropriately Military Airlift Command was different. Instead of dedicated crews, MATS depended upon Standardization whereby everyone knew the same thing about their crew position and could be used independently with any other crew member. It could be argued either way, but I enjoyed flying with different crew members each time, knowing everyone would do their job the same way.

Well, that took a little longer than expected, but I hope it explains the transition from Staff Sergeant to First Lieutenant. I dearly loved both enlisted and commissioned ranks. The frozen enlisted ranks made my decision for me. For better or for worse? I will never know. I enjoyed both!

HICKAM AFB, HAWAII AND BEYOND
NADI AND KOROLEVU, FIJI

"Once in a While, There is a Rainbow"

After my last trip in a C-118 to Travis AFB and return to Hickam AFB and home to Kailua on the Windward, or opposite side, of the Island from Hickam AFB and Honolulu, which required two days crew rest, they called me a day early which restarted my crew rest. Our crew rest time was sacrosanct. This time though they made a slight exception. By calling me during crew rest period, they owed me another two days off. The call was definitely worth taking. They wanted me to be ready to go on a trip to the South Seas. Hell, I was ready to go right then!

This trip would be a little different from what we considered a normal trip. They would brief me on what to expect when they called to alert me for the trip. That call came three days later. It would still be one of the first trips since I had passed my check ride and was now able to take a plane to some destination on my own. But I would be having company on this trip. We had an augmented crew meaning that there was an extra Navigator, Pilot and Engineer. It also meant a longer crew duty day, but no one minded, although the range of the C-118 would be tested on this trip.

The destination was Nadi International Airport on Viti Levu, the Big Island of Fiji with refueling stops at Canton Island (which would close four years later) and Pago Pago, American Samoa. When we arrived in Samoa to refuel and for the pilot to check in with the local 1009th SWS team. (No, I was no longer associated with that outfit. Now I was just on the crew picking up their seismic samples. Knowing that it would take some time, we decided to go into town and get a feel for this American possession just about thirteen degrees south of the equator. As soon as we opened the main cabin door, we knew one thing about Samoa. It was very hot and very humid. It was like a steam-bath had just engulfed our aircraft. But the thought of going into town made us embrace the weather. We could endure! And we could enjoy! This was one of the first stops on a very long trip.

To begin this adventure, let me explain what we had to do to get here. First of all, Navigation in the Southern Hemisphere was a brand new ballgame, and especially trying to one who had navigated only in the Northern 'spheres and was really new to navigating itself. Everything was completely backwards! Toss in the fact that we were also in the Eastern Hemisphere now. The Southern Hemisphere didn't act anything like its northern counterparts and we had a problem. Normal long celestial calculations turned into real challenges. We even had to use a completely different set of books because we had a different set of stars! Getting our heads together, the other Navigator and I finally figured how to think exactly opposite of what we had been taught. I always thought a little bit in the strange direction, but I don't really know if that helped or hurt. The fact remained that we were over large expanses of water with very small destinations. We had better figure out how to get from "A" to "B" real fast. There was no reliable North Star ("Polaris"). It only varied by one degree around its axis. Our best hope was the Southern Cross constellation which was beautiful, but it followed a predictable, but varied path.

Both Navigators worked almost full time with one "shooting the stars" using our sextant while the other tried to extrapolate meanings and put them on paper which would result in the point where we were most likely located about seven to ten minutes ago. In celestial navigation, three lines of sight were necessary to pinpoint where you were some few minutes ago. A speed line was needed, which was taken from a star roughly ahead or behind you. Another line needed was a latitude line. That is where the North Star was so great. It only wandered about one degree (sixty nautical miles) from the celestial North Pole depending on time of year which was the closest thing to a sure thing available in the world of Celestial Navigation. A third line at an "off-angle" was necessary to make a pinpoint which normally resembled a small triangle, or sometimes a large one. Theoretically, you were in the middle of that triangle some minutes earlier in your life. Supposedly, adjusted for time, that was where your aircraft and you were when the time line was shot.

"Dead reckoning," using best time and distance information from your latest celestial fix, put you in your current position. At our now relatively slow speed of two hundred forty knots, we were probably thirty or more nautical miles down the line by the time the location could be determined where the shots were observed and transferred to the flight chart. This experience was, to say the least, an interesting experience. Yes, I purposely used the same word twice! I could say exercise, but that would be misleading. It was not an easy or exacting chore to determine your position over vast expanses of ocean which, in some instances, found you at least one thousand nautical miles from the nearest land. It was comparable to being in the middle of the expanse of the Pacific Ocean between Hickam AFB, Hawaii and Travis AFB, California. Our only navigation aides were Long Range Navigation system or LORAN, developed in World War II. Even that was accurate only within about three nautical miles. I believed it implicitly when I could get it. But it was not always available, especially in this area. LORAN stations were few and far between in the southern hemisphere and their lines on our charts so far apart as to render them useless, leaving our location determination up to primarily celestial navigation. Our old standby celestial was available when it wasn't cloudy. Otherwise, it was "dead reckoning," which was basically using your ground speed and heading determined by using the distance and time between your last two fixes. This should be more accurate than the flight plan. I compared a flight plan kind of like the plan for battle. Things change so rapidly in battle that the plan is thrown out of the window almost as soon as the battle is joined.

Now back to Samoa. On the way in, we passed a small park. It was lush with tropical foliage and flowers everywhere and on the edge of the park, near the road was an open shower occupied by one of the local women. She was huge! She was also naked from the waist up. We commented on this phenomenon and were assured that this is not unusual in this area. I also thought to myself, "What a lovely custom. Perhaps it would sometime, somehow wend its way to the United States," though I knew my wish was all in vain. Localized public showers were in every park and topless bathing was the norm. Good by me! They evidently had no showers in most homes. The indigenous people lived a simple life. But in my view it appeared to be a good life. I wondered why they continued to wear a sarong from waist down while showering. It seemed a little bit unfair, but I figured, "Let's not get too greedy. There was enough pulchritude in what was within viewing distance." It was hard not to stare at this woman, but I knew that a gentleman should just casually gaze upon the personage of this large, but shapely wahini. I hoped to myself that a more winsome lass would be partaking of the facility upon our return. Alas! It was not to be. The showers, though running, were void of any of the local fauna when we drove back by. More the pity! Oh well, someday maybe I would return? Nope!

We didn't tarry very long on the Island. Just long enough to refuel and get lunches for everyone which would be devoured by crewmembers after takeoff. More importantly, Major Cinniman, our Aircraft Commander, had huddled at the Team with our contact point man for all the different islands which we would have to visit to pick up seismic readings if this damned bomb would ever go off. The last one took over a month. Everything had to be just right! On the way back to the airplane, I couldn't help but mutter to everyone and no one, "Good grief, the folks on this Island were HUGE! No wonder there are several in the NFL. I saw one who could play the entire left line!" And that one was a female!

However, we still had business to attend to so we departed Pago Pago for Nadi, Fiji. Both cities were pronounced as though there was an "n" in front of the "g" and "d." I'm not too sure why they didn't just insert an "n" in each place, but this was only one of the strange things I encountered on this exotic journey. I guess it was similar to the situation in Hawaii where the Missionaries used only thirteen letters to establish the Hawaiian language. But this was their land, not mine. Now, if we could just hack the navigation to get this group of aviators to where we would crew rest and await the nuclear explosion which was counting down on Bikini Atoll (an atoll is a ring-shaped coral reef that surrounds a body of water called a lagoon, a not so little known fact). That detonation would send tremors through the earth and sea and would be picked up by several seismic stations scattered among the islands. That was the reason for our exotic vacation. We were here to work! We were tasked to pick up these seismic results and take them back to Hawaii where they would be further transported on to the mainland for deeper analysis. Was it our fault that the detonation was delayed time after time for ten lovely days? Could we help it if everyone had a good time? Or should that be, "Everyone was had by a good time?" Old Irish proverb. Hmmm, did the Irish have proverbs or was that the exclusive domain of the Orientals? It really didn't matter. We were here for business and if a little enjoyment got in the way, who was I to complain?

We hit our first snag as soon as we landed. No room at the hotel for an indefinite stay. Other crews had hit this same problem so Major Cinniman knew what to do. He just needed to rent two houses and wait for the bomb to cooperate. We would be near our aircraft and be ready to get going immediately to pick up those seismic readings and whatever else they might have. We had another one of our C-118s and crew waiting at Eniwetok Atoll, located much closer to Bikini Atoll, doing the same thing which was supporting the U.S. Nuclear Weapons Testing Program. However, there was just one problem. There was only one house available. The Major immediately rented it for the enlisted crew. That old axiom of "Take care of your men first" was instilled in all military leaders.

The five rated crew (Pilots and Navigators) would just have to take their chances on going down and around the island toward Suva, the Capitol tomorrow. For tonight, we found availability for a one night stay. We gladly took it, checked in and headed for the showers. It had been a long twenty hours and we were yet to have dinner. Fortunately, an Indian restaurant was next door.

Fiji had a lot of parallels to Hawaii. Lots of the same flowers, the natives were content with their leisurely lifestyle and there was an ambitious foreign nation, looking for new territory to occupy. They were more than eager to take over the mundane and not so mundane chores in those beautiful Islands that the natives would rather not do. Therefore, the passive invasion from India was not really much opposed. Soon, the indigent population was relegated to what they really wanted to do. Raise tapioca on fiercely protected plots and lay around out in the jungle drinking a mind and mouth numbing locally produced drink. It was actually a mild sedative which was taken in by drinking from a quarter or half of a coconut shell. It tasted like dirty water to me, but I get ahead of myself.

After cleaning up and dressing in our familiar tropical wear, we sallied forth to the Indian restaurant. Curry! That item immediately shouted to us from the menu. We all knew that Indian curry was the finest in the world. They, unlike some, always used coconut milk in their recipes. It made a world of difference. By the time our pre-dinner cocktails had arrived, it had been decided that we all wanted curry. They had the choices of mild, medium and hot. That was the only dilemma, and it was discussed thoroughly. Being from Colorado, I was used to good hot Mexican fare. A couple others were from states that served similar foods. The guy from Louisiana said that nothing could be hotter than his mother's gumbo or red beans and rice. So, it was unanimous. Hot it would be! We were no wimps. Having started the second round of drinks, we were all feeling pretty good. That twenty-hour crew duty day didn't seem so bad now. What other way was there for us to have a vacation, albeit a working one, on a tropical Island? None of us could afford it on

Air Force wages that is for certain! Of course, we were all getting extra pay for living in Hawaii, on Oahu, which was no bad deal in itself.

The Indian waiter came to take our order and questioned our choice of "hot" for our dinner. We all enthusiastically wanted to see just how hot it was. Couldn't be hotter than Mexican! So, there shouldn't be a problem, right? We should have asked for a sample! After we tasted our first bite, we all decided that "curry" was really the Indian word for FIRE! And no use trying water. It was like pouring gasoline on a home lit fire. HOLY CRAP! Our heads were about to explode, much to the delight of the locals around us. Our waiter was completely distraught! He looked like all the blood had left his face! Have you ever seen a completely white Asian Indian? The only thing that wasn't white was his red Bindi. It looked like he was more likely to have a stroke than any of us.

After what seemed like an hour, but which was probably mere anguished minutes, some others rushed a liquid potion to us. We cared not what it contained or its consistency. We were willing to try anything to get rid of that heat! It actually cooled us down and after we had gathered our collective selves together, our now dark again waiter asked us if we would like to try the medium or mild. As if with one voice, a brave, but chastened crew, allowed a request for "mild" to almost echo throughout the dining room. WOW! Lesson learned amid light laughter throughout. We actually did have curry again. In fact, we had it several more times, but never again did we choose hot! The mild was plenty hot enough!

Then it was time to hit the rack and get some shut-eye for the next day. We knew not what it would bring, but felt confident that it would definitely not bring more HOT curry! We were able to take a fairly late breakfast, but had to hit the road to find a semi-permanent place to stay and Suva, the Capitol City, was a long way away. It was clear on the southeast corner on the waterfront. It was far enough away that we were hoping to find some little shack we could rent along the way.

It was well before noon when we started our trek into the un-known. We checked with the enlisted crew. They had made them-selves at home, had rented a car and found a watering hole that served food and made themselves at home there. Major Cinniman's only caution was that they check on the airplane every day. We left Nadi feeling comfortable that they and the C-118 were in good shape.

Then onward, but not upward we went, bent on finding a tem-porary home. The road was not much more than a dirt trail after we got about five miles out of town. So we went merrily along on a bumpy ride to our destiny. It definitely wasn't looking very good!

As we were wending our way along the narrow two lane "high-way" that paralleled the coastal waters, we couldn't help but roll down the windows so we could smell as well as see the abundance of flowers and bushes, some of which we were familiar from the Hawaiian flowers. This was turning out to be pretty nice. I com-mented, "We could just sleep under the stars in the flower beds at night and on the sandy beaches during the day." My random thought was met with more scorn than approval, but most just con-sidered the source. Along the way, the other Navigator said he re-membered a few words from a previous trip. He said that "Hello" in Fijian sounded like "Car shine." As we passed a few natives along the way, he tried it and got the same sound in return. He also told us that the native relaxing drink was called Kava.

However, before we could relax "with all this loveliness," (Al-fred Apaka), we needed to find an abode within which we could abide for an indeterminate amount of time. Lo and behold! We ac-cidentally ran across a nice looking resort hotel. We found it less than half way to Suva and only about ninety minutes from Nadi, all on the island of Viti Levu which translates to "Great Land." It was the "Big Island" of Fiji.

The resort was gorgeous and had plenty of room, but it was probably out of range of our limited budget. The gods were smiling down upon us when we found out it was their "off season!" Great rates! In the tropics and especially in Hawaii with the goddess Pele, we began to halfway believe in many gods after hearing some of the goose-pimple raising stories told by the locals and they swore they were all true. I actually witnessed a few myself, but I'll spare you the suspense.

Even with the great rates and being on an Air Force budget, the Aircraft Commander set us up in the annex across the street from the main hotel. I glanced in the direction the clerk was pointing and it didn't look too bad, but I had a feeling of foreboding when I heard the desk clerk say, "Be sure you are careful when getting into your bed that a mosquito doesn't get in behind the netting with you." Mosquitoes? Netting? They said this was a four-star hotel. Shit! Even the ground stars are all messed up as was all the navigational stars around here!

But with all of that, Tambua Sands Beach Resort in Korolevu is one vacation (oops, I mean TDY) that I will never forget. So beautiful in so many ways! Looking around the resort grounds, we all kind of hoped the nuclear shot would be delayed so we could get acquainted with this beautiful island. It was approximately twenty-three degrees south which was the same as Honolulu was north. Many Hawaiian flowers originated in Fiji, notably the Frangipani or as they are more popularly called, Plumeria. They were everywhere. Their unique smell was even more entrancing than their beauty. Plus, the Pikaki was in bloom and the scent near those tiny white flowers was the most intoxicating of all.

Adding to the overwhelming appeal were the normal tropical beaches. Not the powdery white sands of the Florida panhandle or of Cancun, they seemed related to the light tan of Waikiki. They looked so inviting, I think we had found a great place to stay for a while. Hopefully the nuclear shot would be delayed for at least a little bit! The drive around the bottom western-most part of the island had been nice, but it had been trying and we were ready to get cleaned up and try their restaurants. Having been living in Hawaii, we were well equipped for tropical living. Aloha shirts it was.

To our, at least my, amazement, they were identical to the wear of these islanders.

Food! That's what we needed now. After quick showers, we gathered in the spaciously beautiful lobby with its normal exotic, comfortable, overstuffed, rattan furniture with a fire pit in the center. Onward into the dining room we went. Whoa! Such a dining room! We were not accustomed to nor had we expected such accommodations. It looked like the Royal Hawaiian Hotel on Waikiki! Quietly, we were ushered to a round table set for five. We were informed that this table would be our location for dining during entire our stay. Wow! It definitely looked good enough to us peasants!

We settled in as the nicely clad hostess seated us and gave us our menus. Good Grief! What a lineup. This was fancier food than any of us had imagined. We recognized some the gastronomical delights, but not all. A couple of the crew had been around a little more than I had and could explain some of the more unfamiliar dishes. We knew we would be here for at least a few days so most went with the familiar island foods like Ahi tuna simply seasoned and seared. Others had shrimp and one fell back on teriyaki. We couldn't wait until we felt less tired and could venture into some of those new delights, though I did have the turtle soup as an appetizer. After completely removing most of the silver and glass ware, they were replaced immediately by a new set which was even more fanciful. Having eaten way more than my normal meal, they brought out desserts that appeared to be so fancy it would be a crime to even taste them. I became a criminal and devoured mine after we all sampled each-others. Each of us thought we had the best one. I was thankful that there were only about three other tables seated a distance away so they could not observe our lack of decorum and knowledge of the finer dining arts.

Next, when I was ready to hit the sack (or mosquito-netted, futon-like sleeping area) for some needed rest, came the call for entertainment set up in our honor as the newest guests.

Some typical island type dances, a flaming sword dancer who was one of the best I've seen. There were also a couple of solos by a beautiful island girl with an even more beautiful voice who entranced us with songs like "La Paloma," "Coo Coo Roo Coo Coo" (Little Dove) "Love Song of Kalua," my favorite, and others. I was immensely surprised that they loved Alfred Apaka as I did. Then came the invitation to dance with some of our young hostesses. Who could resist that? As I stepped to the dance floor, I was approached by a nice tropical maiden. One of the pilots was invited by a drop-dead gorgeous girl. These fair maidens were obviously being assigned to us for the duration of the evening. They were all conversant in English and told mainly island stories of what we could visit over the next few days, but mainly, they just glided across the floor. I was a pretty darned good dancer, but I had met my match in "my" chaperone, Queenie. We were all having a wonderful time. That needed rest was but a distant thought now. We were all energized by the rather enticing entertainment.

One thing stuck out to everyone and to the bemusement of our escorts, we couldn't get over the size of the monstrous frogs surrounding the several tall lamp posts. Each post had a big electric bug zapper. These frogs knew what they were doing because there were many bugs and the almost constant buzzing of flying insects being fried must have been music to these amphibians. (do they have ears?) The biggest, fattest frogs I have ever seen sat many deep atop one another with open mouths waiting for toasted bugs to just fall into their enormous maws. The locals got a kick out of us getting a kick out of these enormous and opportunistic amphibians. Cycle of life!

Finally, the night wound down with fond farewells and promises of meeting tomorrow and a visit to the local Fijian Chief in his own hut. That sounded intriguing, so we went hurriedly behind our netting, taking care not to let one of the many monsters trying to get in. Actually, if you could get past the fact that the noise was coming from hundreds of mosquitoes, the steady buzz was like a white sound machine and a well-earned dreamless sleep was not far behind. Thus, a second activity-filled day fell into the background with the expectation of more to come.

I'll not detail everything about a ten-day visit, but I would like to hit a few high points. That waiter, during our entire trip never took a note. All evening meals were at least four courses and he dazzled us. We even began changing our selections after he had gone several orders past the one trying to cause the confusion. One day, we even changed our places in the morning because he knew what each one preferred, down to kind of coffee and juice. He delivered the proper things to the proper place. He just flat impressed us with that smiling memory. Speaking of flat, his feet were about as wide as long. No kidding! His feet were a good eight inches wide! Of course, none of the natives wore shoes or even flip flops or thongs. But even so....

I mentioned the visit with the chief. What a memorable hour or so, probably less! We were led into his hut, bending down to get inside. We could barely see the chief through the smoke, laying on his pillow of an approximately four by four inch block of worn wood. He was lying on his side smoking something. I didn't know what marijuana was at that time as I was an innocent, very naive twenty-eight year old. All I remember was that it stunk! We had to share a toast with the chief after a brief discussion. We had a drink of Kava with which to toast. Though a non-alcoholic drink, it is used in Fiji, Tonga and Hawaii. It is psychoactive. It tasted terrible and I could feel some numbness in my mouth. The Chief insisted we have another. We couldn't refuse. As we left, I wondered if the chief had even realized we had been there. There was just no way to know.

A few days later, the hotel set us up to go with a couple of the fair damsels on a fairly long hike up a streamside trail in a narrow canyon. We made a turn in the path after an hour or so, and, can I say it again? Lo and behold! A large cardboard box was sitting beside the trail. It was loaded with fresh sandwiches, fruit and dessert along with the favorite beverage of each individual. For me, there were a couple local beers which were very tasty! We had no idea how it got there and the girls weren't talking. After the meal and a short nap, we continued on up the trail and made a turn. Wow! A big, beautiful waterfall and a sizeable natural pool! It was framed by a beautiful rainbow. A rainbow that was as serene as the rest of the scene. We all stood there, drinking in the beauty of the moment. Fortunately, I had a camera. It was one of the most enchanting scenes I have ever witnessed. Suddenly, the girls, full of giggles, ran to the pool and dived in. Several of the crew followed suit. I would have, but I don't know how to swim very well. Later, the presence of Queenie and the other escorts, just standing in the pool only served to enhance the beauty of the moment. It lives on in my mind! Some of the guys and girls swam under the waterfall to an indent behind. I once again regretted I couldn't swim!

But, I did a clumsy side stroke under the falls and climbed into the cave-like structure behind the plunging waters. I couldn't believe it. The rainbow was again there in the mist created by the falls. Gorgeous! After a few pleasant hours frolicking in the pool and waterfall, we wandered, taking our time, back to the lodge. I slipped away and went to a magic beach I discovered the night before. I sat on the sand for a while just thinking about life in general and my current situation in particular. After a lot of soul searching, I went back to the lodge, but returned to the beach two nights later. It was truly magical! The next day we wanted to take a little boat to a small island which we could see in the distance. We couldn't because that bomb could be detonated any time. We asked ourselves, "Good grief, how are we being held captive by a bomb a few thousand miles away from us?" I knew why. My entire old enlisted outfit, the 1009th Special Weapons Squadron, was standing by as we were, in spots all over the world. We still had to be ready to react at a moments' notice.

Back to reality and the beach.

The ocean water was great and I did a lot of wading and thinking. I found several large starfish along a section of shallows. They were florescent UCLA Blue. I wanted, in the worst way, to take the biggest one out and lay it in an ant pile to get it cleansed before I took it back to join my shells and coral in Hawaii. I couldn't do it. I still regret not doing it! Needless to say, we had many pleasant evenings and wonderful days at Korolevu, but the weapon finally exploded and we had to leave our Shangri La to pick up the seismic readings.

Someday, you should Google Korolevu to see for yourself.

Our Aircraft Commander alerted the enlisted crew and we began checking out of the resort. A soft rain was falling. One of the lovely ladies observed aloud, in a wistful voice, that the clouds were crying because we were leaving. Nice sentiment to carry away with us. I felt like crying too!

The Flight Engineer had the C-118 ready for flight. This was going to be a long day. We headed south, again trying to solve the riddle of navigating in the southern hemisphere. We went to several islands picking up the readings from the Team stationed there. On either Tongariva or Tongatapuu, we had to make a low pass over a grass runway to get the cattle off of the field. They fled the noise of our roaring engines, but by the time we got around to the field again, the local natives were crowding the field with their trinkets, grass skirts and other things for sale. I still have the gorgeous five-layered, shell-waisted grass skirt. It really doesn't fit me too well! I can't do it justice anyway. It needs a Queenie! I did, however, wear it a few years ago to an Assisted Living Home Hawaiian Party. I was in sandals and was wearing a palm frond woven hat. To much applause from the eighty and ninety year old residents, I wandered from area to area showing off my Hula skills. It still needs a Queenie

The rest of the trip was just tedious navigating of our aircraft through unfamiliar skies, but that is what we are paid to do. This was one trip out of hundreds that I will remember clearly the rest of my life!

WAKE ISLAND

"Where America's Day Really Begins"

"The Enemy has Landed, And it is Me"
Pogo's favorite saying. Not sure why.

There are several ways, in my mind, of looking at Wake Island. I will present some of them. As many times as I have been to and through Wake Island, in seven and a half years of line flying, the place always seems to stir up different emotions. I have spent as much as six individual days during three trips to Tachikawa in one calendar month. I have also spent at least ten days waiting for a replacement engine. I have also spent six weeks without ever staying there when I was being sent on successive trips to Travis AFB. Each trip to Wake was a different experience. I will lay some of my feelings about the Island in front of you for your examination, and will continue with the real story toward the end. There is truth in all. The second approach is more me, but I have seen many others with the attitude which could easily cause at least some of the emotions which may seem a bit extreme, but are real.

Wake Island, # 1
"The Enemy has Landed"

What can I say about Wake Island? I griped about it. I bitched about it. I hated it! I hated the communal showers, I hated to put my warm feet on those cold cement floors at 3:00 in the morning. I hated the FAA dining hall. I hated that it was the only place to eat. I hated that the menu changed every day. I hated that it always changed to something I hated. I hated having to check out towels and soap when we checked in after landing. I hated that the only things to do was fish, or walk. I hated both. I hated to walk because when I walked there, I always had to walk back. I hated to fish because I hated to catch anything. I hated not catching anything because I got shut out. I hated the caves because they held guns. I hated the guns because they had belonged to the occupiers. I hated the Drifters Reef. I hated that Tony fed me too many martinis. I hated when someone told me I had enough.

Wait, no one ever did that!

I hated the beach because it was too sandy. I hated the water because it was too salty. I hated checking for mail at the billets office. I hated that I had none. I hated when I had some. I hated that some guys even got mail from their wives. I hated that I stayed up too late to get up early. I hated that the reason I stayed up was the Drifters Reef. I hated the movies they showed. I hate that I stayed at the Drifters' Reef instead of going to see what movie was showing. I hated the poker game next door. I hated that I didn't get in. I hated I didn't have the dollars get in. I hated I didn't have the guts to get in. I hated getting restless. I hated that someone was shaking my leg or some other body part. I hated I was sweating. I hated that I couldn't just lay there and, make the world go away. Thru my haze I thought someone should write a song. I hated the haze I was in. I hated getting out of that haze.

Oh, crap, I hated that I had just had one of the weirdest dreams or worst nightmares, I don't know which, that I had ever had. Man, I hated that.

We had just been alerted at three o'clock for a four o'clock show and six o'clock go. And, we had no idea where way we were going yet, but I knew it would be west of here. I hated it could be Mactan. I hated it could be Clark. I hated that Guam was in between. Damn, what a dream. I hated that. Wait, that was part of my dream. Warm feet on a cold cement floor at three o'clock in the morning at Wake Island. I hated that I didn't have time to consider my dream. I hated that I'd be airborne before I could figure it out. I hated that I would be that busy. I hated that I hated.

Though there is an element of truth in all of the above, the following would be more like it, though the preceding was true and had their affect one each crewmember. The net effect was different for each one. Two of us could spend the entire layover together and come away with a different opinion of what had occurred.

MY REAL WAKE ISLAND!
"...And the Situation is in Doubt"

Wake Island wasn't made for too many things. Snorkeling, fishing walking or the Drifter's Reef. I partook of all, but spent the most time in the "Reef." But the walks! Everyone walked, but normally by themselves or with one other person, but normally alone. The walks gave everyone a clear area to think. And think we did. I mostly walked up to the big gun on the end of Peale Island, the island just across the bridge from the "Reef."

Then there were those long, lonely walks when you have been stuck on the Island for several days. Sheer boredom! Everything went through your mind, some good and some bad. Normally, bad! On Wake Island, things were just different. It was like no other place I have ever been. It seemed everyone walked alone and at different times of the day or night.

One thing that didn't sit well with me about being west of the International Date Line was the fact that I was always a day older when I crossed over it and when I went back over the Date Line, I never felt the satisfaction of having gained that day back again. It was gone forever and I just had to live the same day over again.

Another paradox involving the International Date Line: My Mom, being a devout Catholic, was a stickler for attendance at Sunday Mass. I couldn't help myself. I offered the proposition that if I left Honolulu on a Saturday night and, because of the International Date Line, I arrived at wake Island on Monday, did I commit a sin by not attending Sunday Mass that week because I had no Sunday?

Conversely, when flying back to Hickam AFB, if I attended Mass on Sunday at the Wake Island chapel, would I, because of the International Date line, have to go to mass again in Honolulu because it was the same day again, Sunday? She started muttering a lot.

It drove many folks, not just my mom, to distraction, and though some actually carried an absolute hate for this necessary place, I loved Wake Island and spent many wonderfully long hours and days there.

And so, for the sake of quenching the thirst for knowledge for those who have never been there, with the proviso of feeling sorry for you, I'll start with a description.

Wake Island was an enigma. The whole place was just one big area of transit and transitions. Wake Island, "Where America's Day Really Begins." A motto both trite and true. Wake Island had its own fickle personality. And that personality made it one very hard place in which to live.

Wake Island, formerly called Halcyon Island, is a coral atoll in the central Pacific Ocean. It is planted firmly atop a long dormant volcano and is located two thousand nautical miles (about two thousand three hundred statute miles or three thousand seven hundred km for those so disposed) directly West of Honolulu. This coral phenomenon rises about twenty-one feet (six meters) above sea level and is actually comprised of three separate Islands connected by causeways. These three small islets are Wilkes, Peale and Wake. They were discovered in 1568 by Alvaro de Mendana (yeah, I don't care either) and lie in a crescent with a four and one-half miles long and two miles wide lagoon with very smooth water within the crescent. Strangely enough, and I never heard the reason, there are no sharks within the lagoon! This glassy lagoon really added to its value as a stopover for the famed Pan Am Clipper. It is surrounded by a sub-aquatic lagoon following the dormant volcano's rim. The atoll receives little rainfall which could explain the absence of inhabitants or else, maybe no one else could find it? These islets are named for explorer British Mariner William Wake and were charted by Lieutenant Charles Wilkes in 1841. The reason for Peale Island's name is lost to me and maybe to history. Note that the names, plus all or some of this description, are from Encyclopedia Britannica. All action is by me and my fellow aviators. I'll just say that for these 2.7 square miles of coral, its value and place in history far outweighs its size. The extremely great value of Wake Island is inversely proportional to its extremely small size.

Now I yearn for the Island and especially the Drifters' Reef. Suffice to say, the United States (U.S.) laid claim to it in 1899 for the site of a cable station. I didn't even know we had cable back then and especially there. I guess I spent so much time in the Drifters' Reef, that I never saw any TV. Anyway, these guys were many years ahead of themselves. They started building a submarine base and air base in 1939, making it a very strategic outpost for the United States. Unfortunately, that didn't last long. The battle for Wake Island began on December 8, 1941. Remember the International Date Line. They are the first piece of land to be a day ahead of normal U.S. time. Remember their slogan: "Where America's Day Really Begins." It was attacked simultaneously with Pearl Harbor on Dec 7th and the Philippines on Dec 8th in 1941. Though terribly out-manned by a reinforced enemy, the few Marines fought and flew F4F Hellcats heroically. The civilian population fought and died as well. They held out until the Japanese brought in a large number of reinforcements and by sheer numbers, overwhelmed the defenders before those fateful words, the last words to be telegraphed from the beleaguered island, "The enemy has landed and the situation is in doubt!"

It was the 23rd of December, sixteen full days after the attack on this tiny piece of real estate began! Because the Japanese, had to bring in a large group of reinforcements to take the fiercely defended piece of coral, their overall strategy of a quick conquest of all the strategic islands in the South Pacific was disrupted. After the battle was lost, the garrison of sixteen hundred and sixteen troops and civilians captured by Japanese forces was forced to sit on the runway facing a line of Japanese machine guns. The plan was to execute the Americans, but the Admiral of the conquering fleet stepped in and halted the planned execution. The entire action of the furious battle that had the ebb and flow of an uncertain outcome was made famous by the movie "Wake Island" which starred Brian Dunlevy and Robert Preston.

At the beginning of the conflict, the initial forces totaled eleven hundred American military and twenty-five hundred Japanese infantry. The Americans suffered one hundred twenty killed, forty-nine wounded and two missing in action. The Japanese forces, reinforced several times, suffered eight hundred twenty killed and three hundred thirty-three listed as wounded. Most of the prisoners captured by the Japanese were sent off to Asian POW Camps. Ninety-eight of the most able-bodied prisoners were kept at Wake Island primarily to improve defenses. After a successful raid by American planes 5 Oct 1943, these prisoners were taken to the north end of the island, blindfolded and machine gunned to death. One prisoner escaped and carved in a big rock on the north end. "98 US PW 5-10-43." It meant: "Ninety eight U.S. POWs, May Tenth, 1943." He was soon captured and executed by the Wake Island Commander, Captain Sakaibara with his own katana, a ceremonial sword. Captain Sakaibara was executed in 1947 for this horrendous deed. His aide, Lt Cmdr Taruibanos sentence was reduced from death to life in prison.

The United States never did land troops to retake Wake Island. They so effectively blockaded the island that the Imperial Japanese Fleet gave up efforts of trying to re-supply their troops. Every American ship transiting the area would bombard the island as they passed. The last re-supply ship which attempted to land at Wake Island was grounded purposely on the southeast end of the westernmost (Wake) island and was still there on my early flights to Wake Island in the summer of 1962 and during the next few years until salvage operations began.

The Japanese occupation troops became so desperate for food that, after they tried to exist on fish caught the ordinary way, they resorted to using hand grenades to stun the fish in the lagoon. They would then just wade in and pick them up. Soon there were no fish to be grenaded (My new word). They also ate all of the tern eggs available and the terns themselves when they could catch one. The starving Japanese troops hunted the Wake Island Rail, an endemic bird, to extinction. On Sept 4th 1945, the ragged, emaciated group of twenty-two hundred soldiers of the Wake Island garrison surrendered without a shot being fired. It was several weeks after the official surrender of the Japanese Empire on August 15th 1945.

During their occupation of the island, thirteen hundred soldiers died of starvation and approximately six hundred from U.S. airstrikes, including bombs delivered by aircraft from my older brother's ship, the Aircraft Carrier CV 11, the Mighty USS Intrepid. It was the most often hit ship in World War II. Somehow, along the way, it was grounded, I suppose purposely, to become a museum in New York City.

The bottom line is that even though there was a substantial loss of lives on both sides, the capture of Wake Island did nothing for the war effort of Japan. Indeed, it kept a couple of thousand Imperial troops trapped on the island so they could not take part in any other part of the war. And the island was still there when the war ended! So were the remaining Japanese soldiers and American civilians.

There were many remnants of the Japanese occupation including the Suwa Maru, a Japanese merchant ship, which had the biggest prize. The Suwa Maru was destroyed when she tried to run the American blockade of Wake Island. She was hit by two torpedoes from USS Tunny commanded by Lt Cmdr John Scott on 28 March 1943. The first torpedo blew off her stern while the second was a dud. She was purposely run aground on Wake Island to prevent her from sinking. For some reason, the wreckage was hit on 5 April 1943 by Lt Cmdr Tyree (later Admiral) in USS Finback.

Her main value for salvage was the bronze screws. She had two. Just salvaging one of them paid for the entire salvage operation. The rest was all profit! Nice! In addition, there were many caves with shore battery guns pointed out to sea and they were everywhere. These were also salvaged. They didn't leave a thing behind.

There was also a nostalgic item that makes you wonder just what the pilots and later, the passengers, of the last Pan Am Clipper flight to arrive at Wake Island would have been thinking as their luxurious flight fell apart around them. Wake Island had become an integral stop for Trans Pacific Flight, especially for the iconic Pan Am Clipper which was a beautiful, graceful, amphibious luxury airliner. This particular flight set down in the deceivingly calm lagoon right in the middle of the fight for the island. They had nowhere else to go! Wake Island just does not have an alternate. It is Wake Island or nothing! The north island part of Wake Island, the largest island, is where Pan Am normally docked and where their hotel was located. When they splashed down in the lagoon, that area was pretty much in enemy control. They had no choice. There was no more dry land within eight hundred miles of Wake Island. They had to try to dock it in the more shallow waters on the easternmost island to get away from the fighting which they did. Since this area was not configured for the flying boat, the pilots lowered its landing gear and ran it up on the shore. The Clipper's landing gear was quite short, but with it, The Clipper could roll up further on shore, where it would hit coral, rocks and Kava trees until it was pretty well stopped well out of the water. From there, I do not what happened to the crew and passengers, but I would speculate that they were gathered up among the other civilian populace on the island. I'd just about bet that this was not the adventure they had expected when they started out from San Francisco or after an overnight stay in Honolulu. Personally, I'd be scared to death landing in the middle of a pitched battle for the island on which you were scheduled for a leisurely overnight stay. I'd be checking my ticket to see if this was really on my itinerary. I've been on a bad flight and a cruise that I thought unpleasant, but looking forward to four years as a Prisoner of War is just a tad different.

That is the story normally associated with the forward end of the fuselage which contained the engineer control area among other things. If you do the research, you would find that the Pan Am

Clipper was able to get airborne leaving one tardy passenger behind. A Philippine Clipper, a Martin 130 amphibious flying boat had happened by and was unscathed during the first air attack. It was able to depart with the Pan Am employees along with their own passengers before any more air assaults and a couple of days before the initial ground attack, which was repelled by this tiny garrison of mixed Marines and civilians. This was the initial setback for the Japanese forces.

The Marines fought gallantly on the ground as did the civilians, but the Marines in their four remaining F4F Wildcats. (Eight of them were destroyed on the ground during the initial air raid by Japanese Mitsubishi medium bombers from Kwajalein.) The Marine flyers led by Major Putnam under their overall commander Major Devereux were instrumental in blunting both air and ground attacks. Captain Henry Elrod was awarded the Congressional Medal of Honor for his heroic flights and fights in his Wildcat. Future President of the United States, George HW Bush flew his first combat mission over Wake Island. They held on for fifteen harried days. The tiny garrison suffered one hundred seventy-two casualties including one hundred nineteen personnel killed. The Japanese force suffered two hundred and eighty-eight casualties. Wake Island was retaken on September fourth nineteen forty-five without a single shot being fired.

The reason I mention all of this is that the forward portion of a Clipper was still basically intact when I began flying into Wake. When I got tired of the Drifters Reef or was with a non-party crew, I would walk among the remnants of a not too long-ago war. I would imagine the happenings on those crucial days when we could not get any support to our beleaguered fellow Americans mostly because of the fog of confusion caused by an unexpected attack. I would go into some of the caves where it appeared the gun crew slept and perhaps even ate when they had food. Each was buried deep in the coral with cutouts in the cave for beds and probably for relaxing. There was a great view of this portion of the Pacific Ocean which they were guarding against an enemy who would never show for the final fight. Each day, they would become hungrier and more disconsolate. Some, it has been rumored, committed suicide rather than slowly starve to death. They knew they were too weak to fight and win.

Some years later, one of the Flight Engineers with whom I had the good fortune of flying, brought along some special tools and removed the entire throttle assembly of the Pan Am Clipper which was made of solid brass and was in great shape. He had told me on an earlier flight that he was going to do it and on our way back from Tachikawa he did! A gorgeous souvenir for a flight engineer! The throttles still actually moved in their full range! Who better to have it? I wonder if Wake Island or Pan Am owned it. By now, they had not flown Clippers for years, so it was a moot point. Probably the only better place for the throttle set would be a museum. But, if he had not salvaged it for himself, it would have been tossed in with all of the other salvage and would have been enjoyed by no one.

After the war, the Island once again became a vital stop that made it possible for military flights as well as commercial flights to again reach Guam, the now free Philippines and beyond as well as northwest to Formosa (now Taiwan), Tokyo and on into Seoul, South Korea. Wake Island was vital in opening the up the Far East as well as southern Pacific islands to commerce and was even more vital during the Vietnam War. Virtually all transport planes carrying supplies and personnel to the places of war, needed to stop on Wake Island for refueling and crew rest before they could reach their destinations. At times, I have seen more than forty aircraft of various makes and models sitting on the ramp awaiting fuel, another crew or, normally, maintenance. For one extended period of time, I could almost be guaranteed to see a C-133 strategic airlifter sitting off to one side with at least one engine missing from a wing. Dubbed the "Flying Hot Dog," it had more problems than a dog had fleas or so it seemed. Some sat there for weeks. It was a constant maintenance headache. Though it resembled an elongated C-130, it was built by Douglas Aircraft Corp, as a strategic (long range) air-lifter while the very reliable Lockheed C-130 was a tactical (short range) airlifter. Powered by four large turboprops, the C-133 was replaced by the C-5 in 1971 and not a moment too soon! The C-5 could bypass Wake Island and fly directly to Japan or whatever their destination may be, so once again the vital necessity of the Wake Island experience was diminishing, but the poker game went on.

My favorite part of the Island, was the Drifters Reef, the comfort zone of Wake Island, affectionately known as the "Reef." It was a lounge, bar or whatever you wanted to call it. I just called it necessary! I spent so much time on Wake Island that they almost ran me for mayor. Not really. However, I did spend enough time sitting at the Reef bar that Tony, the bartender, asked me to be the godfather to his soon-to-be-born child! I checked on the responsibilities of godfather in the Philippines and they were so onerous that I opted not to accept the honor. It did make me ponder about the possibility that I was spending too much time at the "Reef." NAH! I didn't ponder very long. It was my home on Wake Island. "One more please, Tony."

Most of those who crew-rested in the cement block billets spent at least a little time at the "Reef." When the jets like the C-141 started transiting Wake, they did not appreciate the "Reef" as much as all of us did in the prop days. I spent most of my time there. One of the more likely stories, or fables if you will, to be told about the "Reef" was the time one of our young pilots danced with the jukebox! I knew this character well. He was big enough to completely fill the co-pilot's seat. The short sleeves of his uniform shirt had to be let out several inches to accommodate his huge biceps. One time in the Officers Club in Tachikawa, he challenged our pretty waitress to an unusual contest. He bet her that his bicep was larger than her thigh. She hoisted her very short skirt and with all of the remaining crew taking their own wistful measurements, it was obvious who had persevered. His was larger than hers by some measure. Now, that didn't sound too good, but it looked pretty good. I saw it myself. That was the only time I ever saw a "You show me yours and I'll show you mine." Nice! It should happen more!

Now the story of the jukebox dance at the "Reef." It supposedly happened that it was one of those rare times that a stuffy superior officer was in attendance in the "Reef" when this same young pilot picked up the jukebox and started dancing with it. The grumpy Officer got upset and demanded loudly in a commanding tone that the young Second Lieutenant put the jukebox down. He did! He just dropped it. I don't know to this day whether it was out of spite, following orders immediately or just plain stupidity. We were without music for months afterward. Thanks, General! They were going to charge the Second Lieutenant for the repair or replacement. They really couldn't though. He was just following the order of a General!

Next door was possibly the longest running poker game in history. I know for a fact that it ran continuously with normally more than one table and sometime three to five tables or more for the seven years I flew through there. I also knew that it had been running since the early '50's which was years before I got there. I also understand that it lasted long after my last stopover in a C-124 in 1968. The main table was always full with another crewmember always there waiting to take the place of a crewmember who had just been alerted to go fly, got tired or just ran out of money. For personal reasons, I never played although I could at least hold my own in a poker game. These stakes were just way too high. I've also seen as many as seven tables running at a time, some in an overflow room during a bad weather hold or just the normally huge volume of aircraft that transited the Island.

Wake Island! Just the words seem like magic. The air world could not operate in the South Pacific without this tiny coral atoll sitting on that dormant volcano rim. It was here or nowhere when flying in this area in those days. With no alternate airfield, they loaded an extra one hour and forty-five minutes of fuel in case we had to loiter. That happened to me only once. It was one of my first Airborne Radar Approaches. It took two tries, but I got us down, just barely busting minimums.

The rainfall averaged only a little over two inches, mostly provided by the edges of typhoons so the vegetation was sparse and there is no way it could support a human population. Yet, it could be argued that it was the most important 2.7 acres of islands in the world. Even today, it is still important as a Forward Operating Location for a rotating flight of F-22 and KC-10 refuelers and various other aircraft. By now, I would imagine that the F-35 is in the mix.

Even arriving at Wake Island could be a pleasure in several ways. For three years, I was the navigator on many round trips to Tachikawa AB, Japan. We always left at about midnight and would be airborne for only about five and a half hours. We flew C-118B's which was the military equivalent of the civilian workhorse DC-6B. At night and in this northern clime, we could climb right up to our cruising altitude of 18,000 feet. Well, it so happened that the C-118 had a small compartment, just above and to the rear of the nose gear, which had no utility of which we were aware. But it was just the right size to hold a case of beer. Tom Kuhns was my best pilot friend and was a navigator before he lost his mind and went to pilot school. He showed it to me and I showed it to others. A case of beer fit in this small compartment perfectly. Flying at eighteen thousand feet for five hours plus cooled the Heinekens beer down to just above freezing. Can't you just imagine arriving at your destination and having a case of ice-cold beer waiting for you at the aircraft? Then you could have your first cold, cold beer on the crew bus instead of having to wait until the Billeting office where they had a dispenser of just cold beer.

Speaking of having something to drink, the Drifters Reef was one of the main reasons I felt like Wake Island should even exist. Without Wake, where would you put the Drifters Reef lounge? They just went together. The first time I saw it, it was love at first sight and a mutual one at that.

These three islets are of great importance for many reasons. This small piece of coral was so isolated that we did not have an alternate airfield for it. It's one of the few spots in the world with this condition and the only one I have ever visited. I've flown into Wake with water spouts in all quadrants at night and in so much rain that the spouts couldn't be picked out from the downpour. We could still get on the ground. But this day Wake Island was a weather phenomenon. There were clouds from about twenty-five thousand feet down to the minimum ceiling of three hundred feet. That is a real rarity for this kind of weather in this location.

The weather was almost always gorgeous at Wake Island or so it seemed to me. The average temperature is about eighty-four degrees, and rarely hit ninety degrees and never over. The water temp was a constant eighty-one degrees! The nights cooled to an average of about seventy-seven degrees and like Hawaii, the little rain that falls, falls mainly at night. When the showers fall in the daytime, it didn't matter. The rain was normally light and warm so you would soon dry out. I'm not much of an ocean guy and I've mentioned that before. The possible reasons are that the one time someone talked me into snorkeling, I saw what I thought was a huge barracuda which was actually probably a pretty small barracuda, but still a barracuda. Then I was face to face, which was much too close, to an eel in his hole sticking part of his body out of the coral. I always figured it was a moray eel. Then a little puffer fish directly below me in about three to four feet of water suddenly puffed up and scared the living bejesus out of me! It scared me so much that I think I learned to run, not walk, on water. I have always maintained that I love the ocean and beach except for the sand and the salt water. Now I can add those horrible critters to that equation. I have never set foot in an ocean since and plan to keep it that way and it's all thanks to that lovely day in the lagoon at Wake Island!

I have also flown into Wake on a very wet edge of a typhoon of which no one had any knowledge. Who could have predicted something like that on one of my first flights as a Navigator? After we landed, we watched the resupply ship bobbing off shore for about three days until they gave up and moved on. During that time, the dining hall had only brisket on their menu. I made the mistake of convincing the rest of the crew that brisket was terrible meat. My reasoning was sound or at least in my mind, it was. On the ranch where I grew up, when we butchered a steer for our own use, Dad always threw away the brisket as junk meat. I think he just didn't know what to do with it. That time on Wake Island, we existed on all the peanuts, candy and other nuts in the small panic pantry which adjoined the Drifters Reef. We also consumed our ration of booze from Okinawa.

Wake Island is special to me for another, not so wonderful experience. I was on the C-118 ready to take sixty-eight passengers on to Tachikawa when our Aircraft Commander, Major Booth came aboard and solemnly announced, "President Kennedy and Texas Governor Conley have been shot."

Everyone was in a minor state of shock, but I figured communication was not too great and the message could have come in gar-

bled. Later, I just happened to be looking toward the terminal out of the seldom used right side crew entrance door when I saw the flag go to half-staff. At that instant, I knew that we had lost a great man. Minor shock just now turned to major. That was the most quiet five and one-half hour flight with which I was ever involved.

As soon as we landed, Major Booth and I went to the base chapel and prayed for our fallen President. That picture in my mind of the lowering flag will live with me forever.

It is obvious that Wake Island was a different kind of crew rest. I, who has an opinion on everything, can argue either way or agree with any and all opinions. In my seven and a half years of transiting this hardy garden spot, without a garden, I became convinced that Wake can effectively affect your mood in any and all directions. I have experienced literally all of them as someone once said something like: It is an enigma in a conundrum wrapped in a riddle with a few crosswords mixed in.

Wake Island was an integral part of my flying career and, oddly enough, I miss it.

IWO JIMA FLIGHT

"Semper Fi"

After a normal twenty-four hour crew rest at Wake Island, we were alerted at our normal three o'clock a.m. feet-on-a-cold-cement-floor time. I hated that! We were picking up a relay flight as usual and were anticipating another trip with a full load of sixty-eight passengers on their way to Tachikawa Air Base, on the northern edge of Tokyo. When we arrived at Wake Island Airlift Command Post (ACP), we were all pleasantly surprised. We had a load of Taiwanese soldiers returning from a joint training exercise which had been conducted somewhere on a U.S. Army Post. This could be the same group that we flew from Wake Island into Hickam Air Force Base, Hawaii on their way to the Mainland a few weeks ago. No matter, we were excited to be going to a different end airport than normal. I was also excited because I had never been to Taipei, the capital of Nationalist China, Formosa or, as it was now called, Taiwan.

Flight planning, weather briefing and all prep for flight were as normal as they ever were. We were rolling down runway One Zero, a nine thousand eighty-seven foot asphalt runway (3,000 meters for those so inclined), on time as usual. The C-118 was the most reliable plane in the inventory. You rarely had to worry about delays when flying in this baby. Best plane I ever flew in and we were off to a new destination with twenty-four hours planned crew rest in a new city. That was always exciting to anticipate.

Now, if I could just get to Bangkok, my main three cities in the Far East would have been visited.

Those were Taipei, Bangkok and Tokyo, our normal destination out of Wake Island. "One at a time, my boy, one at a time." as my dad would say.

As is normal with a C-118, takeoff was smooth and normal. We turned slightly to the north from our 276 degree magnetic heading of the runway to get more aligned with the direction to Taipei. Taipei, a place of storied fantasies, was home to Madam Chiang Kai-shek and her husband. He had taken his defeated Nationalist Army from mainland China into exile on this island fortress.

His Dictatorship was harsh as was Madam Changs after the Generalissimo would die in April of 1972. Born in 1887, he would die at age 87. Pretty good timing! Madame Chang, actually Soong Mei-Ling, would die in New York City at age 103. Notably, for some, she was the sister-in-law of Sun Yet-sen, the founder and leader of the Republic of China.

After hours of flight, we were cruising along at eleven thousand feet when the oil low level light started blinking. It was not a severe emergency, but worthy of note. Automatically, I began searching for the nearest Air Base or emergency landing strip. We were way past the Equal Time Point (ETP) so returning to Wake Island was out of the question. I began to track our progress a little more closely and frequently in case we had to make an emergency landing. We were hoping that the engine would just stay running long enough to get us to where it made sense to continue on to Taipei. A low-level oil light just blinking was enough to cause me to start looking around. It was bad enough to have just a blinking low-level light, but what we had feared was going to happen really did happen! It didn't take long for the blinking red light to quit blinking and to go on steady. It looked like a red-eyed cyclops, like all steady warning lights do. This was a cyclops who was daring us to continue on as normal. Almost immediately, I heard, "Flight Engineer, we need to shut down number one engine now, and feather the prop." "Roger Wilco." Literally, "Received and will comply." Those words came calmly over the intercom. Next, it was the voice of the AC. "Nav, get me a heading to the nearest landing field where we can get some more oil. Get me an ETA as soon as you can. I think we can make it on to Taiwan if we can get enough to fill it up again now."

Within two minutes: "OK, Nav, destination and ETA?" My immediate response was, "Iwo Jima. Forty-two minutes, heading three hundred thirteen (313) degrees." "Iwo?" came the surprised response. "Roger that! Iwo is the nearest viable airfield. Eighty-six hundred and ninety-four feet. Plenty long, even for you!" "Smart ass!" came the reply. I continued, "They have about twelve hundred station-keeping and maintenance troops there and a landing strip which is in constant use, so they have to have maintenance capability. You may want to contact them to verify availability of oil, so we don't land and get stuck there. It appears that the middle airstrip of the three which were active in World War II is the active. Notices to Airmen (Notams) say that they have improved and lengthened the runway on this little, famous eight square mile island."

Once committed and on the ground, we would never get back off the ground with only three engines turning. It is against the rules, common sense and is nature's way of keeping big aircraft from running around without enough engines to keep it airborne. It has worked that way since God invented gravity.

"Call them on 121.5 on VHF or 243.0 on UHF. They are a twenty-four hour emergency field." "Thanks, Nav." These two radio frequencies are airborne emergency frequencies commonly known as "Guard." Moments later the Aircraft Commander came back over intercom, "Good work, Nav. Iwo Tower is clearing us to land as soon as we arrive. No other traffic in the area. They indeed have as much oil as we need. Hopefully, with a new casing full of oil, we can make it to Taipei before we have to shut it down again. The flight engineer can look it over to see how bad the leak is and see if he can pad the leaking area so it won't leak again or at least as badly. If he can't, we should still be able to get back off the ground and make it to Taipei. And, if it is too bad, it looks like we might have to get an engine change in Taipei. That could take a few days.

I hope I don't hear any complaints about a nice vacation in a great city." There was nary a sound over the intercom.

Now, me again, "Iwo in twenty-three minutes, heading 321 degrees. Confirm they are using the center runway of the three runways they had at the time of the battle." Another thought popped into my head. And I always let the others know what I am thinking. "Hey, guys, a little known fact. We had a few P-51's and a couple B-29's use the south runway in emergencies while the battle was still going on. How much fun would that be?" Later, many US aircraft and lives were saved because of the sacrifice of those sixty-eight hundred Marines and others who died securing an emergency landing field for our wounded planes. This island later provided a departure point to make the bombing runs shorter and so that the P-51's could escort the big boys all the way on their bombing runs. I don't think we lost another bomber to enemy aircraft after the P-51 and later the P-38 fighters began ruling the skies over Japan."

I ended with the obvious statement, "And I wouldn't mind a week in Taiwan!" I then started with all these thoughts running through my mind, "What do I know about Iwo Jima? Really quite a bit, but not enough." I was old enough at eleven and very interested in the war, especially the Pacific Theater. I had a brother and two brothers-in-law in the Pacific Theater of World War II. In fact, one of the Brothers-in-law, one Maury Notch, had given Lt Col "Jimmy" Doolittle a haircut on the morning of his earlier than scheduled takeoff on the famous raid over Tokyo and other heartland cities on 18 April 1942. At an annual reunion of the Aircraft Carrier Hornet, Doolittle tried to buy back the chit. Captain (0-6) Maury Notch, USN Retired, refused. He had it to the day he died. "Thirty Seconds Over Tokyo" is a very exciting movie starring Spencer Tracy as Doolittle and Van Johnson as Army Capt Lawson, author of the book and pilot of the "Ruptured Duck" on the raid. Worth a visit to Netflix.

I remember well the newspaper reports and RKO newsreels in the local theater about the bloody progress of the US Marines against the Japanese empire. I also remembered that it was some of the fiercest and bloodiest fighting in the Pacific War. It began on 19 February, 1945 and would last for five weeks of constant, fierce fighting.

We should have known they would fight to the death. It was the first enemy (American Marines) landing on their homeland. That would make anyone pissed off and ready to fight! The only prisoners we gathered from this battle were those who were so wounded or infirm that they couldn't fight or commit suicide which many did. The wounded amounted to a few hundred. American casualties were over sixty-eight hundred *Killed In Action* and nineteen thousand two hundred wounded. Eighteen thousand Japanese were killed. Only two hundred sixteen enemy soldiers were captured while over three thousand were hiding in the tunnels and were eventually killed or captured. This was the only battle in WWII where American casualties (dead and wounded) outnumbered Japanese killed.

It was far different than was expected after the battle began with heavy shelling and aerial bombings prior to the February landings. But, the ten days of intense shelling immediately prior to the battle requested by Major General Schmidt, commander of The Marine Landing Force was turned away. Rear Admiral Blandy would give him only three days of bombardment which turned into only about thirteen hours of shelling out of the thirty-four hours of available daylight. The refusal for more shelling days was because the Admiral feared a lack of munitions when they might need them. As it turned out, the intense shelling did little good anyway. As we later discovered, the entire island was honeycombed with tunnels which went as deep as ninety-five feet below the surface in one bunker and another bunker was fifty feet. The average of tunnel depth was about twenty feet. As a result of the eleven miles of tunnels, the months of bombardments had little or no effect.

Several probes were conducted by various naval units, including vital Explosive Ordinance Disposal (EOD). These were the guys that detonate mines and other traps before the main troops arrived. Even their trips as clandestine forces were discovered and repelled with casualties. Each attempt to conduct surveillance on the island was surprised and turned back by this resilient enemy. Unknown to the United States forces, the Japanese Commander of Iwo Jima, Lieutenant General Kuribayashi, had constructed a spectacular defense for the island. Every inch of the island was covered with the capability of withering fire against any landing force. Miles of tunnels were constructed. They were even supposed to honeycomb the bowels of Mt. Suribachi itself. Unfortunately for the defenders, the last six miles were never completed, leaving the strongest defenses on the mid and north parts of the small island. This was where most of the oh-so-dangerous tunnels existed.

Though several tried, the Japanese had defenses that couldn't be breached by small units. It would take one huge bloody push onto beaches, completely vulnerable to fire from Japanese hidden and protected artillery which would withdraw back into the mountain after being fired, as well as anti-personnel weapons and small arms.

Unaware that the underground defenses constructed by General Kuribayashi's genius were influenced by the success of the defenses devised and used effectively on the Island of Peleliu, that dug-in defense worked very well even though they were eventually overrun by superior American forces. The Americans expected that most of his army would have been killed or incapacitated by this months-long bombardment, especially with the final exclamation mark insinuated by days of concentrated fire from battleships, Naval and Army aerial bombardment plus every gun on approximately four hundred and fifty warships.

Twenty-two marines, four naval corpsmen and one sailor were awarded the Congressional Medal of Honor for the battle of Iwo Jima. It was the second bloodiest conflict of the war in the Pacific, second only to the battle for Okinawa which was yet to come and would be, thankfully, the last action by our Marines or Soldiers on Japanese soil. Iwo Jima was a Japanese island and everyone knew that as bad as Iwo was, Okinawa would be even worse! I also re-membered thinking, "My brother Bill almost got killed by a Japa-nese Kamikaze attack while serving on the Aircraft Carrier CV-11 during the battle for Okinawa. The Fighting "I" (The USS Intrepid)! The USS Intrepid was the most frequently hit ship during the war.

After the war, Lieutenant General H.M. "Howling Mad" Smith complained bitterly that the lack of the navy's shelling support throughout the entire island campaign cost many Marine lives. This obviously caused many hard feelings between the U.S. Navy and its auxiliary arm, the U.S. Marine Corps! By the way, to the best of my knowledge, the only military base ever named for a living being is a U.S. Marine Base overlooking Pearl Harbor in Hawaii. It is Camp H. M. Smith and was named for the Howling Mad, World War II General, Smith. We held our promotion party there when I was promoted to Captain along with about twenty others. Now back to our current flight.

After landing and taxiing to the ramp, it was discovered that their oil replacement equipment was ill-fitted to the C-118. The only way we would ever get oil into the engine was with a hand cranked oil transfer mechanism. This would take a while, but it was all they had. The commander of the Iwo Jima Air Base was an Air Force Captain and he volunteered to take us to the top of Mount Suribachi if we were interested. I immediately thought, "In-terested? I've been thinking about that mountain ever since the de-cision was made to use this small rock as an oil station." He said it would take about an hour to refill the engine cavity. It was very nearly empty, but the flight engineer with help from the local main-tenance folks said he could pad the engine to slow the leakage if not stop it entirely. That meant the rated crew of two pilots and a lone navigator (me) would be taking one of the most exciting and meaningful trips we had ever taken in an old World War II Jeep. We wended our way higher and higher, passing old gun emplacements everywhere we looked. Some we didn't see until the good captain pointed them out hidden within the mountain caves. And then the crowning moment! The old Jeep came to a stop atop one of the more famous mountains in the world, right along with Pikes Peak in Colorado. The thought occurred to me, "Hmmm, maybe I'm a little prejudiced here." But the local mountain! What a sight, looking down upon those dark grey beaches with the fine volcanic soil. I tried to visualize how the Marines, loaded with an eighty pound plus pack and carbine managed to slog onto the island. They came ashore unopposed for the first hour until they were bunching up on the unyielding fine volcanic sand upon which a person would have trouble just walking without anyone shooting at them. Even so, they were easily landing upon the sands of Iwo Jima, but finding it very difficult to move, especially upward and inward. They were not expecting much, if any, opposition, so this ease of landing had been anticipated. Fleet Admiral Chester Nimitz was famously quoted as saying, "Well, this will be easy. The Japanese will surrender Iwo Jima without a fight." This quote is understandable considering that the preparations against Iwo Jima began in June 1944, nine full months before the campaign ended.

Then, Kuribayashi unleashed his heavily defended forces. The Marine positions were so vulnerable that to the Japanese forces it was like the old saw of "shooting fish in a barrel." The Marines couldn't even dig in and develop the most remote resemblance of a foxhole. Each shovel of sand was replaced with more sand filling in from the surrounding fine dark grey sand beach. They stayed completely vulnerable. They were being cut apart by the withering enemy fire. It seems a miracle to me how they ever got ashore and captured the mountain in the first place!

I have often wondered: "Why this landing zone? Why not land on the other four and a half mile flat part of the Island?" I have been able to find no answer, but some charts I have researched suggested there may be barely submerged parts of the jagged lava and coral covering the approach to the flat part making it completely impossible to land troops with our landing ships. That's the only reason I can think of, and that is only my theory.

We stood where both flags were raised atop the 546-foot mountain. The first was considered too small. The second and larger one was the one featured in the Pulitzer Prize winning photo by Joe Rosenthal which was used as the model for the huge Marine Memorial hard by Arlington Cemetery. They were raised only five days after the Marines landed. Though heavily defended by an inside tunnel network, the Marines encountered very little resistance going up the mountain twice, the second time to raise the battalion flag. Secretary of State James Forrestal landed at the foot of the mountain as the first flag was raised. He wanted that flag, so another Marine patrol climbed with the larger flag photographed by Rosenthal. It is possibly, and most probably, the most reproduced photo in history. Three of the flag raisers were killed in the days following the event. Two of the Marine PFC's and a Navy corpsman lived to return to a heroes' welcome and became celebrities, selling war bonds. One of the marines who raised the flag, Ira Hays, was immortalized in a song by Johnny Cash, "The Ballad of Ira Hays." A full-blooded Pima Indian, Corporal Ira Hayes died in poverty, an alcoholic at age thirty-two. He is buried in Arlington Cemetery, Section thirty-four, Plot four hundred seventy-nine, A. The trip to "the top" was one of the highlights of my life!

We rode in silence back down the famous mountain, each man lost deep in his own thoughts. We barely talked about it. It was as if we had experienced a very private spiritual experience. The Captain told us as we were boarding our now ready aircraft that almost all of the folks who reached the top reacted with the same reverent silence. "The Sands of Iwo Jima" is an excellent film starring John Wayne as Sgt Stryker. John Agar and Forrest Tucker also star. It tells the story leading up to the landing thru the final surrender, although the last two Japanese soldiers didn't surrender until 6 January 1949. Other stragglers on Guam and several other places surrendered much later. The last known surrender was in January 1974!

We were soon in the air on our way to Taipei where indeed we would choose to stay near Generalissimo Chang Kai-shek's bright red Grand Hotel in downtown Taipei. He had a large suite with his wife of many years on the top floor. We wandered through a bunch of downtown as we waited for three days before a team from Tachikawa Air Base could replace our engine. Now it was time to return to Wake Island and begin our section of the trip which would take a new group of soldiers to train with the U.S. Army somewhere. What a wonderful lay-over!

On the return trip, we had a fresh load of Taiwanese soldiers who were headed for the U.S. to replace those we brought back to Taipei. The flight attendants gave them box lunches just like the entire crew had for lunch. I had to go to the restroom located in the back of the airplane on our military passenger plane. On the way back to the crew compartment, I noticed that one of the passengers and several others were chewing in a strange way with a strange look on their faces. I was walking up the aisle which was separated with three rear-facing seats on each side. I finally stopped to see if I could figure what was wrong. Then I kind of laughed inside so they couldn't see me. They were trying to eat the wet naps! As gently as I could, I had the flight attendant get me one out of a box lunch. After she gave it to me, I shouted, "Attention!" which was an order they hopefully knew. They did or else they just responded to my loud voice. I then had her demonstrate the proper use of a wet nap. They all smiled and laughed and some even applauded.

Another international incident diffused. It wasn't really that bad, but it would save some of these folks from eating some weird kind of American dessert. We motored on and got them to Wake Island with knowledge they didn't have before. Twenty-four hours later, we were flying back to Hickam with the normal load of re-turning GI's and families. Everything was back to normal.

One last remembrance of my C-118 flying days: It was a rar-ity and perhaps my only C-118 trip into Tan Son Nhut AB just outside of Saigon. With staging being the type of flying we did in which a plane load of passengers would be boarded at Travis AFB in California and would be destined for somewhere beyond Wake

Island. These passengers would get breaks only for about an hour at each stop at Hickam AFB and Wake Island, on a trip which would require the passengers sit in narrow, rear facing seats, six across with an isle down the middle. The normal flying time for a C-118 from Travis AFB to Tachikawa AB added up to roughly twenty nine hours in those seats with only those two breaks.

On this trip, we had picked up a full load of replacement troops heading for war in the jungles of Vietnam. Upon landing at Ton Son Nhut AB we were marshalled to our parking spot on the ramp near some out buildings. The passenger door was opened and the new troops were aligned in formation as they exited the plane. I did not notice it until the cockpit crew exited the same doors to prepare for our return flight, but as the troops, and later the crew, exited, we were walking directly toward a stack of body bags. This normally would not be a problem, but the United States had run out of coffins. The body bags contained bodies. The bodies of those whom the troops would replace. Now, that must have been tough viewing! It was in 1965 during the big troop buildup after the contrived Gulf of Tonkin Incident. President Johnson used this incident as legal justification for deployment of American troops into Vietnam as well as the bombing campaign known as "Rolling Thunder."

HALLOWEEN, 1968
TAN SON NHUT AIR BASE
SAIGON, SOUTH VIETNAM

"Sometimes Four of a Kind Does Not Beat a Full House"

"What in hell just happened?"

This mission actually began in an empty Douglas C-124 Globe Master II, four days earlier from our home base at Hill Air Force Base (AFB), just below Ogden, Utah. The C-124 was an unpressurized monster that flew at eight to eleven thousand feet and cruised at a steady 205 knots True Airspeed (TAS). We always picked up something at Travis AFB to forward on. On the fifth day, we departed Mactan Air Base in the southern Philippines late in the afternoon. There had been virtually no crew rest because of the heat and humidity. We had been trying to sleep on a cot in a tent with only a fan for cooling. All the fan did was stir the hot air! The Air Base was on Mactan Island, across a bay from Cebu City. Mactan Island is where Chief Lapu Lapu ran a spear through Magellan, killing him and putting a rather traumatic end to his dream of circumnavigating the world. It is lost to history just what ol' Magellan did to make the Chief so pissed that he killed him. Obviously, it was enough!

Though I had transited Mactan Island more times than I'd like to count, I never saw anything on the island to become excited about and certainly nothing

I would consider exciting enough to dirty a clean spear. I guess, like so many other things, you just had to be there. And now we were there. We had arrived twelve hours earlier from Wake Island after crew rest stops at Travis AFB, California, Hickam AFB, Hawaii and Wake Island. When we got to Mactan Base Operations on 31 Oct 1968, we had already been tasked to fly our big "Old Shakey" to deliver a cargo of approximately 39,000 pounds of Class A explosives to Tan Son Nhut Airbase in Saigon, South Vietnam in support of the war effort.

By the way, the C-124 was an oversized cargo plane with four of the largest piston engines ever used for aviation purposes. It was the Pratt & Whitney R-4360 with its four curved banks of seven cylinders with two spark plugs each, giving it the nick name of "the corncob." With a mechanical supercharger providing even more power, the engine was so powerful that the propeller speed had to be geared down so the tips could be controlled so as not go supersonic and lose its effectiveness. It also had clamshell doors which opened the entire front of the plane below the cockpit. In addition, there were two ramps, which unfolded outward, making it ideal for loading troops or cargo. Unfortunately, the only load/unload apparatus in the rear of this monster was a smallish platform, which was lowered by cables. Another drawback, which the crew actually liked, was that it flew at 205 knots. This was the speed at all times except takeoff and landing. This is how so many of us logged many, many flying hours. It averaged twelve hours to fly from Travis AFB in California to Hickam AFB. (twenty two hundred nautical miles). The flight from Hickam AB to Wake Island was another ten hours, (two thousand mile. You see how we could take one trip to DaNang or Saigon (both in Vietnam) and have almost 100 hours at the end of the trip. If we lucked out and "had" to go on to Bangkok, the trip could take about 110 hours or our normal maximum for the month in about ten to twelve days.

One beautiful thing about starting your trip with an empty C-124 at Hill AFB, was that you could basically choose the time for your departure. Often, and depending on the Aircraft Commander, we would set up our departure so that after arriving at Travis AFB and cleaning up after checking into the Billets, it was time for Happy Hour at the two Clubs. With the speed at which "Old Shakey" flew, the normal crew rest period at Travis and the approximately twelve hour flight at 205 TAS would get us to Hickam AFB just in time for Happy Hour. This in turn would set up, after a normal crew rest, to arrive at Wake Island in time for Happy Hour at the Drifters Reef. If we would be going to Clark AB without a stop at Guam, the crew would arrive at Clark AB in time for Happy Hour at the CABOOM (Clark Air Base Open Mess) or Officers Club. If we had to stop at Guam, we would miss Happy Hour at Clark and the drinks would be up to thirty five cents. Sometimes you had to accept the bad with the good!

The biggest problem was that this "flying overcast" was so big and complex that it was a maintenance headache. This headache caused me to spend many days on Wake Island in the middle of the Pacific Ocean waiting for a replacement engine. Ah yes, Wake Island. We have discussed that "garden spot" in another part of this tome.

Though exhausted, we had an uneventful flight (even got some sleep), we arrived at Tan Son Nhut AB at about 2245 (10:45) in the evening on Halloween, October 31st, 1968.

A side note: Not admitted at the time, we had called Airlift Command Post (ACP) at our home base at Hill AFB in Utah, telling them that we didn't get much sleep and the navigator (yeh, me) wasn't feeling very good. Out of safety concerns, we requested a six-hour delay to our flight. They knew that we just wanted to get credit for two months (October and November) in the combat zone for combat pay purposes. Even though they were a little exasperated, they granted the delay because they knew that as Squadron Admin Officer, I couldn't get "in country" every month. And that's how we happened to be in Vietnam on that rather interesting Halloween Eve.

Since we got virtually no crew rest at Mactan AB, the five-man flight crew (three officers and two enlisted men) with the exception of the loadmaster, crawled into the bunks on our airplane after we had been marshaled to the offload area. We had shut down the engines and secured the aircraft so the loadmaster and ground crew could exchange our dangerous cargoes using the elevator. With the entire crew, 39,000 pounds of Class "A" explosives and the extra locals to help offload the explosives on board, we truly had a full house. Actually, I guess most crews had a full house with three officers and two enlisted crewmen.

It was toward midnight and with windows and hatches open, it was cool enough to get some sleep for our return trip. We were supposed to take about 40,000 pounds of expired and unstable Class "A" Explosives back to Mactan. We were all sound asleep about midnight when an enormous explosion awakened us with a jolt. It was extremely loud and it was powerful enough that it shook the hell out of the aircraft. It was so sudden and so hard that it knocked me almost all the way out of my bunk. Trying to recover our sense of where we were, the two pilots almost trampled me getting to the side crew hatch in the most rapid egress I have ever seen! The three rated cockpit crew rapidly exited from the top deck of the C-124 and were on the ground next to the front landing gear in record time. The crew was all in a state of shock. No one knew what had just happened. The pilots beat me down even though my bunk was nearest the exit hatch. All I could think of was: "What in hell just happened?" We knew something big had happened, but were not sure of what yet because we were still in a bit of a sleep stupor. The engineer had to come from the rear of the plane and use the same hatch, He and a few others joined us.

Assessing the situation, I realized we were under enemy attack (duh!). It was most likely from 122 mm rockets and mortars as well as small arms. We knew that we had to seek protection immediately, if not sooner. There was a lot of smoke and one flip-flop between us and the safety of a flight line bunker. There was also a large, smoking hole next to the flip-flop, so the option of going to the bunker, in my mind, was gone. My thinking was that if they were going to send in another rocket from the same tube, it would land in the same place. I was also thinking of that one flip-flop and wondering what had happened to its owner. He obviously had been standing right next to where the rocket hit and exploded. I didn't like that! (An aside: The Aircraft Commander, being relatively new to the area, just stood around). I knew we shouldn't do that, so I kind of took over the crew. Mortar rounds and small arms fire were still flying all around us. We had to have shelter and we had to have it fast!

I just happened to remember a deep ditch between the ramp and taxiway that I had seen on my many flights into Saigon. That would work. Being the most experienced officer and the one most familiar with the area, I started leading the flight crew and some of the ground crew to that deep ditch. We were at least safe from the small arms fire. Though the night was pitch black, I knew about where the ditch was located and with the intermittent light of mortar explosions and small fires around the area, I found the depression. I wished it would have been a little deeper, actually it was about six feet deep, so by crouching or laying down, we were pretty well protected from all of the small arms rounds we could hear whizzing overhead every few minutes. We kept low while running there and felt a little safer in the deep depression until the firefight had wound down.

A short time later, after things had almost completely stopped, we started to make our way back towards our C-124 to see what happened. We also wanted to see if we could get to the bunker and some real safety with sandbags. We were working our way back to the bunker next to Base Ops, running from one piece of ramp equipment to another, waiting and taking another sprint. We were getting close to our objective when I led our little band to another trailer apparently loaded with pallets. As I rose up to see if it was clear enough to safely make another and possibly final run to the bunker, I could barely make out some writing on one of the pallets:

C, L, A, S---OH CHIT! CLASS "A" EXPLOSIVES! "Well, shit oh dear!" I had led our group back to the unstable ammunition we were supposed to take out of here. Oh Crap! Talk about from the frying pan into the fire. This was from possible doom to KABOOM! I rapidly hollered for them to follow me closely in running to the bunker. I never did admit to them that I led them to hide behind the most dangerous thing on the ramp! We busted in through the open bunker entry point and about scared the living shit out of the current occupants. They didn't know that there were others out there. After we convinced them that we belonged in there with them, we settled down, caught our breath and got our bearings. It was decided that since the ground fire had subsided, we could possibly check out what may have happened.

We moved hesitantly back to the aircraft and found that the Viet Cong and/or North Vietnamese had fired four identical 122mm rockets that had landed simultaneously. The four holes that had been blasted into the concrete ramp by the four rockets attested to their power. Surveying the scene, we saw that one rocket had landed in front of the nose of the aircraft by about eight feet, one landed about five feet off the right wing and one landed about ten feet off the left wingtip. The fourth exploded about ten feet behind the aircraft, between the Class "A" explosives we were to remove from the ramp and the Class "A" explosive cargo that had already been partially off-loaded. Those four were the only ones for which we found evidence. Near the hole, about five feet in circumference and sloping to eight to twelve inches deep, was a blue flip-flop. I immediately looked for human remains. Finding none, I assumed that someone had just run out of their flip-flop getting away as fast as possible. I'll always remember the fear of potentially finding the scattered remains of a person dismembered in the attack. During this lull in the firefights, we made it to the minimally protected ACP. The Major in charge of the ACP wanted desperately to get those out of date explosives off of his ramp because they were quite unstable and he wanted them gone. He asked if we would be willing to undertake the risk of taking time under fire to finish offloading our aircraft, loading the decaying class "A's" and taking them away to make the ramps safer. I suggested that we should do it and all agreed to help him out. He had recently been stationed at Hill AFB with us and we felt we owed it to him.

By the way, immediately after the rocket attack, two C-141's, a commercial Boeing 727 with a full load of grenades and a couple of other large planes had rapidly taken off and gotten out of harm's way, probably filing their flight plan after they took off.

The navigator of one of the C-141's was working on a flight plan when the explosions shook up everything. It knocked a florescent light loose from the ceiling, hitting him on the head on the way down. It cut his head open and he was bleeding quite a bit. They awarded him a Purple Heart on the spot! And a short time later, at the request of our friend in charge, it had taken us but seconds to volunteer to stay and remove the unstable explosives as requested which could be classified as a "Stupid Idea!!!" I actually think we were still in shock.

We were the only aircraft remaining on the ramp! And therefore the only target!

The regular local ground offload crew had disappeared when the attack occurred so we basically had to offload and load the explosives ourselves, following the loadmaster's instructions. I say we, meaning primarily the loadmaster and a couple of enlisted folks we enticed out of the bunker. I figured that the Loadmaster thought that a couple of stupid officer flight crewmen would be of little or no help. He was probably right! Though standing by to assist, we stayed out of the way!

Naturally, it took longer than normal to swap out loads, because we were bothered by intermittent volleys of mortars followed by intense small arms fire. This seemed to be their preferred way of attack. One of the flight crew muttered, "Don't these guys ever sleep?" They just seemed to keep coming on. Then a thought came to me as clear as a bell (Ding!). "We are putting up with this for a few hours and trying to show no fear. Putting on the fake strong guy show because we didn't know any better. But these guys who are stationed here have to put up with this all the time. Maybe we are just making too much of this?" It was a common method of warfare fought this way for the ages with an intense volley of mortars or cannon followed by a charge with smaller arms. Each time the mortars started coming in, we would immediately head for the bunkers. I thought, "Crap. We're going to get ourselves killed here. It is like playing a game of Post Office with a cobra or Spin the Bottle with the ugliest witch in the world. You are going to lose either way if you play long enough." But, we had made a deal and we would stick with it. "Remind me, Lord, not to make deals so quickly when the other guy has everything to win and you have nothing to gain except knowing you helped a fellow GI out in a very tight pinch. That is really enough anyway."

We ended up being on the ground for almost five hours on a normal three hour turn-around while occasional small arms fire and mortar explosions broke out around us. During those times, when the firefights were close enough, we would take off for the bunkers where we stayed in relative safety until things calmed down again. Then back to the task at hand until the next round of firefights began, hoping they didn't bring in any snipers or rocket us again! We didn't go back to sleep!

Firefights continued to break out around the perimeter and occasionally small arms fire would come in our direction. There were no more rockets and the few mortars had basically stopped or were far enough away to not hamper our work. Or possibly, we were just getting used to it.

After those four hours plus on the ground, we were all loaded up with the old Class A explosives and ready to go. We cranked engines and taxied to take off on the active runway where the Tower cleared us for a rolling takeoff, which was not normal for a C-124. This time, we just wanted to get gone so, since it was a long runway and we could do the takeoff checklist while rolling, a rolling takeoff it was! Right after takeoff, we received the usual ground fire on climb out. They rarely hit us because they never did learn to lead the aircraft. So, on those rare times we were hit, it was normally in the rear, so everyone was always in the cockpit or up front whenever on approach or departure from any Vietnamese base. Guess they never hunted ducks! After we reached the altitude we considered safe from any small arms fire, we began to relax. It dawned on me then that it seemed like the first time I had exhaled since the first explosions shook us out of our dreams. We were safely on our way back to Mactan Air Base for more time in those unbearably hot tents, but this time we weren't going to bitch about it. We were glad to be back to a safe place, even if it was in a C-124. No one really admitted it, but during our time on the ground, we were probably completely terrified!

The trip back to Mactan Air Base was uneventful, but it was also the strangest return trip of my career. For about the first forty-five minutes, until I had to give a heading change to the aircraft commander at an intersection called Shark (if I remember correctly), there had not been a sound on the intercom! When I gave the heading to Mactan, those were the first words spoken since having taken off out of Tan Son Nhut AB with their tricks. Need I say, we never got the treat part. After some period of time on the new heading, someone said: "Do you realize what we just did?" Suddenly the intercom was full of chatter. Everybody finally exhaled, the adrenaline had quit pumping and we all started talking at the same time about how stupid we were to stay there and remove the volatile Class "A" explosives from the ramp, even if it was for a friend. We had made the conscious decision to help an old friend when he asked. Had we left them on the ramp, they would be a constant threat to everyone within a wide range until someone finally took them out. We did it for a friend and for a good reason. And, it eventually turned out to be uneventful and routine, except for those few mortars and firefights!

We did not turn out to be crispy critters as we would have been if even one of those rockets had connected and the thirty-nine thousand pounds of new Class "A" and forty thousand pounds of the old unstable Class "A" had exploded. It would have been a hell of a mess, but we would have known nothing about it. We would probably have been vaporized in the explosion of the 79,000 pounds of Class "A" explosives and the roughly forty-five thousand pounds of fuel we had on board. It also would have set an NCAA record for the biggest explosion ever on the Tan Son Nhut ramp and possibly one of the largest of the Vietnam War. By the grace of God, it didn't happen! He had to be saving us for something larger in His plans.

All in all, they have a hell of a way to trick or treat!

Meanwhile, back at Mactan AB, after that harrowing experience, we had other things on our minds. When we were figuring out how to get two months combat pay, we neglected to consider that we would be back for crew rest from early morning thru the heat of the day again. Now it would be all middle of the day. After we landed, we hoped they would send us across the small bay to the Diamond Hotel in Cebu City like they often did. Cebu City was a little over four hundred miles south of Clark AB and is the second largest city in the Philippines. No such luck!

As I was lying there once more, probably in the same cot and someone else's sweat, I began to review the night before. How did we live through that rocket barrage? If any of the four rockets, especially the one which landed between the ammo carts, had hit a couple feet closer, it could have set off a tremendous explosion. An explosion which would have evaporated the entire crew and the personnel around us! It made me start thinking of some of my other close calls in my life. I thought it was just part of flying, though I always wondered if a hand might be protecting me. But, I wondered, for what purpose? Maybe someday I would find out, but God mostly keeps these things a mystery."

As I lay there, miserable in my own or some else's sweat, I couldn't help but think back on a couple of other times when it seemed I was in a potentially disastrous situation. As I started to doze in an unsettled, light sleep, my mind wandered back to when it all started. I was going to college, working almost full-time and dating full-time. Then things kind of went to hell. My grades were going down and my girlfriend, Mimi, told me to get lost. I didn't like my job at J.C. Penney's, having to open or close and making about ninety cents per hour. Solution; "Let me get out of this town!" I was still smarting after having to give up my partial scholarship to Notre Dame as mom wanted me to, so off I went into the United States Air Force, and to Lackland AFB in San Antonio, Texas. I thought at the time, "Best thought I ever had." I still believe that! But by now, I was lost between dreams and reality. That area where you land after sheer exhaustion catches up with you. My mind drifted to what caused me to be here right now. It had been a hell of a trip and I had enjoyed every bit of it. Well, almost!

SCOTT AFB
AND
BELLEVILLE, ILLINOIS

"My Assignment from Hell"
Everyone has one

Saint Louis, home of the Gateway Arch, Saint Louis Cardinals and Blues and Budweiser. What more could one ask for? Well, I could ask that I never was stationed near the place.

What more can be said about Scott AFB, Illinois, just about forty miles east of Saint Louis. Well, for one thing, as my friend Billy Wood told me when I arrived there, "This is the only place I have ever been that had Alabama summers and Minnesota winters!" Bingo! Right on the head! For another thing, unfortunately, East St Louis was between Saint Louis and Scott AFB. It has been reputed that it was in East Saint Louis that the Cosa Nostra began its existence in the United States. I believe that story because I became friends with a few of them in Belleville in the lounge called Constantine's. They relayed the same thing. Also, just north of East Saint Louis was Cahokia Downs Horse Racetrack. It was so bad that Las Vegas wouldn't even carry the odds on the races there, about the only track in the U S to be so singled out.

I had the gut feeling that if anything bad was going to happen during my life, both personal and professionally, it would happen here. And so, it did. Which one, take your pick. I won't even get into the things that happened here, just how I ended up here and the fortunate way I got away.

Fat, dumb and happy in Utah in a dream assignment, it all came crashing down. Just like the 48th MATS at Hickam AFB in Hawaii, the 28th MAS was shuttered in Utah. Unfortunately, to go along with that very sad end to a great assignment, well what do they say? "No good deed (in this case job) goes unpunished." The Big Boys came thundering down from MAC HQ to give us a briefing on the closure of our great squadron of which I was the Administrative Officer. Because it was now unclassified, I asked if it would be OK if I taped the briefing so that after they left town, and some of the personnel claimed they promised or said something that they really didn't, I could play the tape back and prove my point. It was used to great benefit many times during our Squadron closure.

Well this must have impressed those high-ranking idiots, who must have been very impressionable. They had carried my new PCS orders with them sending me, like many, to C-141's in Norton AFB, San Bernardino California, another dream assignment. They were so impressed that my dream assignment became my assignment from hell. They changed it from Norton AFB to Scott AFB in the Directorate of Personnel, which would have been OK, but then they added MWR! Morale, Welfare and Recreation. Let me explain a few negatives about this assignment. The chief was a civilian GS-15. The Lt Col I worked for gave me only one assignment for the first six weeks: Study the Regulation. It was SIXTEEN PAGES LONG! 16! SIX WEEKS! Holy Crap! I knew I was dumb, but sixteen pages that were too dry to even memorize? As I said about the razor seller: "Really?" I should have used my Hate soliloquy here instead of Wake Island. I would have meant it here! In retrospect and in all fairness to Lt Col Gomert, that is basically all I had to do. It was a nothing job! After about six months in this miserable job of which the only good point was a nice VIP trip to Europe to "inspect" the overseas bases, I was transferred to a job where they had promised me I would go in the first place: Officer Assignments. Had they done this to begin with, well, my career path would have been different, probably on to Military Personnel Center (MPC) at Randolph AFB in San Antonio. These HQ assignment people took care of their own, real well. I may even have gotten those eagles, but I would have had to have gone to the Pentagon in DC, or as many call it: "The Puzzle Palace." But here again, I wouldn't have ended up in Broken Arrow, OK.

I won't go into the official and unofficial on base and off base hell that I went through stationed in the worst combination of happenings that I even endured. MAC HQ, which would have been a dream assignment for others, was not a match made in heaven for me. When the soon to be Squadron Commander of the Air Rescue and Recovery Service (ARRS) at Lajes Field in the Azores, Lt Col Bill Hoskings asked me if I would like to tag along, I think I was half way packed before he was finished kicking the waste basket down the hallway. I left this HQ assignment with pleasure and with the only regret being that I had ever been stationed there! This would be the first time leaving an assignment, that I would have major regrets for my time spent there. I guess I was fortunate. It was the only assignment in my career that I didn't really love. Well, though I wasn't that wild about it, Test Flying, away from the confines of an Air Force Base, was an easy end of the road assignment and gateway to the civilian world. My talents could have well been better utilized elsewhere.

Scott AFB was behind me, but my life was changed forever! I had more of a jaundiced outlook on life until I decided I needed to bury that two and a half years and get on with life. Those years are still tucked back in my mind and every so often sneak out and bite me. But not often enough to make a difference anymore.

LAJES, DUCK BUTT & ICELAND

As seen from an HC-130H
"Faster than a Speeding Bullet or SAM"

After a six week course at Eglin AFB in the Florida panhandle where I lived in a small apartment on the beach (unfortunately it was April) I had passed my check ride in the HC-130H ARRS aircraft at Lajes Field in the Azores, about six hundred miles west into the Atlantic from Portugal, to whom the islands owed a loose allegiance. Another dream assignment. "Damn, I should quit dreaming these silly career dreams and face reality for once! Nah! I was having too much fun with my dream assignments! This one would work! They needed a rescue outfit here." Here, I should tell you a story about my check-ride. Maybe I shouldn't, but I will.

A group from Wing HQ at Ramstein AB, Germany came down for the purpose of a No Notice Operational Readiness Inspection (ORI), the most feared initials in the Air Force. Knowing that I just been newly checked out, they chose me to be the Squadron Navigator for the inspection ride. We were having a big party that night. It was a mess dress affair so it was probably a base wide event. I had landed from my check-ride (my first solo one in the outfit) just at about the time my new boss had to be at the big event. He was in a rush and asked how I did. I told him that I really messed up. He was a worrier anyway, so he stewed about it all through the event formalities, and kept glancing furtively at me all throughout the dinner & speeches. Ya see, if I busted my check-ride, the whole 57th Squadron would fail the ORI. The Nav Section was his responsibility so it was cause for concern and he knew he was in trouble though he should have noticed that no one had come to talk to him about it. Not the Squadron Commander nor any of the ORI team. When we began partying I finally had the chance to tell him that I had instead Aced it. First one in the squadron to get 100%. He and his wife almost killed me for ruining their evening. I pointed out that I didn't say I had busted it and he could brag about his section on the morrow, which he did! We stayed friends!

Now it was my turn to get to work. I found myself as the navigator on the aircrew that was going to fly to Keflavik Naval Air Station (NAS), Iceland, for a normal one-week rotation. As is often the case on Friday's, we were having a big party the night before I was leaving. And, as usual, I was having my normal good time bouncing around chatting and laughing with each little group that had formed. Naturally, I had a Beefeaters (Premium 90 proof) Gin on the rocks in hand.

It was then that one of my cardinal rules was sorely tested. Ya see, to this day, I still have this rule that you should never eat on an empty stomach. Now, I had already made sure I had a drink, OK! Several were had before I wandered over to the large glass windows overlooking the runway and flight line buildings. The view also delivered a vista of the inner mountains on this eight by thirteen-mile island. Either fortunately or unfortunately, depending on how you look at it, there was this very large, maybe about a thirty-six inch, tray of just one fantastic looking fish. The fish was already scored with toothpicks sticking out like an imitation porcupine. I had my Beefeaters on the rocks in one hand and a filtered Kent cigarette in the other. Normally, it would have made no difference. I almost never ate anything on party night. I don't know why I even wandered over to the table.

I looked first at my Beefeaters, then at my Kent. Then back. That went on for several moments. I figured that it probably looked like I was watching a miniature tennis match. I was in a conundrum. "Which one do I put down"? Damn! What a decision! "But, that damnable big ol' fish looks soooo good!" So, being a good Irishman, you can probably figure out the one I put down. As I ground out my Kent in an ashtray nearby, I made a momentous decision. I remember thinking, "Since I was not clutching a lit cigarette in my fingers or mouth, for the first time in quite some time, why don't I just give them up altogether?" My carton at home was almost empty and I could give the rest to my fellow navigator and close friend Laird Hanson. To put the clincher on it, earlier that week, I had burned a hole in my new double-knit pants from the head of a match that flew off during the process of lighting a cigarette. So, I continued thinking even more strongly, "Why not quit altogether since I made that choice so easily?" That's when I quit smoking.

It was 1971.

The biggest obstacle to my decision to quit smoking was that I was shipping out with an Air Rescue crew next morn on our normal rotation of a week out of every six at Keflavik NAS, Iceland. The routine was that we would alternate with an AARS crew out of England on standing alert and taking the day off while we were there. Either way, night time was poker time in a room full of smoke filled fun. That was tough, not lighting up. But that was one of the reasons I quit then. I figured if I could quit in that environment, I could easily stay quit.

This was not one of those rotations where you don't want to go. These were always good trips. Normally, they were enjoyable and sometimes very interesting. Rather than trying to relate a full story on each incident, I will just enumerate a few of them to give you an idea of what we did while on alert and on our every other day of free time.

The other crew was from the 67th ARRS which rotated out of Royal Air Force Base, Woodbridge, England. They would be on alert with us, taking turns with the days on alert. On our "off" days, since there was little or nothing to do up there, the crew not on alert would often check out the non-alert aircraft and go exploring the area, normally up north of the Atlantic Ocean. We would be able to find, from the air, new territory to explore while logging flight hours. We once flew over the Norwegian Sea and clear across Greenland to the Davis Straight. Wherever we went, when we arrived at our destination, we would drop down for a close look at whatever beautiful was spread out before us. Not much here! And, still, the favorite of all crews was Iceland. I really don't remember how many times I flew over the Island, there was always something new to find that was even more beautiful than what we raved over last time up. We found really cool things, but it makes for complex navigating once we left the Island to the north and got out of TACAN range because the magnetic North Pole is nearby, making magnetic compasses relatively suspect. The Magnetic Pole is a few hundred miles southeast from the physical North Pole. If we flew more northwest, it would make the magnetic compasses absolutely worthless and Grid Navigation would be necessary. It was rather a strange phenomenon to watch the "whiskey" compasses go nuts! It would whirl around inside its enclosure like crazy and then just go into an erratic dance. Nope, not erotic, just erratic!

The "whiskey" compass is almost as old as flying, and possibly older because they probably use them at sea, but I don't want to go there! They call it a "whiskey" compass because the heading indicator device floats in a pool of alcohol. Alcohol has less friction than most other liquids with a much lower freezing point. Maybe that is why the Beefeaters and Johnny Walker Scotch was so good for me. Of course, since we didn't often stray too far away from the island, we were in constant touch with the Approach Control folks. They liked it because it gave them a little relief from the normal boredom between the hectic times when they had to handle several planes at a time.

On our way to Iceland, we were sometimes tasked to fly a "Duck Butt" mission which is the name of a mission that provides a special type of rescue service which would keep a rescue aircraft within thirty minutes of the aircraft requiring the Duck Butt. These were normally special missions flown out of Lajes for just that reason. We were required to be within thirty minutes of the requesting airplane at all times, no matter how fast or slow the target is flying, this was a normal ARRS mission where we would fly to a pre-determined position along the route of whatever needed to be "mothered" that day or night along its route. This could be a flight of fighter aircraft, Air Force One or any other flight which needs to have a rescue capability within thirty minutes of them in case things go awry. I don't know how many "Duck Butts" I have flown, but the number is up there with "quite a lot."

In one case, on our way to Iceland, we were tasked to fly Duck Butt with an SR-71. As they zipped overhead at well over fifty thousand feet attitude, they seemed to be speeding along faster than normal, I radioed them and asked how fast they were going. There was a moment of silence, and then a very casual and perhaps a bit of a cocky voice said, "We are clicking off about twenty-four miles per minute." That's about 1,440 knots per hour or 24 miles minute, folks. They must have had a hot party to get to at their home base at Beale Air Force Base, just north of Sacramento, California.

There is a story which I read in a reputable military magazine. An SR-71 was overflying a country in the Middle east when some folks on the ground took umbrage and launched a supersonic surface to air missile (SAM). Their sensors were suddenly screaming in the back-seaters' ear. It was screaming, not whispering, "Let's get to hell out of here!" In response, the pilot firewalled the "Black Bird which rapidly picked up speed. The missile gained for a little while, but the SR-71 actually outran the super-sonic missile! A few minutes after the sensors quit screaming and went silent, the back seater calmly mentioned to the pilot that he might want to pull back on the throttles since they were out of any danger. "Oh crap!" Could have been the minimum response. The article stated that the bird was doing over three thousand knots. That is a serious bunch of miles per hour (MPH)! My thought was that it was probably red, from friction, not black!

On another of our missions for another SR-71 Super-Secret, high flying Strategic Reconnaissance aircraft returning from a classified trip by way of Europe. I would suspect that they were coming back from an over-flight of the Soviet Union which they constantly did with impunity. They could fly high enough, up to at least one hundred thousand feet, that Russian air defenses are helpless to do anything about it. It is also stealthy enough that at that altitude, the Russian radar probably couldn't even "paint" it which is the buzz word for seeing it on their radar scopes. In this case as with all others, we would be orbiting on their flight path though not at their altitude. When I determined they were within a thirty-minute range, we would start running ahead of them on their flight path. It wouldn't take long for them to catch us and pass over us. We would then "run" with them until they were thirty minutes out of range in front of us where another HC-130 aircraft would pick them up and perform the same procedure. It didn't take long! In this manner, no flight which we were protecting was ever more than thirty minutes from a fully equipped Air Rescue aircraft. On one flight, I was in an HC-130H airplane that flew "Duck Butt" for President Nixon's VC-137, tail number 26000, known as Air Force One when the Big Boss is on board. They also outran us, but not like that SR-71!

When these cocky fighter pilots or SR-71 fast movers, acted too high and mighty, I would tell them that I was getting up and going downstairs to relieve myself, stretch my legs and heat up a TV dinner. I'd be back in touch in a few minutes. It was not too unusual to hear a "you-son-of-a bitch!" in response, and even worse wording when they told me what I could do, sometimes to myself. I didn't know that some of those things were even possible! It really ticked them off when they heard our whole crew laughing over the radio. They were tied to their seat for sometimes hours in the teens, often with their leg strapped relief container ready to overflow and with them only half way through their flight. One flight was going non-stop from Holloman AFB, near Alamogordo in New Mexico, about eighty miles north of El Paso, TX to Torrejon AB, Madrid, Spain. I won't bother figuring out the number of flight planned hours, but they were considerable, and the pilots were strapped in all the way. Most of the pilots were not too cocky on those flights. One time I talked my HC pilots into seeing if we could fool these sharp-eyed fighter pilots. We always exchanged a "Talley Ho" when we spotted them. We normally chatted, gave them current and forecast weather and a change of heading if they were a little off course. On this particular flight, I talked the AC into climbing to over thirty thousand feet altitude. Thirty three is supposed to be the service ceiling of the "H" Model. I had picked up the fighter flight earlier on my radar and we maneuvered into their path, a normal procedure. and knew in which direction they were coming. We called "Talley Ho" and did the normal chatter. There was much consternation because they were looking for an aircraft considerably larger than what they were driving and they kept complaining, "We can't find you." We played this game until they got within about three miles of us and were getting antsy. Then we told them to look up. That really pissed them off. They were used to being the high flyers at about twenty-five thousand while we were normally at eighteen. I think they forgave us when I gave them an eight-degree heading change and updated wind speed and direction. They were headed way north of their intended track. They would have missed their next Duck Butt!

All Rescue aircraft always carried Paramedic Jumpers (PJs). They were absolutely fearless men who would jump from our perfectly good planes and parachute down to whatever emergency needed their attention. On one of our rescue missions, on which I was the navigator, they jumped in complete darkness, in the middle of the night into the path of a Russian ship which had a severe burn victim aboard. While I was calculating an intercept point, the Russians mentioned that they were applying butter to soothe his severe burns. That alone gave us a sense of urgency to get our medically trained jumpers to the ship as soon as possible.

I picked up the ship on my radar and gave our PJs a pretty accurate jump time. This would allow us to know when to have these intrepid men ready to jump into the night and land with their equipment a little ahead of the ship. At this point, the ship had slowed almost to a stop to accept these rescue folks and I had refined their jump time. It was imperative that they jump ahead of the ship so the ship would come to them. Then they could be pulled from the water and perform their magic on the needy victim. In this case with the butter, they had to argue vehemently with the ships' female "doctor" in order to let them scrape the butter off of the burn victim's body (Ouch!) and give it a chance to breathe. I gave them the jump signal at the exact time so they could make a successful intercept and pickup. Now, imagine for a moment that you are one of these PJs. In the dark of night, you are getting ready to jump out of a perfectly good, warm and dry aircraft which was now flying slowly at low level. You were going to land in the middle of the very cold and wet North Atlantic Ocean which is well known for its rough waters. You are going to jump at a time based on the best estimate of the time and location determined by your navigator. I had already calculated the wind speed and direction at the ship's location by having the pilot do some prescribed maneuvers so I had calculated the heading of the aircraft, the speed, the jump time and place which would allow them to land where they needed to be while flying at about one hundred thirty-five knots. They had pure blind faith in our ability to get it right!

Precision was the key here. From takeoff until they jumped into the dark void of night, it was my job to get them to the right place at the right time to accomplish the very difficult mission of saving a life. The motto of the Air Rescue and Recovery Service is:

"That Others May Live."

These jumpers were putting their lives on the line and in my hands. They trusted me to deliver them to the afflicted member of an enemy ship, not knowing whether we would ever see them again. Once they went out that side door of the HC-130, they were on their own until they returned to us, hopefully in one piece and upright. In this case, they would be stuck on a Russian freighter which was on a long voyage of a couple of months, possibly with a cargo of munitions, destined to help the North Vietnamese fight their American brethren in the United States military. We just didn't know, but such is the life of a PJ. They would be leaving a perfectly good aircraft and taking a large chance in order to save the life of an enemy who needed their help in International waters. I always had a strange, half empty, always helpless and all concerned, but confident feeling after I had given the jump signal. "Was it at the appropriate place and time?" That was the question that always crossed the nav's mind. If the jump time was even just a few seconds off, they could land on the ship and probably be severely injured. Even worse, they might miss the ship's path by a few hundred yards and be lost in the night forever. The worst-case scenario would be if they landed behind the ship because I hadn't figured the drift of the wind correctly. This was precision work and I sweated every jump.

After the drop, we flew around the ship, circling it until we received the radio transmission from the PJs that they were on the ship in good condition. In this case, they were met with suspicion and some hostility because they were there to take over the ship's medical doctor's duties and reverse the orders. It was even a little more hostile this time because it was a female Doctor. I understand that this situation got a little tense on the ship until the captain ordered his crew to back off. He turned his crewman over to these strangers. They had arrived in full scuba gear with about a hundred pounds of equipment on their backs looking like creatures from the blue lagoon. They seemed to come out of nowhere, but were accompanied by flashing lights which made a lot of noise then passed over them in a flash and disappeared into the blackness of night. They couldn't be sure we were there to help them until they picked up the PJs strobe lights and then the PJs them-selves with their own shipboard spotlights. After the PJs jumped and were picked up, we circled until they radioed that things were as they should be. We would then climb to our return too base (RTB) and leave them to their own devices.

In this case, all went well. The PJs were plucked out of the heavy sea and finally were able to take over the medical situation and saved a crewman on a Cold War enemy's ship. Now they were bound for who knew where, stuck on that Russian vessel, eating strange food and trying to communicate. In addition, they had to try to get along with a semi-hostile crew until they got to land and disembarked which in this case was at the Northwestern USSR Port of Murmansk. They finally disembarked after months at sea and a visit to Haiphong Harbor, North Vietnam, among many other communist ports like Havana.

We never did know when they would return to our squadron. I barely remember, but it seemed like it took them almost four months from their exit of our HC-130 until they just showed up wandering down the hallways into the squadron with tales that were worthy of a book themselves. They had made their way from Murmansk, USSR across most of the European Soviet Union and through the Eastern Europe Warsaw Pact countries which were also on our "unfriendly" list. They finally made it to civilization in Eastern Free Europe. I imagine they took their time from there to get home. That's OK! They deserved a little vacation. Nonetheless, these brave airmen completed their round trip and took a week off before they were ready to go back to flying with us again. What a life! No way could I do it, starting with the severe training required to become eligible to wear a PJ beret.

It was after we dropped these heroes that I knew it would be my turn to go to Iceland in a few days. So, I continue the story of this lovely country with some of the most beautiful women and most stubborn men in the world.

Among the many oddities of Iceland is the fact that they are constantly in a very low pressure area. In fact, almost all of the northern hemisphere's weather systems get their start just a few hundred miles northwest of the Island. When flying into any Icelandic Airport, they will relay the current local pressure by prefacing it with "low, low" 28.78 or whatever the current setting. Normal flying never encounters such low altimeter settings. They are normally in the 29.+ inches of mercury range. Before they started the code "low, low," they had some accidents because setting an altimeter at 29.82 instead of 28.82 causes your altimeter to give a false higher altitude than is real. Therefore, when trying to get down to the runway, the aircraft would plow into the ground far short. Both pilots and the navigator had to set their altimeters, so a crosscheck normally caught anyone that missed the "low, low" instruction. Upon reaching assigned altitude and saying goodbye to departure control, all aircraft set their altimeter to the standard day setting of 29.92 so that all aircraft out of range of some controlling authority are using the same altimeter setting.

Because we were an alert crew, we always had reserved parking outside the door of every place we went, including the Officers Club. The enlisted crewmen had the same setup with their Non-Commissioned Officers (NCO) Club and elsewhere. They had their own vehicle. Several times in either Club or the base theater, the alert crew members in the audience would suddenly get up and run out of the facility to the waiting vehicle. In fact, at the theater, the first row of seats on the right, as you enter the theater was reserved for the alert crew at all times. The off-duty crew also had a vehicle which was an extended cab pickup with the ability to get us around, if needed, in the snow. Of course, we had the flashing lights which would give us the right-of-way to get to the flight line when we received the emergency call. I don't recall ever using lights nor siren. There were just not too many vehicles on Keflavik.

One strange and wonderous phenomenon during the summer months, when there was no complete darkness, only a dim twilight, was the teen ritual of making out behind the theatre. In spite of being visible to everyone who cast their eyes in that direction (the theater was right along a main street so it was hard to miss) the wonderful pastime of wrestling through the usual entanglements of hugs and kisses as if it was completely dark continued. Kids really are kids, in spite of obstacles!

CANADIAN AIRCRAFT RESCUE

"It Could Ruin Their Whole Day"

I was the navigator on alert status on the 6th of June, 1972. The whole crew was bored, as usual when on alert. It is akin to being on duty at a Fire Department: Nothing going on except regular housekeeping chores, and then all hell breaks loose! I was used to this from my enlisted days when I flew with the 1009th SWS in B-36 and other aircraft (written about elsewhere) where we sat around and became expert chess players while awaiting another surprise bomb test by the "bad guys" for us to go check out. Then we were busy beyond words. On this particular day, the weather was getting gradually worse, and we were joking with each other and trying to guess when the cross wind component was going to put the field out of limits for takeoff and landing in a high winged HC-130H, the premier C-130 of the fleet. Our planes had a large dome on top of the aircraft, just aft of the crew compartment, with a very powerful radar which enhanced our capability to obtain more clear radar images from farther out than normal C-130's. They were also equipped with a folding pair of booms which could be extended forward from both sides of the nose Radar Dome (radome) to form a "V" in front of the aircraft with which an aircrew member could gather in a bungee type rope that had been lofted into the air by a balloon on the high end and with an individual attached to the other end. These were normally used to extract an agent from a hostile environment. The method of extraction must have given the person being extracted quite a ride. The bungee effect was that the person being extracted would suddenly be pulled straight up into the air, level off and be pulled into the extracting C-130 by an electric pulley system which exited thru the open rear ramp. I don't know of any use of them for Rescue purposes except that they really looked neat! I did not fly Rescue in Vietnam.

We were getting ready to pack up our things and go home as the Field was beginning to go below minimums. Then, just like in a firehouse, the bell rang, scaring the hell out of everyone. Oh, Oh! It was our call to action. Our squadron radios had picked up a MAYDAY call. We quickly ran out to our HC-130H alert aircraft and started taxiing with only two engines turning, starting the other two on the roll to the runway to save time and beat the deteriorating cross wind component. Making contact with the pilot of the stricken aircraft, on VHF radio, while taxiing to the runway, we all garnered the following information:

1. They had no control over the horizontal (up and down) movements of the aircraft.
2. It was a Canada RCAF (Royal Canadian Air Force) Electronics Warfare airplane whose job was to search for USSR Submarines, similar to the U. S, Navy P-3's, which were stationed with us at Lajes Field.
3. They were preparing to ditch (a controlled landing on the water) in the rough and cold North Atlantic Ocean.
4. We needed to get to them as soon as we could with a clean exact intercept and try to talk them out of this extreme notion! Ditching under ideal conditions was an iffy proposition at best. Ditching an aircraft with twenty-one Souls on Board (SOBs) in the North Atlantic Ocean was tantamount to purposeful suicide. (I guess all suicides are purposeful?)

I figured out and called an Estimated Time of Intercept as we were starting a rolling takeoff. I was standing behind the engineer, looking over the copilots' shoulder as we increased our speed down runway 33. As we lifted off, the aircraft was blown so hard to the right that we were face to face with our hangar. "Holy Shit! What a way to die! Running into your own aircraft hangar!" The Aircraft Commander, banked hard left and barely avoided a disaster. We had slipped by our hangar only because the Aircraft Commander had the aircraft turning away from the hangar banked at about a forty-five degree angle so the right wing went over the hangar roof! For us to be blown that far right immediately after liftoff, "Damn," the conditions just HAD to be out of tolerance before we started our takeoff run. I think the winds were out of tolerance for our aircraft as we lifted off, and the field should have been closed to high winged aircraft such as our HC-130H. I realize that our ARRS motto is; 'That Others May Live,' but if we are supposed to die, it is NOT by crashing into our own hangar. It is supposed to be by sacrificing to save others, not being stupid!"

But twenty-one SOB's needed help!

The Canadian aircraft was preparing to ditch their aircraft in the North Atlantic Ocean in heavy seas and a very cold water temperature. We convinced them to keep flying toward us and let us take a look at their problem. They told us that they had no control over the horizontal stabilizer. (Which made me wonder how they were going to get down for a ditching anyway). As we got within range, I picked them up on my radar and set up timing for a 09/270 (90 degree right turn until level then bank into a turn through 270 degrees to the left. This should bring us out directly under the left wing of the target aircraft. Earlier, I had given the pilot a compass heading that would put us about 10 minutes down-stream and on a head-on collision course. It takes three minutes to execute the 90/270 procedure. We drove toward the stricken aircraft which was now flying at the same speed as were until we were exactly three minutes from them. I had warned the pilot to be ready for the call to turn. He initiated the anticipated 90/270 turn. Incidentally, the closing speed of the two aircraft was just under six hundred knots. We rolled out of our turn barely below and left of the wounded Canada Goose on the exact second of the ETI that I had radioed to them approximately two hours and forty-five minutes before. I must admit. That was the only time that this exactness happened during my many rescue flights in one and a half years of flying with the 57th ARRS. We pulled in so close to the crippled ship that I took a picture of one of their crewmen taking pictures of us from his aft bubble window. The two aircraft were almost touching while we were searching for the problem with the horizontal stabilizer.

It didn't take long to find their trouble. This dropsonde did not eject properly from its chute, was caught in the aircrafts' slip-stream and was forced by aerodynamic pressure into the area between the fuselage and the horizontal stabilizer (tail) where the aileron normally moves controlling the attitude of the airplane. A jammed aileron makes the aileron absolutely useless. The crew was fortunate that the dropsonde did not cause the aileron to jam in a position that could force the aircraft to go nose down into the water or up into a stall. The crewmembers of the stricken EWO plane were still planning on ditching their aircraft and were glad that a Rescue Aircraft was with them and could provide rafts supplies and medical aid when our Para Rescue Jumpers (PJ's) jumped to help them.

After a series of discussions, the pilots came up with an ingenious plan: Use their tiny trim tabs for slight and gentle control of attitude with a resultant adjustment of altitude. There was, practically, no other choice. We couldn't undo the damage so, instead of trying the impossibility of ditching, which was a stu,... an unwise choice at best, the Canadian Flyers decided to do as our pilots suggested: Try to control their altitude using the trim tabs only. The Trim Tabs are small tabs that were designed to facilitate the movement of the ailerons. The only problem was that trim tabs could cause only a small rate of decent, so after we found out at what rate they could descend, we had to figure out a long glide path that would put them at almost sea level when we reached Ponta Delgada on the Big Island of Sao Miguel, because Lajes Field had been closed because of high winds. Imagine that! In other words, I had to come up with a time and place to begin this shallow downward glide. It took a few minutes but I figured that at their current rate of descent, which was the most they could get with only the trim tabs, they would not yet be able to be at desired level when they reached Ponta Delgada on the more southerly Big Island! I did some calculations and decided we should plan on going about 60 miles south of the Island, do a flat 180 degree turn and then initiate a very long final approach to the airport. It didn't matter if they reached the desired altitude above sea level before we reached the airport. Minor changes to altitude could be made with the trim tabs. I wanted them at about two hundred eighty feet above sea level when they crossed over the "fence," or about twenty feet Above Ground level (AGL), which was well below the fifty feet for normal approaches to landing. This was anything but normal. It was a much flatter approach. I wanted them to be at about twelve feet AGL just short of the touchdown area, to get on the runway which was eighty seven hundred seventy eight feet long. We would be using Runway 22. Now it was up to the Canadian Aircrew to execute my plan. They did, and as they touched down we roared past them doing a double "Wing Waggle" acknowledging that we knew they were on the ground safely.

They contacted us again and said basically, "free drinks for your crew all night!" Unfortunately, when we contacted the Rescue Command Post on Lajes to give them the results of our successful mission, they informed us that we would have to land and spend the night on Sao Miguel, maintaining an alert posture because Lajes Field was out of tolerance for landing or takeoff. They said that we had to immediately go into crew rest in order to be ready to go if another rescue request came in. We were still basically standing alert, but away from home base. "You guys can still get off the ground from down there, so we need you to be ready. By the way, you did well in bringing those Canadians in safely." That killed an all-night drinking party with the Canadians, and they really know how to drink and party! The sounds of revelry echoed down the hallway long into the night and morning. The situation was painful and tempting, but I behaved myself. I finally drifted off to sleep after slobbering like Pavlov's dog. It was a very sober and fitful sleep.

The only redeeming factor was the fact that we could feel good tonight because we had saved 21 Canadian Air Force personnel from a very wet and cold night, at sea. Instead, they were in there having one hell of a party without us. The weather improved overnight, so after a great breakfast of some of the local fare, we eagerly went to our HC-130 and began our preflight duties for the short trip home to our Island of Tercera, the third largest island in the Azorean chain of volcanic islands.

Tercera means third in Portuguese. They are the third largest island in the chain.

The short hop back to home base was uneventful. I still have the plaque that a grateful and gracious Canadian Aircrew sent to the 57th ARRS as a token of appreciation for that rescue. It is on display at the Military History Center in Broken Arrow. All agreed on one thing: It was better that they stayed dry that day. And, the word held true: A ditching in that angry sea *could* have ruined their whole day.

GREENLAND ICECAP

"Like the Inside of an Eggshell"

After a leisurely breakfast at the Clubs, we all motored down to the flight line at Keflavik NAS about thirty miles east of the Capital city of Iceland, Reykjavik. This was our off-duty day, so fun flying was going to happen. We met the enlisted guys at Base Operations at the pre-arranged time and did our flight planning for a comfortable little trip of about twelve hundred miles round trip, plus whatever time we spent wandering over that area, to the western fjords of Greenland. We all wanted to go see what Greenland looked like.

Legend has it that Eric the Red discovered both islands. Greenland is so large that it, like Australia, is sometimes considered a continent. After a couple hours of flying over a vast ice field under clear blue skies, we arrived over the western coast and descended to about one thousand feet and, drawing down our airspeed, we began a leisurely drive up and back down the western coast of this huge ice packed island. We saw several fjords with small villages. We picked a fjord at random and flew over it at almost full speed. We were low, fast and noisy.

We made another low pass at a lower speed returning out to sea. All or most of the villagers came out to see this huge plane, one like they had probably never seen. We gave them what they wanted with a slow speed all flaps and landing gear hanging flyby. They could get a good look at this workhorse of, not only the United States Air Force, but that of many other countries, including Denmark to which Greenland belonged. We made another low pass, again with everything hanging out. I didn't check to see how slow we were going, but it couldn't have been over one hundred twenty-five miles per hour. We were in no danger of falling out of the sky, but we gave them a good look at our aircraft. Stall speed at this weight is about ninety-three knots. One more low and slow pass on our way back out to sea. We went out farther this time gaining speed as we did. Coming back in, we cleaned up the airplane, we gave them what I thought would be a thrill. Almost maximum power and everything cleaned up with gear and flaps in the "up" position. As we roared low over the village doing about two hundred and ninety knots, we could see the natives shouting and waving at us. We gave them a double "wing waggle."

We made a couple low passes over the other two villages we had seen. Then it was time to return over the Greenland icecap back to our beautiful Iceland. That's when things got eerie. "Spooky" is what the engineer called it. I couldn't argue. All of a sudden, we were in what appeared to be a bottle of milk, with the milk still in it! I compared it to being inside an eggshell with the yolk and white removed. There was nothing but a soft opaque white color in all directions. None of us had experienced anything quite like this. It affected all aspects of our bodies and minds. I felt lighter. It was as if we were going down in an elevator or pulling negative "g's." I also told the Aircraft Commander that we were in a left turn. All instruments read straight and level, but we all voiced the opinion that it felt like we were in a medium bank to the left. We all wanted to turn the aircraft to the right, but the instruments said, "Straight and level." It was a horrible feeling. We all wanted to turn right, but the instruments started hollering at us, "Straight and Level!" It was about to drive us nuts! This went on for a good or you might say, bad forty-five minutes. Our stomachs were churning as the left turn seemed to accelerate, but we all knew that crews had died because they didn't believe their instruments. They followed their feelings and instincts instead and ended up dead!

Then, possibly a hundred miles out on the horizon, a little black dot appeared. Suddenly the world was right! That little dot brought order out of utter chaos. We now had a reference point that we could relate to and the feeling of a left bank disappeared for all of us. I can unequivocally state that I DO NOT EVER want to feel that way again. It was almost as scary as some of the times I should have died. This time it was our choice. Actually, it wasn't really. It was the instruments' choice and we never faltered in believing them though sorely tempted to do so!

Getting back to Eric the Red who discovered both islands, there's more to his story. His name was mentioned before, but his little skullduggery wasn't. He obviously saw the potential in both places. He knew that other explorers would follow his lead to these new lands and would attempt to colonize them. Well, old Eric, being the clever man that he was, didn't want any more adventurers to find the richness and beauty of his favorite of the two. He made a very clever and astounding announcement when he returned home. Eric the Red knew it would be transmitted by word of mouth and perhaps in written word that he had discovered two new islands which came before reaching the large mainland. He named these islands Greenland and Iceland. Now if you wanted to establish a new colony, which one would you choose? That's exactly what ole' Eric thought everyone would do. His plan worked to perfection! All of those adventurous souls headed out for the place where they could most likely succeed in establishing a new flourishing colony. They were drawn to the best sounding island name which was the one Eric had dubbed Greenland and when asked, Eric gave (or maybe sold) the navigational chart to their desired destination. Meanwhile, the colony established by Eric the Red on Iceland grew and flourished. I know not what happened to those hearty souls who ventured on to Greenland. I do know of several villages in the fjords of Greenland because I saw them. This was proof that it was colonized, but none of them are of any great size.

Meanwhile, the folks on Iceland even developed their own language which to this day is spoken nowhere else. Eric fooled everyone with his naming of the islands. He named them just the opposite of what they really were. His plan worked to perfection. I thought to myself, "I'm so glad that our trips up north were to the beautiful green of Iceland and not the solid ice of Greenland." That sounds strange. But, I guess it did to the early explorers, too! It worked exactly as Eric the Red had planned. Of course, we do have an Air Force Station at Thule, Greenland.

It needs to mentioned someplace, so why not here? The world record for distance of continuous non-stop flight without aerial refueling in a turboprop aircraft was set by one of our planes. Major Tony Liparello (sp) was the Lead Navigator and Lt Col Allison the Aircraft Commander. It maybe should be pointed out that the record had been held by a Navy P-3 sub hunter aircraft like was stationed at Lajes Field. The way the record was taken from them was also a little sneaky. The children of the Lajes schools were invited to take a Saturday waxing the subject HC-130H. They turned out in droves, as did the parents, to thoroughly wax the plane which cut the air drag considerably. Any little trick would do. But, not sneaky here!

Tony did a masterful and thorough flight planning including when to step climb to get the maximum distance out of fuel expended. Now to put plan to action! I can't remember what all had to be done in order for this to become a new NCAA record flight. It seems that some FAA guy or other official had to bear witness, but I don't know who. Now, the sneaky part. The plan was to fly from Ching Chuan Kang (CCK) AB, ninety miles south of Taipei, Taiwan to Scott AFB, Illinois. Long day! With augmented crew, they set sail for Clark AB in the Philippines. They planned to arrive with almost minimum fuel left in the tanks. Then sneakiness was put into effect so it could affect the overall effect of the flight. They flew over a small mountain range to Cubi Point, the NAS part of Subic Bay Naval Station and took on a great big bunch of Naval JP-5 flight fuel. The Air Force only had JP-4, a lesser fuel. I'll not get into specs of fuel, but rest assured that JP-5 is superior to JP-4. Completely topped out with Navy JP-5, they flew the relatively short distance to CCK where they again topped off. They had waited until winter in order to get maximum tail winds and hopefully be able to catch the jet stream somewhere which blew lower in the winter time.

They waited at CCK for a few days until the winds and the weather in general was favorable for this historic attempt.

It was 20 Feb 1972 when this intrepid augmented crew set the world record of eight thousand seven hundred thirty two point zero nine miles. (8,732.09 miles or 14,052.94 km).

Officially from the Ching Chuan Kang Air Base web site: "On 20 February, 1972, a Lockheed HC-130 set a world record (that still stands) for a great circle distance without landing with a turbo-prop aircraft of 8,732.09 miles (14,052.92 km) flying from Ching Chuan Kang AB to Scott AFB, Illinois." It would be a fools game to try to figure time involved because we do not know the reality of the event. Affecting factors which would have an effect on the flight: Especially, average TAS, Altitudes involved and Average tail winds. I'm not sure where you could get those or the actually flight time. This was a flight to set a distance record so the time made no difference.

The second mention is more oddity than history. Picture this, if you can: You are driving south on I-65 from Huntsville to Birmingham, both in Alabama, when you see a giant C-130 camouflaged aircraft actually flying backwards across the Interstate right before your eyes! The plane is going in reverse! It happened. We were at about eight thousand feet.

I was up to my normal nonsensical things when I figured a nice trick if I could get the pilots to do it. We had already completed the test flight and were cruising around Smith Lake, North of Birmingham to see the sights. Pretty! I was fooling with the doppler when I discovered that we had a pretty good wind from the west! Doing some quick calculations and not knowing if we would ever be up flying with these conditions again, I started talking and finally convinced the pilots to go along with a stupid stunt. It was winter and I figured the winds were about one hundred twenty five (125) plus knots. Our stall speed was eighty seven (87) knots. Ergo, if we would safely head into the wind at about one hundred knots, our ground speed would be an estimated negative twenty five knots. We would be backing up across I-65 at twenty nine miles per hour! I appreciated the humor in it at the time and for years until I forgot about it. Writing about it now, I wonder if we caused any wrecks. Our reverse flying would be quite obvious either going up or coming down I-65! Now, causing a wreck would not be humorous! We did it several times starting west of I-65. Well, a boy has to have his fun!

LAJES, EUROPE & ADEUS (GOODBYE)

"I Remembered to Forget what I should have Remembered"

My dream tour of flying in HC-130 ARRS Aircraft out of Lajes Field and Keflavik, like all of my dream assignments, came to an abrupt end just as I was getting ready to apply for an extension of my two-year tour to become a three-year working vacation.

The word came like a cold wet cloth across the face on an Icelandic winter morning in an outdoor washroom. We were being curtailed by six months! The 57th ARRS was being disbanded! Discontinued! Closed down! Our next trip planned for the near future to Mallorca had to be scrapped. I was down to being a crewmember on the base C-118 to various Mediterranean bases with a three night layover in Athens, Greece. And this, only because I convinced BG Aldrich that I was qualified in C-118 aircraft and they needed a Navigator. All of this was true. I was qualified in C-118's having flown them, racking up almost four thousand hours on a three-year tour at Hickam AFB in Hawaii. Obviously, I had all the bad tours, Huh? Unfortunately, they were all curtailed, primarily due to Squadron closures. This made three consecutive dream tours that stopped suddenly because of discontinuation of the squadrons! My defense mechanisms have made Scott AFB disappear!

And so, it was: In the current situation, I was qualified in C-118's but that was in C-118B models' about eight years ago. Now, in a C-118A, there was little noticeable difference looking at it from the outside. I don't know from a pilot's perspective, but the navigator station looked very strange. The difference was probably more critical for a pilot, but for a navigator it was just that the equipment was different, that's all. Instead of the simple and easily mostly accurate LORAN B, the "A" model C-118 had LORAN A which I had last seen in Navigator School and which I was promised I would never see again. That was ten years ago. In electronics, that is a multiple life time.

It was in these conditions that we made our way into the air and over the Atlantic Ocean with an initial heading of somewhere around 090 degrees, roughly toward our first stop at Torrejon Air Base near Madrid, Spain where we would stay for a couple of nights. At least we would if I could find it. Fortunately, it was only about an approximate eight hundred fifty-mile flight on a clear day so I could get two star (sun, moon and maybe even Venus) fix lines if necessary to cross my semi-accurate LORAN A fixes.

Brigadier General Aldrich wandered back to the Navigator station which was about five feet behind the cockpit, to see how we were doing. He had been in the copilot seat as an observer. He wasn't even qualified in the aircraft, but he was the Commanding General, so who's to argue? I explained to him that we were rough- ly midway between the Azores and Portugal when the question of my qualifications arose. My situation was that though qualified in this type aircraft, I had not been current for lo, all those many years but that it was all coming back to me and maybe I could extend my tour of duty at Lajes Field as his personal Navigator? Well, you can guess how that turned out. He didn't say much though, because he needed a navigator to get back home and he had been piloting a plane in which he was not qualified. Nothing was ever said nor heard about it, again. I did not get the base navigator job! And, not even another trip.

But, all was not lost. I was on my way to another plum assign- ment. I have to quit saying that. This one would be an isolated tour for one year (without my family) at Ching Chuan Kang AB (CCK) Near Taichung in middle west Taiwan. At least I knew this would be only a one-year tour. I dropped off my family near Ent AFB in downtown Colorado Springs, Colorado, where they would have to suffer looking at Pikes Peak every day. Unfortunately, it turned out to be one of the worst winters on record, and I had unwittingly rent- ed a house with a northern exposure, so the winter weather was no piece of cake for our four daughters walking to school, nor for my wife keeping the driveway cleared of snow. At least, they had a garage. Meanwhile, I would be attending Water Survival Training for a few days at Homestead AFB in sunny Florida, south of Miami, and C-130 Tactical Training School at Little Rock AFB, Arkansas, for roughly twelve weeks.

SURVIVAL AND DEATH

SURVIVAL—HOMESTEAD AFB, FLORIDA AND DEATH—LITTLE ROCK AFB, ARKANSAS

"Diarrhea of the Mouth and Constipation of the Brain"

I had gone to Little Rock AFB on January of 1973, but it was on the way there that that they had me travel to Homestead AFB, for my Water Survival School, a condensed class to teach a body how to survive in a water related emergency while flying over the ocean. This, after I had accrued over fourteen thousand overwater hours, and was heading for an assignment(s) which would happen almost exclusively over the green (or brown) earth, with the main exception of flying "feet wet" a few times. "Feet Wet" was a term coined in Vietnam to alert the friendlies that we were flying off shore mainly to avoid detection and secondarily, enemy gunfire, I suppose.

The school, at an off-base site from Homestead AFB at Flamingo, Florida, was a snap except for a fool like me whose greatest fears were height and copious amounts of sea water. That, and with some NCO's who got back at me for my wise-ass attitude.

The first incident was when (after they schooled us in these arts) they tied me to a parachute whose canopy was, in turn, opened and held spread out against a large square screen and held by the suction of a giant fan, built into the front of our watercraft. A sinister looking speedboat was idling at the rear of the boat. Soon enough and much to my chagrin, I was tied to this speedboat by a cable which was wound into a large winch firmly attached to the boat. About the only instructions I received at that time was something like "when you began to be pulled forward start running and keep running no matter if you were already off of the deck. In this fashion, I found my sweating, fear saturated body dangling from that parachute over Florida Bay. When they had me frightened enough, and I had reached their estimate of the correct height of seven miles (it was actually about six hundred feet), I received a pre-arranged hand signal to cut myself loose from my lifeline to civilization. I considered disobeying the signal, but I realized that would only result in doing it again, under duress, with the threat of loss of wings, and I do not mean water wings!

With a one-finger salute to my tormentors, who in reality were my instructors, I released my umbilical cord. I listened to the worst noise an aircrew man can hear: SILENCE. The speedboat, my last hope for survival, had disappeared, the sound of its motor gone with it. I was hanging in a world of blue (normally my favorite color but not too enticing today) everywhere I looked. I searched for land with the unattainable hope that I could guide my parachute in that direction. It was like a preview of my frustration in my very distant life where I lived in Broken Arrow, Oklahoma. I had no idea where I was, I had no idea which direction was, which, and I didn't know how to pronounce Apalachicola and I was completely lost! "Oh, Oh," I had better get back to reality. I was sinking fast and I had to review in my mind, the actions I had to take to insure my survival. All I remembered was that I pull the inflation tabs on my Mae West flotation device, and to disconnect from my parachute canopy, but not until my feet touched the water. I was also doing my best to avoid letting it collapse on me, which was an endeavor in itself. After I was certain that I was not going to get tangled in the parachute cord, I proceeded to figure out why I was having these drowning feelings. Hell, I discovered that I was drowning because I was lying on one side. Those dirty #@<)*&%^'s had let one wing of my life jacket with a used compressed air cartridge in that device. After about ten times of trying to get it to inflate, I faced my problem. I would just have to blow the damned thing up with my own breath, which I had planned on saving for salvation in case I started to sink. "Well, hell," I reasoned. "Why not do it in the comfort of home?" Of course, I was referring to my one-man life raft which had sunk under me because it still had to be blown up too. Good grief. Next thing you know, I'll be inflating a blowup doll! So, I pulled the trigger on the compressed air cartridge to inflate the raft. Finally, SUCCESS! The damned thing filled up like it should. I turned my attention back to my life vest because that was my primary life-saving device. Then I noticed a kind of a hissing sound. CHIT!@!!!! My one-man "lounge of the sea" was leaking nicely as was everything, including my brain! Or what was left of it.

Now I had to concentrate to gather what few wits I had left and evaluate the situation. Aww hell, it wasn't that bad! One lung of my life jacket was holding. As far as I was aware at the time, the other one was good, just flat as a tire on an abandoned '28 Chevy. The raft had to be patched if it was to be of any use. They had warned us about this situation, but I must have dosed during that part of class because I had no idea in hell as to what to do about it. "OK smart ass. Get yourself together and get things done. You are going to be out here for several hours." I hadn't slept through that part of it! The raft had to be patched, but the life jacket just needed air, compressed air and the only air compressor within quite a few miles were my own lungs, so I had best get on the task. I had blown up mattresses and other bladder contraptions that needed blowing up, which brought to mind this little girl in the Catholic School across Canon City from the Abbey School. She seemed to have a different sized top every time I saw her, which wasn't very often. But I had my eye on her from across the dance hall just in case I figured out what I was supposed to do. It seemed we never danced at these dance parties but just stared across the empty dance floor at each other.

Oh, how my social development was left utterly undeveloped. Sixteen years old and still didn't know what to do. Actually, I had an idea of what I *wanted* to do but had no idea of how to go about getting it done. Of course, I was still like that when I graduated at barely eighteen years old. And then I went to Regis College, which, at the time was another, all male institution. "Damn my social skills, or lack thereof!" I wish I knew what to do. It wasn't because she looked bad. As a matter of fact, she looked pretty good and made me feel that same tickle tummy that June Allison did many years ago. But right now, she just reminded me of my life jacket. One size full the other almost empty as she had looked one night. I wish I had the guts to find out why. I still don't know.

OK, here I was in deep trouble and I was daydreaming about my favorite subject. And that was not about blowing up football bladders! I had to figure out my current plight. I already assumed that I would best be kept afloat if I had more than one water wing capable of keeping me out of that deep trouble. So, I started to huff and puff until it would hold my body above sea level. After a time, I began floating somewhat evenly. Now to pull up my raft, which fortunately, was tethered to my life jacket. After expending too much effort pulling this thing that was about as flat as an old truck tube and weighed about as much as the tire, I had to find where the hole was, and to do that, I again had to huff & puff. I began to feel sorry for the big bad wolf. After an extensive search I found where the air bubbles were escaping. Now to get the knife and the rest of the patch kit gathered in one place. I had them gathered together before, but they had been scattered again while I was figuring out where the leak was.

Finally, I had everything together again. Strangely, I thought of another song, once again. Now, I just hoped I remembered the salient points of that fascinating instructions period. One thing I must have gotten wrong. "Cut open the small leak you have found in your raft." That must have been the result of a nightmare instead of just dozing off. What fool would cut a bigger hole in his leaking singular water conveyance. It made no sense to me! So, now that I had discounted those dreamed of instructions, I proceeded to initiate repair of said flotation device commonly known as a one-man life raft. I do remember you had to stick this part of a patch thingy through the hole in the raft. "Tab A into Slot B." Ahhh So! Now I understood why I had to cut a hole in my only means of getting out of this damnable wet salty water. You had to use the dull knife to enlarge the smallest hole to accommodate the inside part of the patch. Man, did I ever hate to do what I thought was making my situation worse, but I did faintly remember this was a proper procedure. I don't remember the rest of the patching operation except push through elongated hole and screw together. Well hell, I thought that together was the only way to go anyway! I was right! But after I had the patch installed so I thought it would hold air, I once again started huffing away. That poor damned wolf! I'll never be on the side of those fat little pigs again! After blowing into a tube in which I felt I was losing almost as much as I was forcing in, I had the raft filled enough for me to climb aboard. WRONG! The raft immediately sunk like the flat side of that little girls'---. "Damn it, Jack! Get your mind on survival! Not as enjoyable, but more necessary!" It was obvious that I had to blow it up way beyond what I thought was reasonable but knew was physically necessary, if difficult. After several more underinflated attempts, I finally was able to get on board and started bailing. Soon I was high if not dry, but drying out, and getting ready to settle in for a long wait for rescue. The waiting was part of the training and I was bored already. I was hoping for a boat. No such luck. After several hours, which seemed like weeks, a helicopter appeared over an unexpected horizon. I was even happy to see that loud, flying threshing machine! Painfully ignoring my Uncle Emmett's admonitions of "never trust anything whose wings go in circles." Well, in those wings I now trusted. I didn't care how, I just wanted to get to hell out of there. Well, as I watched the whirly-bird approach I recalled Emmett's many accidents back in the nineteen twenties and thirties, including the one in Death Valley. All of his accidents were in fixed wing aircraft, so I thought I'd give the rotating ones a chance. It worked! It whirled me away to safety cause whirling is what they do. I took a base cab to my VOQ, a shower and a chance for a nice Beefeaters on the rocks to start the night of celebrating that I was still alive!

I thought that was the end of it. Not So! They had one last little trick up their sleeve. Next day, we were bused to a "high" hill, probably what they would call Mt Trashmore (a Florida name for reclaimed mountains of trash) and which had a long cable running over yet another body of salt (ugh) water which ended just short of the far shore in fairly shallow water, but deep enough that you would be glad that you had your water wings inflated. They were tucked behind you for training purposes. You were to pull them out from behind and Velcro them together in front for a nice stable end to the training. They would definitely not keep a person from getting wet, again, but they made it easy to reach shore. Naturally, I had been spouting off to the training guys. I had been harassing the Survival experts, a group of highly qualified NCO's. It seems I had caught a bad case of diarrhea of the mouth while having constipation of the brain, again! Not necessarily a highly recommended combination in a survival situation! Of course my mouth got me in trouble again, but I made sure that they knew I had been a SSgt so they would have a little empathy for me. I also reminded them that I was over six years older than their average victim. They just laughed harder!

As I kept mouthing off to the instructors and hoping they understood that I was talking too much just to hide my fear of this entire needless (so I thought) exercise, my turn came up. I had to make the slide down the cable to the water below in a sequence meant to establish the speed to hit the water at approximately the speed at which one would hit the water after bailing out at ten thousand feet. Getting the wings from behind your back to under your arms was supposed to simulate the time it took for the wings to inflate (I think)! The NCOs were meticulous in getting each man prepared for his ride. This was to be our last exercise before graduation.

I sarcastically observed how they prepared each man that went before me. Seems I said something about like putting pampers on a baby, or something like that. I went on commenting on various aspects of the preparation process and how no one had any trouble after they hit the water and pulled their water wings around and attached them in front. Then it was my turn and the preparation was as meticulous as those who had gone before. Tied in properly and this time with fully aired up water wings, I figured I was as ready as would ever be. Actually, it didn't matter if I figured I was ready. It was when THEY figured I was ready. These full wings, when pulled from behind my back would help me get to shore more quickly and put an end to this horrendous survival torture. I noticed that when they attached me to the zip line, it seemed a little hurried, and I hated it, but with a shove, off I went on my first fun zip line ride to the waiting water below. After I hit the water with a smack at the speed simulated to be the same as if I had bailed out of a fatally injured aircraft, I realized that my over active mouth had gotten me in trouble again!

Those wise asses had Velcroed my water wings behind my back so that when I hit the water, instead of easily pulling them forward under each arm, they were holding my body up while my head was plunged into the salty, brackish Florida Bay! Yep, as those bastards laughed, I was fighting for my life. My head went under again! Their skullduggery was not completely unexpected, but even so, it took much sputtering and threshing of legs to keep my head above water as I tried to tear the Velcroed wings apart. I finally successfully separated the Velcro and moved the wings from behind my back to where they should be: Under my arms. I meshed the Velcro in front of me where it belonged and went sputtering and coughing out onto dry land. After gaining control of my senses and sensibilities, I looked up the zip line to find a group of NCO's damned nearly falling down all over the place laughing uncontrollably at this poor old Major, laying on the shore, almost spouting water out of his mouth like he had spouted his words earlier at the top of the hill. Now, he was swallowing as much as he spouted. He was probably swallowing those unwisely chosen words of early on also. Now his spouting was to keep from drowning. They had thoroughly enjoyed giving this officer a thorough and embarrassing dunking that he would never forget. I have not forgotten it yet, and if any of you out there are reading this book, believe me, you are NOT forgiven, but ya are complimented on a hell of a trick on a wise ass old fart!

LITTLE ROCK AFB
TO CCK, TAIWAN

"That Damned Hill was Higher than they were"

I entered this Tactical Drop Training as a Major with approximately fourteen thousand, five hundred flying hours primarily between California and Japan by way of Hawaii and Wake Island. I did this for over seven and a half years in C-118's and C-124's, so I considered myself fairly well qualified in the art of getting an aircraft from one place to another. Navigating is what I did! In fact, I was so qualified that I corrected more than some of the instructions which were being given in long range overwater navigation LORAN and some other things. This was the navigational aid of choice during this period of time. I had accrued many flight hours earlier as an enlisted man flying in WB-29, WB-50 and RB-36 long range aircraft mostly over water. But I wasn't navigating then, so I don't know why I mentioned them. Oh well!

I thought that after that many over-water hours, it was a little late for training in overwater flight, but it happened anyway, just like needing water survival after that many hours over the seas! Now in this Navigational part of my Little Rock training, I would go back to Colorado Springs after I had taken classroom exams and passed a test without getting any classroom instructions. In the flying area, I finally talked them into just giving me a check ride on my first time up instead of taking several instruction flights before a check ride. I spent at least half of my TDY back with my family in Colorado Springs. But I did need training in tactical troop and equipment dropping. It was different and important but not that difficult except for some pretty interesting computations taking into consideration wind, drift, airspeed, weight and other variable factors.

The instructors were very good. One of them, John Davis, had flown with me out of Hill AFB. He was a great instructor. Just before I was due to rotate back Stateside from Clark AB a year later, John was killed when, in a three ship formation, they encountered some unexpected heavy rain which called for a split of the formation so the closeness of aircraft in formation wouldn't cause a problem by running into each other.

By the command of the lead Aircraft Commander to engage evasive weather related maneuvers, the two outside aircraft split forty five degrees to the direction away from the lead aircraft. John's aircraft just happened to have a hill at higher elevation ahead. Evidence indicated that the C-130 was climbing when it hit the hill in front of it. I have no idea if the return started looking larger on the Navigator's radar and the repeater scope in the cockpit or if they had a visual, but it seems they were aware that they were in deep shit just before impact. All crewmembers died!

Back to training. I needed this Tactical Training. I made a few drops of some unfortunate troops out of a C-124 at Hill AFB. I put them on the drop zone, but several ended up with broken legs because there was a crust a couple inches thick. Beneath the crust was mud. Hill did some drops, but I was made instructor after my first ride. I knew nothing, but they needed the figures. Stupid! But dropping was not stressed so I learned virtually nothing about the many complicated computations nor the nuances of Tactical Air Drop.

My extensive training in radar interpretation at Navigator/Bombardier School at Mather AFB had an immense impact on my drop capability. In fact, there was a long running conviction in the school that radar drops of troops was impossible. Not so! One night after we had finished our required drops, the pilots wanted to get in some extra night hours, jokingly one of them said something like, "We should have the navigator try a radar drop. He has aced everything else!" "Hey nav, want to attempt a radar drop? No one has ever been successful at it yet and we only have one other aircraft in the pattern." "SURE!" I was always ready for a challenge, and this was a good one. They didn't know I had been through the Nav/Bomb school. I had hated that school, but now it could pay dividends. We went quite a way out from the drop zone and started our run while I began identifying little radar returns that a navigator without that training would not even notice. I started with the old bomb run technique. Pre-IP, IP (IP=Initial Point of entry to bomb run) and selection of offset aiming points as well as keeping track of where we were, ground speed, drift and more observations taken quickly but accurately as I had been taught so long ago in that hated school.

I started giving them headings, speeds, altitudes and whatever other pertinent information, even more than they were used to, for a successful run. When the pilots contacted the ground troops at the drop sight and told them what we were going to attempt, I could actually hear them laughing with the pilots through my headset. I said nothing, but was determined to shut them up! We began our final run and I gave them the required instruction and number of seconds before drop. They followed my instructions to the letter. Ten seconds to drop, pause, five seconds, four three two one DROP. The loadmasters tossed the simulated paratrooper out of the open duck tailed ramp. Silence as we roared past the drop zone at six hundred feet Above Ground Level (AGL) and continued into the night on our way back to base. Suddenly, over the UHF radio, "Holy Crap! We have a shack (Landed on target). Man, that guy is lucky! First radar shack ever that I know of!" "Even a blind hog finds an acorn once in a while." Came from someone. They all had something to say. Laughter, including the pilots. I spoke up and asked what was so funny. They all laughed more at my blind luck.

"Hey, AC," I mouthed over the radio. "Can we stay out long enough to try another drop?" Silence! Then, an enthusiastic "Yeh man!" from the ground troops. Give it another whirl and see if the nav really knows what he's doing." By this time, we were out of the drop zone area so I gave them headings to get us back to my Pre-IP. That kind of amazed them in itself because they normally had to get the nav set up on the right track to start his run. I set myself up. The pilots radioed that info to the ground troops. A cautious "We'll see," was all the ground troops responded. We went thru the same routine and again gave the loadmaster the order to drop. The AC said, "now let's see." Silence. Then, "Shack!" Came the cry over the UHF radio. He did it again! "Guess he's real lucky." I cut in and said, "Let's do it one more time. That should settle if it is luck or skill. Do you ground folks agree with that?" "Yep" was all I heard, "OK. Mr. AC, take up heading 295 Degrees. "What? That's going the wrong way!" "If I'm making a drop, I'm in control of the aircraft. You'll see what I'm doing in a few minutes. Tell the ground troops that this will be a little different and a lot more difficult. Also, get permission for unrestricted maneuvers and altitude changes up to eight thousand feet." The AC came back after a pause, and said, "OK, nav. You've earned our trust. copilot, notify our control that we are going out of the area for a few minutes, but we'll be coming back in from another direction." Tower: "Roger, Understand," after they noted our call sign. The ground troops said, "He's going to bring you guys in from another direction instead of you bringing him in the normal track? We won't be able to recover the dummy when he misses." My quick response was, "Who in hell says he is going to miss?"

The AC asked me why I was going out here. I told them I wanted to show them that I could find the drop zone alone and drop on my own on the much more narrow cross zone. He said that I damned nearly had him lost. I told him not to worry. This will be our last run. At eight miles out, I started giving the same info needed for a successful run. The ground asked where I was going. The AC told them to stand by for one more radar pass from a different direction. "Well, good luck with that!" "We've started our run. Expect us from the south instead of the west this time." I started the new headings and told them that I took us out far enough so I could figure a drop from a different flight level. "take us up to seven hundred fifty feet AGL." The pilot started to object, but then said, "This I have to see!" Tower, request permission to seven hundred fifty feet." "Cleared." We climbed to the new altitude and began our close in drop prep. This time direction and altitude were different, so the effect of the wind etc... would be completely different, the ground voiced their skepticism over the radio. The AC said he would buy the beer when we got back to the Club if I pulled this off. I said, "Two rounds?" OK, you'll have earned it!" "Ten seconds." That caught them off guard, but they let me ride it in. "Drop!" Tense waiting as we changed headings to get home. "SHACK!" three for three. "Good work nav," came the call from the ground troops. "This one was dead on. Guess you're OK after all!" I took this veiled sarcasm with a few choice words and thanked them for waiting for the last ride. They actually said, "It was worth it, nav. First shacks we've seen. Good luck and good night." I had free beer until the club closed!

A week later I graduated and after trying to give a crash course on offset radar drop navigation, I went to Colorado for a week or so before my departure to Southeast Asia (SEA). I should probably have requested instructor duty after my SEA tour, and I probably would have gotten it. But then, I wouldn't have ended up in Broken Arrow! Fate again? Or Providence?

TRAVIS & ALOHA, HAWAII

"Hell, we're in no Rush.
They don't even know where we are."

Next stop "Snake school" in the Philippines was what my orders read and then on to Taiwan and further Ching Chuan Kang (CCK). But a strange thing happened trying to get out of Travis AFB, CA, our Port of Embarkation.

After having more toddies than I needed at Bill and Sam Bayless's home in Fairfield, Bill took me to check in at Customer Service in the terminal at Travis AFB, CA, and much to my surprise, they had no room on the aircraft for me. This, after I had arrived on time with a flight number. I enquired when the next plane would be and could I book it then. They politely informed that I would have to place my name on a "Space Available" list and there were seventy names on it now. "Well Shit," I slurred! I could be stuck here for weeks, and I would have to check in for every flight which meant packing, unpacking and checking in and out of my quarters. Of course, this didn't make much sense to me, and Bill started fussing with the clerks that it shouldn't have to be that way. Then it slowly dawned on both of us that it was April 30th and if I didn't get out before midnight I would have a departure date in May which meant that I wouldn't get back form SEA until a month after I had planned. This did not set well with me or Bill, but he didn't say much to the passenger service personnel. He just kept egging me on to find a way out.

And so it began!

I started with the passenger check in folks. They promptly wanted out of this situation with a major fussing with them. They quickly called the on-duty officer at the terminal. His response didn't satisfy me. After some very loud wrangling, he called the Officer of the Day. This exercise turned out about the same. They really couldn't refute my reasoning and didn't want to be the deciding officer if things went bad, which was the way I was heading. My reasoning was simple. How and why would they place me on a Space Available (Space A) list to go somewhere I didn't want to go in the first place?

Then a simple solution came to mind. I had been flying into Travis for many years but not for the last four and I had damned nearly forgotten about the MAC Airlift Command Post (ACP). We drove over there in Bills' automobile. They had aircraft flying out of there on a scheduled and as necessary non-scheduled flights. As we went in, I thought I would check in with them and see if my old friends were still there. Naturally, not. After this many years, they had moved on up and out and these guys looked so young. I was getting old! I explained my plight, and some of these young officers had gone through the same Southeast Asia shuffle and knew what I was going through. Knowing that I was an old MAC Line Flyer didn't hurt. They said there was a C-141 leaving just before midnight to Hickam AFB, Hawaii and beyond. The C-141 Starlifter was a big four engine jet with beautiful lines and a "T" tail which could carry one hundred fifty-four passenger and was going out empty. It just didn't make sense with seventy military folks on standby to go get shot at in Vietnam. A great crew aircraft, it was not built for luxury. But, they could carry a load of up to over one hundred paratroopers and could easily wipe out the backlog that had accrued, probably by over booking by PAX Services. The C-141s were very reliable. One of the best birds in USAF History. Most folks that flew them loved them.

The feature that I liked best was that they had one leaving the U.S. of A. just before midnight. That was all of the ammunition I needed. I can get out of California (stateside) before May. Believe me, that was a big deal. I normally sit back and let things go. When I am backed in a corner or see something that is seriously wrong, and I can solve the problem, I will stand up and do it. This was one of those times!

I went back to Passenger Services with the news that we could get, not only me, but lots of people out of there. I thought they would be glad for this solution for a lot of problems. Not so. They wanted nothing to do with the idea. Time was running out. I raised enough hell that they got the PAX Services Officer back to the counter. He almost immediately went to the Officer of the Day. He was reluctantly back on the phone. He finally yielded to my mysterious logic and gave up. He called the Wing Executive Officer who was having a party at his place. After some more arguing with the XO and with neither of us satisfied, he thought he'd get my ass in trouble and threatened to call the Wing Commander who was a full Colonel already selected for a star. I told him to do it. He said, not too politely, "By damn I will! This Colonel knows how to chew ass." I told him that I had one that was ready. He uttered a couple obscenities and told me to stand by. The Exec called the Wing Commander who was already in bed. He asked one simple question. "Was this important enough to wake me up?" I said, "yes Sir, I do, and I need to get out of here in that C-141 that is empty and ready to go to Hawaii. There is no reason that I can't." I gave him my, by now, practiced line of reasoning. He told me to standby for a phone call that I probably wouldn't want to get. I waited, fidgeting all of the

time. Did I mention that time was running out? I soon, very soon, received a call from a two star, (Major General) asking the same question, "Do you think this is important enough to wake up a Numbered Air Force Commander? This better be pretty damned important." With Bill still urging me on, I replied "Yes General, I do, and it is well important."

I did my best to assure him that it was. I probably stood up a little straighter when I answered him. I also told him that I had seven Second Lieutenants that needed a ride also. He repeated, "Why Do you think it is that important? I told him that we should not have to stand by on Space Available to go somewhere we didn't want to go in the first place." Silence! I thought "Oh shit! He is going to kill me." Finally, he responded, "You know Major, you are right, and this is wrong. Now, damn it, get off of the line and stand by there for a phone call." The phone rang and I heard a very exasperated voice of the wing commander telling me to get my ass down to the MAC ACP right away to catch that C-141. I asked him about the seven lieutenants, "OK, damn it, get them on board too. You evidently know the drill. Don't call me again!" "Yes Sir," I said as I was hanging up the phone while I heard him slam down his. I had to hurry! We went back to Pax (passenger) Services to get the other guys down to Base Operations which was practically next door. "Hurry up and get on the manifest. We're going to get out of here tonight." Since we were going on an unscheduled cargo plane, we did not have to clear through Pax Services. We grabbed a flight line driver and had him take us directly to the C-141 which had been ordered to hold until we could get on board. We hurried so they could button up and go. They had already done all of the required checklists and had engines running. They were a little puzzled by this unusual order to be put on hold for a Major and seven Second Lieutenants. They followed the hold orders, but made sure that we were logged in the air before midnight after I told them my story. We indeed were going "Space A" as they said we would have to.

We barely had time to get seated when we started to roll. They had to get off the ground in April also. Off the ground at seven minutes before midnight! I logged on to the manifest as an Additional Crew Member (ACM) to log some time and to prove that we were airborne in April. To this day I don't know if I thanked Bill for egging me on and damned nearly getting me in trouble. Getting a two star out of bed at a little before midnight? I would not recommend it. Maybe it happened because I ended up between a one star and a two-star arguing about getting my family and a few other folks out of Germany two years earlier to get a C-141 diverted from its destination, McGuire AFB in New Jersey, to drop off a few folks including my family as well as the Ops officers' family at Lajes in the Azores. The crew was not happy. Their Squadron Christmas party was that night and this would make them a little late. If I hadn't been able to get them to do it, we may miss Christmas altogether! I still don't know why our Ops Officer didn't take care of it. He was a Lt Col. Oh well. It may have been a little easier at Ramstein AB, Germany this time because I had done the same thing the previous Christmas. This time when I requested diversion of a C-141, the Airlift Command Post ACP Duty Officer asked if it was Major O'Connor again. "Yep!" I didn't have to wait so long this time. I think the decision was made by the local Wing Commander. He may have remembered me too. Who knows? But, at Travis AFB, I could have been on the wrong end of a bad situation if it wasn't for that logic of having to go on "Space A in order to go somewhere I didn't want to go to begin with."

About a half hour before landing at Hickam AFB, I finally roused myself and took inventory of how I felt and where I stood. I finally figured that if they were expecting me to get to SEA "Space A," then they had no idea where I was nor when I would get there and perhaps, even if they knew I was coming. So, feeling tired and with the remaining feeling from the inordinate amount of booze that Bill "forced" me to drink, I decided that I had gone far enough. I had no desire to fly that leg to Wake Island and then on to Clark AB feeling like I was. So, I informed the Aircraft Commander that I was going to stay here in Hawaii for a few days. He had no choice and it didn't matter to him. He just scratched me off of the manifest and gave me the form for my flying time. I gathered my things, told the Second Lieutenants that I'd see them at Clark AB and had the flight line driver take me to the billeting office. I needed a practice nap before I contacted friends here on Oahu.

No need to go into what all happened during my eight lovely, what could be called AWOL days, but needless to say, I had a most enjoyable time with Bruce and Novie Barnes, my longtime close friends and a few other lesser known but well remembered acquaintances. As a surprise bonus, Novie's lovely cousin Faye and dentist husband Ed were in for a six day visit. Bruce and Novie picked me up at Hickam AFB and we went onto Honolulu International Airport where my presence surprised Ed and Faye. We all had a wonderful time together at the Barnes household until Ed and Faye had to go across the island to attend a conference in Waikiki.

Bruce and Novie were always ready to share a toddy when I came wandering through. I had lived within a half mile of them when I lived in Kailua, on the windward side. Many times, Bruce would come home to find me sipping an Asahi beer at his lanai bar or me finding him at my bar. It all evened out, actually more in my favor. Asahi, a great Japanese beer for three dollars a case at the Marine Corps Air Station in Kaneohe BX Panic Pantry, just a few miles away. It actually worked out that I would buy a case frequently and we would drink them at his much more pleasant lanai bar. He called it "ass high." I'm still not sure if he was joking. He had been in the Submarine "Silent" Service way before WW II when Shanghai was still a great port for any kind of entertainment that you might want. I never got a chance to go there, but I enjoyed and envied his stories. But, he also did North Sea escort duty, self-tied to the railing of a Destroyer Escort (DDE) in freezing cold, covered in solid ice. I didn't envy that! I was even going to stop at Honey's lounge. Don Ho was no longer there, but Honey was still Honey!

I was still completely worn out. What happened to resting up? Maybe Clark AB would be more sedate? After those eight sensational and memorable days, I jumped the next contract DC-8 that would take me to Clark AB, after I spent a night on Waikiki. I wanted to see Don Ho one more time. He was sold out, but with Faye and Del in Waikiki, that night and next morning were not wasted. I wasn't in much better shape when I left the Outrigger before noon than when I landed in Hawaii, but happy with my reason for exhaustion. Now, it really was time to get to work.

CLARK AB, PHILIPPINES & SNAKE SCHOOL

"Do you know how many Hiding Places There are in a Thick Jungle?"

Clark AB, Philippines! Many tales are told about Clark, some of them even true. But, those soiree's will not be tattled here. Instead I will jump off to my jump off of a huge helicopter somewhere deep in the Luzon Jungle. The beginning of Jungle Survival School. Now, this is one school I possibly could really need! I hoped not. They immediately took us into the jungle surrounding the helicopter clearing. Triple canopy jungle, the same as in Vietnam. We were greeted by instructors who were eager to treat us to the legendary capabilities of the indigenous Negrito Tribe who inhabited the local area. They would teach us how to forage in the jungle. Actually, you could eat quite well. Covering your tracks was the problem. Escape and Evasion (E & E) was the main purpose of the training.

I knew I was in trouble when they gave each of us a net and a hammock, and vanished into the departing helicopter. I didn't have a clue of what to do with them. By the way, I was getting pretty damned tired of survival schools. But, I guess they were all necessary IF you remembered anything they taught you when and if the need ever arose. I did not have a good track record with that. Three Marines were in from their Marine base, camp Futema in Okinawa. They felt right at home and had volunteered, again, to go through the training in order to get away from their normal duties at the Marine base. One told me that this was his fourth time to come to "Snake School" for that purpose. It was a vacation for them and I never saw them do much but wander around. After the instructors had walked us back to the bivouac area, treating us to hearts of palm, bamboo shoots and other delicacies upon which we could exist for the five-day school. It was almost dark when they quit trying to teach us to do uncommon things which would make us more comfortable during our training. Unfortunately, they neglected to tell us how to prepare for the night so I found a wide clearing, rigged the net so it would afford some protection from the reunion of hundreds of bug families. I ended up just collapsing in this clearing which I found out to my chagrin during the night that must have been a major intersection for cross jungle trails. I really don't know how many animals ran into me until I finally moved to the edge of the clearing. I was only run into once after I moved, but by then it was almost daybreak.

Of course, a few mosquitoes got into my jury-rigged screen. Fortunately, they didn't know much about evasion themselves. After I slapped them all into submission, I got as much sleep as you would imagine I could get sleeping on the ground knowing that there were snakes and all sorts of wild things running around out there.

A tired group of jungle novices gathered a little after dawn for more education which we would need if we ever went down in the jungle. A frightening thought indeed. Today would be a split day. We would be trained and then given the chance to put our training to test. We received a lot of verbal instructions which after 45 years have escaped my trap-like mind. The problem with a trap-like mind like mine is that it is always closed. Anyway, it was time for demonstrations by these very small natives.

The instructor pulled us to one side of the clearing and gave us just a very few minutes of what we were going to do next. It turned out that he wanted us to find the Negrito who had been standing amongst us not but a few minutes ago. No one had seen him leave the group. The American instructor had been explaining a few pointers about Escape and Evasion and how there may be times we would have to hide in just minutes if not seconds. The little Negrito was said to have hidden himself and was supposedly inside this thirty-foot circle right behind us. There were about fifteen aviators who became hunters of the elusive indigenous individual hidden very close to us. We had seen him just a very few minutes before. Now, not even his shadow remained.

We started tramping over the place and could not see any sign of another human being in our immediate area. "Ok, came a smiling voice, he is within this circle." And he indicated an area about 20 feet around where we had already searched pretty well. About five minutes, that same voice came to us. He is within this five-foot circle, Damn, were we blind, dumb or just plain stupid, We spent another five minutes basically bumping into each other and throwing dead palm fronds and any other thing loose. We finally figured it out. The instructor was just fooling with us. When we confronted him with that accusation, he smiled, moved over a little and said, "OK, ya got me. I misled you a little bit." Ah hah! We caught him at his own game. He moved over very slightly. He began to confess; I misled you again by dimensions. He is within three feet of you. Gather around. We formed a circle as tight as you could with that many shoulder to shoulder. Or more like back to belly. "Ha! He would have to admit to us now that the guy was somewhere else." We accused him of misleading us and a few other things. The instructor gave us about a minute to either fuss with him or stare at this tiny area. There was no room for us to search. Then, the instructor whistled three times. An apparition arose before us! A real live person came out of virtually no-where. In a matter of seconds, he had straightened his hiding place under the jungle flooring of local flora so you couldn't even tell it had been disturbed except for our foot prints and the mess we made stumbling around for about twenty five minutes looking for him. We stood there aghast or whatever word you would like to use for a bunch of officers that had been unable to find a living being in a three-foot circle when, rolled up, he took up about a third of the space. Jaw hanging stupid is how I felt, and I was no city boy!

We all immediately decided that he had just crawled into a premade hiding place. The instructor told us to form a fifteen-foot circle in a location of our choice and watch. Honest to God! He just seemed to disappear before our eyes in a spot we pointed for to him to try. He was hidden in seconds. And, I swear, that if we walked away for a few seconds and then came back, we wouldn't be able to find him. Then we were given our assignment. "You will be given a forty-five minute head start and then we are going to turn a few of these folks out to find you. Use the secrets we have shown you here. There are no limits of where you can hide. It is a big thick jungle out there, but we're not very concerned about your getting lost. I would bet that none of you will escape detection. If you do, we will blow an air horn to get you back in. It's been used only once! These folks will find you and then let you know how they did it. They do not speak English, but they will indicate that they found you with their eyes, ears or nose. After they find you and indicate their detection method, give them that little piece of paper you have been given. Write the method by which he found you and the time on it. For each one of you they find, they will receive a little bag of salt. Yes, that is their only reward, so there is competition among the hunters and No! They are not Head Hunters. The Head Hunters live way farther north and are now non-cannibalistic, but still do minor head hunting, strictly for ceremonial reasons, So, not to worry!"

Off we went in any direction we could. We scurried out of sight like a bunch of cock roaches when you turn on a light in a dirty kitchen. I was soon alone trying to find a hiding place. Do you know how many hiding places there are in that deep dark old jungle with all the trees and underbrush? NONE! I knew I could never disappear into the jungle floor as he did. I ended up undecided among about ten likely spots. I picked one a little before the whistle sounded that the hound dogs were on our trail. I wormed my way under the exposed roots of some kind of tree up on a hillside covered in undergrowth and pulled as much of the stuff over me that I had gathered from some distance away to stockpile in order to use it for my cover, I was set! Boy, was I ever. I can't remember for sure how long it took one of them to find me, but the size of their bag of salt was somehow measured in the amount of time they took to find their quarry. Mine must have received a quantity! I was found in less than ten minutes and he indicated his nose. Damn, I didn't think I stunk that badly, but you didn't need to have to stink but normal and I guess these Negritos can smell you. But by now, we had been out here for five days, so... Most of the Hiding airman were found by nose. Only one by sight.

After a couple more nights, spent in hammocks hanging between trees as the Marines demonstrated, it wasn't too bad. Hell, I'll be honest. They felt sorry for this helpless old Air Force Major and fixed my neat little swinging bed. They knew that Air Force "K" rations, instead of stale biscuits and canned chicken was a couple martinis followed by a medium rare Ribeye, a baked potato, and a glass of White Zinfandel, followed by a nice after dinner toddy or a few and a good nights' rest between clean sheets. And that this, their good time, was considered roughing it by us when we were away from home. I bartered with our Negrito guide for his machete, now on display at the Military History Center. It is still sharp as is a second one I bought for very little money, but for no reason.

We were herded together again and made our way to that same jungle clearing used for transferring troops in and out of the training area. Now it was time to go to war! But first, I decided to spend a couple more days at Clark, getting a little pre-R & R under my belt, anticipating the hardships that I was now as prepared as possible to face during the ensuing by now eleven months. Yeh, real hardships! CCK and C-130E's. Can't get much worse than that!

Oh, did I mention? The seven Second Lieutenants that got a ride with me to Clark AB on that C-141? Well, they waited for me as I suggested they should. In fact, several were in Snake School with me. We decided it was time to get to our ultimate duty station. Destination Taipei so we could catch a flight hop or a train to CCK. I told them I was going to take the train so I could take in the countryside and see what kind of service they had to offer. Strangely, they all opted to do the same. Snow white & seven dwarfs? Not really, but the corollary isn't bad. More like an old hen and seven chicks. What I did, they did. I knew in my heart that this was going to lead to no good somewhere along the line, but why worry now?

One more night at the Fire Empire, The Officer Club and our Officer billets at the six story "White Elephant" VOQ. There was a fairly early C-141 flight to Taipei on the board, so we all signed on. I'd just about bet that this group of seven very young officers had more fun following me around than if they had waited and finally got out of Travis AFB on a scheduled DC-8! What's that old country western song by Buck Owens? "Together Again." One of my all-time favorites. That suited me and this gang to a "T!"

TAIPEI, TAIWAN & CCK

"Good People, Good Eating and a Big Taiwan Beer. What's to want?"

We arrived in Taipei by lunchtime. How nice. As far as I was concerned, it was too late to bother trying to catch a train to CCK, but a couple of the gang went on to CCK with the C-141. I discussed it with several of the more outgoing type 2nd Lts. I explained to them before we got off of the C-141 that it wouldn't get to CCK until about two o'clock and I doubt if they would want to in-process newbies this late on a Friday, though everyone worked on a Saturday morning also. No use in cluttering up our logic with common sense. Five from our Butter bar group stayed behind with their ipso-facto leader. We all checked in near Madame Chang's Imperial Hotel for the weekend. We went to a nice restaurant, amazed by the inexpensive but savory fare. I had been to Taipei several times before so I led them to some of the worlds' finest massage parlors, jewelry stores and eateries. I also pointed out the main area where the "girls of the night" normally operated and if they wanted to lean in that direction, I'd think about it twice. You can be taken advantage of in those places with no recourse. These girls had very tough "managers." I cautioned them to wait until they got to CCK. The base and locals work together so no one gets hurt if they use their heads. No "managers" to take a cut of the action, and with all that competition, the costs were more manageable. In Taichung, it would only be an agreement between two compatible parties. Just have a few toddies and be careful.

The second night in Taipei, it was everyone for themselves, I opted to go with a couple of them to an area called the Beitou District, northwest of downtown. It was an area on the hills outside of Taipei with fantastic hot baths and massages, not as good as a Bangkok vibrator massage at the White Tower, but still very good. The others probably went to a movie which were good American flicks in complete cushioned luxury. Next morning, because all were out late, we drifted into the lobby and restaurant and got together to plan our day. I knew of some of the sites to see, like giant Buddha's and a few of the other things. Mainly we just wandered around. Earlier return to our rooms that night. We all enjoyed our time in the Taiwan (formerly Formosa) capital. But, it was beginning to get boring and we were getting antsy to get back to our flying duties. Also, we couldn't get any pay until we got signed in and it had been set up through the base clearing in process. Mine, of course, stayed partially in Colorado Springs and my family with a certain sum coming to me for my comforts such as lodging off base, sustenance and sundries.

On to the train depot for a comfortable ride south about one hundred and twenty miles to Taichung, the town which hosted CCK. We all grabbed cabs to get to the depot on time and I scurried to help these guys with their passports, and just anything they needed. I spent too much time making sure they had everything they needed. I should have been taking care of myself also. Crapola! I discovered I did not have my own briefcase so I could get myself headed south. Oh Shit! My briefcase was in the back window of the cab I had just vacated. I told the guys to go on without me, and that I appreciated their offers to help, but they couldn't do anything for me. I had to figure this out for myself. Besides, they needed to sign in today. One of them had already run back to find the cab we had shared. GONE! Now what to do? Few spoke English around there and I was trying in vain to get someone to call the headquarters of the cab company. Someone understood through sign language and pointing out in his cab, the relative location of my missing bag. He finally contacted dispatch of the cab company. The dispatch relayed my plight to all cabbies. Everyone was relaying my pathetic story.

My hopes of finding the case were really dim. Very valuable items were in the unlocked case including my PCS orders which were essential, some cigarettes which were good for barter, cash which was good for anything. My cache of Greenbacks (US Dollars) would be cherished. I even managed somehow to get the radio station to which most of the cab drivers listened, to broadcast my plight to all cabbies. Discouraged? Yes. Depressed? Getting there. Frightened, Oh hell yeh! What was I going to do without official Permanent Change of Station (PCS) Orders which were requisite for doing almost anything. I was in deep doo doo and wasn't sure what to do about it. I even had my wallet in the briefcase as a precaution against pickpockets which are prevalent in any foreign country. I couldn't even prove who I was. By now, I wasn't even sure. My bags had been checked (Randy was going to retrieve and take care of them for me). I was just in one hell of a fix!

Then I heard and noticed a big commotion. There he was, breaking thru the crowd like a broken field runner shouting something in Chinese, a man running amidst cheering and waving of hats and scarves holding my briefcase over his head. My Cab driver himself! Man, talk about a sight for sore eyes. Against all odds, everything was intact! He probably had not even opened the case. In broken English, he explained that he was going straight back to his dispatch when he heard the distress message. I'm still not sure if he heard the plea from dispatch or over the radio. He checked his back window and immediately headed for the train station. He just abandoned his car exactly where he had left us out and came looking for me. I was not far away. He was hollering and jabbering when he saw me. I don't know what I was doing but it probably was not within the decorum normally expected of a field grade officer. Screw it! I didn't care. As far as I was concerned, that cab driver was my savior! My salvation. Without his return, I'm not sure how things would have turned out. After arguing with him, I convinced him to accept a gracious reward for his honesty and effort to find me. I was finally successful because of the kindness of these Taiwanese whom I grew to love. As it did turn out, I was on a later train, in Taichung and quickly out to CCK by that evening.

Next day, I caught up with my buddy from Little Rock AFB. He had rounded up a couple other folks, one of them, Randy, who was with me from the Travis AFB fiasco, and had retrieved my bags at the train station. Rick had rented a six bedroom home in Taichung close to the Main Street and one door down from the infamous Maggie's, the biggest party house in the CCK area. It would be ready for us in a week. Meanwhile, a hotel downtown. That week was about a years' worth of experiences. The hotel was across the street from a USO. That's why the housing folks on base recommended it. I was surprised. A USO right in downtown Taichung!

One of the fascinating sights was a Chinese funeral parade. A large contingent came down the main street with blaring bugles, horns, cymbals and all sorts of banners, flags and noise makers. I became confused when one part of the group continued straight while about an equal number turned and went down another main street. Fascinated, I watched from my sixth story window. I later learned that these funerals have two main groups. One group has the body of the deceased among them. The other group, identical except no body. It was a decoy to lure the bad spirits from the corpse. They kept the parade going until they were sure that the evil spirits had been turned away and couldn't find the body. Brilliant!

The other mini incident was when I was soooo bored. I had already filled the audio tape to be mailed tomorrow. The hotel did not have air conditioning so I was in my skivvies and my pants were hanging on a chair by the dresser. I was dozing off & on. While I was dozing, I got a kind of sixth sense tingle. Something was going on. I stayed very still. But had maneuvered so I had a view of the small entryway, the chair with my pants hanging and my dresser. Then I thought I saw something, but it happened so fast that I wasn't sure I really saw it. There it was again, A hand quickly in sight and then out of sight. Once more only farther in this time. A short wait and then the hand and arm came out and came within about six inches of my slacks with my wallet in it. I waited. There it was again. This time, he touched the pants and I noticed that my wallet was sticking up a little out of the pocket. Ok! That was enough. I was ready this time. The hand appeared and I hollered at the top of my lungs and scrambled to get out of the bed. Damn, that slamming door was really loud. I ran and looked out. Hallways empty! One of the sneaky boys had attempted to get my wallet while I slept. I called the front desk, but in broken English they managed to get across that they knew nothing and could do nothing. Oh hell yeh! He had a key to my locked room! That kind of theft was fairly common in oriental areas. They are good at testing to see if you are alert or awake.

The house became available earlier than planned. I was very glad and relieved. It didn't take long to get tired of hotel living when you didn't know a thing about the town and had no wheels to get around. I moved in immediately. The house was near the bus stop which I would need until my little Red Rambler station wagon which had become almost a part of me arrived from the Azores. Most military and civilians who worked at CCK rode the bus which was derisively and accurately dubbed "The Smoker." Everything was GOOD! Rick had also hired an Amah (maid) who was almost as inexpensive as in the Azores, but who had many fewer duties. Her main chore was to cook our evening meals when we were home and to do the laundry. The other three, two captains and a second lieutenant spent most of their time "In Country" on a varied schedule. It wasn't often that I was there by myself. As Squadron Exec, I couldn't go in country as often as they could, nor as I liked, but I really enjoyed being the XO. It tested all of my skills! That changed after we were forced to move to Clark AB in the, Philippines and ended up with a new Full Colonel Commander and three Lt Cols who didn't have a job. I quickly put them to work on various projects which needed attention and nabbed the one I liked best, Bob Regal, for my assistant XO. Yep, strange set up, three Lt Cols working for a major, but when operating under combat operations rules, strange things were not so strange. Bob would rather stay at Clark, and I would rather go in country. With all four cooperating, I think we had the CO completely baffled. He pretty well left us alone as long as we were taking care of everything, making him look good and left him alone to preen and talk with his four star buddy at Pacific Air Force HQ (PACAF) at Clark, I went in often and mostly with him not even knowing.

At both places, the flying was great, with a few exceptions. Missions were actually flown out of the 374th TAW Forward Operations Location (FOL) at U Tapao Royal Thai Naval Air Base outside of Sattahip in southern Thailand. The FOL for B-52 Bombers and KC-135 Tankers was also located here on the opposite side of the runway. By now, we were basically through with flying in Vietnam and were relegated to Thailand Bases and selected areas in Cambodia which was becoming like an "Old West Shootout." Cambodia was being overrun by Khmer Rouge forces of the Pol Pot revolutionaries.

CCK was a great assignment. The Taiwanese people are the greatest in the world. In seven months there, I never felt that I was taken advantage of or disrespected. If you agreed on something, it was honored. In selling things they called the agreementa "Chop." It was an inviolate code. And the military personnel were advised that if they entered a deal where a "Chop," a small wooden design which was stamped on the contract, was made, they were obligated and the base would back whatever local made the chop, no matter they found a much better deal. This was an honorable agreement and how most of the American appliances were legally passed on to the local populace.

CCK also, like all other bases in the world at any time in history had its own area, some of which were OFF LIMITS! It wasn't really bad, but you could get most anything you wanted. It was a triangular piece of land on the CCK end of town known as the "Dirty Dozen." I never understood the name unless it came from many years before I arrived there because this triangle was filled with probably, more than a hundred bars. The surrounding streets accommodated the overload. It was a great place to go and let off some steam. I always laughed at these places and others downtown because it appeared that they were all called "shoot pool bars." Succinct and effective. These were the places where you could play western songs, drink enough and lean on the juke box and cry about what could be happening back home. I caught myself doing just that myself! After that I didn't listen to a western song for the rest of my isolated tours. It was tough enough to be separated from family without the music making your mind wander needlessly into water deep and dark! CCK turned out to be at least as good of an assignment as others had told me it would be. Good people, good eating (I had one restaurant that would just bring my Mongolian Bar-B-Que and a big ol' Taiwan Beer when I walked in) and good flying. What's to want?

CLARK AB, PHILIPPINES

"Just not in the Same League"

Then, what was it I said about dream assignments? Something on the order that the come to a crashing halt. This end, or crash, came about because of a secret summit meeting in which Chairman Mao demanded and President Nixon acquiesced. We were forced to leave CCK and move the entire 374th Tactical Airlift Wing out of CCK. Two squadrons of C-130E aircraft, the 50th and the 21st Squadrons, I think, transferred to Kadena Air Base on Okinawa, which had been newly returned to Japan. The 776th TAS of which I was the XO went with the Wing to Clark Air Base north of Manila in the Philippines. I much preferred Clark AB to Kadena since it now would be affected by the Japanese government, and the great prices for booze and other necessities were going to be shot to hell. It was from the FOL that I would fly most of my memorable missions though I had many good missions out of CCK earlier.

Clark AB was another great assignment, though not in the same league as, and not as well liked as CCK. I'm not even sure any other place was better than CCK but home. And for some folks, CCK was even better! The exec for the Wing was going to retire at the end of this tour and move back to Taichung and marry a local girl. One of the Captains with whom I shared the house, a good Mormon guy, divorced his stateside wife and married one of the local bar girls. He went to Kadena with one of those squadrons. I don't know how it worked out, but CCK/Taichung was mesmerizing to a lot of folks. When I learned in nineteen sixty-two that I would be flying into many oriental countries, especially Japan, I self-hypnotized myself (strange statement) to believe that I did not like oriental women. For the most part it was very effective. I was successful in self-hypnotizing to dis-like Beefeaters Gin at home. If I try it now, I have to throw it down the sink. It tastes horrible! BUT: I dearly love it when I go out to a restaurant. Just the way I want it to be! I've handled hiccups the same way. I hurt myself by holding my breath until I almost passed out and it hurts like hell. Now, If I start to get them I threaten myself that I will hurt myself in the same way. I just threaten now, and they're gone!

From either home base, we all still flew out of the FOL at U Tapao. I didn't have roommates at Clark. I lived off base by myself in Angeles City. There was a great big rat which lived down in a hole in the sidewalk right in front of my small house. He seemed to be there every time I left the house in the morning. I could get within just a few feet of him before he would quickly dash down his sidewalk hole. I also had a houseboy whose main job was to keep my refrigerator stocked with San Miguel beer.

I know that there should be more to write about being stationed at Clark AB, but I spent most of my time "In Country." I do have one where the TDY began and ended at Clark. I was given command, on very short notice, to proceed to Iwakuni MCAS, Japan. I was to take four C-130s and a group of about one hundred fifty Maintenance personnel and cause a Squadron of Marine F-4's to be moved from Iwakuni MCAS to Naha NAS in southern Okinawa. There was not enough rooms on base for everyone and I didn't want to split up the guys so we set up a bunch of rooms in a down town hotel. Things started out with one of the guards at the hangars where the planes were housed got wacked with an airplane chock. Yes, an approximate 4x4 piece of wood. He was completely blind for about twelve hours. It was about midnight and I called out all maintenance folks to go through all four planes looking for whatever may have caused this to happen. They found nothing so I started dispatching the aircraft in the morning. One of the planes broke so I had to do it with three aircraft. I got it done two days early and got my ass chewed for not following the schedule. Damned if you do, etc...

I had arranged it, with a broken aircraft that one of the crews and a portion of the maintenance folks go into Hiroshima, next to the base, to see the Monuments remaining from the "Fat Boy" atom bomb explosion. I was the only one not to be able to see it. I had a room on base also, and was on duty twenty four hours. After we completed the mission and were ready to go back to Clark AB, I launched the three aircraft with the maintenance folks but stayed to make sure they got off OK. I was ready to get the last plane started home when I heard that one of the planes was coming back with only three engines. No beeg 'ting! I called the same hotel to get our rooms for another night. They said they couldn't. "Filled up." That didn't make sense so I argued a bit. Then it dawned on me. Did someone take your robes, slippers and other things. "Hai" (Yes in Japanese). "Ah so" I said quietly. "They are coming back. If I can get them to return all of your things, can they stay again?" "Hai." And so it went. I had the maintenance NCOIC put the men in formation when they got off of the plane. Only group ass chewing I ever had to do. Not bad for some of the positions I held. The aircraft was fixed next morning and we all went back to Clark AB. It dawned on me later. I should have had the customs Security Police check when they got back to Clark. I'd bet that more than one re-stole their "souvenirs" Damn!

Maj Jack O'Connor transferring a Marine F-4 Phantom Squadron from Iwakuni Japan to Naha NAS Okinawa.

CAMBODIA TRILOGY–PART I

Quick Offload and F-4's

"Nothing Really Bad Has Happened To This Crew"

After a normal night at The Officers' Club, we got home for a few hours' sleep and then, after some breakfast, we proceeded to the Forward Operating Location (FOL) Operations office. There was the CO smiling at the looks of this motley crew. We may not look real purdy, but he knew he could depend on us.

Another priority mission today, fragged to an unknown, unimproved red dirt airstrip. It had a name that I can't remember, but it was up toward Battambang, Cambodia. We were warned that it was another little strip typical of those inside the many battered Cambodian Army outposts that were surrounded by the Khmer Rouge. In fact, this area was still known as Kampucia in the Khmer language. We were to go into this short, dirt runway through Khmer Rouge ground fire to deliver of all things a load of Marston Mat, more commonly known as PSP, an acronym for Perforated Steel Planking. These were strips of steel ten feet long by fifteen inches wide with three inch holes (eighty-seven holes per mat) held together by the hook and slot system.

Now, we were supposed to take a load of this stuff into a little unimproved landing strip which somehow will save this brave little garrison from being overrun. Really? I asked the Boss if maybe we could take them something better. He told me that this was General Westmoreland's world and we were fragged for this mission today. Man, I really felt like we were saving the world with this load of junk, but what the Boss wants, he gets from this crew. We proceeded as though it was a load of ammo, which they probably needed and would have preferred! Man, just by looking at my chart, I could tell this strip was truly in the middle of nowhere. If something bad happened to us, help would be a long time a'comin'! Nothing really bad has happened to this crew, except a few hangovers that were theirs, not mine. I didn't do hangovers so no worries there!

Off we go into the wild blue yonder, again, wondering just why. But as they say, "Ours was not to reason why, etc..." That's a good thing because you'd go nuts trying to figure the reason why! The landing strip was about one hundred fifty miles into the hinterlands of Cambodia. It was located in one of the dry spots of Cambodia that has its middle about fifteen degrees above the equator and has a huge lake.

On this mission, we received a blurb on the Notice to Airmen (NOTAMS) and also from our operations briefing that we needed to get in and out as fast as possible. The bad guys were very close to the airstrip. So, we were planning on a complete combat procedure which means we would fly in close to the strip at five thousand feet, drop to five hundred feet for the last two miles, drop in over the trees at the end of the runway, have the pitch in reverse almost before touching down, drop the load off to, hopefully, friendly forces and get out of there ASAP. Neat! No problem for this crew. Yeh, right. We broke open the box containing our .38 caliber handguns for the first time in my career. The first time I had ever been in this situation in all my flights into Vietnam and Cambodia during the last seven and one-half years and they didn't seem concerned. We were! We inserted real ammo! So, we launched anyway!

We were getting near the drop zone and for all practical purposes, we were out of touch with anyone. There was a little puffer cloud about a quarter mile wide and a few hundred feet top to bottom, but it was directly in our line to the "popup" place so the pilots decided to just drive on through it. No problem with a small cloud at this level. We entered and almost immediately came out the other side. Oh, my God!!!! Two F-4 Phantoms were almost in our windshield, climbing out from the same field into which we were already committed. They immediately split, one right and the other left, causing our C-130 to pitch, rock and bounce like an over-wrought bucking bronco and I don't mean a Denver Bronco. I was standing between the seats as I normally did which was a real no-no for landings, but I always did it. It wasn't very smart and a Flight Check buster, for sure. When those two Phantoms buzzed us, I was damned nearly knocked to the floor. As it was, I ended up in a squat between the seats, holding on with just one hand. Good Lord!!! That was unbelievably close! Had we collided, everyone would have lost!

I have endured a lot of turbulence during my many hours of flying, but I have never been rocked as hard as we were by the jet-wash of those two F-4's. The shock waves of four big jet engines at full throttle, plus the turbulence stirred up by those two big airframes flying at probably four hundred twenty-five knots, really kicked us around. I guess they had just done some close air support for the surrounded troops who needed help. We're talking about some real help, not PSP! Perhaps, the F-4 bombing and strafing run might make the Khmer Rouge keep their heads down until we got in and out of there. No time to think about the very narrowly missed mid-air collision now, but it could have ruined our whole day!

As it was, we were ready to drop unannounced over the tree-tops onto a rough dirt runway. We hit hard and short. I doubt the field was too much over three thousand feet long. Even with pranging (or crashing it hard) on the ultra-short landing and being in full reverse pitch, perhaps even ever so slightly before touchdown, we weren't stopping very fast. He kept it in full reverse until we came to a full stop, just short of the trees at the end of the runway. Why they had the runway in the middle of a grove of trees, I'll never quite understand. I remember thinking, "Whew! I thought we would have some trees in the cockpit there for a while." With full reverse pitch on the props, we still used almost all of the dirt available. There just is not too much that compares with doing a combat approach and hitting a dirt (red if possible) landing strip in a loaded C-130 with props already in reverse. But, we were safely on the ground. Not really safe, but on the ground. We saw a Cambodian Officer waving to us to drop the load along the side the runway. Since we were in a hurry and seeing a mortar round drop into the clearing every so often, we decided a quick combat off load was in order.

Now for the off-load. With the props still in full reverse pitch, we backed the plane like you would your car. This would be a little different though. The pilot backed a little way down the runway, then backed into the space where they indicated they wanted the load. I wondered, "What do you think they will feel when they find out these crazy Americans went on a very dangerous mission, braving small arms fire and mortars to deliver a bunch of stupid strips of metal with holes in them?" With the holes in them, they couldn't even use them for protection. They probably thought, "Stupid Americans! No help at all!" I wouldn't blame them if they started shooting at us after raising their hopes that some really badly needed ammo was coming and then finding a pile of worthless steel that would probably sit there until it rusted away in a hundred years or so.

As I said, this was like backing your car into a parking spot, but with a couple of big differences. This would be your biggest ever car with a large appendage, mostly full of Avgas sticking out each side with spinning propellers. Avgas is the aviation fuel used to propel the aircraft. We intended to drop about thirty thousand pounds of steel on the side of the dirt strip. The Loadmaster and I had untied the tie-down chains so the load was basically loose on the rollers except the rollers were in the hold position. Now, the Loadmaster and the Pilot had to have very tight timing on the next maneuver. As we were backing up with the ramp in the rear of the plane wide open, all the little kids in the area were running to get behind the C-130 to see what we were going to unload. They were almost up to the drop spot, so the Loadmaster told the pilot that we had better drop our load now before the kids could get to the point where we planned to make the drop. With very tight coordination, the loadmaster released the roller brakes just as the pilot switched to full forward pitch. With a mighty jerk, the monster plane stopped going backwards and suddenly sprang forward, driving right out from under the now free rolling PSP. A text book example of how to drop a load in the right spot.

I had gone down to the cargo compartment to help the loadmaster retrieve the tiedown chains, which was unusual, but this was a combat offload and procedure was a little different. We all helped where we could. On a non-combat or normal offload, the loadmaster would do all of this by himself, but as I said, this crew was different and didn't worry about breaking a few rules if it enhanced the mission. As the plane lunged forward, the Loadmaster and I hung on for dear life. As soon as the PSP was clear, the pilot went immediately back to reverse pitch in order to stop the forward progress of the aircraft. Oh, yeah, the kids. When the AC went from full reverse to full forward pitch, the prop-wash was very strong from four Alison turboprop engines and it blew those poor kids ass over teakettle. They flew like little plastic bowling pins being hit by a monster ball. They went end over end, rolling and flying in the wind of the prop-wash. Fortunately, they were all laughing and having a great time. It was like this was a big carnival ride to them. I hoped that not many of them were hurt. It may have been my imagination, but I would swear that a couple of the smaller ones actually went airborne for a short distance.

We were very short of tie down chains back at U Tapao, so the loadmaster and I went out to recover them off of the pallets of PSP. The neutral pitch still caused a little wash and I was really surprised at how quickly it dried out our sweat-soaked flight suits. We had come in unpressurized, naturally, and with the cargo bay being open, the ultra-humid Cambodian air, plus working undoing the chains inside and out, had us all soaked. Now, suddenly we were dry.

From out of nowhere, a Cambodian Lieutenant Colonel showed up with a neat little package in his hands. Actually, he must have come out of somewhere, but I just hadn't seen from whence he came. He approached me and handed me a little container made of woven palm leaves, a common item in Southeast Asia. I didn't have time to check to see what was in it. The loadmaster was just gathering the last chain and I had to get on board or jeopardize the crew and aircraft as well as myself. Mortars were becoming more frequent and closer. I hollered a thank you to him and saluted. He returned my salute with a nod and a smile. He was an outstanding man. Very sharp in a neat uniform and quite tall for a Cambodian. I was very impressed. I jumped into the rear ramp and as the loadmaster gave the go signal, I ran to my station on the crew deck. Since there was virtually no breeze and no control tower, it was our choice of which way we wanted to take off. We chose the nearest and backed up until the tail was virtually touching the trees.

With brakes on, the pilot turned the blades to maximum forward pitch. Applying maximum power, he released the brakes and we literally jumped forward. We gained speed rapidly, but those trees were getting mighty close. I was getting ready to remind him of that little barrier formed by those trees when he pulled back on the yolk and, I mean, he pulled it back. That airplane literally jumped off the runway and pointing the nose at what seemed to be straight up, we cleared the trees with some to spare. Then, he put the nose down so we could gain speed rapidly to get by the small arms fire. We soon were going so fast and so low that we were past them before they knew we were coming. After we hit a nice speed of about 300+ knots, it was up, up and away again. That empty C-130 Hercules climbed faster than a lonely angel missing his girlfriend! We were out of range of small arms in a split second. Well, almost. After we reached fifteen hundred feet, the AC eased off on the gas and we settled into a normal climb. Not much was said, just a "normal" mission with a little added excitement of the two F-4's, a short dirt strip, trees, small arms fire and a couple of mortars that did no damage. Soon we could relax. When we hit cruise altitude on the way home, I said to the Aircraft Commander, "That was fun. We ought to go back and do a crash and dash (touch and go) just for the hell of it." That suggestion didn't get much response!

Now, I had time to look into the container. It had some weight to it, so I knew we had a nice gift. WOW! Five small bronze statues of dancers in various poses. I guess the Lieutenant Colonel knew there were five crew members. He trusted me to give one to each. I did exactly that and kept one for myself. It is displayed in a place of honor in my home as it has been ever since I returned from my Southeast Asia tour. Sadly, I knew the Lieutenant Colonel would probably be dead by nightfall or at least by morning. I hoped and actually prayed to God that he would be killed instead of captured by Pol Pot's Khmer Rouge's vicious thugs. I couldn't help but think that he may not have had to face that fate if we had brought in thirty thousand pounds of ammo instead of that damned PSP. But, eventually, the entire country fell to Pol Pot's Khmer Rouge regime with Phnom Phen being the last to fall. It has been estimated that between one and three million Cambodians were murdered over the next two years. God's way of population control, I guess?

We flew back to the Forward Operating Location (FOL) in almost complete silence. I guess that none of us could get away from the obvious fact that the Lieutenant Colonel as well as all of those laughing children would be tortured and murdered soon. We went to the club straight from FOL Headquarters after the mission de-brief still in our flight suits. Not that uncommon, really. A couple of strong toddy's helped that night, but I still think of those smiling little faces every so often even today, all these years later. But, I take comfort thinking that the dancing statue in my home represents the happiness they eventually found in their heaven.

We were all still pretty somber the next afternoon. None of us could shake the thought of all those kids being massacred, along with the Lieutenant Colonel. There was not a damned thing we could do for them except give them a show delivering that junk.

From experience, I knew things would right themselves after a couple toddies, hot red peanuts and more banter at one of the lounge tables at the U Tapao O'Club. We didn't know it yet, but the next mission would certainly do it. While we were starting to loosen up after our first drink, our fearless FOL Commander came wandering in and joined us. Naturally, since he outranked us, we all stood when he joined us.

Sit down and relax guys, how was this last trip? We explained our feelings especially taking in that damned PSP. "Yeh, that was risking my men for nothing, and you guys know I don't like to do that, but when you get a direct order it has to be taken care of...." He got a wistful look on his face. I wish I could have had you dump the damned stuff in the middle of that dry area up there. And too bad about those kids. From what I've heard about what they do to the youngsters, well....

"Well, it's done! And, I have a trip to offer that I think might take your mind off of that abortion of a mission you just flew. Maybe this will even make up for that one." I'm looking for a good crew to take the Peace Negotiators up to Hanoi real early Wednesday, but l guess I could give it to you if you want it. One of the pilots broke in and with a grin asked: "Are you talking about the real Hanoi?" "Yep, that very one." Suddenly, the excitement at the table was palpable and could be noticed from anywhere in the room. We all suddenly felt better. If you're in the flying business over here, it's best to have a short memory. That last trip took a little longer to get over, but the thought of that new trip got us up and ready to go again. We all said "Hell yes, coach, put us in! We'll sacrifice and take that one. We're going home next Friday and it would be neat having a good mission to remember."

"Well, get saddled up for a very early alert on Wednesday then. You'll get several briefings before you go in, so in the meantime relax with a couple toddies. Guess I don't have to tell you that!" I've already ordered your next one.

GIA LAM AIRPORT, #1 HANOI, NORTH VIETNAM

"No One would Sit in Hanoi Jane's Butt Print"

Our constant availability to do the boss's bidding paid off in spades! He called us into the Office and again gave us the opportunity to make a flight to Hanoi taking the Peace Commission Negotiators up to Gia Lam Airport in North Vietnam. He knew we were pretty down yesterday, so he thought he'd better check again. "Oh, hell yeh!" I answered for all of us. I won't have to fly the plane up there! It would be early morning Wednesday. And I mean real early morning. Make sure you take your passport! You'll stop at Tan Son Nhut AB to top off your fuel, get a briefing essential to the trip and pick up the negotiators. Be nice to them. They are foreign, doing a job, and you do not to even have to have contact with them, except the crew compartment will be pretty crowded if all of you stay up there, so the first five seats downstairs are reserved for the crew. It will be an augmented crew, so it will be a long day. They will brief you on Air Control. They won't be of much help."

"But, I will let you know, confidentially, that the last crew to fly up there got so screwed up that they were refused permission to land and were even threatened with a shootdown. They actually got far enough off course that they overflew downtown Hanoi, obviously a restricted fly zone! They came back without landing. They almost didn't let us make the trip last week. I don't want that to happen again so, O'Connor, be ready to use those nav skills you claim to possess. I want you to be the main Navigator from the coast on in. Use that radar as much as you can." Well hell! I hate to be called out, but it is probably best that he did. Especially since the trouble of the last trip was being blamed on the Navigator. "Sh**!" The damned pilots have instruments too!" I guess it definitely will not be a milk run!" Well, well, at least this will be something entirely different. I secretly hoped so. We hadn't been to any weird places, well, not real weird, lately and we have never been up there before. I always loved going to somewhere new. The pilots felt the same way. North Vietnam, huh? We knew it would be something different when the FOL Boss advised us to try to find some warm civilian clothing. Warm clothing in Vietnam? Crazy! This was a tropical zone. He told us it was not so much up north. I scrambled over to the BX, but the only thing I could find was a bad ugly sleeveless sweater vest. It was the only item there that even resembled warm clothing. I hoped they had warm facilities in their busses and hotels where I heard we would go. Well Hell, we will be flying in enemy territory, they control everything up there. Well shitsky! That could take all the fun out of it!

Alert came at 0030 hours, or 12:30 in the morning. Damn! This wasn't early morning, it was still late night! Breakfast this early after dinner? That didn't work too well but we all scarfed down some scrambled eggs with bacon and burnt toast. I could barely look at the biscuits and gravy nor the SOS. They all looked like they had already been used! We would each have three box meals for the trip, so no problem unless we ran across a honey bucket. But I haven't seen one of them since the good old WB-29 days. After breakfast, we gathered again in the crew bus, and began the trip across the stinking klongs*[1] to get to the flight line.

Believe me, at 0200 hours, the Klongs stunk at their worst! I was afraid I was going to be seeing those eggs again, but we all made it to our battle wagon, our C-130E. It was fired up and ready to go. At least the pilots could use their VORTACS and other nav aids to get to Saigon. Since I would be taking the last leg, I grabbed the

---

* A klong is the name for huge drainage ditches that have a mix of almost everything on earth that stinks. I never could understand how the local Water Buffalo, called Carabao in the Philippines and many other Asian countries, could sink under the surface and stay for the longest time. Yeh, I know they were avoiding the flies, but, really? It was not unusual to see one of these very large plodding beasts rise out of the water like an apparition. They have scared more than one person doing that, including me. What I liked about them was their steaks. I guess the stinking klongs must tenderize the meat.

top bunk. It was generally considered the navigators bunk. I'd get a little (damned little) sleep on our way to Saigon.

First stop, Tan Son Nhut AB outside of Saigon. Many memories here, none which were pleasant except seeing those two gorgeous women in long flowing, very colorful dresses walking toward the terminal one day. Good Lord! I've never seen anything like that before or since. They rivaled the beauty of the women in Iceland. But those also were faded memories.

We would get off on time: Wheels up at 0400 hours or 4:00 AM. That would get us to Saigon at about 0700 and after topping off our fuel tanks, were ready to accept the Peace Negotiators on board at about 0800. I would take the first leg out of Saigon and let the other navigator get some rest. It was going to be a long day. Probably pushing twenty-four hours.

Flying out of Tan Son Nhut AB, Saigon, South Vietnam, with the peace negotiating team? The importance of this mission was finally sinking into all of us. We had been the swashbuckling crew who flew within the rules, most of the time unless a rule had to be bent a bit to get the mission accomplished. There was no one watching us out in the middle of Cambodia, so it was pretty much a "Let 'er rip," outlaw country.

Our eyes were opened even more when our briefers began laying a lot of restrictions on us, and guess who would be watching over our shoulder for the entire last half of the trip going to Gia Lam and the same control freaks looking for any violation on the first half of our trip returning from Hanoi until we passed abeam Danang. North Vietnam kept a very close eye on anyone stepping across the line.

The briefing in Saigon was different from any I had ever had. First, we were ordered to change into civilian clothes before we exited the plane. No surprise. They told us that at U Tapao. Next one was tough. Also, be nice to your North Vietnamese "hosts"? That *would* be tough. These were the guys trying to kill us. And they did a pretty good job of it some years ago, times have changed and the killing had stopped, but it was still tough to accept. But orders were orders. Another surprise that especially got my attention. We were directed to fly the whole trip all the way to the mouth of the Red River "feet wet," meaning we would fly the entire trip overwater. In this case, they, the North Vietnamese, demanded we fly within a five-mile corridor thirty miles off shore. No problem, but the navigators will have to work monitoring our progress while making sure that we were staying within the five mile corridor. The pilots would keep us in line with VORTAC while abeam South Vietnam, but after that, it was the navigators job to keep us in line. We will probably be able to do that with radar, but after we get "up north" we will take a lot of LORAN fixes to verify that we were where we should be. Things felt good except that "be nice" thing, but: We were on our way!

After the final briefing in Saigon, our C-130E (with augmented crew) left Tan Son Nhut AB and headed north "feet wet." We flew about 30 miles off the coast, staying within the prearranged five mile wide corridor, basically aligned with the ADIZ. After a few hours, and with Haiphong Harbor in sight about 40 miles ahead, we came abeam the mouth of the Red River and turned upstream toward our destination, Gia Lam Airport, just east of Hanoi. The weather we were encountering was the typical broken clouds. After going over Thuan Nghiep, the river straightens out considerably so it was easy to follow on radar.

I then briefed the crew, as I had been in Saigon, to beware of "spoofing" of Navigation Aids and false directions from the Gia Lam Control Tower or any other "Controlling Authority." Spoofing" is the subtle moving of ADF (Automatic Direction Finder) and other radio navigation aids to lead your aircraft to the wrong location. It almost always consisted of moving the ADF beyond where it is located normally or moving it closer so you would make your turn earlier and stray out of the corridor.

I had been told that If you're watching closely enough, the pointer needle on the compass will quiver a little each time they change location. They are good at it, though, so I had the other navigator and the pilots continue watching for that little quiver in case we lost visual and/or radar contact. I was mainly making copious mental notes on my radar returns. But I had my head in the cockpit frequently, looking out the windows, cross referencing my radar sighting points.

We made contact with Hanoi Approach Control and advised them of our impending entry into their airspace. This had all been prearranged, so no problem there. It was farther upriver that they started screwing around with us and trying subtly to get us confused. They were trying to spoof us by moving the ADF and VORTAC ever so slightly to locations, which would cause us to fly into restricted airspace. I briefed the rest of the crew about the screw up that happened earlier, and I thought it important to repeat it here. A C-130 crew had been threatened if they didn't abort their mission. They had believed their Nav Aids and they had over flown Hanoi. They returned to Saigon without landing at Gia Lam Airport. North Vietnam cancelled the next trip, so that made the success of this mission even more critical.

Then, they really tried to get us fouled up. Hanoi Approach Control called us and told us to turn right to heading 022 degrees for approach to final (it is the actual runway heading to Gia Lam), but it was waaaay too early. The pilot started to turn and I virtually screamed into the intercom mike, "Negative, Negative, Negative," Maintain Heading!" That was the first of three times they tried to get us to turn too soon. After the second time, I told the Aircraft Commander to ignore the tower and go by my direction only.

Then I saw on radar and visually, a very nice return. It was the Cau Vinh Bridge right at the turn in the river. Now, do you remember that Damned Bridge (the Paul Doumer bridge) that our fighter bombers tried so hard to bring down? It was still there and intact on upriver. I used that bridge as my off-set pre-I P (pre-initial point) to provide an aiming point for the real turn to final. We lost a lot of Thuds (F-105's) and Phantoms (F-4's) there. Whenever they knocked out a span of the bridge, the clever North Vietnamese would use pontoons while they were fixing the bridge. Our guys never did really disrupt the flow of traffic very much. Now, I was glad they failed to destroy it!

That bridge, and the Long Bien Bridge just beyond, a smaller return but great for verification, and a huge sandbar which I could tell was permanent from its size and green clumps of bushes, about 5 miles downstream, were perfect radar returns. They were my aiming points to tell me when to start our turn to final approach to Gia Lam Airport. I checked radar and found all those neat things about 15 miles ahead. I alerted the pilot to be ready to turn in about four to five minutes They feebly tried to get us to turn once more and finally gave up. They realized that we knew where we were (We were basically flying VFR, after all) and that they would get the next plane the following week. So, eventually they gave us the proper time to turn, but the pilot turned on my command. Landing, roll out and taxiing to the parking spot went without incident. Then it was time to meet our new "friends." We quickly got out of our flight suits and into our "civies." Then the crew bus took us to a fairly large rectangular room inside the terminal while the Negotiators went down town.

The hosts immediately started taking our pictures (individual close-ups) as we sat around a table for their briefing. They then took us downtown. We were advised that we could take photos, but only in areas when they told us we could take our equipment out. I

Jack O'Connor with Chief Interrogator/ Propogandist- North Vietnamese Army.

have photos of folks in the street and of the War Museum. We went by a block long area of overturned, severely damaged locomotives. They claimed it was their repair yard. Yeh, sure. Complete with bomb craters. No photos here! I did get some unauthorized photos with my little Minox "spy camera." Our tour guides also allowed us to take photos of their downtown area. For the most part, very plain. Little color obvious. They had hundreds of manholes in their sidewalks. They were very proud of this network of "bomb shelters" which they had used when our bombers headed their way. We eventually ended up at what I had been advised was one of their finer hotels. I believe them. I wish I had taken a photo here. But, if I did, it is lost among all the others. Having been known as Indo China with over two hundred years of French influence, I couldn't argue with the subtle elegance. In a plain but spacious dining area in the hotel, they served us a ten to twelve course meal in a large banquet room. Several of the crew swore it was more like fourteen.

Banquet room at the hotel where the North Vietnamese took Jack O'Connor and the C-130 crew for lunch. The hotel was considered the best hotel in downtown Hanoi.

I don't care, it was a fantastic meal. The copious amount of food was delicious. It was one of the finest meals of which I have ever partaken. I had learned a little bit of Oriental protocol the hard way early on at a banquet celebrating an engagement in Taichung. When the eldest visitor attending the meal quits eating, everyone must stop. I thought I was only being polite, but I killed the meal.

Looking back on this banquet, I was seated at the head of the table honoring my "elder guest and rank" status. I wondered if because I kept eating so as not to curtail the gastronomical delights for my crewmates that our hosts may have begun to serve the same foods over again. I really don't think so. I had taken small portions so I could continue enjoying the delicious fare. Perhaps I overdid it? They were probably trying to show us the prosperous side of their society. I just do not know. New dishes just kept coming. I even knew what some of them were! We were ordered (by our briefer in Saigon) to drink their beer when offered if it didn't go against your belief. My belief is, "The more beer the better." The beer was actually quite tasty. At around 1% alcohol, the brass weren't concerned about us being able to fly afterwards. I had more than one.

During the time we were at the hotel, before, during and after the meal we were bombarded with propaganda. They had a magazine similar to our Life magazine. Taking up the entire front cover was a photo of Angela Davis, a black activist professor from University of California, Berkeley. One of the lower ranked Vietnamese soldiers proudly took some of our crewmembers to the table with the photo. Jane Fonda! He espoused in a loud voice. Of course, we pointed out who it was. He would have none of it, Jane Fonda! She visit us! After an ongoing harangue from the Vietnamese soldier, one of the flight engineers took exception, and told him who it was. The soldier kept repeating: "Jane Fonda visit us." The engineer decided to tell his escort the difference between the two women. He said, "This is not Jane Fonda. Jane Fonda is pink, not black and has jowls for cheeks, has a flat nose and goes "Oink Oink." We all erupted in laughter. Our escorts all immediately put their weapons

Outside the War Museum in downtown Hanoi. The North Vietnamese claimed that the small gun displayed was the same gun "Hanoi Jane" was photographed on during her tour of Vietnam.

at the ready. Our eruption of laughter had startled them because they couldn't understand it, nor why. Normally, we just let them spout their regular propaganda.

Since I was the ranking man in the group, I was subtly isolated from the rest of the crew (it was a large room, so isolating a crewmember wasn't too hard) and interrogated a little more strongly. I had been briefed to expect this, and I think I acquitted myself reasonably well, especially since I didn't know anything anyway. He proudly explained to me how their wives work out in the fields to release the men to go fight. He looked at me with a smug grin and asked what our women do to help their government. I gave him my best smile and shaking my head in a negative response, I said, "Our wives just lay around the house looking good and having babies." They weren't too appreciative of that observation.

They had lots of propaganda so I asked for some, including one of the copies of that *Life Magazine*-type picture of Angela Davis. Unfortunately, that magazine and several other pieces of their literature along with the chart and log of the mission are lost to history. Evidently all of this material which would have been of some value to the Military History Center, was thrown out at some point in time, either during a move or in my sometimes mood that nothing military mattered anymore. Most likely the latter!

After that great meal, they took us to their "War Museum." They had parts of our warplanes. B-52, F105, F-4, A-4 among others, which had been shot down during the war in a park-like setting, and also showed us and invited us to sit in the seat of the anti-aircraft gun where "Hanoi Jane" Fonda sat for that infamous photo. I don't know if it was the actual gun or not, it didn't matter, I think they just wanted a reaction. They got none from any of us. Our entire group just turned and walked away. No one chose to sit in her butt print or even make a comment. Our "hosts" seemed shocked and quite offended. We didn't care!

After we returned to the airport, they took us to a quite small gift shop in the terminal. I bought several items including some local money and stamps. They also encouraged us to send mail to whomever we could think of. I was careful how I worded things. If I told the truth about what all I had seen, the mail would have been censored and destroyed. (Just my opinion)

The return trip to U Tapao was without incident.

CAMBODIA TRILOGY – PART II
PHNOM PENH

"Watch for the Telltale Corkscrew Smoke"

Things were going pretty well back in the 776th TAS at Clark Air Base so, as was fairly normal, I sauntered over to the Operations side of the house. I checked on my favorite pilots and saw that they were both scheduled to go "in country," which meant to the FOL at U Tapao AB in two days.

Since we all operated under blanket Temporary Duty (TDY) orders, meaning that we could use them our entire tour instead of needing new orders each time we traveled somewhere, I quietly put my own name on the navigator side to go in for an undetermined period of time. The Squadron Commanding Officer (CO) was being so full of himself, as usual, that he would not know I was gone for a few weeks. He would then issue a call for me to get back to my job as (XO) even though my best friend, Bob, had everything under control with two more Lt Col's working with him. They were not as keen on going "in country" as I was. I really enjoyed the atmosphere in that southern Thai base and the folks that were flying. I felt more like I was earning my pay when I was flying, though the work was far more intense back at the squadron. My "assistants" were using that time at Clark AB to study various aspects of Squadron activities for their upcoming assignments to Air War College while on their way to being promoted to Full Colonel. All four of us were happy with this arrangement.

After alerting my two favorite pilots that I was going in also, we sent a message to the FOL commander to set us up as a team again. Being set up as a team insured we would be in the same trailer and would fly only with each other as an integrated crew which meant we would be back to our old tricks of flying as a team.

We would arrive at U Tapao after about a five and a half hour flight. I always utilized that flight time to rig my nylon net hammock in the ramp section of the aircraft to catch up on a little needed sleep, rocking to and fro with the sixty second sine wave (a smooth periodic oscillation) of the plane's natural flight profile. After landing, I immediately checked in with the FOL Commander. Everything was set. Since Pol Pot and his Khmer Rouge gang pretty much owned all of Cambodia except for a little area around the Capital City of Phnom Penh and the coastal area near the city of Sihanoukville, that was just about the only flying that was being done. It was so slow that it would be a week before our first flight so we took advantage of the time off. We went to some islands just out of sight of Pattaya Beach which was building up for the anticipated increase of tourists from Europe. I had never been there, but one of the islands was reputed to have the best seafood in the area. So, we rented a boat and proceeded to check out the rumor. After hours of stuffing ourselves on all types of shellfish and other seafood which we washed down with a few Thai beers, we were convinced. This was the place. The warm water lobster was absolutely the best! We took this time of being too satisfied with that island cuisine to lay around and take a practice nap again. I practice a lot! We all slept some as the skipper took us back to Pattaya in a following sea.

We finally got the call that we would be taking a load of something into Phnom Penh the next day. We rarely knew what we were carrying. We just knew there was something in the cargo hold that weighed "X" number of pounds. All the navigator ever knew, or even needed to know, was where we were going and the Command Post made that easy. They had our flight plan and the weather already planned for us. Pretty easy going. We always received a briefing on the destination and weather, but our primary mission was to fly the stuff to wherever they wanted. I have no idea what we were taking into the Capital City. We just knew we had a 0900 hours "go" time. We were supposed to take off within a three minute window on either side of the "go" time, which was almost always easy to make. And, so it was with this flight. It would be a milk run that would take about eight hours round trip which would make for an easy day. We liked this kind except for a few trips around the Thai bases which were beginning to deactivate. They were closing most, if not all of them, because the fighting in Vietnam was through and it was sad to see them closing after so many very active years. But, it meant no more lost lives. This was all that was left. A sad chapter for our government and a proud few years for our fighting men!

We were airborne on time and in about three hours, we were coming into Phnom Penh. It was not an easy mission anymore. The Khmer Rouge owned the countryside and now had Russian made "Strella" shoulder fired surface to air missiles. We had to be careful. The Strella's capability was ten thousand feet, a considerable distance for a shoulder fired rocket, so we had to come in and then spiral down to the runway in a tight pattern directly over the airstrips so we wouldn't stray out over the airport parameters. As added "protection," we put a crewmember, usually a spare navigator or loadmaster who was tied in, but standing in the open doorway of the cargo compartment looking for the tell-tale corkscrew smoke pattern of the Strella. If one was spotted, the individual so designated was supposed to fire a Very (flare) pistol at the incoming rocket. The flare burned hotter than the C-130 engine exhaust so the Strella was supposed to change targets and go chase after the hotter flare. I was never certain if the Strella was briefed on that or understood it. It supposedly had a mind of its own. I never heard of this tactic being actually employed so I have no knowledge of its effectiveness.

Some of the newer model planes coming in had a rudimentary rack of flares that could be shot out to intercept the incoming rocket with a barrage of three or four flares. That guy hanging out of the cargo door didn't really make me feel much safer.

Fortunately, I never did have the "honor" of hanging out of the cargo door looking for incoming trouble. I enjoyed the relative comfort and safety of my navigator station in the crew compartment. Our idea was just to get on the ground as soon as possible. Not that it was that much safer on the ground.

There were occasions when the bad guys would start lobbing mortars as soon as the C-130 was parked. I was told of one incident where they just "walked" a barrage of mortars one at a time, getting closer with each one until they dropped two on the aircraft, one in the cockpit and another about half-way down the fuselage. They dropped a third one directly between the first two on the center of the wing, rupturing the fuel tanks. That one blew up everything and started a conflagration, which basically consumed the entire plane except for the tail section, which remained upright and defiant. It was still standing straight and proper in all of its olive drab beauty after the flames cooled. I understand that the crew had seen the explosions getting closer to them. They had no time to start the engines and taxi out of harm's way so they just got out of the aircraft and started running for the safety of the terminal. They got there in time to see the plane get hit and burst into flames, burning the plane and the few personal belongings they had on board. They ran to another C-130 which was getting ready to taxi out for takeoff. That crew spotted them, and took them on board for the ride back to home base. A tired, but excited crew was soon spiraling upward to the safety of 10,000 feet. They were not too worried about their stuff. They had their lives and that was good enough for now.

We were now over what used to be Phnom Penh International Airport, one of only three International airports in the entire country. At this point, it was pretty much limited to military flights, though there were a few commercial missions still being flown. Now, for the normal downward spiral to deliver whatever cargo we had onboard. We had no problem getting down and we were brave fellows, but just for the hell of it, we left the plane for the locals to unload while we sauntered to the relative safety of the terminal. I got a little bored sitting around watching nothing, so the entire crew opted to go around behind the rather small terminal to see what was happening there. Nothing! Nothing except a few locals who were selling some trinkets. I spotted one guy trying to sell four-faced statues that he claimed he had stripped from the temples in the countryside in order to barter for something to eat or whatever he could get. I bought a couple of soapstone statues, one for each of my four daughters, when I saw a larger one that really caught my eye. It had a greenish white look to it. I asked him about it and though I had given him a dollar for the small ones, he wanted more for this one. I haggled with him. I don't remember his going price, but it was ten to twenty bucks. I hefted it up and quickly offered him thirty US dollars. That amount would be enough to last him a nice period of time on the local economy. That was some bargaining, huh? He wanted twenty bucks. Hell, I didn't want no cheap-assed statue so I gave him thirty. Now I had a more expensive statue. Nope, I can't figure out the logic in that one either, but it was typical of my bargaining prowess! Actually, I felt sorry for these folks and wanted to give him a fair price for what I thought was a nice statue. It was.

Years later, long after my retirement, I ran into a little bit of a hard stretch and I needed some dollars to get me by. When I couldn't get it anywhere else, my mind and eyes turned to that little statue. Perhaps, now I would be rewarded for taking it out of harm's way. I finally had it appraised and arranged for an auction house to put it up to bid for me. Highest bidder, come on! It wouldn't be much if it even sold, but anything would help. Then I remembered what a Thai friend told me about it. He said it was an old statue from Cambodia, Thailand's next door neighbor. Hell, I already knew that! He said that they carried a curse. He wouldn't even touch it and wanted me to take it away. I complied. I was going to sell it anyway. I was going to take it to an auction house to get what few bucks I could. I should have listened to my Thai friend. He had told me I probably shouldn't. It really carried a curse!

The following things happened to me in about a seven-day period of time and I found out how quickly life could fall apart. First, starting in May 2008, we lost our Arizona home to foreclosure. The market had just plain old crashed right in front of us. Orders for our company almost quit coming in. I had a mini-stroke (TIA) and I was hospitalized for a few days. Following that, I had an aneurysm which landed be back in the hospital for a stent in the upper colon and a few days more rest, which I didn't need! I did enjoy watching them, on color TV, inserting that stent. I was amazed at how colorful it is in there. Adding to the first two health scares and having to move a complete household back to Colorado, my automobile showed signs of immediately blowing a head gasket! That required me to purchase a new automobile (three year old 2005 Cadillac) which I am still driving today. There were two other happenings of lesser magnitudes, but still with negative consequences. However, I can't recall what they were now, but at the time, they were meaningful!

I got the message loud and clear. That four-face statue was cursed and mine, and it was to remain in my possession whether I wanted it or not. I decided pretty quickly that I wanted it and will keep it. I'm certain that another person possessing that statue would, in turn, become cuursed. I have put it away and am doing fine now!

HANOI, ONE WEEK LATER – PART II

"More of Same. Propaganda is Still Propaganda"

On my second trip into the capitol of North Vietnam, the same tricks were tried to get us confused. Damn, these boys were good. If you paid attention to them, they could easily get you off track, and the river was the only source of distinctive radar returns but they had to be considered very carefully. Several bridges, small harbors and sand bars in the Red River could throw an inexperienced navigator off and get him confused. If I had not had that radar training which I hated, it would have been much more difficult for me to keep track of our position. I continue to be amazed at how many times that training has come in handy and how much I hated going through the school. As it was, using triangulation of various radar returns, or targets, I could discard and add according to their worth. I settled on the ones I had decided on during my first run up the River. The Paul Doumer Bridge and the permanent sand bar were by far the best for close in maneuvering. They could put you in exactly the right position. For the larger perspective, just the river and Haiphong Harbor were excellent returns. The river itself has many distinctive turns. It almost has its own personality, with a bridge at a curve down river from my main aiming points. Very radar friendly for the trained eye.

After successfully negotiating our way to the airfield by radar navigation, we landed and the same procedure was followed. More close up photos. Now, I'm on their wall of fame twice!

We once again took the same routing to the same downtown hotel. (I wondered: Just how many did they have?) Again, as on the previous mission, they had a feast of many courses for us which we devoured while they spouted their propaganda. Our hosts were the same soldiers as last week. Damn, had it only been a week? Yep! It was probably fortunate that we were forbidden to argue with them. I just drank their beer and nodded. Although we had the same escorts, all the crew members except me were fresh meat. My "guide" didn't bother me very much. He knew I was either too dumb or else too smart for him to get any information of worth. I'll let him worry about that. We were courteous, but instead of trying to converse in different languages, we simply ignored them as best we could. Again, they showed us the Life magazine cover and they continued to put forward the same words. They still identified Angela Davis as Jane Fonda. This was typical of their propaganda. Same stuff over and over.

This time they took us to their Peace Museum. An absolutely beautiful edifice both inside and out. Absolutely stunning! More than many HUGE white jade figures were on prominent display. It was, and I assume still is, a beautiful, even gorgeous museum! Of course, the largest white jade statue of all was that of Ho Chi Minn. Bigger than life! One which would rival that is that one of a peacock. There may be a photo of me with it to show the size, way larger than me. There were many others. Now, I am just assuming the statues were white jade. I am not an expert of statuary nor rocks, so I wouldn't swear to it. I understand that there are two types of jade and I discovered that the most desired green jade comes from Burma, now Myanmar, on the Thai western border. Again, I know not if they are jade, but still I marvel and wonder at the size and beauty of these statues and carvings.

For the most part, again, we were not allowed to take photos. They did allow us to take photos in certain areas of Hanoi such as the War and Peace Museums and the downtown areas. They would not let us take pictures of the rail marshalling yard, which was full of bomb craters and wrecked train engines, same as before, nor any part of the airport. I got some of both anyway with my little Minox spy camera. This time, they told us that the rail marshalling yard was their engine repair facility. We all laughed, which seemed to upset them more than a little bit. There was no sign of bomb damage to any of the buildings bordering the train mess nor any of the earthen banks of the surrounding dikes.

The flight back to U Tapao was same ol' same ol'.

CAMBODIA TRILOGY—PART III
SIHANOUKVILLE

"One Barrel of Oil? Ya gotta be Shitting Me!"

The boss was an excellent FOL Commander. He was all business, but in a friendly way. Our crew was a little unusual for this job being comprised of a Captain, a Second Lieutenant and an "old" Major. I was the "old" Major which referred not only to my time in the Air Force, but my actual age. I had served flying as an enlisted crewmember for over six years, but I knew Airborne Radar Approaches from an advanced Navigation School. Now, this was 1974, I was thirty-nine years old and had completed nearly twenty years in the Air Force. And now I was here in Southern Thailand in early 1974. Our FOL was right outside the little city of Sattahip. There was another town in the other direction with even more great restaurants. You could find fun and adventure in either. There were many eating and drinking establishments. Once again, "Shoot Pool Restaurant" seemed to be the theme. In addition, there were enough haircut, hot bath and massage parlors for anyone. Some of the missions we flew were easy missions, but the FOL Commander seemed to have us pegged as a crew he could depend on for most anything, especially on short notice. We worked hard, drank hard and flew hard, and we had fun doing any of them. We enjoyed each other's company while flying, eating or drinking at the Officers Club bar or downtown. Cabs were really cheap. Tell them what sounded like, "Lao Lao" (Hurry), and they would deliver you in a short time and even stay waiting for you all night if you would so choose.

I guess I taught my two young pilots to drink martinis as I had others. One of my greatest achievements was also teaching them how to drink Beefeaters on the rocks with a couple olives! But, I also taught them not to over-do it. They were a quick study and before my tour was over, they could hang with me pretty well!

We were kind of a strange looking crew because we had one of the youngest and one of the oldest crew members at the FOL. It really looked as if I was their father! We purposely became friends with the FOL Commander by offering to take any missions at any time for him. We liked to be in the air! It was a matter of avoiding the boredom when you weren't flying. In return, my pilots and I were assigned a few "plum" trips which were sometimes called "milk runs." Some actually were, others not so much. One of our rewards was that trip transporting the United Nations Peace Negotiators to Hanoi, North Vietnam. In reality, it was not really too much of a "plum" though the destination itself was intriguing. It would also be up to a twenty-four hour crew day with an augment crew. The augment crew meant we had an extra pilot, engineer and navigator. It was still a real day killer, or killer day.

As I said, we flew some easy missions but the FOL Commander knew damned good and well that he could depend on for most anything, even the worst.

On one of my last "adventures in country," we flew one barrel of oil to Sihanoukville Airport right on the tip of a peninsula. Yep, just one barrel. The FOL CO knew we could have poor weather most anytime, which means fairly well covered with clouds and perhaps some fog since it was so close to the sea. It was defined as clouds if above fifty feet, but if it was less than fifty feet, it was officially fog. This was considered an essential (highest classification) mission because the Cambodian military air fleet was grounded and couldn't pound the Khmer Rouge with their T-6's and A-1's without oil for their engines. Who did he choose? "Hey guys," he said jokingly, "I have a tough mission here that you don't have to take. No prejudice if you turn it down. It's just that it is essential that we get that oil to the Cambodian Air Force down south. Your plane is ready, but you'll have to go north of here to Ubon Royal Thai Air Force Base (RTAFB) to pick up the oil. However, first you will have to drop off some "stuff" at Nakhon Phnom Royal Thai Navy Base (RTNB). The cockpit crew rarely knew what we were carrying on our aircraft. The weather is good in northern Thailand, but not too hot at Sihanoukville and surrounding areas. In fact, it could be pretty bad when you get there, so don't take any chances. I thought, "Yeah, right! That sucker knows I can do airborne radar approaches and he also knows that we're crazy enough to take it below minimums if necessary." He knew us! Especially if it was an essential mission, we would find a way to complete it somehow, even if we had to loiter! Though we had a late night, this was pretty early and we weren't at our best, the Aircraft Commander said, "Sure." He made it sound like we really wanted it and with as much enthusiasm as he could muster. The conversation was on the phone so, fortunately, the Boss couldn't see us. As this was our scheduled day off, we would have rather lain around in our bunks for a little longer. But duty, and the boss, called and we took pride in always responding to that call even though sometimes, it hurt!

We trundled off to Base Ops for flight planning and a weather brief. The boss must have already spoken to them because they gave us basically the same thing only in "weathermanese." Good up north, potential for not so much down south. After our briefings, we motored out to our wonderful flying machine and took off for Nakhon Phnom RTNB and Muang Ubon in eastern Thailand. We were going to be "punching holes in the sky" in our aerospace machine for what seemed to be a stupid mission. But, the boss said it was essential and he trusted us. We weren't going to let him down! Sure as hell, the weather man was right! Both bases in Thailand were "hot, dry and dusty," but when we reached our final destination in deep southern Cambodia it was less than desirable. We were sort of anticipating this weather and had discussed it along the way. First, the airfield was a decrepit piece of dung.

They had no Ground Control Approach (GCA), no Instrument Landing System (ILS) or any other kind of landing aids. For a place named after King Sihanouk, it had shitty or no facilities. I'd bet they had some of these systems and either didn't want to bring them on line for only one aircraft or, more likely, they were broken. Well, that left only one way and that was the Airborne Radar Approach! I wasn't really sure if our radar scope was centered or not, but these radars were much more reliable than the old APS-42 in the C-124's and I had not found one very much off center yet. I had done OK with the APS-42, but only once in weather this bad. Another negative factor was that hill about five hundred feet tall just off the right side of the runway. No problem with a seven-hundred foot ceiling, but not too good on a day like this. The C-130 is a rugged airplane and can cut through the clouds and fog real well, but it couldn't really drill holes through rocks. One mistake here and it could ruin our whole day! I heard, "Hey, nav, what do you think? Ready for a little adventure?" I replied, "I've already had about enough excitement for one lifetime, but we're here so let's go down and take a look." I was a little concerned about that hillside to the right, but I could keep it on radar. I just didn't want to get too close and clip a wing. Damn, according to the letdown plate, that hill was really close to the approach. I don't want anything but a straight in-approach. The angular approaches just bring in too many unknown factors and decisions have to be made way too fast. But, it's still the hundred and fifty foot towers off to the left that I couldn't see on radar that really concerned me. I hoped they were marked true on this "let down" plate which is a chart drawn showing runway heading and elevations and locations of all obstacles in proximity to the airport. However, the plates had been known to be way off in this part of the world. I hoped the towers weren't any taller and they kept me from going very far to the left and away from that mountain. I've seen fifteen hundred foot towers down in this area, so I wasn't about to mess with them. The hill I could see on radar. The towers? No! I told the pilots and engineer, "I'll bet I know why no GCA nor ILS today. I'd almost bet this is a Visual Flight Rules (VFR) approach only landing strip, though it didn't indicate that in the Notes to Airmen (NOTEMS) at U Tapao or on the letdown plates. To hell with it. We're here to do a job, let's try at least one pass." Our intrepid commander said, "Let's take a chance, Columbus did!" "Yeah," I replied, "but he ended up in prison, too." Then came the wise guy reply from the AC, "Well, if we get caught busting minimums today, we could end up there, too, so be careful" It always seemed that in flying, the more hazardous it got, the more smart-mouthed the intercom talk became and the sleepier I felt. "Yeah, but at least he didn't kill himself and the crew." I added. Strangely, whenever we approached a dangerous situation I always became sleepy. I did my job well, but It always seemed like I was getting sleepy. Nature has its own way of coping.

We had no idea of what the cloud ceiling was, so out to sea we ventured to make a radar approach from the South China Sea and find out. It got a little tense for a while when we didn't get out of the clouds. I gave the initial approach heading to the Aircraft Commander in the left seat and briefed them that I would be giving them the appropriate heading and whether they were drifting off course, and I would advise them if they were above or below the glide slope. I gave them optimal airspeed. A typical advisement from me to the AC would be something like this:

"AC, Nav. Current heading 033 for approach to Runway 03. 033 (degree heading), (True Air Speed) 164 knots, (elevation) 848 feet (AGL-Above Ground Level), glide slope 3 degrees, distance 5.3 (Nautical) miles."

Those items in parenthesis are not repeated, in fact, not even used at the start. The pilot acknowledges that the Navigator is in charge and only listens and doesn't respond to instructions unless he thinks something is amiss. So, the Navigator keeps up a fairly constant chant with pauses after a full set of instructions were completed.

None of us had ever been to Sihanoukville before, so we were all flying blind except I had my radar scope, and they had a small repeater up centered on the dashboard.

"Ok, Pilot, this is Nav. Starting Airborne Radar Approach. I'm going to try to bring us in a little on the left side of the runway because of that damned hill, so be ready to break a little right when we pop out of the soup. Take heading 065 to get to alignment for approach to runway 03. (Pause) OK, we are on alignment. Turn to heading 033, maintain 164-knots. Start three percent descent rate.

Adjust heading two degrees left. You are drifting a little bit. Speed 160, increase and maintain 164. Altitude 485, heading holding at 033. On course, on glide path, descent rate good. Descend to 300 feet then pick up same descent rate. Two miles from touchdown. Advise when you have visual on runway. Drifting right. Stay left if anything. We have a mountain on right. Take heading 020 degrees for five seconds, then back to 033. If you are going to drift, damn it, make sure you drift left. This plane is rugged, but it can't fly through mountains. Glide slope just a little high. Bring It down a little bit. Now one mile from runway. Maintain 300 ft altitude. That's minimum for IFR Approach. The flight engineer had a good view of the Repeater 'Scope on the dash. "That mountain is getting a little close, sir!" He said it quietly, but there was urgency in his voice. He was not a crew "regular." "Yeh, I noticed." Mountain about 200 yards to right. That's a little too close. "AC take a 10 degree "S" turn to the left. That should give us enough separation. Speed 145 knots. Over land now. Begin four degree descent. We are busting minimums. We're one-half mile from runway. Prepare for missed approach. Descend to 250 feet and if you can't see the runway, begin missed approach sequence on my word. On glide-slope, on heading, airspeed 148 knots. Everything looks good. Ok, if you can't see the runway in ten seconds, initiate missed approach procedure. New airspeed 143, descend a little more. You are still a little high. High and a little hot. OK now. We go around in five seconds, four, three..."

Suddenly, the pilot came on intercom, "Tally Ho! Runway in sight. We are just left of center line. Good job, nav, I got it." "Roger AC, you have the airplane. That was almost too close! 195 feet when we broke out." Our AC repeated my words, He also said, "We are a little high and hot. "No problem! Doing a Combat Short Field Landing Procedure." Engineer replies, "These boys will get their oil and I hope it is still in the barrel!" I had gotten up behind the copilot as I always did. I knew there would be a jolt, so I flexed my knees. I mainly wanted to see the excitement too! WHAM! We hit the runway and stayed planted. I just hung on standing behind the copilot. After a firm landing and with full reverse pitch, yoke full forward and heavy braking, we finally came to a stop nearly at the end of the runway. They had no overrun which we didn't know. I opined, "Shore glad we didn't need that overrun which doesn't exist. Plates say five hundred feet dirt overrun. Not there!" The Engineer came on and said, "Know what? I needed a little pucker time anyway." I said, "Just don't let anyone know." The engineer comes on and says, "Know what?" "Nice job Major. That took brass balls." "Thanks. You guys are the ones that had the brass gonads to let me take you down that low." Bull, shit. Nothing ventured, etc... I wasn't concerned about my two pilots saying anything. They never did. The flight engineer talked with the loadmaster. He was good with it since we made it OK and he really didn't know what was going on except for listening to the approach instructions. I didn't feel sleepy this time until after we had landed!

No one ever knew until this book that we busted minimums that day and really, by more feet than we should have. Added to that, I was standing behind the co-pilot for take-off and landing as I always did. I like the idea of another set of eyeballs looking out of the cockpit windows looking for potential trouble. Anyway, by now, who cares? What happens trying to get into Sihanoukville, stays, etc...

Hell, in reality, with no landing aids, we shouldn't even have come close to landing. We really should not have even tried. As a result of being stupid and always feeling bullet proof, we did it anyway! But they needed the oil!

On an Airborne Radar Approach, I have to watch about five parameters: Heading, Glide Slope, Altitude, Speed and Distance to touchdown. Altitude (feet above ground) and Heading are probably the most corrected variables. I can normally talk the aircraft clear down to touchdown. It is a good feeling when the results turn out well!

One fine day, during my annual check-ride, we were on final approach into U Tapao when I saw a little dot turning onto the active, runway. I called "AC, we have a B-52 that looks like he is going to enter our runway, but continue approach. He's moving. I called him entering, in the center of runway and then, over a slow minute later, almost clear of runway. Prepare for missed approach if he stops." I had been ready to call for a missed approach in a few seconds, but after the bomber cleared the active, I cleared the pilot to continue his landing approach. The Navigator Flight Examiner pulled back the curtain we used on check rides so the navigator couldn't use visuals to pass the ride. I was seated and with my head in the scope. He couldn't figure out how I called that plane crossing the runway. I said, "Well, shit, boss (he was a captain), with all that radar training in Nav/Bomb school, I could pick him out plain as day, that flat sided B-52 return on the scope was big enough not to be anything else. Even a KC-135 doesn't have much of a radar return. This one was just too big of a radar signature (return)." I called the final approach all the way to touchdown giving the pilot precise instructions. I passed the check ride!

Back at Sihanoukville, we had to wait around until they took that barrel of oil off of our plane and until the low cloud ceiling raised to take-off limits or at least a little higher than it is now. We didn't want to take any more chances. We sat around watching them put oil into their attack planes. A-1's were first because they can do the most damage. We watched them takeoff and disappear into the too low clouds. They would probably land at another Cambodian Air Base instead of trying to come back in here with this low ceiling. Judging from when the A-1's disappeared into the clouds, we guessed the ceiling was now almost two hundred and fifty feet.

At that point, we were getting bored just sitting around and decided we'd rather be sipping a cool one back in our trailer. We were going to crank engines to head back to U Tapao, but were informed that because of the bad weather, we had to wait until all of their aircraft had been recovered to base. The runway was closed to all traffic except the returning Cambodian fighter bombers. We had nothing to do back home anyway, so we grabbed our box lunches and sat under the wing shooting the bull, eating and just killing time until the strike planes returned. Soon we heard the rumble of the A-1 engine. It came in low and trailing a little smoke, but still did a Tactical Approach. This is an approach where the pilot takes his plane down the runway at about two hundred fifty feet high, does a 180 degree right turn, away from the mountain, to go down wind (with the wind) and come on around to land against the wind. There was virtually no wind, so they were going to land on runway fifteen, coming in from the north. Good move. The tower wouldn't switch landing directions for us when we requested them to do so. That way, we could have avoided the possibility of hitting that mountain. I wish they had, because that would have taken the mountain completely out of play. But then, we wouldn't have had all that fun!

Right after all their warplanes had been recovered and they had parked their planes in a row while waiting for more bombs to be installed, the Cambodian Flight Leader came over and thanked us for flying in under these conditions. They had just blunted an incursion and the next flight should stop it altogether. He said, "Thanks to you, we will be able to keep flying until our normal supply arrives. They can't cut off our supply lines now. Our ground forces are now in control, thanks to your oil and our bombs and machine guns." We all rose, he saluted his thanks and we saluted back our "you're welcomes." No words were necessary. Now, feeling even better about our mission, we prepared to return to base. We took off, knowing by now that the FOL CO would have another mission for us if we still had enough crew duty time.

Sure 'nuff, when we got back, he asked if we would take another short run. He told us, "I've extended your crew duty day so you have enough time." We responded with, "OK, Boss, take us to our mighty steed and we'll deliver whatever, wherever." We went to our C-130, but it didn't take long to find trouble. A hydraulic leak ended that mission as of right then.

We went back to FOL Operations to tell the boss. He was disappointed, but allowed as how it had already been a pretty long day, so he told us, "Take off before I find something else for you." "Well," I suggested, as was expected, "let us wander to The Club for a beer or two, take a shower and a practice nap and then go for some real toddy's and a steak to get ready to sally forth tomorrow. We still have time to hit The Club for Happy Hour before dinner." It was decided. The club it was. The three of us stayed in the same trailer so coordination was simple. Go or not go were the only options. With this Captain and 2nd Lieutenant under my sterling leadership, it was always "go!" I wish I could find them again. If you are out there, get in touch.

This was the last month of my tour, so I was getting close to flying my last mission here and the CO had given up keeping me at Clark. But tonight there was always the O' Club, martinis, hot red peanuts and my buddies!

After a few days, I was ordered to return to Clark AB. I figured the boss missed me again. However, and surprisingly, I would be ordered back to the FOL in a few days. I found that even more than "kinda" strange. I normally wasn't ordered to go to the FOL. My return this time was for a classified mission, which would remain unknown until we got to Saigon for a final briefing. We were also told to take our class "A" uniforms with us, which was very, very unusual. In fact, it was the first time I had ever heard about it happening. I assumed we would be evacuating embassy personnel out of Saigon or doing something with some VIPs, but, I didn't know, so I didn't worry about it. That was someone else's job. To aircrews, it would just be another mission among all the others. The crew would stay up front and the passengers would stay in back as normal. But, for all practical purposes, that would be my last action on this remote tour to Southeast Asia.

RECOVERY OF POW'S WHO DIED IN CAPTIVITY IN NORTH VIETNAM PRISONS

"They had Touched our Heroes for the Last Time"

This was by far, the most emotional mission of which I was honored to take part during my rather exciting and unique Air Force Career.

Many folks believe that the first of our Heroes who Died In Captivity (DIC) were recovered by bright shiny C-141's as were the living POWs recovered eleven months earlier. Not so!! I felt honored to be chosen to be the lead navigator on the (Pathfinder) Olive Drab C-130E, which went up to Hanoi, North Vietnam on March 6th, 1974 to recover those gallant men. The second (Recovery) C-130E, also Olive Drab, would bring the remains of our Heroes home. I disagree with the official record of the names (not call signs) of our two C-130s. Ours were the names given to the crew that early morning and, in my mind at least, better describes each aircraft mission. That is one of several disagreements I have with the official record. That record was probably written by a clerk in the 374th Tactical Airlift Wing at Clark AB in the Philippines, or even at PACAF. Bear in mind that this mission occurred in the skies over Thailand, South and North Vietnam and the waters about 30 miles off-shore of South and North Vietnam as well as on the ground in Saigon and Gia Lam. He (or she) was sitting at a desk at the 374th while I was flying the mission. I'll stick with my version.

I was there!

Having volunteered to take any mission any time for him, The FOL Commander kind of looked upon our crew with favor. He used us often on non-fragged missions, and as a result, we became friends with him. No, I do not know what "fragged" means. However, it is not "to kill your superior officer with a hand grenade." (That was the Army definition). To us, it was just a term used to describe a scheduled mission. Some of our more interesting, and sometime most dangerous, missions came about because of our reliability, no matter if hung over or not. I was lucky. I have never had a hangover no matter how much I drank. No headache either. Some wags say that is because, medically, where there's no sense there's no feeling. Can't argue.

As stated before, although unaware of the reason, right after I returned home to Clark AB, I was ordered to proceed TDY back to U Tapao. Not only was I given short notice, I was also instructed to take my Class A dress uniform. I thought that strange, but I said, "Yes Sir" and proceeded. Neither of my Pilot buddies were coming in with me. "Well hell, that'll be no fun!" I forgot my uniform shoes. I had to borrow some.

Ironically, recently while looking for more material on this trip, I found two letters I had written to my wife. Both on the way home from a Hanoi trip. Strangely, they were from the previous two Wednesdays, the dates of the Peace Negotiators meetings. I can't say that The FOL Commander set this up so I would get familiar with the trip and the extracurricular harassment the North Vietnam Traffic Control and Tower gave us, but if I had to guess?????

The Mission

It was very early morning, 6 March 1974, when we left U Tapao RTAB for Tan Son Nhut AB, to get our final briefing on this flight. That's when we found out the true nature of our mission. The briefer somberly told us, "You have been selected for a very special mission. You are going to go into Hanoi and pick up the first remains of our Heroes who Died (were murdered, I thought) in Captivity (DICs)." Naturally, we all got excited and were fully "Gung Ho" for the mission, but we sobered a bit when we got the weather briefing. Though barely manageable, the weather in the Hanoi area was forecast to be pretty bad for our arrival time. We gave no thought to scrubbing the mission. Scrubbing (cancelling) because of weather would have been not only unthinkable and even unforgiveable, it would have caused an international incident. North Vietnam had finally agreed to release the remains of some of our fallen Heroes, and if we had not recovered them, it would have probably stopped all negotiations. It was clearly obvious to everyone that *this* was a very important mission.

We topped off our fuel as usual in case we had to loiter up north until we could get sufficiently good weather for at least an airborne radar approach.

Having gone through that damnable Nav/Bomb school, by habit I had picked out several radar returns on my previous missions, which I would use to keep me on track and to establish the correct position to change to runway heading instead of trusting those treacherous bastards in the Hanoi Approach Control and Hanoi Tower.

That was another reason that I was selected. The boss knew I had gone through Navigator Bombardier School. They schooled me long and hard in the art of radar navigation. In fact, I had also made several low visibility airborne radar approaches throughout Southeast Asia and Wake Island with excellent results. I also liked to do simulated approaches to many airfields. Because of the forecast bad weather, I wondered if they would try to confuse us even more on this trip than they did on my earlier trips. That was probably why they directed that I be the lead Navigator from the time we approached the Vietnam coast, I would be the navigator with the second Navigator on this augmented crew backing me up on whatever I needed. I had to be and was prepared. Another reason I was chosen to be the lead Navigator was simple. I was one of only a few crewmembers, if not the only one, on either crew to have been to Gia Lam Airport. I couldn't then and still can't figure that one out. I had already been to Gia Lam twice, the two Wednesdays prior to this run. Now do you think I was being set up? I still don't know, but it is almost obvious. I'm just glad I was chosen to be there. I wanted to get those Guys out of there!

By 0800 we had received our "Treatment of the North Vietnamese Troops" briefing. This one was different. We weren't going to have to be nice! They had loaded everyone who was going along for this little ride. That included: Our mission commander, Col Albert Navas, the Vice Wing Commander of the 374th Tactical Airlift Wing, at Clark AB who owned the 776th TAS of which were a part. Army Brigadier General Joseph Ulatowski, Commander, Joint Casualty Resolution Center, was on board our aircraft with an open line to the White House and with direct access to President Nixon. Obviously, it was a very high priority mission. An official Air Force photographer was also on board our plane. The General kept our President updated as we proceeded on our mission.

The mission north was completely routine, keeping within the five mile wide corridor thirty miles off shore. We were cruising at twenty-four thousand feet, our assigned altitude. When we hit the point in our corridor that we were heading for the coast, they shook me out of a fitful sleep. I was ready to take over in minutes. We were about fifteen minutes from the main mouth of the Red River. Showtime for everybody! I double checked Haiphong Harbor to make sure. Yep! About forty miles to the northeast.

Good Lord! Look at those clouds. They must to up to twenty thousand feet or more, but they were not solid. There were plenty holes between the clouds that we could wiggle through at first, but we needed to stick within a few miles of the crooked Red River. I hope that there were no imbedded thunderstorms in there, but the tops looked fairly stable, and they look broken and layered. They should be alright. We hit the North Vietnam coast and the weather at about the same time. Damn! It turned dark in a hurry! We had been descending and were penetrating the coastline at ten thousand feet, the agreed upon altitude. I tried to brief the crew on the spoofing that I was sure would come, but they seemed bored. I don't know if any of these folks have ever experienced that action.

It was any one's guess as to whether the spoofing would be worse or not at all. I would think the former. They kind of blew it off as a "no sweat" thing. I hoped they would be right. Damn, I wish I had my regular crew. They would know about the spoofing without my telling them again.

We contacted approach control and requested unrestricted descent to fifteen hundred feet. They told us that we could begin descent at Thuan Ngheip which was the point that the river straightened and headed straight upstream to Hanoi. They told us to take up a heading that I felt would take us slowly off track to the south, trying to get us to overfly Hanoi. After having fooled around with these guys twice before, I trusted them with nothing. I told the pilots over the intercom to go ahead and take up that heading when we crossed our turn point, but to gently turn back right until I told them to straighten out again. We can play the spoofing game too! "You flat don't trust those people, do you nav?" the Aircraft Commander challenged. My response was: I don't know if you have been up here before, but if you haven't, you'll soon see why I do not trust them one iota." "Why not? They have to give you correct headings like everywhere else." I just told him this was a different world up here and begin watching for the needles of their instruments to start quivering. That will mean they are changing locations of ADF or other stations. "They can't do that!" Newbie, I thought. "Just watch your instruments and follow my instructions. It appears that they have already moved the ADF slightly to the south to get us to head toward Hanoi. We'll discuss it later. Just watch it." By now, the weather had really deteriorated. We were getting to the critical area and I began to think that this mission was so important that they weren't going to try to spoof us. Just about then, the same Pilot mentioned that the Pilots' Direction Indicator (PDI) had drifted off a little bit so he was going to adjust course. "Negative, Negative, maintain heading!" They just spoofed us and they did it very well! "But," the pilot started. I said loudly, "Maintain Heading!" He replied, "Aye Aye, Major, sir." We were farther out when they started this time. By now we were down to the fifteen hundred feet we requested and we told them we were leveling but request one thousand feet immediately. "Negative, maintain previous altitude" was their response. They sounded like they would play hardball. Well shit! Just what we needed! Then came the first heading change. "Pathfinder one, turn to heading 022 for final approach to Gia Lam Airport. The young pilot started to make the turn. "NEGATIVE, NEGATIVE, NEGATIVE! MAINTAIN HEADING!" Yep, they were starting early. I gently, but firmly, told the Pilots we were about forty miles out.

From my previous trips, I knew we were still about 30 to 45 miles out and they were doing their best to get us off course and lost in that bad weather with low ceilings and limited visibility. They wanted to get us into an area with which we were not familiar, and as importantly out of our prescribed corridor. The weather was rapidly worsening. The cloud cover was now full instead of the previous broken layers. I would get a quick positive visual when we would get a break in the undercast every couple miles or so. We descended to less than 1000 feet, which helped a little bit. Approach control came back on. Turn to heading 022 as directed and climb back to assigned altitude of fifteen hundred feet. I quickly said, "Do not respond." He didn't. Nothing for about five minutes. We had lowered our altitude to eight hundred feet and I could see the river through infrequent breaks in the clouds. No problem, I had it on radar too. They contacted us again, "Turn to heading 022 for final heading to runway zero two. Maintain one thousand feet." Again, the pilot started to turn. Again, my shouted admonition to maintain heading. Col Navas broke in and told the pilot to follow my instructions only. Next time they come on with their instructions, tell them that they are coming in garbled and we would follow previously stated instructions. It was good that Col Navas directed the pilots because now, Hanoi Tower identified themselves and directed a turn to 022 degrees. This time, it was Col Navas who responded that they were coming in garbled and we would follow previous instructions.

Now, do you remember that Damned Bridge (the Paul Doum-er bridge)? I used that bridge as my pre–I P (pre-initial point) to provide an aiming point to the real turn to final. We lost a lot of Thuds (F-105's) and Phantoms (F-4's) there. Now, I was glad they failed to destroy it!

That bridge, and the Long Bien Bridge just beyond, a smaller re-turn but great for verification, and a huge sandbar about five miles downstream or two minutes from my turn point, were perfect ra-dar returns. Cruising in at about one hundred and eighty knots, they were my aiming points to tell me when to start our turn to final ap-proach to Gia Lam Airport. I was getting a little concerned when they weren't coming into view as fast as I thought they should. I guess I was just overly anxious. I checked radar and found both about 15 miles ahead. I alerted the pilot to be ready to turn in about six min-utes and he relayed to #2 aircraft to be ready to follow us on our approach. They had been hanging on tight with their station keeping radar. Because of the heavy cloud cover, they had not had a visual on us for well over ten minutes.

Hanoi Approach Control had given up trying to get us to turn early, but only after many loud and probably profane ass chew-ing's from them. They complained that we were ignoring their instructions. And so we were! We repeated that they were coming in garbled and that we would continue as previously instructed. Because we couldn't trust the Approach Control people at all, we were now and have been flying VFR (Visual Flight Rules) in IFR (Instrument Flight Rules) conditions, but I had a handle on it with radar, so things were OK. In fact, we had been navigating only by radar since we hit the coast. We descended a little farther so I could try to get a visual on both the sandbar and the bridges, though I didn't need to. No good anyway. Nothing but clouds. We were strictly in the soup. I was ready to bust minimums again. In fact I had already cleared with the Mission Commander that we should go to zero, zero (clouds to ground) in order to get on the runway. I assured him that I could do it. He knew that was the reason I was here. We Were Going to Get Our Heroes on This Trip — come hell, high water or fog! We were radar approach only. I told the pilot to start descending at standard rate and prepare for turn to heading 022 in two minutes. I knew exactly, from my previous trips, where we would make our turn to final approach. "Relay to number two ship also, please." We flew about five seconds past the sandbar, and with the Paul Doumer bridge on radar, I told the Aircraft Commander to turn to the appropriate heading of 022 degrees, and this time he could turn! Decent was begun and both planes broke completely out of the overcast at a little below four hundred feet. (I agree with official records here) There it was. Gia Lam runway, elevation fifty feet, about one and a half miles ahead. Perfect! The runway was right in front of us, dead center. I strapped myself in and, with a sigh of relief I exhaled and quietly said: "Pilot, you got it from here!" "Roger that nav, good work." The other Recovery C-130 radioed a "Tally Ho," so we knew everything was fine. Or, so we thought. Should have known better!

After we landed, Ground Control took over and directed us toward the proper area to pick up the remains of our Heroes. For the first time, we saw where our Guys were patiently waiting for us. There were two olive drab tents standing in a remote area on the ramp, far away from any building. Many North Vietnamese soldiers were guarding them. After landing and rollout, we taxied to the proper ramp where the Ground Marshalling Crew took over from the tower and directed us toward the tents. They were having us come in and turn us in a manner that the prop wash from our engines would flow directly on the tents, probably blowing them away. Our Aircraft Commander quickly recognized what they were doing and called for a neutral (zero pitch) prop setting and warned the second aircraft to do likewise. Both planes coasted to a nice easy stop, in their right spots without causing so much as a ripple in the tents, I'm sure to the disappointment of the marshalling crew.

After surveying the situation Col Navas immediately made the decision to set up an Honor Guard in front of each tent. By this time, we had changed into our class A uniforms and were not under orders to associate or socialize with our "hosts." We all felt good about that!! I felt even better because I had to put up with their bull crap two times which was two times too many. Col Novas decided that two men at a time would stand at Parade Rest for fifteen minute intervals in front of each tent. The order was forwarded to the other aircraft so four U. S. Air Force Officers departed two aircraft in unison and assumed Honor Guard status in front of both tents at precisely the same time. I was watching from the cockpit windows. Colonel Navas and our senior navigator were the lead men on our tent. I did not know the other men. The North Vietnamese were standing fairly close to the tents. They were taken aback when four of our uniformed men marched straight at them with no sign of hesitation wearing some real serious faces. I could tell that the soldiers were getting nervous, and weren't sure what was happening with these unsmiling men they were staring at for the first time in full dress uniform and not in the friendly civilian garb they were used to seeing. By voluntarily moving back, the North Vietnamese gave our crewmen room to do facing movements and take up their positions, first at attention and then with a whispered command to Parade Rest. Two things stuck in my mind. The amazement and commotion caused among the North Vietnamese by this display of honor for the deceased that was being carried out by crew members in dress uniforms. The second thing was the completely shocked looks on the faces of Col Navas and Major Schofiield. I would be in the next duo to relieve the first two in fifteen minutes. They would not have the opportunity to tell us what to expect. I wished they had. We knew it would be bad, so we steeled ourselves before we took our turn. All crewmembers, commissioned and non-commissioned, took turns for the honor of standing facing our Heroes, silent in those tents.

The tent flaps were tied wide open. What the first set of Honor Guards, and ultimately all of us saw, came as a complete shock. Much to our dismay, we saw a couple stacks of small green boxes. Each was accompanied by a rock. Each rock had a white painted name and date. The name of the prisoner and the date of his death!

The sight hit us like a slap in the face. The boxes, which in reality were the coffins of our deceased Heroes, measured about thirty by eighteen by eighteen inches. Think about it. One of our Heroes remains was in each of these little boxes. It tore us up to think that our fallen comrades, who had suffered so much, were in those tiny green boxes. The little green boxes were long enough to fit a femur fairly well with about four inches to spare, and they were long enough that a human spine would also fit; *Without Their Head!!* We were beyond shocked, we were pissed and couldn't do a thing about it! Unfortunately, I do not remember any of the names. I tried to commit at least one to memory, but my mind was so conflicted over this that I couldn't remember after I returned to the plane to await another turn. I guess my mind would not accept the shock.

The Honor Guard rotation was maintained for well over two hot hours while the final release papers were being signed at the government offices in downtown Hanoi. It was obvious that the North Vietnamese didn't know what to think of the Honor Guard. We saw the North Vietnamese soldiers who had been our escorts on earlier trips. They smiled and waved at us. We stared blankly back at them. Some civilians tried to get close to watch, but they were chased back over the dikes by armed guards. It was hot! My interrogator "Friend" worked his way forward to smile and wave at me. I glared back at him.

After a ten minute formal ceremony to complete the paper transfer of the remains, we were ready to begin the real transfer. We were finally given the okay to board our precious cargo onto the Recovery C-130E. With cargo ramps open, the silent aircraft sat waiting for the most precious cargo it would ever hold! The word came that we could begin returning our Heroes to American soil, in this case, our Recovery C-130E. The North Vietnamese moved in to begin loading our Heroes, their deceased captives. Their MURDERED captives. We immediately formed a cordon around the tents and though unarmed, we shook our heads in a negative way and motioned with hands for them to stop. We basically dared the armed North Vietnam troops to try us. They stopped with a puzzled look on their faces, but never tried to cross the line.

They had touched our Heroes for the last time.

It was now late afternoon and after a short transfer of remains ceremony, making it official, General Ulatowski joined in setting up a new Honor Guard on both sides of the ramp leading into the cargo bay of the aircraft. I was part of three pair of crewmen from the planes who tenderly picked up a little green "coffin" followed by another crewmember with the "headstone," and proceeded, one of us walking up each ramp, keeping the green, box coffins level. Two more crewmen were inside the plane to take our "coffins" and place them in an appropriately sized coffin. They secured the now sacred box in the coffin and draped an American flag over each one. We exited through the front crew entrance door to retrieve another Hero.

With General Ulatowski on one side and Col Navas on the other, the remaining crewmembers formed an honor guard. The general called for a Hand Salute as each box of remains passed on board. We only recovered twelve bodies, the number had been negotiated with the North Vietnamese. We took our time to insure that all of our fallen Heroes were properly cared for. It took a considerable amount of time, but we didn't care. As their former captors looked on in puzzled amazement, we felt reassured knowing that each former POW was honored by what we were doing. After our final Hero had been boarded, properly secured and draped, we finally began preparations to take our Fallen Heroes home.

As we were getting all four engines turning, the Aircraft Commander contacted the Gia Lam Control Tower to get instructions to proceed to the runway for takeoff. The Ground Marshals were still in charge and gave us the signal to start rolling. As they motioned for us to turn, we each started to smile. Unknowingly, the Ground Marshals had turned us in such a way that our prop wash would soon be aimed directly at the now empty olive drab tents. We listened on a discreet frequency while our Aircraft Commander contacted the second ship and pointed out the obvious. You could hear the joy in the response.

Both planes turned as one, and as they aligned with the tents, a short burst of full forward pitch was applied. While we continued our turn, we saw the now empty, useless tents, impressive officer hats and a few of the smaller former guardians of our Fallen Comrades flying and/or rolling across the Gia Lam tarmac, A fitting end to our visit. We had done that one thing in an act of revenge for our Guys to show the "American Wave" to their former captors. They had attempted to get us to blow the tents away with our prop wash earlier, and now we had complied with a few seconds of full forward pitch. Things went flying!

Now, the "Recovery" C-130E would leave first. We would remain short of the runway, to make sure they got off the ground OK and were well on their way back to U Tapao AB. After about twenty five minutes or so, we received the word from the Recovery C-130 that everything was in the green, that they had passed the coast and we could proceed. Receiving clearance from the tower, we taxied into position.

As we started our own takeoff roll down Gia Lam Runway 02 and began our turning right hand climb, I knew, with a little nostalgia, that this would be my last time to roll down that runway. I was leaving Hanoi for the last time, going DOWN the Red River this time. Continuing our climb in the right turn, to return to Saigon and eventually U Tapao AB staying behind the evacuation aircraft which was taking our now Silent Patriots home, I still had control of our progress to assure they were not screwing round with us again. I continued to monitor the radar, still following the Red River: Check! Haiphong

Harbor about forty miles off our left wingtip: Check. Though our mission was not physically complete, in our hearts we knew that we had extracted our Heroes from a hostile enemy. We all had that sense of pride and patriotism that you get only rarely. This was one of those rare times!

We received our initial instructions from Departure Control, and this time, they gave us a proper heading. They probably wanted to be rid of us as badly as we wanted to be gone. As we climbed out on our way back down the Red River, General Ulatowski came on the radio with a connection to both aircraft. He informed us that he had delivered the message to President Nixon that the mission had been accomplished in an honorable and totally professional fashion.

He relayed the following message from the President of the United States, "Job Well Done. And Thank You from a Grateful Nation!" Never has those few words meant so much to us.

We received further instructions to proceed on our pre-arranged flight path and altitude, again "feet wet" in that same five mile wide, thirty miles off shore corridor to our destination. The other navigator kept us within the corridor until the pilots could pick up DaNang VORTAC. Then, they took over. Our trip back to Tan Son Nhut AB was quiet and uneventful. We dropped some officials off in Saigon, the last time I ever stepped on Vietnamese soil. (I actually did not leave the C-130, but I still considered that I was on Vietnamese soil). We taxied, took off and proceeded to U Tapao RT-NAB, Thailand. The evacuation aircraft had turned the remains of our deceased comrades over to Brigadier General Ulatowski's Samsung Army Remains Identification unit stationed near there. Further ID would be conducted at Hickam AFB, Hawaii as necessary.

A personal footnote: In September 2005, I was attending the 45th anniversary of our graduation from Officer Candidate School (OCS) with Col Mike Gilroy and others. Another one of my classmates came to my table and informed me that his wife would like to speak to me. I wondered what kind of trouble I was in now!

I went to find out. She just wanted to thank me. The remains of her first husband had been on that first flight!! We both cried, holding onto each other

That mission to retrieve those who Died In Captivity was the most important single mission of my Air Force career, and will probably end up being the most, important, satisfying and yet, most emotionally trying thing I have ever done in my entire life! I thank God I was able to be there!

Seven days later, March 13th, the 61st TAS retrieved 11 more of our heroes. The mission encountered no problems.

That ended the recovery missions. Those twenty-three are the only known members of our military to have died in captivity.

GUAM IS GOOD

(Sign over entrance to flight line exchange in Guam)

"Sometimes there is no Answer"!

This was it! It was finally time to go home. I had come to the end of my one year isolated tour, the term used for spending a full year, normally overseas, without your family. It seems like forever when you start, but like no time when it ends. Strange how time plays with your mind.

Time, or whatever you want to call it, was playing with my mind. It was time that was leading me on this crazy chase on how to go home. Time, my mind, a few martinis and my best friend at

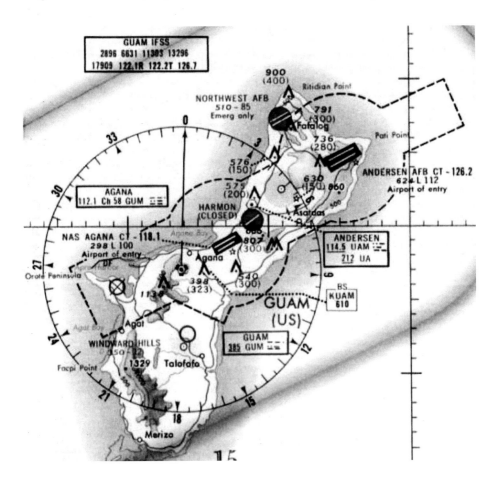

Clark Air Base and his crew had me running back and forth between their C-130 and the DC-8 contract jet "Freedom Flight" back to Travis Air Force Base and stateside.

My best friend over there was Bob Regal, the navigator of the C-130E crew. Bob and I had hit it off as soon as he arrived at CCK. Something just clicked. I started lending him my car each time I went "in country" to our Forward Operating Location in Southern Thailand at U Tapao Royal Thai Naval Air Base. We rarely spent time together during off duty hours, but then, I spent off duty time with no one. For some reason, I was a "loner" during my entire isolated tour and I still do not know why. Now, I had an opportunity to fly with him as a crewmember, all the way back to Colorado Springs. That opportunity had me running back and forth, killing time, from his C-130 and my scheduled DC-8 jet "Freedom Flight" because of maintenance problems on both.

So, finally, now it was my time to return stateside and to my family. Most GI's don't have a choice of transport, but I did. As I said, Bob was on the crew, Jim King's crew, taking a C-130E back to Birmingham, Alabama, my next duty station, but I had a reserved seat. A "Freedom Flight" seat. The "Freedom Flight" was a DC-8 which would whisk us back to the states with refueling stops in Guam and Hickam AFB, Hawaii. They were both scheduled to depart Clark AB, Philippines with the C-130 scheduled out a little before the "Freedom Flight."

I was having a real tussle in my mind over which way to go. Both planes would make the same basic stops until they got back to the States. The jet (DC-8) would get me back to California more quickly, but the C-130 crew would drop me off in Colorado Springs, and I could wander about and crew rest with them on my way to my ultimate destination, where I would be reunited with my family. What to do?

I had my bags on the C-130 and was ready to go home with the crew from the 776th TAS, of which I had been the Executive Officer (XO) or second in command of the administrative side of the

Squadron. Then, it broke! The C-130, which was being ferried back to Birmingham, Alabama, had developed maintenance problems. So, I removed my bags and returned back to the Officers' Club for a toddy or two. Oops, the C-130 is back in commission with takeoff two hours from now. I took my bags back down to the Airlift Command Post and asked the crew to take my bags out with them. They did.

I guess a couple things need to be explained. First, I was still in possession of my little red Rambler station wagon which we had purchased when I received orders to go to Lajes Field, the Azores in 1971 to fly with the 57th ARRS. Here it was now in the Philippines. So that little red car had been from Colorado to the Azores, then to CCK and on down to the Philippines to Clark AB from which I would depart in some manner this day. I figured that the little red Rambler station wagon most likely had visited all four hemispheres. Quite a feat! Especially for a car that wasn't even trying. Second, I was friends with all of the crewmembers, including the ACMs on the plane being that they were all from the 776th TAS, the only C-130 unit at Clark AB. I was using that little red Rambler to run back and forth from the club and the terminal ACP and had to give my main key to Bob. That covers just about everything that anyone need to know about the red Rambler. However, it did have a mushroom about eight inches tall growing out of the passenger floorboard and it was almost a solid moss color green throughout the inside when I picked it up in Kaoshiung, the more southern port city. It was a mess after five months sailing the globe in a cargo ship. I did a lot of wiping before just the drivers side was inhabitable.

I was at the Officers' Club again when I got the call that the C-130 was once again being delayed because of maintenance problems. So, being of sharp mind and wit and boosted by several toddy's by now, I decided that someone was trying to tell me something. Upon figuring that out, I committed to the Freedom Flight and checked my bags at the terminal. Fortunately, I had time to whip back to the Club for a quick scotch and water and a grab couple of miniatures of Johnny Walker Black to slip on the plane with me. I then whipped down to ACP for a final goodbye and thanks to all of these fine gentlemen. I also gave Bob the second set of keys. I was leaving the little red Rambler with him. They were back in commission, but my bags were in the Freedom Flight. I told him I'd see at Maxwell AFB in Montgomery Alabama in a few months, he promised to give me a call when he got settled. He thanked me for the key. And so it was when I went to the terminal and found the DC-8 had gone belly up again. I was beginning to have my doubts about that plane. This time they gave a hard Estimated Time In Commission (ETIC) of six hours, instead of sliding it an hour or so each time. I had already boarded once. Knowing the flight line and Base OPs system, I grabbed a flight line driver and had him take me to the White Elephant (the club was closed) so I could grab some shuteye on the sofas in the Rathskelller. As I got into the flight line cab, I heard a C-130 taking off. Damn!

Earlier, I stayed as long as I could at the club to enjoy a couple of my friends who were toasting my departure and wishing they were me. As a result, I barely made my flight, but they had a reserved seat saved for me. So, we are on our way home. First, fly to Travis AFB and then try to figure out how to get to San Francisco International (SFO). Then, fly on to Colorado Springs. What began as a long year suddenly became a thing of the past, a very memorable past. I had just finished doing the most enjoyable, sometimes dangerous, but always intriguing flying of my career. It had been one great, wonderful isolated year. Now it was over! I was on my way! I would miss it as most men missed their isolated assignment.

After spending a night in California, I caught an early flight to Colorado Springs where, after receiving a warm welcome from my wife and four daughters, my wife presented me with a telegram.

It basically asked, "would you be available to return to Guam and perform the duties of casualty escort for an officer who died in a crash a few days earlier?"

That paraphrased message sent chills down my spine. "Oh, Lordy! Who could they want me to escort?" I could think of only one crew with whom I had been connected that would have been transiting Guam in the last few days.

Then my wife gave me a second telegram, which canceled the request in the first telegram. As soon as I got to the house, I was on the telephone to the number listed in the telegram. After several attempts, the Casualty Assistance Office at Pacific Air Force, (PA-CAF) Headquarters picked up the phone. They told me to ignore the request because of a new rule that did not provide for body escort from an overseas location to stateside. I asked whom I had been requested to escort. They said they didn't know. I had to find out.

Remember, this was 1974 and spontaneous worldwide telephone intercourse was difficult at best. Instant contact was still in the distant future. I felt my best bet was the Red Cross. They had been able to put my wife through to their office on Clark AB where she notified me of my favorite aunt's demise. Perhaps now, I could work it in reverse. I made a phone call to the local Red Cross. The Philippines was fourteen hours ahead of Colorado Springs or almost opposite our time.

After a considerable amount of time, we worked out a deal whereby I could go to the Red Cross in the middle of the night and call my old unit and have my fears verified or, hopefully, allayed. Either fortunately or unfortunately, my call was finally answered by my ex-secretary. She burst into tears as soon as she heard my voice. Jim (can't remember his last name), one of the XO's for the 776th, took the phone from her. "Jim, what in hell is going on? I was requested to be a body escort and then the request was withdrawn. Who was it?" I was asking questions without giving Jim a chance to answer. "Jack, Jack, Damn it!" he screamed into my ear, "Give me a chance to explain things as I know them." I couldn't help myself. I was almost screaming back at him, "Was it Bob Kings' crew?" I heard nothing but silence. Oh, please, no. "Jim?" I heard a quiet voice say, "Yes, Jack. The whole crew." Again, I almost screamed, "What in hell happened?" Struggling to maintain my composure, I asked again, "Jim, what happened? I'll keep quiet while you fill me in."

"Well, as near as we can tell, they had just lifted off after a re-fueling stop on Guam. Now, this is according to the Control Tower at Andersen AFB. Right after they got airborne, they noticed #3 engine had started to deteriorate and were checking out the problem. Well, I guess from what the Tower could tell, it seemed to them that everyone in the cockpit was looking at the gauges and no one was really flying the airplane. Now, you know how the runway at Guam goes down and then bends back up like it has a shallow valley in it?" "Yeah," I said. "We used to get a kick out of the B-52s trying to negotiate it" "Yep." he said, "Well, no one was watching the runway and their C-130 stayed at very low level while picking up speed. They flew right back into the upslope of the runway, tried to recover, which caused the plane to balloon into the air, come back down and then, bounce again. There is no way a pilot can catch up with the porpoise action without roughly planting the plane hard onto the runway. But, by the time they tried to do just that, it was too late. They hit the runway a final time, bounced and the landing gear caught the rocks at the lip of the cliff, which slowed them enough that they dropped straight off the edge of the six-hundred foot sheer drop. This perpendicular cliff with jagged rocks below was the place where many Japanese jumped to their deaths rather than surrender to the conquering United States military (Marines, I believe). The C-130 fell those six-hundred feet into a kind of rock bowl at the base of the cliff where they exploded and burned with over seventy eight thousand pounds of JP-4 fuel on board. Big explosion, bigger fire."

"Oh, no!" I said. Then I had to ask, "Nuh, no survivors?" A long pause. Jim quietly answered, "None." I responded, "Those were all of our guys on there. SH**!!" Another long pause. I told Jim, "I was almost on that airplane with them. I almost tried to get home with them. They were going to drop me off in Colorado Springs. I had my B-4 bag on that airplane two different times! Oh, God! They all died?" Again, in a solemn tone, Jim said, "Yes, Jack, they all died. Died in a huge explosion and bigger fire. They are gone, Jack." I stood there stunned. Tickle tummy would not adequately explain how I felt. I almost felt like throwing up. My best friend in Southeast Asia, (SEA) was the navigator on that crew.

I just hung up the phone without even thanking Jim for the terrible news. I just stood there. I have never felt so empty in mind and soul. Then another thought hit me. I could have been on that C-130. I could have died with them! My mind came alive swiftly pondering over the fact that a C-130E, loaded with my friends, crashed and burned. "Crashed and burned" is a phrase that aircrews use in a light-hearted fashion. Now, it was true. They actually DID crash and burn!

Then a thought occurred that would haunt me for the rest of my life and one which my defense mechanisms had kept basically hidden until I started talking and swapping stories with those Docents. "Shit! Why didn't I leave that one alone and let it remain buried?"

The haunting thought that came to me while reminiscing was: If I had been on board and in my usual takeoff position looking over the copilot's shoulder, would I have noticed that we were not gaining altitude? Would I have thought to or even have the audacity to yell at the pilots? And if I had, would my warning have been taken seriously and acted upon by one of the pilots? They were very inexperienced. Normally, in a case like this, the copilot would check the gauges and the Aircraft Commander would fly the airplane. Obviously, this didn't happen. That thought has haunted me off and on for years. It stayed buried while I was still on active duty, even though my new assignment was four years of test flying B-57s and, mainly, C-130s at the facility, which was the destination of the doomed aircraft.

It really did come home to me in a startling letter I received at my new home at Bluff Park in Hoover, a suburb of Birmingham, soon after I assumed my duties at my new assignment. It was about a month later that I received that strange letter. I don't even remember from whom it came. Suffice to say, it was just a small, slightly bulging letter. Inside the letter, causing the bulge was a portion of a key, a partially melted and blackened car key. The letter requested that I respond whether I recognized the key or not. Stunned, I was staring at the burnt remains of the key to my little red Rambler station wagon. The same little red Rambler key I had given to Bob Regal the night we both left Clark AB in different planes!

I stared at the key and had the emptiest feeling a person could ever have. I don't know how long I stared at that blackened piece of semi-melted key while holding it in my shaking hand. I recognized from the small burnt piece (it was less than half, but enough of the big end was recognizable) that it was the key to my Rambler that I had given to Bob. My stomach was churning. This may have been the ONLY thing recognizable from that burning disaster. I have been told there were not even any recognizable bones. When the fire died down and had cooled sufficiently, they found only an ash of metal debris and one small piece of a key. I fell back on my bed, staring at the ceiling with tear filled eyes. I didn't wipe at them. I let them run down the sides of my face onto the bed. They weren't really falling, they were just oozing. MY GOD! DID I LET THEM DIE? OR DID I JUST SAVE MYSELF?

No one would ever know! I thought that crying might ease my pain and conscience a little more. It didn't! Not just Bob Regal, but Bob King and the rest of the crew had been killed. I had known all of them. l and had flown with most of them. And now they were gone! Bob and I would never get together at the Maxwell AFB Officers' Club, as we had planned when he came back from Clark AB to attend Air War College. None of our plans were to happen!

I finally got up off the bed and with shaking hand wrote a letter back acknowledging previous ownership of the key. I also acknowledged that it indeed had been in Bob's possession. That was the only thing they had to positively identify one of the crewmembers, my best friend. I have no idea how or if they identified the others.

Years later, I found out that the crash had occurred about four hours before we arrived at Guam. Bob had been dead while our jet refueled at Guam! The only thing I noticed as we waited to re-board our plane was that innocuous sign over the entrance to the flight line exchange:

"GUAM IS GOOD"

I never did understand. Why that sign? This time, it wasn't good to my best friend and his crew. But, I will never forget that sign which had always intrigued me as to why it even existed. Now it is a haunting reminder of a tragedy which I may have been able to prevent. Maybe the reason for its existence is just to haunt me?

The entire incident made me think all the way back to 1972 when I served as an escort to a woman whose husband had been killed in the crash of an identical C-130E. It crashed shortly after takeoff from Taipai International Airport on the northern end of Taiwan. After the crash with its ensuing explosion and fire, they had not been able to identify the bodies. They buried the remains of the crew and passengers in three caskets. To this day, I still remember that there were thirty-eight bodies contained in three coffins.

After being her escort for three days, we were on our way to Jefferson Barracks National Cemetery, a little south of Saint Louis overlooking the Mississippi River, she asked quietly, "How do they determine who is in each casket?" I had to speak the truth. Uncertain of how she would react, I pulled the car over on the shoulder of the highway. We looked at each other. "They place thirty pounds of remains in each coffin until all of the remains are deposited with proper respect." She said, "Oh." Certain that she was OK with that. I pulled back on the roadway which was winding toward this sacred burial place. During the three days, she had asked many questions. She accepted each answer with strength and acceptance. I was very impressed with this young widow.

Later as the ceremonies were winding down, there will be, normally, a three rifle volley, followed by the bugler playing Taps. I knelt and presented her with a United States flag, tri-folded in the proper tradition.

"On behalf of the President of the United States, the United States Air Force and a grateful nation, please accept this flag as a symbol of appreciation for your loved one's honorable and faithful service." I stood up at attention and rendered a proper slow motion salute. Doing facing movements, I proceeded to take my place behind her.

Those words were more difficult to memorize and especially deliver than any I had the honor of uttering in my life.

After the culmination of the ceremony I took her back to her hotel in Saint Louis. I said, goodbye and thank you!" to as strong of a woman that I had ever met.

I have to assume that all of the members of this Guam Crew were buried in one casket. I know not where or if at all!

To this day, when I drink my beer on special military related occasions, I always use the pewter mug Bob Regal bought for me in Jakarta. He gave it to me just before we parted. I had to send the burned/melted key back to Remains Identification Unit. As a result, that pewter mug is my only tangible remembrance of Bob Regal. A very powerful remembrance!

The mug also a reminds when I'm using it at a party, even if I am still having fun, that he died for his country just as much as anyone on the Wall. I will never get rid of the feeling that maybe, just maybe, I could have saved their lives if I had been on board. Then my mind flips and tells me that more likely, I would have died with them.

The phrase "Cheated death again" comes to mind when I look back at this time. That used to be an old joking refrain, often spoken by Martini Jim Cannon after landing from any routine flight, but it seems to have taken on a very new meaning. I very nearly believe it now.

If I look back carefully, I can think of nine close calls with death and a couple close ones left over from the nine, when by all rights and logic, I should have died. Was God sparing me so I could get down here to Broken Arrow and be with these docents, many who flat told me that I needed to write this book? This was after they attended a ceremony honoring seven kids from the local Broken Arrow High School who were Killed in Action (KIA) in Vietnam at which I was the featured speaker. My speech barely touched the lives of the KIA's, but told of the day I was the lead navigator selected to go on that very special mission to Hanoi, North Vietnam in a C-130E. They all heard or read my speech. For some reason, it affected them enough that they said I just had to write my story. Obviously, I yielded.

The following is an official word for word transcription about the Guam Crew accident:

"June 22, 2017, 04:28 AM

This aircraft was assigned to the 776th TAS, 374th TAW, Clark AB, Trying to make Hawaii in one hop, the crew overloaded with fuel. On takeoff, they suffered over-speed on #3 engine. The crew lost situational awareness and allowed the a/c to sink and strike the lip of the cliff at the end of the runway. Plane fell over cliff and burned in the jungle below.

Except for the Flight Engineer (FE), the crew was relatively inexperienced and had not flown together before this mission. The aircraft commander was a Lieutenant Colonel who had married a general's daughter. He received an age and vision waiver to enter pilot training at an advanced age with poor vision."

NOTE: Why this report is dated 2017 is a mystery to me. It takes a long time for Air Force investigators to wrap up an aircraft accident, but forty-three years? The accident happened in 1974. What is written in the report coincides almost exactly with my memory. I heard that #3 was deteriorating. They say over-speed. Either one can, and in this case did, lead to disaster! I had known that it was an inexperienced crew and had considered that in making my decision to just go on the "Freedom Flight" instead of waiting for a plane that was constantly having maintenance problems. I was aware of the waiver Bob King had received. I had briefed his four-star father–in-law while in the Officer Assignment Control Section at Military Airlift Command (MAC) at Scott AFB. The referenced General was the MAC Commander.

And one of the Best!

To this day, this mission still affects me. I want to relate how a television show that I recently watched caused this mission to fall in place. I had watched "Hawaii Five-O" just to see the landmarks I loved when I lived there for five years.

However, this particular show in the series finally, after all these years, brought home a very obvious fact that I had missed. This episode focused on one of the cast members who had been requested to escort the body of an Air Force Staff Sergeant Forward Air Controller back to Oahu, Hawaii. I had a very hard time watching this as they went through all of the honors and protocol that accompanies all aspects of the special honor of escorting a hero that sacrificed his life for his country.

I found myself tearing up as they brought the flag-draped coffin from Afghanistan through Dover Air Force Base Delaware and on to Hickam AFB, Hawaii. This in itself was unusual. The "Hawaii Five-O" Task Force Sergeant had received a telegram requesting him by name to accompany the body home, though he didn't even know the man. He finally realized why this Sergeant requested him. He had given an inspirational speech about joining the military at one of the local high schools. After hearing that speech, this student was especially inspired and made the decision to enlist in the Air Force.

Then it hit me. My experience paralleled the show. In two ways. It reminded me of the flag draped coffins carrying the remains of twelve Heroes wo had died while in the care of the North Vietnamese. When I finally made it back home to Colorado Springs and my home on the Freedom Flight, I too had a telegram waiting for me. It was a tough episode to watch. It was like re-living the past. I didn't like it! I continued to watch "Hawaii Five-O" through tear-filled eyes. I would normally have walked away from this type of show, but this time, for some reason, I didn't leave the room. And then came the awakening of why I didn't walk away. I was also reliving the Guam disaster through this Hawaii 50 segment.

The request that I received so many years ago was cancelled because, I found out later, they said there was no reason to return to Clark AB now. I had thought going back to Clark AB was a little crazy since the accident happened sixteen hundred miles closer to home, at Andersen AFB in Guam. Since I had taken several days visiting a friend en-route home, I assumed that someone else had taken the body back to Ohio, so, I let it go.

I thought about trying to go to Ohio for the funeral, but I had just signed into my new Flight Test outfit, so I didn't go. That is not true. I just do not know why. I sorely regret that decision now. I thought I would be of no use to the family. I thought which I now understand was wrong-headed thinking, that they didn't need my support.

Now I understand that they could have used any amount of my support. It would have been significant to have a dress blues uniform complete with ribbons, one which belonged to one who was a close friend. I could have lent support and honor to a man who had worn the same cloth. I know better now.

After watching the rest of "Hawaii Five-O," through tear-filled eyes, it all became ultra, crystal clear just how wrong and insensitive I was. I don't know if I thought it through enough or just flat missed the signs. I hope I didn't use it as an excuse, which I may have. But now it was all so obvious. The key should have given me the answer that maybe I didn't want to hear. Perhaps my subconscious would not let me process the thought of such a traumatic, horrible occurrence. Perhaps it was too soon for my mind to accept the happening properly. No matter what, I now knew. And then it hit me. The total reality of the Guam crash in 1974 was more similar to the one which killed the thirty-eight men outside of Taipei. The remains of the Guam crash, if there were any, would have all been buried in one casket. Eight bodies in one coffin, and I didn't even know where they were going to be buried, and yes, they would have had a full military funeral with many uniforms, a three gun salute. And…….Taps! Echoing……Taps!

There was nothing left to escort home! I still have a hard time accepting the fact that my partially burnt car key was the only thing left to identify my closest friend, then there could be only one very clear conclusion. Everyone and everything was basically evaporated by the explosion and intense heat caused by over eighty thousand pounds of high octane aviation fuel. The C-130 and crew fell over six hundred feet into that rock bowl at the bottom of the cliff. Possibly, all that remained was that burnt key!

And then I knew. And then I cried!

B-57 TEST FLIGHT #1 BIRMINGHAM INTERNATIONAL AIRPORT 1974

"This could Ruin our Whole Day"

Coming back from my remote one year assignment in the SEA, I was assigned as Chief of the Navigation Test Section at DCASO HAYES, Birmingham International, Airport, Alabama. The assignment wasn't really that good!

I had turned down another dream assignment, this time to MPC, which was at the top of my dream sheet. I was in my usual post work hour(s) in my favorite corner of the CCK O'Club Bar when the Wing CO, Colonel Baginski and Vice CO, Col Navas approached me with an offer which I may have been foolish to refuse. They offered to change my current assignment to Flight Test and to re-assign me to MPC at Randolph. Being full of righteousness, for some reason, I refused their offer because "If they had to change the assignment given me by MPC, then the system doesn't work." They didn't argue. They had offered what I wanted on a silver platter and I turned up my nose. They wanted to sponsor me and I was leery of what they may want in return, such as assigning or reassigning against my judgement. I would not be my own man. In retrospect, the probability of an eventual two star sponsor causing me to win my eagles may not have been such a bad deal. No, I probably wouldn't have ended up in Broken Arrow, but who is to say that it may have been better for both me and Broken Arrow?

Years later, long after I retired, it dawned on me that when I had been in Assignments Control at MAC HQ I had changed many assignments for friends and wives of friends of folks coming back from and going to Vietnam, including choosing the best C-118 pilot to go to SEA and become General Westmorland and the US Ambassador's pilot. Each change of assignment was a win, win for the two subject officers, the one coming home and the other who was diverted to an assignment which also suited him better. Oh well, At least I didn't take a dream assignment that could blow up on me. Did I mention that Colonel Baginski made his first star out of his 374th TAW CC assignment at CCK and Clark and his second star later. And he had offered to be my sponsor! Col Navas sacrificed his own star while stopping the preening asshole of a full bird Commander of our Squadron at Clark AB. It helped the Air Force greatly though It cost him dearly. Col Navas did it in the best interest of the Air Force. Back to reality.

I was to be the test navigator in KC-97 Refuelers, all manner of C-130's and the light/medium Bomber turned Reconnaissance, "Recce" twin jet, bat-winged aircraft, the RB-57. It was as beautiful as it was deadly! The KC-97 was a modified cargo and passenger version of the famous B-29 bomber, but with much larger Pratt & Whitney R-4360 engines. These aircraft, commonly known as tankers, were reaching the end of their productive lives in the years in which I flew in them from June 1974 thru June 1978. In order to refuel the B-47, the KC-97 had to go into a shallow dive, reaching max speed for this type aircraft while the B-47 had to slow so much to almost fall out of the sky while being refueled. It was rapidly being replaced by the far superior four engine pure jet, KC-135, the military version of the timeless Boeing 707 which could refuel the B-47 or B-52 flying at normal speeds. The KC-135's are still flying and will fly for many more years refueling today though being supplemented by KC-10 Extenders, an adaptation of the commercial DC-10 which is no longer used by the major airlines. They are also being re-enforced by the KC-46 Pegasus, an extremely modified Boeing 767, an aircraft which, for the first time, has been designed strictly as a refueling tanker! I also had the opportunity to fly in every model of the C-130 available up to that time, including the new H model as well as the Roman nosed three bladed prop, C130A, one of which was so old that it was built in late 1953. That would be one year before I enlisted in the Air Force. There is a story about those airplanes also buried in here somewhere. In fact, there are several stories, some of which you may have read. That would be eight models, including variations, of the workhorse C-130 turboprop tactical cargo/troop carrier/counter intelligence/rescue/electronic...I could go on for perhaps pages covering the versatile aircraft. I really do not know which has more variants: C-130 or C-135. They both have many! We were commonly known as "Trash haulers" in the C-130. It was officially known as the Hercules and affectionately known as the "Herkey Bird." I was also introduced to the low slung twin engine jet, batwing RB-57.

In the late '60's I became acquainted with one of the more colorful characters who flew these planes as pure B-57 light bombers in Vietnam. "Nails" Nelson wrote quite an amazing story of his time as a Pilot flying these rugged planes out of Da Nang and, I believe, Phan Rang AB, South Vietnam. If you can find a copy of "Doom Pussy," you should get it and gain great insight into piloting a plane that could come back completely ruined almost in pieces and still deliver its crew safely. It could also blow up killing the crew when it felt like it. The Doom Pussy was a statue of a cat, I'm not sure, but if I remember, correctly, it was black. That cat was turned to face the wall each time the squadron lost another pilot. It did a lot of "wall time" during that little skirmish. I knew "Nails" from the stag bar at Hill AFB in Utah while I was flying in the C-124.

But this tale is about my time in the back seat of an RB-57. It was a twin jet Fighter Bomber/Reconnaissance plane with a two man cockpit. The two men sat in a tandem cockpit (Navigator behind the pilot). In the original Canberra, they were side by side. The engines were imbedded in the oversized "bat" wings. Because of the huge wings, it was very maneuverable. That aircraft alone turned this assignment into a pretty interesting four years!

I was about to say "ya know," but I use that too much so I'll just give you my true feelings about the RB-57. "I hated the flipping thing!" But, to be truly honest, it was a love-hate relationship. It loved me and I hated it! But then, really, in all honesty, just because something tries to kill you, doesn't mean you can't love it in return. That's what happened with me and this strangely beautiful looking piece of aluminum and various other components.

Our Chief Pilot, Major Dave Harmon and I had a lot of fun with the old flying bat-mobile. After a quick and sometimes simple test flight, we would stay out to get more flying time, but mainly to have a little fun. Dave had been a pilot in the F-89 which was an ultra-dangerous aircraft. To the other fella. Another twin jet, these jets were mounted close to the fuselage. It was a heavily armed all weather interceptor which was normally stationed at our northern bases in Alaska and Laborador. Just don't get one angry at you. It was called the Scorpion for a reason. Originally with six machine guns or cannon, it could fly at five hundred thirty MPH and carried fifty two 2.75 unguided rocket in each wingtip pod. That is how Dave became qualified in the B-57. Because it had twin jets also.

To be really honest, (again?) once we finished the test flight and knew we had a flyable aircraft, we just liked to screw around with it for a little while before we went back to our respective offices with nothing to do. One of our favorite thrills or whatever you want to call them, was for Dave to push this batwing aircraft up to about four hundred knots or so at low level and aim at a thunderhead that was rapidly building, pull up just before we reached it and go straight up until we topped out barely above it, do an Immelmann (this is a maneuver in which you invert the aircraft, normally at the top of climb) and then drop down the other side. Falling down the other side made it relatively easy to regain the airspeed lost from the rapid straight up climb. The whole aerobatic stunt was pretty neat, except for having to pull negative 'g's but though I did not appreciate negative 'g's, it was OK here. A negative 'g' is caused when your body is lighter than its actual weight by whatever factor the maneuver caused. We would normally pull about two negative "g's" at most. My helmet would be pushed tight to the canopy of the inverted aircraft. I always hoped that Dave was able to keep in touch with the controls. Then we'd just fall out of the sky, nose down, on the other side of the thunderhead. We would drop about ten or fifteen thousand feet, depending on how good the storm was, pull out starting at about twenty five hundred feet pulling several positive "g's" pushing us down firmly in our seats while we felt like we were weighing a few hundred pounds above our real weight. We would finally level at somewhere between five hundred and one thousand feet, probably scaring the be-jesus out of anyone under where we leveled off. I have often wondered how many folks would see this aircraft, which would look so tiny against a monstrous thunderhead, going straight up and then disappearing over the top. After a few excited comments, we would normally go look for another thunderhead to conquer.

On one certain day, we quit our fun a little early. We did the normal approach and climb to the top of the rising thunderhead, and had just turned on our back when I heard a very loud "Oh Crap" over the always open "live" intercom. I looked up, which was really looking down from our inverted position. I immediately understood Dave's consternation. I think I probably said something like "Oh Crap" myself! I realized just what had him a tad upset. There was another, basically as large thunderhead just on the other side of the one we had just turned over. Nothing we could do but drop right into that tumultuous group of rising and falling extreme air flows. Man, did we ever get the hell shaken out of us until we had regained enough airspeed that we could extricate ourselves from that mess. That is the absolutely worse turbulence I had ever experienced, except those F-4's in Cambodia, and neither of us wanted any more of it. Chastened by mother nature, we called the tower after switching our IFF back on and requested vectors for landing back at the Birmingham Airport. I was happy that it was such a rugged plane and that it would have no lingering effects from that drop into the middle that roiling thunderstorm like I would.

But back to the original point of this part of my test flying career.

My very first test flight in a B-57, also known as the British Canberra, almost turned out to be my last flight in ANY aircraft. Had it not been for an exceptionally strong pilot, we would have gone inverted, crashed & burned off the end of Runway 05 as several others before us had done in a similar situation at other airfields. Same problem. It happened quickly.

Naturally, being the back seater and brand new to testing B-57's, I was quite apprehensive to begin with and up until now, I had been involved in testing low, slow and steady KC-9's with their reciprocating engines and all eight models of C-130's with Turbo-props. This twin jet fighter-bomber was something entirely new and I was quite reluctant, to say the least, to crawl into the back seat of this low-slung twin engine jet, nicknamed "The Widow Maker," a moniker justly earned mostly in Vietnam. But when the boss said, "Do it!" I did it. We had a lot of fun with this bird. I've been in it up to an altitude of over 50,000 Feet, 10 miles, (illegally), for just a couple of minutes. Almost immediately, both Dave and I began to feel the effect of nitrogen bubbles coming out of solution (blood stream) and bubbling into our joints. That is why they wear pressure suits at high altitudes. My pain was in the elbows at first. I think Major Harman felt the pain in his knee and thigh joints. It was not a pleasant feeling. Actually, it hurt like hell! Checking with me to see if I was experiencing pain, and a quick, "Me too," we immediately descended to 49,000 feet, our assigned altitude. It took longer for the bubbles to disappear than for them to become bothersome. In fact, it seemed we still felt them after we landed at Birmingham. We had pulled this stunt over south central Missouri, directly above a worthless lot I own down there at Theodosia Hills.

Back to reality: On this, my maiden flight, we taxied out, were cleared for immediate takeoff and proceeded to trundle down runway 05 and achieved a normal lift off. But, immediately after liftoff, and as the pilot was retracting the landing gear and resetting the flaps, we felt a sudden tremor and a violent yaw to the left. My Aircraft Commander had previously experienced this recurring problem with the B-57, so he fortunately recognized the problem immediately. A runaway Rudder Power Boost! The rudder had gone, on its own, and with hydraulic assist, to the full left position. Major Dave Harman is a very strong guy, and only his strength of leg to neutralize the rudder kept us from flipping over and crashing in an inverted position, landing canopy first, which could have ruined our whole day. The main thing I remember is: "I'm not used to this crap!" I also very clearly remember Dave declaring an emergency and requesting immediate clearance to land. It was a bright, calm day so the tower cleared us for an immediate 180-degree turn and return for landing on runway 23, the same runway, but in the opposite direction of the takeoff. The tower directed all other traffic in the area to various pre-determined holding patterns until our emergency was resolved. That was another one of those days when I would have given anything to be on the ground rather than to be where I was: In the air.

With extreme effort, Dave kept the aircraft basically level as we made a quick left 180-degree turn. Fortunately, we were still within two miles of the runway and with my hands on the eject handle, I also realized that we were flying very low level over a cemetery. I hope we didn't disturb any of the permanent residents! Dave was able to hold the aircraft steady until touchdown and began immediate braking to minimize the effect of the rudder on the direction of the aircraft. As it was, we ended up near the left edge of the runway anyway. This damned plane wanted to have its way with us. Dave wouldn't let it happen! We immediately raised the canopy and egressed from the aircraft. We quickly but carefully just crawled out of our ejection seats and slipped over the side of the plane and dropped onto the tarmac. Never has asphalt felt so good. Major Harmon could barely stand because his right leg muscles were so exhausted from using all his strength in that leg to hold the rudder in a neutral position. I was just shaking all over, scared shitless! I don't think I had ever been so scared in my life, including when the rockets came in on the Tan Son Nhut attack. Once again, on this flight, I was unable to alleviate the situation and too scared to even pray!

I knew we had been in a desperate situation, but it was not until after we were safely back in our Flight Operations that the full gravity of the incident hit me. It was then that the Dave, leg still shaking, explained to me what had happened and how many others had lost their lives to the same malfunction which seemed mostly unique to the RB-57 type aircraft. That was the first time the RB-57 tried to kill me. My first flight! There were other more minor incidents, but I will write of only one other later.

Following my harrowing escape from death, I refused to fly in the next two test flights, instead forcing our other test Pilots to fly in the back seat. Only when I was threatened with courts martial did I finally relent, and with much foreboding, began flying in the back seat of the B-57 again. I barely slept for the two nights before my next flight, tossing and turning, dreading getting into that back seat again. I never did get over being semi-terrified on each subsequent test flight, and a later one would validate that terror. To this day, I wake up at nights after having dreamt of being upside down heading toward the headstones barely below us.

Thirty-seven years later, I still think of that ride and reminisce with the realization that, had I been with a less capable or less strong pilot, I would not be able to write this story. I still have an almost unearthly dislike and fear of that twin-engine monster! Except for the fun that we had in it!

The B-57 was a very rugged aircraft that could take a real beating, as would be witnessed in some of the shot up bat planes missing half of their appendages as the pilots would occasionally have to crash land their planes at their home field at DaNang AB and other bases prior to that during its tenure in Vietnam. But, though almost utterly destroyed, the Canberra emerged the victor. It got its crew back safely, though it would never fly again except as spare parts on another like aircraft. We only lost one in Alabama. Unfortunately, I was on final approach in a KC-97 when they were beginning their take off roll with Larry Hillman in the back seat where I would have been if the refueling plane hadn't had problems which had to be checked out before it could land.

After normal takeoff and during the testing of the plane, The RB-57 cockpit filled with smoke before the pilot, I think it was Captain Charlie Wiegraffe, initiated eject procedures and they both hurtled into the twilight skies, sans aircraft which landed on down the road after cutting a clean and clear, slanted swath through an Alabama pine forest. (The back seater went first to avoid being turned into a crispy critter by the rocket blast from the pilots seat). They found one of the engines over a mile farther on down the way. Both pilots survived with minor burns and a little shook up. Damn, I wish I could have been on that one. All of those emergency things, as are in this book, are fun when looking back on them. Not so much as you are going through them!

Another example of just how rugged was this sleek looking plane is the beating it took in the middle of an atomic bomb in the desert called Frenchman Flats, about fifty five miles north of La Vegas, Nevada. In a hot clear sky over the Nevada Desert, a lesser plane may have been crushed and torn apart by the intense and sudden change of pressure to vacuum to pressure again experienced as this B-57 flew through the hot, turbulent cloud rising rapidly from a seventeen kiloton (seventeen thousand tons) of TNT rising rapidly from the just detonated atomic bomb explosion. But that was covered in another, hotter story.

BIRMINGHAM TO ANCHORAGE

"If Anyone can Move this Hangar Queen, we can"

We were the Bad Ass Test Flight Crew out of Birmingham, Alabama! We were the brightest and best money could buy (at a cheap Air Force salary rate). We may have been the only crew that could walk on water and not cause a ripple. That is, at least according to our intrepid Chief Pilot at Hayes Aircraft Corporation in Birmingham, AL. The Chief Pilot, actually was one of the best pilots I have ever known, but he had the habit of not really thinking things through sometimes, and if someone offered him a challenge, the bravado went up about three notches. This was one of those times!

And so it happened that Dave Harman received a call from Base Operation on Elmendorf Air Force Base in Alaska. Their problem: They had a "Hangar Queen" (an aircraft which is always in the hangar for maintenance) that they couldn't get off of their base. The phone call came in mid-afternoon, which was mid-morning in Alaska. The Chief of Base OPS, told Dave that several crews had tried and eventually gave up getting this piece of Olive Drab crap out of his sight. Several crews even got it off the ground for a short period of time before maintenance problems made them return the thing to the ramp to be towed into the hangar again. Now, there it was. Sitting defiantly on the ramp. He was tired of seeing it. He flat made the statement that: If anyone should be able to move this thing, that a Test Flight Crew should be able to do it." "Tell me right now, can you or can you not get this plane on its way back to Korat AB, Thailand." Dave thought that he was not giving us enough respect. He told the Base Ops Lieutenant Colonel, "If anyone can move it, we can. No matter why the others couldn't, we could! Moving planes is our business! If anyone on this earth could move it he and his crew could do it and we could be up there in a couple days. Then, he would never have to see that piece of crap from the morning after we arrived." Of course, he did this without consulting with any of the rest of the crew as to whether we would even want to leave home for a week. "Damn, Dave, give us a little say so too." The copilot was a real "homer," but I was always ready to hit the road on a new adventure. Our Commander called us in for a briefing. He asked if we would be willing to go. Flight engineer, Bud Hall was a lot like me. "Spring loaded to the ready position." The "homer" backed out, but Larry Hillman said he would go with us. We were set, so the CO turned the meeting over to Dave. He told us that every crew came back with the same old trouble. All eyes immediately turned to Bud Hall. It would be his job to keep the engines turning! Bud nodded without saying a word or showing emotion, which was not like our loquacious and verbose flight engineer, another way in which we were alike.

And so it happened. With that innocuous exchange, we launched what would turn out to be the flight of our life. But first, we had to enjoy a going away party for the guy I was replacing. It would be a long night and an early wake-up tomorrow to start our trip to Alaska and beyond.

It was a fun party, maybe too much fun. We all had to get up early in order to get to the airport and catch an early departure for Anchorage International Airport, a long day away. For some reason, the airlines have an unwritten rule, or I guess I should just blame Delta Airlines. Anything that leaves Birmingham, has to go thru Atlanta. They claim that if you are a Delta employee, and die, you must clear through Hartsfield International Airport before you can get to heaven! None of us would be going to heaven, yet! As I was taking a quick shower after about two to three hours sleep, I was thankful that I could just grab a little extra sleep time since I had prudently packed the previous day. All I had to do was grab my B-4 bag which was sitting in front of my closet door, ready to go. (A B-4 bag was an Air Force issue suitcase with a long zipper which opened the bag in half for insertion of hang up clothing and huge side pockets for other clothing and various sundries). All in all, it was a very efficient suitcase. I mention the hang up aspect, because in those days, the mid-seventies, Air Force crews still wore suit and tie when going to eat and/or drink at the Officer or NCO clubs. It had been that way since I joined up 22 or so years ago and I wish it still was. But it really doesn't matter. Almost all of the Clubs were dead now. Absolutely no fun allowed! And almost always closed.

Amazingly, a ragged but well-dressed crew of four gathered together at the Birmingham Airport to await our flight. Dave, Bud and I were anxious to get underway. It had been a long time since our last Temporary Duty (TDY) trip, and we were looking forward to it. Once we got to the Philippine Islands, I would, ipso facto, become their leader because I was the only one to have lived in the Philippines and Thailand, and though I had been to Kwajalein before, it had only been for crew rest. I had been to Midway Island a few times, but just for a few short hours to pick up passengers or whatever they wanted us to move. Even in that short time, though, I had experienced the fun of watching the Gooney Birds. A large albatross that stayed at sea for most of its life. I've witnessed a group of them standing around in a circle, like a bunch of little old ladies at a quilting bee would be sitting. One of the thousands of birds circling overhead would decide to join them. No problem, right? Just glide in and land, elbowing your way into the circle. Not that easy with the Gooney Bird. They were so used to being at sea, that they would come in, gear up as on a water landing and hit the group with such force that it looked like a bowling ball hitting right in the pocket for a noisy strike. Birds and feathers flew and the squawking reached an even higher level of decibels than the almost unbearable noise already filling the air. Those on the ground would gather back around squawking and shaking their heads like they were commenting on the intrusion. In the few join ups I have witnessed, the flying intruder would just stagger off shaking his head making weird sounds and go sit for a while to get his bearings after probably six to nine months at sea. Although very graceful in the air with their long wings, they are a complete disaster when landing, they always forget to lower their landing gear which provides us mere humans with hours on end of jocularity. We flew into Midway Island one night after I had been regaling the crew with long and many stories of their antics.

The Aircraft Commander just would not believe me. We were standing in the open double rear door passenger entryway which had a floodlight light trained on it. As we stood there, gazing out on the night, unexpectedly out of the darkness, a huge gooney bird flew straight into the side of the C-118B (DC-6). It hit right beside us, within about two feet. It scared the living stew out of both of us. The AC stood in shock as the gooney bird, now on the ground and knocked even more senseless than normal, shook itself and literally staggered off into the night. I'd swear it was muttering. He was probably wondering just what in hell got in the way. He was used to having the entire sky to himself and his counterparts. The AC became a believer. We were damned fortunate that he didn't fly into one or both of us! That would have been interesting to have the AC and Nav knocked down and hurt, and a Gooney Bird loose in the cabin of a C-118! The good Lord only would know what would have happened, and he's probably not sure, or isn't talking. I know, it would have hurt! They are BIG!

Now, none of us had ever been to the U.S. Naval Station in Adak on the Aleutian Chain of Islands which ran southwest, curving west away from Anchorage where we were picking up the calcitrant C-130. No one needed to be in charge. There was nothing there!

I received my first of many surprises on the trip when, in a very strange hotel in downtown Anchorage, I opened up my B-4 bag to get out my hang up clothes. EMPTY! My hang up clothing would be hanging tonight, but in the closet of the main bedroom in Bluff Park, Alabama, a suburb of Birmingham. I had only the clothes on my back! Fortunately, we also flew in a suit, so at least I could start the trip properly, if wearing the same clothes to a local restaurant was proper. We went to a western or Klondike themed bar and enjoyed a few proper drinks (Oh Boy, they make them strong in this area). Then we went across the street to a "Cook it Yourself" Steakhouse where we also indulged in one order of crab legs, split among the crew. As we indulged in our meal, someone mentioned that he had heard the current popular song "Leaving on a Jet Plane." We all started babbling at the same time. All of us had heard the same song though we listened to different stations and types of music. Hmmmm, the first weird circumstance of the trip, and the first feeling of foreboding. Not to worry, we were that Bad Assed Test Flight Crew! What could go wrong?

ELMENDORF AFB TO ADAK NAS, ALUTIANS

"NEGATIVE ON GO AROUND.
WE ARE LANDING ON THIS PASS"

What could go wrong was the question. Well, for beginners, when we ventured out to the flight line to get our bird ready to fly, we discovered there were two main things wrong with our air machine. It was an AC-130A. It was not a regular C-130. It was a gunship and an "A" model at that. It was one of the oldest gunships in the inventory. That helped explain the problems other crews had trying to get this olive drab pile of garbage out of their sight. Though still a C-130, the gunships carried:

2 ea 7.62 GAU-2A miniguns

2 ea 20 mm M61 Vulcan Cannon six barrel Gatling cannon (2700 rounds/minute) A single 105 mm 4.13 inch M102 howitzer was there with other menacing hardware.

In addition it had on its left side, almost seventeen hundred pounds of lead armor protecting it from ground fire, as it flew in low and slow circles while spitting out its lethal tongue of flame at a soon to be destroyed enemy target on the ground. Thus the name, starting with the venerable AC-47, it was referred to as "Puff the Magic Dragon." Because of the heavy armor, the aircraft needed about seventeen degrees of left rudder to fly straight. Still, for this Bad Assed Test flight Crew from Birmingham, no problem, or maybe! The AC-119 may have been the first "Puff."

Yep, we could see the problem(s). Too old and the wrong model. Still, we were that Bad Assed Super Test Flight Crew out of Birm etc.... Just ask Dave! Even though the AC-130 would fly at a lower altitude and a slower air speed than the normal C-130, we were that Super Flight Test Crew from Alabama who could do anything! We could see no problem, but we all still had that feeling of foreboding which we didn't share until after spending a week in the most beautiful spot on the tour. During our normal departure briefing, we were told that the reason it kept coming back to Elmendorf after departing for Adak NAS, was a hydraulic hose which kept coming loose and either spraying fluid inside the engine or spewing a real fine mist. Neither one was good, but the fine spray was a real explosion hazard rather than just a fire like would happen with the regular hydraulic fluid. So, what's the problem? The Bad Assed Test Flight Crew told them to fix the damned hydraulic hose and we would be on our way and the gunship would be off their ramp for good after camping there for well over forty five days. Now, the Great Test Flight Crew would be able to do what they do best, and better than anyone else: Fly Airplanes. Let's get this hog off the ground! The weather forecast was for hot dry and dusty for our trip to Adak. We were all smiles as we lifted off of the runway at Elmendorf AFB and turned on the heading for Adak Island. I remember vividly, a large fire in downtown Anchorage, but that didn't affect us. In fact, nothing affected us! We were that Super Flight, etc…

It had been a long time since any of us had been on a decent TDY. Dave and I had gone to Malstrom AFB at Great Falls, Montana quite a few time delivering a B-57 after we had passed it on our test flight, but we wanted someplace new. We would find plenty new on this trip. We were ready! Imagine, spending a night in Anchorage Alaska (they had no room for us on base at Elmendorf AFB, so we got to spend a night in a downtown hotel). The hotel itself was a bit of a puzzle. The wall paper was a flocked red and fuchsia colored material. Flocked? I wondered just what type of hotel it was, but again, not to worry. It was going to be for only one night, I hoped. And, we had paid for the full night, and not an hourly rate!

But, the trip: A night in Anchorage, followed by: A night in Adak Island in the Aleutian chain, Midway Island with its famous Gooney Birds and the farthest west of any U.S. owned civilization, Kwajalein with its white sand beaches, coral and perfectly clear water. Watch out for giant clams in that water. They can be huge! Followed by nights in Guam, Clark AB in the Philippine Islands and terminating with at least one night in Korat AB, Thailand.

Then a nice commercial air flight home. Let others do the flying for a change! Who could ask for anything more? And what would it cost? Hell, Uncle Sam was paying us (not much) to do this, what normal folks would pay dearly to do.

We were now airborne out of Anchorage headed toward our second spot on this luxury tour, Adak Island. The weather forecast was for Clear and Visibility Unlimited (CAVU) for our arrival time at Adak NAS. We all felt better now that we were airborne and we all started to relax. A couple hours into the flight, the hydraulic light began flashing on number two engine. As Dave and Bud discussed it, "Should we shut it down now or see what happens? This was the most prevalent problem the previous crews had. We had not yet reached ETP. This is where the other crews quit and went back to Elmendorf as per required by regulation. "Ah, let's just keep an eye on it and see what happens. That's what a Test Flight Crew would do. Find the root problem." About an hour past the Equal Time Point (ETP) where it becomes closer to continue than to go back, Bud went back to check on the engines from the rear which he did about every hour. Our earlier premonitions began to hit home when TSgt Hall spoke those famous words, "Oh Crap!" The reason for this brilliant verbiage: Hey, guys, we have fluid running back between the dry bay and number four engine. Those hurried words came from our flight engineer, one of the best in the business. The AC immediately said, "I'm shutting number four down, Now!" Dave pulled the handle which caged the engine (made it stop turning) and feathered the prop (turned the blades so they presented the least resistance to the wind). One engine out. Normally with a C-130, this is no problem. With a gunship, which can only maintain an altitude of 17,000 ft comfortably with all four churning, not so much. We had to make a shallow descent to 13,000 ft. None of us knew what would happen if we lost another engine. We were trying to ignore that blinking red hydraulic light on number two. We were tempted to put a paper cup over it so it wouldn't bother us! We didn't want to think about it. I knew that if we lost a third, we would become less than a powered glider, rapidly losing altitude until we hit the water. By the way, there is no record of a successful ditching of a C-130 of any type! With this extra ton of lead, there is no question, it would go down real fast!

We were past ETP, so turning back was out of the question. We weren't too concerned. There was a little landing strip on every one of these islands, and a C-130 was built so it could land on about any kind of terrain in a very short distance. Let number four stand at attention and let number two hydraulic light keep on blinking. We'd be there in about two hours. We had just met another A Model AC-130 headed for Elmendorf. We exchanged words on the weather at both locations. "Hot, Dry and Dusty" was the word at each place. It made us feel better even looking at number four not doing its job. We were feeling pretty good about our situation by the time we got within Ultra High Frequency (UHF) contact with Adak Approach Control.

"An unpredicted, fast moving cold front is coming in. Low visibility and ice on the runway is possible by the time you arrive." "Well, how do you do?" I thought. "I'd just as soon be in Birmingham right now." I verbalized on the intercom, "What in hell happened to "Hot, Dry and Dusty?" Silence! That told me more than I wanted to know. When David Harmon didn't speak to his copilot Larry Hillman in this type of situation, he had some serious thoughts on his mind. "Dave was normally serious, but never quiet. This quiet did not bode well." He came on the intercom. He had been in touch with the tower on another frequency. "The ceiling was at one hundred feet." Below minimums! Visibility was half a mile but intermittently three hundred feet and one-mile visibility, right at minimums. It didn't really matter. By now, with the fuel consumption of this damned AC model, we were committed. We were going to land at Adak. We had about one hour loiter time then "Bingo" fuel. We land!

We were now within one half hour of the base and were reviewing our options, which were few. Dave had briefed us on current conditions which were "iffy" at best. To make matter worse, the winds were coming from the north giving us a crosswind component of 18 knots. This was not good for a high wing aircraft like the C-130, but it was coming from the side where we had one engine caged. Dave was one of the best pilots I have ever known, along with Lt Col, then Captain, Tom Kuhns from C-118 days, and he would need every bit of his enormous skills to get us down safely, Oh! I forgot to mention. The runway had an RCR of four, meaning it was pretty damned slick. Ice with snow on top? Have you ever tried even walking on that? And if we can get this hog on the ground, we'll have a lessened result from braking and we just couldn't use as much of reverse (none on the starboard or right, side) as we wanted with that fluid flowing down the wing. We didn't want the fuel to be blown back into the engine where it could cause a fire or an explosion. At the same time, we didn't want to have to use the over run and definitely not the arresting cables all Naval Bases seemed to have.

It was time to start puckering as we began our approach. Another problem was the terrain. The runway started in the open, but about half way down, there was a fairly good-sized mountain on the right side which would change the condition from an 18 knot crosswind to either none or a very turbulent air caused my movement of air over and around the mountain which would meet with the straight line wind at the runway. I was on the radar, watching to assure they didn't get us too close to the mountain. However, they had Ground Approach Control (GCA) whereby a voice will give a constant assessment of the position relative to the runway. He would give Dave the desired heading, airspeed and glideslope as well as any other pertinent information. It was similar to when I talked the pilot down on an airborne radar approach. The difference is that this much larger and more precise radar was on the ground looking at the aircraft. On my radar approaches I was looking at the runway when I gave similar information. The talk should be steady and calm. It was, when he calmly told us to make a go around because the field just went below minimums. Dave took notice of his effectiveness as a GCA Controller. Excellent. That bodes well for if we absolutely had to get down. He could use GCA with me as a backup. Dave added enough power to get us climbing again to go back out over the ocean and prepare for another run at it. We were ready again and were on final when a Navy P-3 called "emergency, minimum fuel." Of course, GCA told us to go around again and hold south of the base until the Navy plane made it down, Damn, now we were eye balling our own fuel level. We had enough for a few more passes, but I wanted this bird on the ground!

It is a strange situation. I don't know if y'all have thought about it but, there are a few times during an aviators' career when he was in the air and was wishing desperately that he was on the ground. The inverse sometimes can be true as in the situation at Tan Son Hnut AB in Saigon. In that case, I was wishing to hell that I was in the air! At those times, you just have to relax, and if you can't do anything to improve the situation, just sit back and wait for the condition to change, which it invariably will. Hopefully for the better. By the way, we found out later that the "emergency" the P-3 declared was that they only had an hour plus fifteen minutes of fuel left. Not their fault, though we could have killed them. Navy flight rules!

We waited south of the field while the Navy P-3, who declared the emergency, finally made it to the ground after he too had to go around one time. Now, we were the only plane in the sky close to the airdrome. It was time to make a real run at it. "Buckle up folks, we are going for a ride" is the only thing I could think of. I have rarely been in a situation here the combination of negative factors combined to this extent to complicate a situation. Now, it was us who would declare an emergency for minimum fuel. Now they *had* to put us on the ground! We started our approach from about five miles out. The weather was going in and out of minimum requirements for landing. I knew Dave. WE WERE GONG TO LAND! Only the GCA didn't know it yet. I was monitoring our situation in case I had to take over and guide Dave on in. We were now within a half mile of the runway when we were advised that the conditions had deteriorated immediately and immensely. As far as we were concerned, we were committed. GCA finally told us to break off our approach and make a go around again. Dave calmly said: "Negative tower, we are out of gas, we don't know if the conditions will get better or worse. We are going to put this thing on the ground on this run. If you drop us, my Navigator can get us on the ground with a radar approach. He is talking us in now." GCA immediately picked up landing instructions again and wished us good luck because for all practical purposes, the weather was now "zero/zero," meaning that we were, for all practical purposes landing while blind. I was counting Dave down in my mind just in case. The GCA controller was doing an excellent job. We were matching exactly. He called us over the fence at 50 feet, perfect! GCA said: "Take over and land." Damn, he quit too soon. I came on the intercom and told Dave he was on heading and on glide slope. Keep everything steady, touchdown in 10 seconds. It was a long ten seconds, but I counted it down. And the last thing I jokingly told Dave was, "You are at touchdown." There was a bump felt by all. "Take over visually and taxi to the terminal." We were on the ground, but not sure where. Dave got the plane stopped. The first zero/zero landing ever for me. I didn't want another, but it was kind of fun. If you ever want to feel the adrenaline pumping, just try it. Tense! We waited. For a period of time we just sat there somewhere on the runway, learning how to breathe again. Fortunately, the cause of our feeling of foreboding had been successfully conquered. Now to get this thing parked.

We enjoyed the U.S. Navy hospitality for the evening with several adult beverages followed by a surprisingly good steak with some crab legs and their huge three-pronged forks that weighed about three pounds. We were sitting at a table with a couple of Navy pilots. Which was actually protocol for the Navy. Fill all the table before opening a new one. Join the group. Good practice! One of the Navy pilots asked us if we really had made a zero/zero landing.

Dave smiled and said, "Had to!" All the Navy guy did was shake his head and said, "Balls!" Dave got a bigger grin, if that was possible. Shaking his head the pilot just looked at his other tablemates. They were the ones who had declared an emergency while we were on that first final approach. Not too much was said, and we turned to general banter. You could tell that they were embarrassed. We didn't press it. Bud and SSgt Martin, the Loadmaster we picked up in Alaska, enjoyed their Club also. Their quarters, though Navy spartan, were clean and livable.

The next morning dawned bright and beautiful. After a great breakfast, we had to confess, the Navy really knew how to eat, but, their huge three-pronged forks still baffle me. We fired the AC-130 up and started to taxi out. But we didn't even get to the taxiway before the cargo compartment overheat light came on and pressurization failed. All of this was run from number two engine, the inside engine on the port side of the aircraft. We turned around and began taxiing back to the ramp when we saw some one of the ground crew come running toward us, waving his arms and pointing to number two engine. He was all excited and looked like he was hollering. FIRE! Immediately, Bud Hall stuck his head up through the hatch. There was a fifteen-foot streak of flames shooting out of the engine. The loadmaster yelled into his mike, "Number two is on fire! Cage number two." In a situation like that, we didn't care who was doing the yelling. Bud yelled the same thing. Fire and airplanes are not a good mix. Number two was shut down and as soon as it quit turning, the fire went out. The engine had quit pumping out whatever was fueling the flame. The ramp marshal cleared us back to our parking spot. The problem we had been warned about was a problem again. The foreboding returned, bigtime! Inspection showed only that a hydraulic hose inside the nacelle (front part of engine) had broken lose and the fluid was burning. As soon as the engine was feathered, the fire went out. No damage was found so the hose was reconnected and we proceeded to take off, though, because of having lost number two engine, we had lost pressurization and didn't want to take the time to get it fixed. Now, because we had no pressurization, we could only fly as high as 11,000 feet. Destination: Midway Island at flight level nine thousand. Farthest west inhabited piece of the United States of America.

ADAK NAS TO MIDWAY ISLAND

"A Beautiful Day for Flying"

THIS SECTION LEFT BLANK PURPOSELY
Nothing happened!

MIDWAY ISLAND TO KWAJALEIN ATOLL

"They Actually Pay us for doing this?"

After a nice smooth flight from Adak to Midway, we had another nice meal, courtesy of the U.S. Navy. I still marveled at their oversized three tined forks. Being bored, I did the same thing at breakfast. Hell, they could be used for weapons! Harpoons at twenty paces?

Though we heard the occasional squawk of a lonely, not sure why I thought he/she was lonely, Gooney Bird, our officer quarters were nice and quiet. The enlisted quarters, not so much. Several planes had arrived during the night and taxied right up to the hangar in which their quarters were located. Even though they were way up on the top floor, it still scared the crap out of them! The noisy engines were bad enough, but they had also shone their bright landing/taxi lights into their room, and cost them some much needed sleep. The officers got some good shut eye. The Navy, in my opinion, had this thing that the officers should be treated very well while the enlisted troops, of lesser rank than Chief Petty Officer, were treated like dirt. Well, at least very poorly. But: We were not going to worry about Navy protocol, or whatever. We were ready to take on the next leg of this odyssey. We lifted off nicely and pointed our bird southwest and leveled at nine thousand feet. Still no pressurization, but we could get it fixed at Kwaj. I was certain that Kwajalein was ahead there someplace. We'd be there in a few hours at the western end of the Pacific Missile Test Range.

Now, as we settled into the routine of watching the beautiful Pacific Ocean passing beneath us we once again began breathing easy. Destination: Kwajalein Atoll. Ah, Damn that is beautiful. Nice big swells which we could see because we were at low altitude, with small whitecaps scattered around. So much more calm than the rough Atlantic Ocean.

I took up residence in the co-pilots' seat while he took a break. Great place for viewing a beautiful day. "Damn, Dave," I said over intercom to the AC. "They actually pay us for doing this!" He keyed the mike and just chuckled. Then said, looking around, "Yeh, hard to believe." The co-pilot returned and Dave said, "Better go back and find out where we are. A Situation Report (SitRep) is due in a few minutes." These reports are due every hour of flight or every five degrees of travel when going east to west or the opposite way. A good tool for the ground folks, but an inconvenience on such a nice day. With a SitRep, we give them our profile including a calculated fuel expenditure line and a comparison of actual fuel consumption. They were staying on track nicely. Our current position in relation to the flight plan is also required as was a position report. But now, at this low altitude, there was no radio contact so we were transmitting in the blind.

I gave Dave what he wanted, including an ETA (Estimated Time of Arrival) at Kwajalein Atoll of fifteen twenty-three (Three twenty-three PM), a little over two hours and twenty minutes 'till touchdown at Kwaj, and went to my bunk for a quick practice nap. After a few hours of watching a very calm Pacific Ocean slip beneath our wings, It was still a beautiful day bordering on getting boring, as all long over water flights do. It was about one thirty when I got back off of the top bunk. About then we spotted some small islands on the horizon. We were soon watching those tiny tropical islands slipping by beneath us. They were real small with tiny beaches and they were covered with Kava trees, a hardy tree common to this area which grew in abundance on Wake Island. Everything was beautiful, including the weather and those islands. A little after two o'clock Bud said he was going to do his routine engine check from the rear cargo compartment. Numbers one and two checked good as did number three and four on the right side of the airplane. He was about to go back up front to his seat between the pilots when he thought he saw something aft of Number Four that made him hesitate. Yep, there it was again. He thought he was seeing little puffs of smoke coming from the engine but wasn't sure. He told the AC and maintained a vigilant watch and it paid off, In spades! This time he thought he saw a little puff of smoke *and* a little flame coming out of the exhaust. "Hey, AC. I think I just saw a little puff of smoke and fire coming from number four tailpipe." Dave scanned the instrument panel. Everything was in the green. No trouble seen here. "Yeh, there it is again! Feather Number Four!" It wasn't so much a request as an order. Dave acted accordingly and pulled the 'T' handle which feathered Number Four engine. Puffs of smoke and/or close intermittent bits of flame coming out of a turboprop engine indicated that the turbine had started wobbling. This was not a good thing. The wobbling turbine, turning at over three thousand RPM, was ready to explode, sending shrapnel in who knows what direction, and possibly causing the loss of the aircraft and crew. It had happened before. It also could ruin your whole day! There were so many things that could. I decided we had really had our share of them on this trip.

"Damn," I muttered to myself. "Here we go again! Is somebody trying to tell us something?" Dave's hand had barely returned to the yoke when number one low oil light started flashing. Dave said into his mike, "Looks like we have an oil leak." He was interrupted by the co-pilot. Larry who said urgently, "number two hydraulic light just came on, steady! It didn't even flash for a little while this time. It just came on steady!" "Damn, what else could happen?" Bud Hall had stayed watching number four to make sure it had stopped turning without causing any external damage. He thought, "A least that was a good thing!" Dave followed with the news (like we needed more), Number one oil light just changed to steady. "Well hell, three out of four are screwed up now!" I was about ready to voice a brilliant analysis when Bud, the Super Flight Engineer spoke up. "Hey guys, I don't know how to tell you this, but there is a stream of fluid about eight inches wide running back off the wing about six inches outboard of number three exhaust pipe." "Well, Holy Shit! That does it! I want off of this thrill ride!" I wondered what in hell do we do now? That exhaust runs at about thirty-two hundred degrees! Not a comforting thought. Damn, that whole sequence from the wobbling turbine to the steaming fuel took probably less than two minutes! Talk about things going to hell in a hurry? This was it! One engine caged, three on Mandatory shut down conditions. That doesn't add up very well, especially on a gunship. I got busy at my position. I couldn't do a damned thing about those engines. Those were the domain of the pilots and flight engineer. The Super Flight Test Engineer and Pilots, that is! What are *they* going to do? Me? I was going to find out where we were. "MAYDAY, MAYDAY, MAYDAY!" "Damn, I guess this is serious?" Yeh, it was serious and I knew it as well as the rest of the crew. We all listened intently on our headsets, straining our ears for a response to our urgent emergency cry, in vain. No Answer! We flat needed help, and none was coming, though I didn't know what they could do. But, a sympathetic friendly voice would be nice! We were up in this big, blue, suddenly lonely, sky all by ourselves. Evidently, no one was near in case we tried to ditch or do something stupid like that. This was once again, one of those rare times when I wished to hell that I was on the ground instead of in the air! We were still over two hours from landing!

Now, to discuss options which, we knew, were basically nonexistent. One feathered and three needing to be feathered. No big deal but cause for concern in an RB-36 in which I had flown in what seems now like a long time ago, even another lifetime. But this baby didn't have ten engines like the B-36's had, we were oh for four in baseball parlance. Four on this plane, but none were supposed to be working. This hangar queen should be in a hanger, not in the sky with five souls on board (SOB's)! That was the term Dave used when broadcasting in the blind for rescue assistance in case things got worse. It was also the required terminology for announcing how many folks, total, were on an aircraft at any time, not just in an emergency. After discussing over and over with many pregnant pauses in between, the Aircraft Commander, copilot and flight engineer discussed the technicalities of our situation. No simulator would even try this. I kept pretty much silent, keeping track of where in hell we were, and broadcasting, also in the blind, our position every 10 minutes, hoping someone would hear my transmissions. After about an hour, they had exhausted every option.

"Well," our intrepid Aircraft Commander said nonchalantly. "Here's the deal. We are in a little bit of trouble. We have one engine shut down and three others on mandatory shutdown conditions. We can't shut down any more if we want to keep flying." I interrupted, "We are also flying over some of the most shark infested water in the world, so consider that before we consider ditching this lead sled." Dave continued, "Damn, thanks for that encouraging bit of information, Jack!" He continued, "Now, we will lose some altitude and I don't know when she will level off, but probably about seven thousand feet. If we lose another engine, we will become a powered glider that is looking for a place to land. So, we have to keep all three turning. We can't afford to take the chance on restarting number four. It is done for the day. We keep all of the rest running unless one catches on fire, then we shut it down and prepare to ditch and you know there has never been a successful ditching of a C-130. We also have about seventeen hundred extra pounds on the left side, so that won't help, but we will set it down next to one of those islands and try to run it up onto the beach. Does anyone else have a better suggestion?" Silence! "OK, then. nav, how long to Kwajalein?" "One hour and seventeen minutes" was my firm answer. No one on the crew will ever forget those numbers! That was the time left before landing!

What seemed like another lifetime passed before the co-pilot was finally able to raise Kwajalein on the radio. He explained our situation. Kwaj tower came in: You are cleared to land in your choice of direction. Winds are light and variable and ceiling and visibility are unlimited. "Thanks, tower." But they interrupted again. "You probably won't want to hear this, but you have to know. Be advised, one half of the runway is closed for repair." "Well hell! That puts the icing on the cake." Thank God that we had one of the best pilots around. We were going to need him at his best.

Dave had to make a slight correction to our heading when TA-CAN locked on. I had drawn my track line to an island just a little west of Kwaj. The change made no difference in the time, but it still should not have happened. Sheer carelessness on my part! Our one hour and seventeen minutes was now down to less than fifteen until touchdown. The left side of the long runway was closed down. This was the business end of the Pacific Missile Firing Range and so, had the best of everything. It was a long and wide runway, and the left side being closed was no problem. Dave greased it in and used brakes only. Reversal of props would have sucked the running fuel right back into the engine causing a fire or, probably, worse. We rolled to a stop, set the brakes and shut down all remaining engines. We got away from that damned machine as quickly and as far as we could reasonably get in case there was an explosion! We did a quick debrief to an unbelieving crowd. We left with the admonition, "go see for yourself and get us some transport to the club. I think we all need a stiff drink or two!"

Then it got bad!

KWAJALEIN ATOLL TO KORAT AB VIA GUAM

"I wanna' go home"

After we landed at Kwajalein Atoll in the southern Pacific, and so thankful that we were safely on the ground and had not blown up in mid-air as it appeared we should have, we all came down with the flu. Like everything else, we did this together. The three officers were living in one suite with only one bathroom. I'll not regale you with all the fun that entailed, but rather go to the point where we were ready to happily leave "Kwaj" behind. When we arrived at Base Operations to check on the status of our plane, yes they were still trying to get it fixed enough to fly after six days of the entire crew being out of commission, we discovered that the aircraft still was not ready to continue its quixotic or should I call it "Chaotic" type mission. We were approached by another AC-130A crew who was stationed at Korat AB and were in no hurry to leave this exotic paradise and return to the humdrum and dangerous duty at their home base. They allowed as how they had a perfectly good gunship ready and operational. Our ship was still acting like a hangar queen, presiding over all the maintenance available but still hiding out in the hangar. Well, this was music to our ears. We were damned well ready and anxious to leave this "paradise." It had not been a paradise for us and held no enjoyable memories. We were ready to get off this chunk of Coral with its beautiful beaches and azure waters. We had been gone way longer than we had planned. Besides, I was going broke buying clothing, after leaving all my hang up clothes in my closet at home in Birmingham Wow! That seemed like eons ago.

We jumped at the chance to get out of there, desert this this dog and get the other gunship delivered to home base and jet our way back home back on commercial aircraft. The swap was made and we proceeded with flight preparations. Just as we were about to board our plane for departure, we received word that our original ship was in commission and ready to roll. So, the swap had gained the Korat crew only a few extra hours away from home base. They would be flying our same route about two hours behind us. About four hours later, we heard, "MAYDAY, MAYDAY, MAYDAY!" Number two hydraulic line had once more come unglued and caused an engine shutdown for the umpteenth time. I guess the crew was tired of Kwajalein, but I think it was more of a delaying tactic to keep from getting back to Korat when we heard them transmitting in the blind that they were diverting to Truk Island, another dot on the Pacific Ocean map about 800 miles farther east and that much closer to Korat AB. There was another big battle there about which I know nothing except we kicked some enemy ass! The stats are astounding! I doubted they would find much maintenance support there, but, no one on our crew, nor probably theirs, even cared. We were rid of that beast and couldn't have cared less when or if they would ever get home. We were just happy that the dog was now someone else's problem. We figured that it would take about two weeks to get help to them. Returning a sick gunship couldn't have been a real high priority. I wondered what Truk Island might look like, but I was way more interested in getting this relatively good aircraft delivered and begin our trek home in commercial aircraft comfort. We were tired of babysitting sick airplanes and our own tired and sick bodies. We had been gone from home way too long.

Andersen AFB, Guam was our intended destination. What the hell. Will miracles never cease and all those trite phrases! This new, to us, gunship delivered us there on time and in good shape. And I mean plane and crew. A few toddies and a good meal preceded a few after dinner drinks and a good nights' sleep.

The next day broke bright, clear and for us a lazy late arising breakfast, preflight and everything went just fine. This was beginning to get scary. Everything was just too smooth! Looking over our shoulders, we ventured out to our new non-hangar queen AC-130A. Everything looked great, so it was on to greater glory! Korat was still about twenty-four hundred miles away and this lead sled would never make it that far, never! I drew up a flight plan for Clark AB. It would have been a more fun crew rest at Mactan AB, if they would send us to Cebu City to spend the night, but that was a huge "if." Clark it was. There can be almost as much fun had there! And so, it was from Guam that we would sally forth with Clark on our minds. We had already planned an extra day in the Philippines, but that seems eons ago now. We were in a different state of mind than we thought we would be at this juncture.

That old Earl Laney song "Detroit City," and "I Wanna go Home" kept running thru my mind. Soon, I thought, Soon! Well, as us old timers say, "That's what we thought at the time!"

Naturally, it wouldn't quite work out quite that way.

Since we got into Clark fairly early because we were still headed west and were running with the sun, we made the obligatory stop at the Fire Empire. I told the guys about the free samples but after all is said and done, they would surely agree that this little place had the coldest beer in town. Soon we were in the mood for something stronger and perhaps a dozen oysters for fifty cents and a steak dinner for about three dollars. By now, having an after dinner drink would completely make all appetites sated for the night. We had decided to get a fairly early start so we could get some kind of transport to Bangkok for a half way around the world ticket to good old Birmingham. Boy, were ever thinking wrong!

It was with pleasantness in the world that we landed our "new" old gunship at Korat AB, Thailand. The end of the road! We were thru flying those damned lopsided things, hopefully for the rest of our lives. Now to get a flight from Bangkok to The U.S.

Fate can be a trickster. Fate can be fickle, Fate can also lull you to sleep. After we had landed the AC-130A, without another hiccup, we were feeling pretty good about the trip and anxiously dreading the long trip in those small coach seats. Another thing we, or at least me, didn't like was that we would be traveling west to east. There is just no good schedule going that direction. I always hated it, but we couldn't go the other way because there were still some bad hombres in that direction, starting right next door to Thailand in Burma, now known as Myanmar.

It was now when that Fickle Finger of Fate showed up. It can appear at the craziest of times! Like now, in the Operations Office.

"Hi gang." Said the Major with the cheery demeanor. Having fallen into traps to do other Majors favors, I was leery from the start of this one. I knew he wanted something! "We've been flight following you for a few days now." I understand that you are the Test Flight Crew out of Hayes Test Flight in Birmingham. Dave seemed pleased with the recognition. I just became more leery. I was right. Someone always needs a favor.

The Chief of Operations told Dave that he just happened to have an H model AC-130 that needs to go back to Birmingham, so if you wouldn't mind, it would save us having to give up a crew for a couple weeks and you can go back on your own schedule instead of having to ride in those damned narrow coach seats with no legroom. Next Freedom Flight is not scheduled for a little over a week and that's the one you would be scheduled to take. You could be home by then if you want to take the gunship. "Want." Once again, Dave made up our minds for us. "Hell Yes, we'll take it. We are qualified in all models of the C-130." I think that "want" word got to him! "Well, crapola! Here we go again, but at least it was a modern piece of junk this time." Bigger engines, longer flight duration, higher altitude faster airspeed. Dave used all these descriptive beauties to entice us. The only thing I liked about the idea was not having to sleep in a 'Hootch" here until Freedom Flight time. Hell, they'd probably be having us fly missions. OK, I'm on board! The others also fell into the trap. A smiling Ops Officer said, "Thanks, fellas. You are doing the right thing. See ya in the morning."

KORAT RTAB TO CLARK AB, PHILIPPINES

"Holy Shit, what was that?"

We rolled out next morning for a relatively late morning show time for our preparation to take another gunship for a ride. Since we were only going to Clark AB for the first RON (Remain Overnight) on our long journey half way around the world we weren't in any rush to get airborne. While we were doing flight planning, I noticed they had planned us for a higher airspeed and altitude than normal. It was comparable to the HC-130H Air Rescue aircraft I had flown out of Lajes Field in the Azores, that group of islands about six hundred miles off the coast of Portugal to whom they belonged, remember? It seemed so long ago!

With some trepidation and in high spirits, we wended our way from Base Operations to the waiting AC-130H, Hercules, gunship. We were finally going home! We saw our bird awaiting us on the ramp looking just like any other "Herkey Bird," as we called our beloved workhorse. Then we started to climb into the cockpit. I immediately knew I was in big trouble and I heard the engineer who went onto the flight deck ahead of me utter a resounding, "Oh shit!" Now I knew damned good and well that we were in trouble, only not just trouble, but Big Trouble! I didn't recognize hardly anything in that cockpit except the windows and crew-member seats. It was a completely different "ball of wax!" Dear Lord, what has Dave done now, and what are we going to do about it? The answer came soon enough. After Dave Harmon, the Chief Pilot, talked to Bud Hall, our Flight Engineer, they decided that being that Great Bad Ass Test Flight Crew from Birmingham, it was close enough to some of the variety of different model C-130's that we had test flown in the Birmingham test facility that they could hack it across the pond and get back home. Yeh, right! What about me trying to find our way back? Hell, I didn't recognize one piece of navigation equipment except the sextant. And going across the vast Pacific with only celestial navigation hadn't been tried since a bunch of intrepid idiots took off in outrigger canoes from relative safety somewhere around Tahiti and accidentally ran into the Hawaiian Islands after making a "U" turn near Chili many centuries earlier. Check with James Michener's "Hawaii" for more exact dates. Right now, I was wondering just what in hell I was supposed to do!

Dave was very helpful. Like so much Bull Shit! Our ever re-sourceful leader spied a crew pre-flighting for a mission in the same model and suggested that I go over there and ask the navigator for some help in figuring out this bunch of black boxes which I have never seen before.

I did.

As suspected, they were getting ready for a mission along the Ho Chi Min Trail running between Vietnam and Laos, the main supply route from North Vietnam to all points down south. I tracked down one of the navigators, they had two, and explained my situation. I said in a rather apologetic voice, "Would you mind coming over to our aircraft and explain how all of this new, at least to me, nav-igational contraptions work?" He looked at me like I was a com-plete idiot. I couldn't disagree with him. After coming out of what looked like a state of minor shock, he said just a few words, very carefully and softly spoken, to this idiot in a green flight suit whom he had never seen before. "Do you know how long it took me to learn to operate this navigational system?" He answered his own question before I could reply. I just stood there with open, noiseless mouth. The sweat was running down my back. Yeh, it was that hot already, but that wasn't the only reason. I hoped his answer would be "maybe a couple of hours," and I knew I didn't even have that much time. But what the hell, why sweat it? Weren't we that Great Bad Ass Test Flight Crew out of Birmingham where they tested ev-erything and solved all problems? After all, we had delivered an AC-130A that had been stuck in Elmendorf AFB, Alaska for three months, defying every (and there were many) crew that tried to get it on its way. Hadn't they called us to get it off of their ramp, and didn't we do just that? Yeh, Man!

Oh wait! Wasn't that the airplane that almost killed us about six ways on the leg between the famous Midway Island, Hawaii and Kwajalein Atoll? Yeh, and come to think of it, we had delivered a different plane and had heard the crew of our original "A" model call "Mayday: Number two engine shut down and we are diverting to Truk Island." Oh yeh, that one. FLIGHT TEST! Yeh, great. It said so on our shoulder patch. No, wait. That was a B-57 there. Well, it must say it somewhere because we were the best and the brightest. It didn't really seem like it just then, when I looked like a pleading hound dog in an oversized, wrinkled green skin. Oh well. We had always said that if God had intended men to fly he would have given us oversized, wrinkled green skin. As the saying goes, "Ever onward and upward" or something like that.

The resident navigator finally answered his own question: "TEN MONTHS!" Damn, he didn't have to shout. I too was a navigator and knew a little about time and months! After shaking his head and looking for someone to come haul me away, he just said, "Come on, and I'll give you a very quick briefing. And you say you are going to take this bird Stateside? All of this equipment breaks down a lot and they don't have too many places that can fix it along your way because it is so new. Are all of you nuts?" I could only speak for myself, so I just nodded my head while he was tuning red, about ready to explode in front of an idiot with an obvious death wish. How prescient!

We finally came to terms and he reluctantly agreed to give me an ultra-quick tutorial on things it took him ten months to learn. What a dumb ass, I thought. It took him ten months and he is going to pass all that knowledge on to me in thirty or so minutes? Either I, a Flight Test Navigator, am brilliant or he is very slow. I had to find out the hard way. I was the incompetent!

As he began giving me a briefing and what little instructions he had time to give, he found a challenge like he had never found before. He said, "See this here Doppler?" (he was a southern boy). I gave a gurgling sound and managed to croak, "What is a Doppler?" Oh shit! You don't even know what a doppler is?" I said, "Well, when a train is coming toward you, the sound gets compressed and so it gets louder and just the opposite after it goes by. The sound waves decompress and the sound lessens." The Captain threw his hat down on the navigator table and started to give me a sub-basic, very condensed cliff note version of some very complicated equipment like Doppler, C-Loran and other evil looking things that I don't even remember now. Boy! Was I ever out of date? Yep! "Crap! OK, here is the deal." With that, he gave me some very rudimentary instructions on how to at least turn the instruments on. He covered the operation, but it seemed that he was speaking another language. A half hour passed very quickly, and I didn't know a whole lot more when he left than I did before he came. I thanked him anyway and wished him luck with the action on the ever-dangerous Ho Chi Min Trail.

Dave was unfazed by my admission that I was completely confused by the new-fangled navigation gear on this bird, but I could at least get it turned on and do a little with the doppler. He figured that was good enough to travel eight thousand miles, mostly over water. THIS MAN WAS CRAZY! INSANE! But he was our only ticket home now.

We finally taxied out and took our place in line among many planes that were taking off to wage war. All of us were anxious to get airborne. We were finally cleared onto the active runway and given the authorization to start takeoff roll and head toward Clark AB in the good ol' Philippines where I was stationed for five months back in 1974. What a five months! But, that is another story that may or may not be told.

Well, Hell! Already this piece of complicated electronics turns out to be a pile of doggie poop and we're barely off the ground. Crap! Already I'm back down to celestial only unless I can figure out this C-Loran, which is doubtful. I'll have to wait until I'm over water for the Loran signal to be valid, so after we get past DaNang, I can cross reference with the pilots' VORTAC. What a way to start an eight-thousand mile mission! Heading the wrong direction and not really knowing what I'm doing with this, to me, worthless pile of rack mounted shit in front of me.

Consider it. We were starting out on an eight thousand mile trip in a plane that I didn't want to be in anyway. Another AC-130 with my main piece of equipment upon which I was going to rely telling me I'm heading the wrong direction to get home. Now, it was beginning to look like another trip from hell!" But, we were barely off the ground. Maybe it will straighten up. Kinda like tapping your remote to get TV to come in better.

We were climbing out from Korat to our assigned altitude of twenty-six thousand feet when I tried out my new Doppler knowledge. I decided to get the heading for the shortest way back to Birmingham. Much to my surprise, it told us to take a westerly heading. It would be closer, mileage wise, to go over Burma, India, the Mideast and the Mediterranean Sea and on across the Atlantic to get home than to go east over the Pacific Ocean. While I was explaining my newfound knowledge from my newfound friend, my doppler, this strange phenomenon or whatever, to the rest of the crew, the doppler hesitated and then switched to an easterly heading. We had just passed a point where we were equidistant, headed east or west, from home. Mileage wise, we were at an equal distance to get home by going either direction, about eight thousand miles. Of course, that was as the crow flies, but, we were in a damned old "H" model airplane. While I was pondering this strange phenomenon, I decided to further inspect this strange new aircraft. I had seen a big bubble in the ramp of this gunship and surmised it was for verifying target effectiveness of the 20mm Gatlin gun, the 50 Caliber heavy weapon and the 105 Caliber Howitzer used for urban renewal when the others weren't doing the job. Wow! It was a huge, neat plastic type bubble slung under the rear bottom of the fuselage. As I had mentioned, it was at least three to four feet in diameter. What a view! There were no actual positions which would indicate where a crewman would sit. An ACM (Additional Crew Member) just along for a hop back to Clark AB and I found positions by the bubble and were watching the world go by. He had found a nice comfy looking mat to lie on. I guess the spotter did lie down. I just sat by the bubble leaning over for a better view. It was an excellent and fascinating view and rather exciting to watch the little villages come and go under our mighty climbing steed. But, it had been awhile since a pitiful breakfast and we were both hungry, so we both went forward toward the crew compartment. He stayed in the forward cargo compartment where there were a few seats, and I went forward to my crew position and get out one of the box lunches. I mainly wanted to get lunch out of the way so I could get back to the bubble in time to see the beautiful valleys and waterfalls of the western mountains of Vietnam and Laos between Korat, Thailand and DaNang, South Vietnam. I was in the process of taking my seat at the navigator station when everything went to hell! Papers flew, fog enveloped the cabin and there was a very loud explosive sound and, "HOLY SHIT!! What was that?" My ears exploded. Oh Crap! What in hell happened now? The flight engineer immediately called that the aircraft had suffered an explosive decompression. Instinctively, our training kicked in and everyone immediately put on their oxygen masks. We were at almost 18,000 feet and climbing. Dave, immediately after donning his mask, declared an emergency and requested unrestricted decent to 10,000 feet. Air control cleared us to descend immediately. They also said there was no other traffic in the area at that altitude, so we were good to go. We went down!

Something had blown out somewhere. I had already put on my headset and mask as my thoughts immediately went back to that big ol' bubble. I called the Aircraft Commander and told him and the rest of the crew over the intercom that I felt that the observation bubble could be the site of the decompression. I told him I would investigate. Dave called back and said, "Keep your butt in your seat until we can perform a rapid descent to an altitude where supplemental oxygen was not necessary," or something to that effect. Upon leveling at 10,000 feet, we first did a quick medical check to see if anyone had suffered any physical damage from the rapid depression. After making sure that I could breathe normally at 10,000 feet, I immediately got up and hurriedly proceeded to the cargo compartment, back to the ramp area of the aircraft, stopping well short of a gaping hole in the floor where the plastic bubble had been. An ashen faced ACM standing just behind me now, was jabbering about the effects of a rapid decompression. It was a new experience to him. He and I were both staring out at that open hole where he and I could have been free falling had we not let our hunger and, in my case, the desire to see all of those waterfalls and valleys, overrule our thirst for gazing at the country side slipping by. All jabbering had stopped. I think we both were in a minor stage of shock, and I'm not completely sure it was "minor." That whole damned bubble was gone and everything not tied down within about ten feet had been sucked out of the plane, including the mat where the ACM had been laying. It was making the kind of noise that only rushing wind can make. It was so noisy I could barely think! Damn. THAT could have been US!

Instinctively I wondered how it would feel to free fall from about 17,000 feet. The free fall would have been bad enough and would have taken some time while we would be flailing wildly trying to grab hold of something that wasn't there. I still have daytime nightmares about that feeling of falling and the helplessness of knowing you were going to die and the extreme efforts to try to stop your fall. I wondered if I would be screaming or just be calm in facing a fate that was certain death, not worse than death, but just plain old death. From that altitude, we would probably reach terminal velocity. The thought crossed my mind that the free fall wouldn't be bad and could possibly be an adrenalin rush, but OH! That sudden stop! At terminal velocity, about 120 miles per hour after 15 seconds, we would have made a pretty good double SPLAT! That would not be good! I suddenly had the urge to check my under drawers to see if I should get into my clothes bag and get a change. It felt OK, so I decided to get back to my navigator station after lending my hand to help the ACM back to his seat and make sure he was strapped in. I ordered him not to go near the gaping hole where we could have easily died. He responded with a very quiet and shaky, "Yes Sir!" I doubt if he could have said more if he tried. He was not a flyer, and I'm sure he now wished he was at his desk job. Shit, I was wishing to hell that I was on the ground, anywhere!

Dave called Clark AB and declared an emergency. Clark AB who had control of our aircraft now directed us to return to Korat. By now, we were about over the Laos/Vietnam border and well on our way to Clark. As Major Harman rejected their kind advice and told Clark Traffic Control that we would continue to Clark Air Base where they had better maintenance and medical personnel, he told Captain Hillman, to take over the flying aspect of this situation. He knew from experience that Clark AB, of all places, did not like anyone to question their supreme authority. Dave was not one to back away. Clark, we are going to continue to your house (old Vietnam Air Force talk which meant your base. In Vietnam, we always said your house, because if the bad guys were listening as they always seemed to do, we didn't what them to know at which base we were going to land so they could get ready to shoot at us at the end of the runway) while he talked some sense into the bone heads of the Air Control idiots at Clark ACP. Dave never did like being told what to do especially by Air Traffic Control folks. Clark ACP told our AC, "I am giving you a. direct order to return to Korat"! Dave very loudly responded, "I am the Aircraft Commander which means that I control all aspects of my flight as long as I am the AC. We are continuing to Clark!" After a few minutes, Major Harman was directed to go directly to the Chief of Wing Operations upon landing. Dave tersely replied: "Roger/Wilco." He told Hillman that he had control of his airplane again.

I think we need to review a few things here:

First: Roger /Wilco in Air Force parlance means Message Received/Will Comply.

Second: The reason for Clark Area Control to direct us to go back to Korat was to get us on the ground as soon as possible. There is always danger of physical harm from an explosive decompression. The air had just been expelled from our lungs at a rate that cannot be duplicated by an individual. It is a weird feeling that can have some detrimental consequences. The nearest comparison I can think of is when you get the wind knocked out of you. It is a helpless and scary feeling. And, though it lasts for only a few seconds, it scares the hell out of you by its suddenness, the noise and fog caused by condensing air, and the frightening physical response of helplessness. For a few seconds, there is absolutely nothing you can do except fight becoming panicked. The fog is real and thick, the noise is piercing, and anything not tied down really goes flying.

Third: Why did the bubble blow out? The bubble is at least three feet in diameter and made of a materiel much weaker than the piece of the aircraft structure (the rear fuselage) removed to make room for this observation post. That makes for a rather large weak spot. We were accustomed to having our aircraft pressurized to about eight thousand feet, a comfortable altitude for flying. But, other aircraft do not have a weak spot like that bubble. They are solid aircraft frame and sheet metal. Though the Aircraft Commander is ultimately responsible for anything that goes right OR wrong on his aircraft, none of us took the weakness of the bubble into consideration as we should have. Naturally, problems were bound to ensue. As we climbed higher, the air got thinner and as we kept the cabin pressure at eight thousand feet, the relative difference between inside and outside pressure continued to grow until the bubble mounts just could not keep the observation bubble attached to the aircraft. The ultimate problem was that instead of leaking air to equalize the two pressures, it just blew out all at once. Suddenly, the inside and outside pressures were the same!

Fourth: The reason for the observation bubble in the first place was to keep an eye out for enemy activity that could cause harm, not damage assessment as I had earlier assumed. Instead of a plain loadmaster as the regular C-130 has, the AC-130 (AC stands for gunship, don't ask. It's an Air Force thing.) Anyway, the AC-130H gunship has a loadmaster /illuminator operator who scans for threats while lying on a pad looking out of the bubble. If he sees or perceives a threat, he has both flare and chaff dispensers at his disposal to alleviate that threat. The AC-130 normally flies at a level low enough as to not need pressurizing, say around seven thousand feet. We didn't know that before, but now we surely did, especially the ACM and me! It is a fact that neither will ever overlook again!

Fifth: Clark Control wanted us to back to Korat AB because they had all the supplies and were manned to replace/repair bubbles.

Back to the story:

In the meantime, while Larry was flying the plane, I was listening to the exchange between Dave and the Control Center. I was wondering just what kind of trouble he was in now? There would surely be repercussions from his blatant disregard of instructions from a controlling authority. I couldn't help myself. I just had to listen in. This is what it really sounded like. He flat told them, "I am in command of this aircraft and I can access the situation in this airplane better than someone on the ground 500 miles away, and I am going to take whatever action I deem necessary. You can take whatever action you deem necessary when I get on the ground." "Roger, Shadow 13, We *will* take whatever action we deem necessary, as you put it, and it will start when you get on the ground. As for right now, I am ordering you to return to Korat, short of that, bring your ass up to Base Operations as soon as you land." Dave couldn't help it, "I'll taxi to the ramp first. Looking forward to seeing you on the ramp, or wherever, at Clark. Nice chatting with you. Over and Out." That basically ended the conversation as we flew over the coast of South Vietnam at DaNang AB. You could almost see the steam coming out of Dave's ears. No one said much to him for a while. Bud Hall gave him some readings, and that was about it. You just didn't want to bother Dave when he was mad. Now, he was mad AND frustrated. A real bad combination for him and us! Naturally, we flew on to Clark at eight thousand feet because there was no way we could pressurize the airplane and we didn't want to have to wear our oxygen masks for several uncomfortable hours. They were that bad! As long as we maintained an altitude of 11,000 feet or less, the requirement for use of oxygen was not met. I watched the waterfalls and valleys go by from the safety of the cockpit. Still beautiful, but not the unrestricted view I had wanted. Shit! That was so f'ing close! How many more times am I going to almost get killed on this trip? I just want it over with!

CLARK AB, PHILIPPINES

"Are we Through Yet"

Upon landing, we were met by a Lieutenant Colonel (Dave was a Major) who gave Dave a direct order to come with him to Base Operations immediately. There was also a Flight Surgeon who carefully looked us over and questioned us as to our physical condition. After questioning the rest of the crew and satisfying himself that we were all OK in spite of the rapid decompression, we were allowed to proceed to the Billeting Office and continue on with our lives. The Aircraft Commander was led away by the Lieutenant Colonel, who looked like he didn't know whether to maintain his stern attitude or laugh at the situation. He knew what punishment would be meted out. Our Aircraft Commander would be punished for not following controlling authority instructions by being forced to attend a day-long period of reading flight manuals on how to fly airplanes. The irony, and the funny part, was the fact that our AC had over seventy five hundred flying hours in a variety of aircraft. Probably five thousand of those hours were in all models of the C-130. To make it worse, they had him reading manuals of all early models of the C-130 except for the "H" model. They didn't have any manuals on that one yet. He was one of the best pilots in the Air Force and his escort knew it. The Lt Col had known Dave, though not well, from a previous assignment and was well aware of his personality and his prowess.

Because the Aircraft Commander has the ultimate responsibility for the mission, the rest of us were free to do what we wanted. How nice! A free day in my old haunts? Hmmm. I didn't know if that was good or bad. After sleeping late, I got up and went to the Club for some lunch. I was getting tired of Clark already. My old flying squadron, the 776th TAS, had been deactivated, so I didn't know anyone here anymore. It was from here and, in 1973, Ching Chuan Kang Air Base in Taichung, Taiwan, where we would go "in country" to our Forward Operating Location (FOL) from whence we flew our combat missions, mostly into Cambodia.

Old habits always seem to return, so I went out the side door to the barber shop. A haircut, shave and manicure for four dollars and fifty cents. "Yeh, I could get used to this again." Then I took a taxi to the Base Exchange to pick up some more clothes. I hoped I now had enough to get me home. At least in this part of the world, shorts were the things to wear and I bought some that I could wash out in the Billets' sink and made sure they were the type that dried real fast. Then, I bought a few trinkets, that I didn't need to take home with me. The girls in the music shop area remembered me and, while giggling almost uncontrollably, immediately started searching for the style of music they knew I enjoyed. After buying several good LP's for the same old price, two dollars and twenty cents for first rate name brand LP's, I went back to my quarters for a practice nap which turned into a real one. By the time I was up and around, our intrepid Aircraft Commander had finished his punishment and was ready for a beer. Since we were staying in the "White Elephant," a six story white concrete building, He burst into my room and said, "O'Connor, let's get out of this damned place. Where is the nearest place to get a cold beer not called the Club"? I responded, "Damn it, Dave, don't you know how to knock? I have a couple places in mind but let's see what's happening in the Ratskeller*." Absolutely nothing was going on, but it was the closest beer, *including* the place called The Club. We had a couple cool ones in the basement as I told him about a few places off base. *Yeh, though of German origin, many clubs around the world called their casual bar in the cellar the Ratskeller. This one was like most others, not a trace of German heritage in sight, or mind.

We called a taxi and went to the Freedom Gate which emptied into my old home of Angeles City. It was not really your optimum city. Dirty and poor, it had that old decrepit poverty ridden charm.

From first glance, not much had changed in the two years I had been gone. It looked like you could still get anything you wanted and probably have it delivered to your room. I wondered if I could find my old, small rental house. It was inside a stone wall compound with glass shards and razor wire sticking out of the top to discourage the "stealie boys." The Filipina people were wonderful people, but by tradition, stealing was just something they did. Pickpocketing was considered an honorable profession. I never did unravel how these two aspects of life worked together and seemed to be the core of these highly principled and mostly devout Catholic people.

I decided not to look for my old place. It would just be a waste of time and we hadn't even had a hot bath and massage yet. I couldn't help think of the place though. I had a houseboy whose main charge was to keep my refrigerator stocked with San Miguel beer, and I had a friendly rat about the size if a small dog that would sit by his hole in the sidewalk and let me get within feet of him while walking to my red Rambler station wagon before diving into his escape hole. Damn, he was the biggest rat I had ever seen and that includes the well-known giants of Bangkok. A few of the folks I flew with and their wives lived in the compound, including a bar girl from the "Dirty Dozen," a triangular shaped tangle of about 100 bars and massage parlors in Taichung, near CCK AB. Why it was called the Dirty Dozen was lost on me. My guess is that it started small? She came down from Taichung with her First Lieutenant husband who was stationed at CCK. I can't remember his name, but as Squadron Executive Officer (XO), I had to counsel anyone who was planning on getting married, advise them on the wicked ways of the world and sign an official permission paper before they could apply for benefits from the Air Force for now having a family. I told him he was crazy for wanting to marry this well known, even notorious, bar girl, or "hostess." He sat at my desk and explained his reason in confidence, which has remained in confidence all these years. This attractive woman, perhaps the most well-known and successful hostess in the "Dirty Dozen," had offered him $40,000 American Dollars to marry her and take her Stateside when he rotated back to the United States. After that, a quick divorce and all would be good. A plus was the fact that he was about ready to rotate back to the States upon completion of his tour in about a month. Though I didn't care for the situation, my guidelines for approving potential marriages had been met, so I signed the papers. This bar girl would soon be an American citizen in San Diego.

Then fate stepped in. Because the entire 374th Tactical Airlift Wing with its three C-130E squadrons was unexpectedly and suddenly being forced to leave our beloved CCK and move to family friendly Clark AB because of the Mao/Nixon alliance, the Lieutenant was extended for a year because he was now accompanied by a wife. It seems so strange how fate has a way of jumping up and biting you in the ass when you least expect it. But all that was in the distant past. The last time I saw this woman, she looked like stuff warmed over. Actually, she looked more like thirty miles of bad road and was looking for a ride to the Club. I declined to offer her a ride. There was just something about her and her situation that made me want to maintain my distance from her. But, every so often, all these years later, I wonder what ever happened to her. As I said, though, that is all in the past. Now it was time to hit the VFW and my favorite: The Fire Empire.

Dave, Bud & I opted to go out the Freedom Gate and venture to the Fire Empire, a small club with wide wooden picnic tables just outside the gate. I had frequented this place when I was stationed here, for a beer and a little entertainment with the indigenous population. When the Jitney (an old WW II jeep that was way overly decorated, but basically the only means of transportation in Angeles City) dropped us off at the Fire Empire, I told Dave and Bud that, "Yep, still the same bar with what they claimed to be the coldest San Miguel beer in the city." After that first sip we decided that, true to its claim, I do believe it was the coldest beer in the city. Of course, that's not saying too much for the rest of the city. I also observed that not much inside had changed either. Everything else going on was the same, just with a different bunch of GI's relaxing and enjoying the end of the workday. To Bud & Dave's surprise, free samples were still being given, but the one thing everyone agreed on was that San Miguel was the best beer in the world. Especially when it was cold!

We hung around the Fire Empire for a little while then the VFW and a couple more nameless bars. Everything was emptying out when someone hollered "Last Call." I said, "Hey guys, I forgot they have a very serious curfew at 11:00. We'd best get our asses in a jitney and get to the Freedom Gate." That curfew was a serious law. They would gladly shoot you if you were caught out after the strictly enforced deadline. I guess it was called the Freedom Gate because there was a military cemetery right inside the gate. It always looks so solemn in the moonlight. Once again I chastised myself for not ever visiting the cemetery when I had lived there. Though cutting it too close, we made it to the gate in time. There were many Philippine Army personnel with rifles showing, positioned in very obvious positions. Fernando Marcus was still very much in charge and his goons were still making sure that it stayed that way.

We immediately caught a base cab back to the "White Elephant." Fortunately, we all had purchased our gallon of duty free booze so we could have a couple nightcaps. It should be a fairly easy flight tomorrow, bypassing Guam and going direct to Wake Island, one of my favorite old haunts. As I said, it *should* be an easy flight, but our record for easy flights was not sterling.

CLARK AB, PHILIPPINES TO BIRMINGHAM, ALABAMA, USA

"I didn't recognize any of the other stuff"

"The LORAN Died a Little Short of Wake Island"

We got off the ground the next day a little after noon. This late departure was to allow for flying against the sun, and would allow us to arrive Wake Island in daylight while Tony had the Drifters' Reef open for business. It would be like old times!

I guess the last time I had spent time on Wake Island was in "Old Shakey," the faithful C-124 which was basically retired now. Other than losing (it quit working) one of the black boxes that I really didn't know how to operate anyway, we were in good shape. I had become a little more familiar with the Doppler and I could actually get a fix on the Loran 'C' though I didn't trust the results I came up with, especially when it didn't agree with Doppler. The LORAN died just short of Wake Island anyway, so it was just one more "black box" I didn't have to be concerned with. I was feeling pretty good about things when we got to Wake Island in fair shape. Only two more overwater legs to go on this nightmare! And, I felt even better when we made it to the Drifters' Reef, the beachside bar. But it wasn't the same. Tony was no longer the bartender. I had spent so much time at the "Reef" that Tony knew me well enough from over the seven and a half years of overnight stays here, sometimes staying for up to ten days at a time, that he asked me to be the godfather of their upcoming baby. After finding out I could become legally responsible for him, I declined the nice invitation. Also missing was probably the worlds' longest running, non-stop poker game. I'd always rather sit at the bar and sip my martinis with one of my favorite pilots, "Martini" Jim Cannon or Tom Kuhns or scotch with our chief navigator at the 28th MATS (Military Air Transport Service), "Whiskey" Bob Wilson. He actually did a "soft shoe shuffle" in the middle of the Travis AFB, CA, Officers' Club dining room to his own made up song he was singing about navigating, on my first instruction flight with him. I didn't know what to do except sit and stare. I couldn't find a hole to crawl into! Do you get the idea here? It was just that way in those days. Drink on the ground and crew rest in the airplane bunks. If you missed "Happy Hour" on Friday, on the following Monday, the Boss would ask you where you were on Friday. You virtually had to drink to get anywhere in this man's Air Force in those days. I evidently thought that if I drank twice as much, it would help me twice as much. Check the credits: Major O'Connor, not Lt Col O'Connor. No, it wasn't the excessive drinking and partying that went on at Hill AFB in Mormon Utah, that I remain a Major. I am where I am in rank because a boss at MAC HQ red-lined me which meant I could not be promoted above current grade, so Major it is and, ya know? I've kinda gotten used to it. What I really consider though, is that I've never been happier in my life. Had I been promoted, I would have had to transfer to another duty station and would have stayed in the Air Force much longer. Who knows where I would be now and if I would be happy? Nope, I'll take what I have and enjoy it. As you read this historical novel, you will notice that a far greater power was watching over me and led my life to be what it is. A combination of my moving to Oklahoma last year and finding these wonderful men and women at The Military History Center and a young publisher joining the group at about the same time. Can you say Devine Intervention? I have come to the conclusion that a higher power kept me alive through these many near brushes with death to "pen" this tome. I only pray that I am doing it justice. But now, my concern is. If He is keeping me alive to write this book, what happens when I am through writing?

RB-57 TEST FLIGHT, EMERGENCY LANDING #2
BIRMINGHAM, AL INT'L AIRPORT
SPRING — 1977 OR 1978

"Tippy Toe Flying"

Before I explain about another RB-57 that obviously didn't like me, I'll take you through some more fun times in that "Bat plane."

One other fun thing we did, after we would dip into Oxmoor Valley, out of sight of the Birmingham Control folks and turn off the IFF, was to climb up high and then dive down pretending to bomb the dam at Lake Smith, a large body of water north, northwest of Birmingham. We wiped out that dam so many times, it is a wonder that it is still standing. Nothing like a good high-altitude approach and then a screaming (simulated) dive bombing run on a local landmark. I would imagine we may have scared more than a few fishermen on shore or out in a boat when a strange looking and even stranger sounding noise converter (we converted jet fuel to noise) came screaming, and I mean screaming, out of nowhere, suddenly flying over your position about five hundred feet above only to disappear into the valley beyond the dam, never to be seen again unless you may be out there on another of our dam busting flights. I don't know if I have ever thought about causing more than one fisherman to dive into the water when he heard these two screaming engines passed over him at low level, and we *did* low level. What would you do? I'm not really sure what I would do or how I would react. I never gave it a thought at the time. I was just hanging on and smiling! Sometimes, we would do a couple barrel rolls as we went by. Normally, the fisher guys would be looking up because they heard our approach about half a second before we arrived, sounding like the devils from hell were screaming at them! I really wonder what happened when one of these fisher people saw us coming at them fast and low. I'd guess that we ruined (or made) someone's day each time.

These maneuvers naturally came after we would have ducked into some valley and turned off our IFF (Identification, Friend or Foe) instrument that allowed Approach Control radar to maintain contact with the aircraft. After we were though having fun or running low on fuel, we would duck into another valley, turn on the IFF so they could vector us to landing explaining that the IFF was intermittent, remember, we were Test Flight. We'd get it fixed on the ground. Because we were a test flight outfit we could get away with a lot because the Birmingham Approach Control and Tower weren't really sure exactly what we had to do to test each type aircraft we flew. We had another division who flew only KC-135's, just to confuse matters a little bit more for those folks. We didn't get that many B-57's in for test flight, so we normally took advantage when we did.

One of my favorites was to call "Smitty" in the Hayes Control Tower from my back seat position. It would go something like this, "Smitty" in the tower, this is Jack in the plane." After he responded, "Would you please call my wife in the house? Tell her we'll be by in about five minutes." "Roger, Jack in the plane, will do." With that we dropped down into Oxmoor Valley, southwest of the airport and again, our IFF was called intermittent. We would come out of the valley south of our house and start our run. She would be sitting out in front on the curb, or sometimes standing there waiting for us. Once again we were cruising at close to four hundred knots and as soon as Dave spotted her, he initiated a series of barrel rolls flying low right up the street and beyond the house in the blink of an eye. One of the last times we did this, Dave decided to go lower, A female postal employee was driving a mail truck straight down the street on which we were coming up. Seeing us headed for her at low level, she leaned out of the little truck instead of stopping. She ran over the shallow curb onto a neighbor's lawn and into his flower garden where it stopped on its own. Again, after two rolls at almost max power so the neighbors could hear us, we ducked back into Oxford Valley, turned the IFF back on, popped up and requested vectors for landing on runway 05, the normal active runway. That IFF, though never broken was blamed for many outages! My only real regret about all of these shenanigans is that I wish I could have seen them from the "outside" myself.

My second serious incident in testing a B-57 was some time after my initial flight described before. By now, my drinking buddy, bowling partner and comrade on many TDY's ferrying RB-57's to and from Malstrom AFB, Great Falls, Montana had been transferred to his dream assignment. Upon receiving promotion to Lt Col, he became the Active Duty Air Force Liaison pilot at Wisconsin Air National Guard at the Milwaukee International Airport. I have only spoken with him one time since. We had some real experiences on land and in the air!

One last tale of woe from my time in this amazing aircraft. On this particular flight, a pilot from the home base of the RB-57, Malstrom AFB, Montana, was in the front seat. The test had been uneventful with the customary single engine climbs, engine shutdowns and restarts, stalls, etc. being completed in routine fashion.

We were about 40 miles north of the airfield at about 25,000 feet above Smith Lake and were about ready to bring a safe plane back into home base when we flew past a single towering Cumulus Nimbus cloud about four miles away. Suddenly and unexpectedly, we encountered just a split second of an extreme downdraft, a high-altitude micro burst! This was similar to the "Honey Bucket" incident, but more dangerous. This downdraft caused the pilots ejection seat to come lose and slide up the ejection rails so far as to come out of the tracks and hang up on top of the rails. This was extremely dangerous because a switch on the rails initiates the full sequence required for ejection. Neither of us knew exactly what distance the seat had traveled, or had to travel to initiate this switch, but we knew the seat didn't have to travel much farther to complete the sequence, hurtling us both onto the clear spring air with only our parachutes for company.

The pilot, unfortunately, was fairly short, and the ejection seat was now hung up high enough on the ejection rails that his helmet was pressed against the canopy, and he could barely reach the rudder pedals with his toes. It was a single control configured aircraft, so I had no controls in the back seat. If I had controls, he could have given me enough instructions that I could help get this hog on the ground. But it was my choice to be a navigator, not a pilot, and had been completely satisfied with my choice coming out of OCS. I was still satisfied! But for the ending of this flight, well, it would be tippy toe flying by the pilot to get us on the ground safely. There have been plenty of times that I wish I was in the air instead of on the ground, but this time was another of those, that, "Damn, I wish I was on the ground waiting for this plane to get back down."

After declaring an emergency we immediately called Birmingham Approach Control, and after the pilot described our emergency, were given clearance for immediate return to either runway at the Birmingham Airport. All incoming and departing traffic were put in holding patterns until our emergency situation was resolved. As we closed in on home base, they turned us over to the Control Tower for final approach. While the pilot was arranging for our emergency return to base, I had contacted Hayes Int'l Corp (the contractor which was responsible for inspection and repair/ replacement and major overhaul of the B-57) to see just how dangerous our situation was. Their experts hit the manuals, and came up with the comforting answer that they were not sure, but the seat had to be very close to the initiation switch. With this information, we had to make the decision of whether to eject now at a time and location of our choosing and let the plane crash, or to ride it in and take the chance of a zero altitude ejection, which were virtually always fatal with this ejection system. I understand that a few had survived with life changing injuries.

While discussing our options, we discussed what could happen if we chose to eject. First of all, we were not sure if the proper sequence would occur. Proper ejection sequence is as follows: Either crewmember can pull the ejection handle to initiate the ejection. The canopy is fired upward away from the aircraft, then the rear seater always goes first and in a split second, the pilot follows. Hopefully, the vertical stabilizer will miss both crewmembers. That upright piece of the stabilizer at the rear of the airplane had killed many, especially the back seater. The artillery shell just couldn't get the Guy In Back (GIB), high enough quickly enough to clear the oncoming vertical stabilizer. A later Martin-Baker Rocket Ejection System solved this bothersome little problem.

One other consideration was that we did not know if the seats were shot from the cockpit by an artillery type shell or by the newer and safer rocket propelled ejection system. If the sequence gets fouled up and the pilot ejects first, his rocket or shell blast will burn the back seater to death. Not a good option from my perspective. Another consideration was that even if the sequence worked perfectly, now that the front seat was off the rails, which way would the pilot be propelled? He could end up looking like a Roman Candle. This was not a good option for the pilot.

Our only choice was to ride it out and try to get this hog safely on the ground. Hopefully, with a nice soft landing, the only viable option.

With its over large "bat wing," the B-57 had a tendency to "float" and the pilot, even with the "rakes" extended, had to force it onto the runway and keep it there. The rakes were a series of square metal spike like devices that rose out of the top of each wing about six inches to break the airflow and thus, help to cut down on the floating effect. This normally made for a relatively hard landing, which was the norm for this plane. This time, the pilot had to overcome the extra lift of the big wings in order to make a smooth landing, because a rough landing could possibly initiate the ejection sequence. Previous Ground Level Ejections from the RB-57 had resulted in approximately 100% fatalities. We didn't care for the odds, but the RB-57 also had the reputation, from its action in Vietnam, of killing the crew, especially the back-seater (me), by hitting them with the vertical stabilizer when the crew ejected, as mentioned. What great choices!

We elected to take our chances on a smooth, gentle landing. The pilot was the best they had at his home base, so I knew that if I were to go, I'd be going out with the best. Having received clearance for emergency landing (the tower had cleared all airspace around the Birmingham Airport) they gave us the choice of landing on runway 05 or 23. It was the same runway, just coming from different directions.

We chose to land on 05 because 23 had small hills short of the runway and 05 was basically free of obstacles for a long, low approach to final, which would, hopefully, contribute to a smooth landing.

The final decisions having been made (primarily by the pilot) we said a quick prayer and began the approach. Because the pilot was busy landing the plane, I continued praying for both of us! The approach and landing were very smooth and with a cautious sigh of relief, we were on the ground safely and rolling out with light braking action, followed by a slew of emergency vehicles, to a gentle stop at the end of the runway. We didn't want to hit ANY switches, so rather than opening the canopy electronically and hydraulically we sat very quietly and waited for the ground crew from Hayes Int'l Corp to crank the canopy manually from an outside access port. After it was raised sufficiently high enough for egress, the pilot instructed me to carefully crawl out first so that, if he triggered his seat, I would not be in the rear seat, which would eject a split second before the front seat. The pilot carefully slid over the side and followed me to safety and terra firma. The hard quiet tarmac had never felt so good.

Since I am writing this episode, it is obvious we were able to exit the aircraft safely. I have no idea how they solved the problem of de-arming the front seat, but inspection for the missing pin that holds the seat to the rails, which had been overlooked by the Periodic Depot Maintenance crew, became a vital part of a new preflight checklist. The RB-57 was such a great aircraft, sometimes. I think of it often and miss seeing that silhouette in the air! I really don't miss being on a test flight with it. I do not remember how many test flights I flew in that scary airplane, but I figure I was almost killed by it least once in every eight flights. An 87.5% safe rate is not good, even for a test crew! It was one of the most construed love/hate relationships I was ever forced into. I'll not miss that aspect of that beauty!

12 Fallen POWs Flown From Hanoi

(Continued From Page 1)

Military officials would not estimate how long it would be before the studies are completed, families and the public are notified and the remains are sent home for burial.

There still was no word on when the North Vietnamese would give back the remains of 11 other men they have reported as having died in captivity, and one B52 crewman reported to have died in the crash of his plane.

The U.S. military lists 1,190 servicemen still missing in action in the Indochina war and about 1,250 more as dead with bodies not recovered.

"I fervently hope that this is the beginning of a breakthrough," said Brig. Gen. Joseph H. Ulatoski of Stamford, Conn., head of the Thailand-based Joint Casualty Resolution Center who flew to Hanoi in charge of the recovery delegation.

The turnover "went very smoothly," Ulatoski said, but he did not know when there might be more progress toward finding and repatriating the other Americans dead in Vietnam.

It took place in a simple ceremony in a tent at the secluded end of Hanoi's Gia Lam airfield. The North Vietnamese turned over death certificates and personal effects of each man.

The Viet Cong's provisional revolutionary government has cited "security" and other reasons for refusing to permit body recovery expeditions in its territory.

A spokesman for the Army's identification laboratory here said experts can make a positive identification from as little as a fragment of skull or jaw. The spokesman said the remains of each of the 12 would be studied painstakingly.

"Before any paperwork is forwarded we have to be 100 per cent sure that we have identified that individual correctly," the spokesman said.

All articles in this attachment are from the Stars and Stripes, 8 March 74, except the article below, which is from the Philippine Flyer, 15 March 74.

374th returns prison dead

The remains of 12 U.S. military people who died in captivity have been turned over to the United States by the Democratic Republic of Vietnam.

Hanoi announced plans for the reparation on Mar. 4. Representatives of the Joint Casualty Resolution Center in Nakhon Phanom, Thailand, and the Four Power Joint Military Team in Saigon flew to Hanoi Mar. 6 to accept the bodies.

Airlift was by two 374th Tactical Airlift Wing C-130 Hercules aircraft temporarily out of U-Tapao Royal Thai Navy Airfield, Thailand. Col. Albert Navas, vice commander of the Clark-based unit served as mission commander.

At the signing of the Paris agreement last year, the North Vietnamese and the People's Revolutionary Government reported that 20 U.S. personnel died in captivity: 23 in North Vietnam and 32 in South Vietnam. Of the 16 U.S. Air Force men who were reported to have died in captivity, 13 were in North Vietnam and three in the Republic of Vietnam.

Of the 16 Air Force men who died in captivity, eight were identified by the North Vietnamese as being among the 12 bodies turned over to the United States. Positive identification will be made at the Central Identification Laboratory in Thailand before the remains are flown back to the United States for burial.

The eight men identified by the North Vietnamese as Air Force men who died in captivity are:

Col. Edward B. Burdett, Maj. Earl G. Cobeil, Maj. William C. Deihl, Col. Benjamin B. Newsom, Col. Gene T. Pemberton, Col. Norman Schmidt, Lt. Col. Ronald E. Storz and Capt. Robert L. Weskamp.

ADDENDUM

That mission to retrieve those who *Died In Captivity* was the most important mission of my Air Force career and will probably end up being the most emotional, important, satisfying and yet, most traumatic thing I have ever done in my entire life. I thank God I was able to be there.

Seven days later, March 13th the 61sth TAS retrieved eleven more of our Heroes. The mission encountered no problems. These twenty-three are the only prisoners known to have died in captivity while in Hanoi area prisons.

Uniform worn by Maj Jack O'Connor at the transfer of remains.

INTRODUCTION TO SPEECH GIVEN
IN BROKEN ARROW, OKLAHOMA

I am not a speaker. Never have been, never will be.

A ceremony honoring the seven students of Broken Arrow High School who lost their lives in the Vietnam War was going to be held on March 15, 2018. I was fairly new to Broken Arrow and the Military History Center having moved from Colorado Springs the previous May. I discovered a home in the Military History Center in June of that year and have maintained an almost daily relationship since.

They were looking for a speaker for the ceremony on fairly short notice when they realized I had taken part in one of the most important missions of the Vietnam War. I was the lead Navigator on a two ship C-130E flight which had the honor of repatriating the first twelve of our heroes back to the United States.

They never asked if I was a speaker and I never told them I was not, so it happened that I was given the honor of speaking to the families of those students who had given their all. There were two widowed parents there, both in their nineties. I toned my story down out of deference to their sensibilities. This was the story I relayed.

DIED IN CAPTIVITY
KILLED IN ACTION FAMILIES
BROKEN ARROW, OKLAHOMA MARCH 15, 2018

Speech Given To Honor The Lives Lost in Vietnam

Good evening, folks. I am almost eighty-four years old and like all old men, I have a story to tell. Maybe two. And though this evening is dedicated to honor those of you who have lost a loved one either killed in action in Vietnam, I want to tell you of a group of virtual kindred spirits. A group that parallels your story. Same time. Same war. Same result. The loss of life in Vietnam.

Like your loved ones, these men made the ultimate sacrifice for their country. It just took their families a little longer to discover just how much of a loss they had suffered. These are the families of those heroes who were captured. These are the heroes who eventually died while in captivity in the stinking, rat-infested prisons of North Vietnam.

To say they were mal-nourished would be a gross understatement. Even emaciated couldn't quite describe their condition. These heroes had been beaten, starved and tortured at the hands of their Viet Cong and North Vietnamese captors until they finally and blessedly yielded their lives to their God! Their families did not have someone walk up to the door to announce the tragedy. Most of these families were notified by a telegram beginning with the dreaded, "We regret to inform you…." It was an impersonal and almost insulting salutation that rips apart the strongest heart. It was normally followed by, "Your son has been listed as being Missing In Action as a result of enemy activity." Or some similar statement. In the absence of any credible evidence otherwise, the Missing In Action (MIA) family members remain in bereavement limbo. Almost literally stuck in time and unable to go forward. The initial shock of not knowing if their loved ones were dead or alive led to an unbridled, complexity of feelings. It was an emotional hell. They could

not grieve completely nor could they relax. They could not celebrate nor could they give up. Their emotions ricocheted between
the hope of seeing their loved ones again and the dread of the alternative. They could and did cry and pray. Other than that, they were
locked in an interminably hellacious, never-ending nightmare. The
families had to wait in anguished anticipation, never knowing....
never knowing!

The Missing In Action status is unique in that the loss is not
final. There is no certainty of death nor of life. No "physical body"
to identify or mourn over. For all the world, they were listed only as
"Missing In Action." And for all the world, except for family, mostly quickly forgotten.

I cannot tell you how their stories began in this seemingly endless war, but I can tell you about how the story ended for twelve of
these heroes.

I'll start in the very early morning at U Tapao Air Base in Southern Thailand about two hundred miles south of Bangkok on March
6, 1974. This base was the Forward Operating Location for B-52
bombers, KC-135 Refuelers and our own C-130 Cargo/Passenger
planes. Because of time restraints, I will skip most of the preparations for our flight and just hit a few highlights.

First, close your eyes and imagine a moonless night on the
southern tip of Thailand. OK, ya there? It was just after midnight. It
was dark. It was hot. It was eerie. And it was time. The Klongs were
stinking more than usual and the normally rowdy crew was silent.
We were all lost in thought. The mission was shrouded in mystery.
We didn't even know our ultimate destination!

The mystery had deepened even more when we were instructed
to bring our Class A uniforms with us. Class A's, though not formal,
were the blue uniforms with full ribbons and aircrew wings worn
for special occasions like a surrender of an airbase to the enemy.

Then, to make things worse, just before they pulled the door
shut, they boarded an Army One Star General who was listed only
as a passenger. That was really strange. But we figured that as long

as he was just a passenger and stayed out of our way in the cargo area, even an Army Brigadier General couldn't screw up the mission too much!

Aircrews hated mystery and unknowns. We liked to know what was going on with our airplane. This time, we didn't have time to worry after going through the normal checklists. We were airborne at about 0300 hours with a second olive drab C-130E following in loose formation. After arrival at Ton Son Nhut Air Base in Saigon and as they topped off our fuel, we finally got the word.

We would be going up north to Hanoi, the capitol of North Vietnam! We would be retrieving the first of those who died in captivity. We broke into grins and a few "thumbs up!" Remember, this was way before high fives had been invented.

But, quickly, the mood in the room sobered when we received the weather briefing. Instead of the hot, dry and dusty we always hoped for, it was....good luck! It would be pretty good weather until we hit the coast of North Vietnam. From there, it was solid clouds up to fifteen thousand feet from the coast on past Hanoi. Even worse, the forecast for Hanoi's Gia Lam International Airport was for a five hundred foot ceiling. That was pretty close to the three hundred foot minimum required for landing. In my mind, we would go in anyway. I had busted minimums before doing airborne radar approaches when it was absolutely necessary, but it had to be extremely important. This mission fit that criteria. We were going in and only the flight crew needed to know! We were willing to do whatever was necessary to get our guys out of North Vietnam!

After we turned inland and crossed the coastline at the negotiated ten thousand foot altitude, we started going up the Red River. The weather deteriorated rapidly. As advertised, except this was even worse than expected. In seconds, we immediately went from a beautiful, sunny day into a dark, foreboding, solid wall of clouds with light turbulence. Now it was just us and my radar.

Haiphong Harbor lay about forty miles off our right wing tip as we were getting ready to turn left over Thuan Nghiep for our final run to Gia Lam Airport just northeast of Hanoi. I gave the pilot heading three hundred thirty-eight degrees and asked him to start a shallow descent. Oh, yes, we had the navigational aids from the ground stations around Hanoi, but there was no way I was going to use them. I had learned well from my earlier two trips the previous month. They had tried many times and ways to get us lost while flying in toward Hanoi. In this weather, it would be easier for them to do and as far as I knew, I was the only one from either crew to have been to Hanoi. That was one reason why I was picked to be Lead Navigator on the "Pathfinder" aircraft. The second aircraft was the "Recovery" aircraft. That would be the plane which would take our heroes back home.

Colonel Navas, the Mission Commander, also knew I was very proficient with radar approaches. He knew I had performed several in Vietnam and Cambodia. He also knew that I was a graduate of ten months of intensive radar training at the Air Force B-52 and B-47 Navigator/Bombardier School at Mather Air Force Base. It's the toughest school I had ever attended. I had already briefed the crew that we would be running into bad information from the various aircraft control agencies around Hanoi. I wanted the crew to ignore them. We would get the job done without them or in spite of them.

Then it started. The Vietnamese started changing locations of their various navigation aids. But, as planned, we would be going solely by my radar navigation. Hanoi Approach Control started fussing at us for being off course. Then Giam Lam Tower came on instructing us to turn to heading 022 for final approach to Gia Lam Airport. The pilot began his turn and I virtually screamed into the intercom, "NEGATIVE, NEGATIVE, NEGATIVE. MAINTAIN HEADING!" Yeah, it woke the pilots up, too!

They had given us the correct heading, but it was about nine minutes too soon. They tried that three times. They were trying their best to get us lost and confused. The second aircraft was hanging on, flying in tight formation, keeping track of us on their station keeping radar. We were their ticket to Hanoi. Approach Control tried their best to fool us in many ways and once threatened to have us shot down! We told them they were still coming in garbled and that we would continue approach as instructed earlier. We felt pretty sure and hoped that they were bluffing about the shoot down part. Colonel Navas told our pilot to ignore them and go by my instructions only. We were going to get this mission done our way!

Gia Lam Tower finally gave up trying to get us to turn early, but only after many loud and probably profane scolding's. Now, flying at seven hundred feet, we could occasionally see the Red River below. A quick break in the clouds gave us a glimpse ahead. I could see some bridges! I had the pilot descend to about five hundred feet so I could get a visual on more of my landmarks to confirm our location. Then there was a short break in the clouds. Now I knew it was the Paul Doumer and Long Bien bridges and the huge sand bar in the Red River that I needed. We were right on track. I timed our turn for eighteen seconds past the sandbar. I told the Aircraft Commander to make a blind turn to heading 022 degrees and to start a shallow descent for landing. We broke out of the overcast a few seconds later at a little below four hundred feet. There it was, the Gia Lam runway, elevation fifty feet. We had arrived! I strapped myself in and with a sigh of relief, I turned the aircraft back over to the pilots. The recovery aircraft radioed a "Tally Ho" and we were both cleared for landing.

After touchdown and rollout, Gia Lam Tower instructed us to taxi to a remote area of the ramp. For the first time, we saw where our guys were patiently waiting for us. There were two olive drab tents that were far away from any building. Many North Vietnamese soldiers were around them. The Ground Marshalling Crew took over from the Tower. They brought us just short of the tents. As the Army Brigadier General and his team went to meet with his North Vietnamese counterparts, Colonel Navas sized up the situation. He assigned a tent to each aircraft. He instructed us to set up an Honor Guard in front of each tent. Of course, after landing, we had *changed into our more formal Class A uniforms before exiting the aircraft.*

Colonel Navas and our pilot were the first to stand guard at "our tent." We could see from the cockpit that they were stunned at what they saw and what we would all later see as we took our turns.

Major Soloman and I were next. They had no chance to warn us. I wish they had! The tent flaps were tied completely open and as we assumed our Honor Guard positions, we were....I don't know what words to use. Shocked? Outraged? Actually, there were no words.

We finally saw our murdered comrades. There they were in two stacks of basic, sage green wooden boxes which measured roughly thirty inches by eighteen inches by eighteen inches. Think about it for a moment. That length of thirty inches is less than a yard stick! Thirty inches is basically four inches longer than an adult femur. Folks, that is a thigh bone! Yes! A stinking thighbone! Do ya know what else it is? It is the approximate length of a human spine. It is the length of a human spine. A human spine without the head! Think of what they may have had to have done to get a martyred hero into that condition. What did they have to do? We could barely begin to think about that. It's best that we didn't. We put our professional feelings before our real ones and soldiered on! We held parade rest positions for fifteen minute intervals for over two and one-half hours facing those green boxes and thinking about what was inside. Damn! A little green box!

Each box was accompanied by a rock, a plain rock which had the name of the victim and the date of death written on it in white paint. As the North Vietnamese soldiers looked on with puzzled amazement, we continued performing Honor Guard duty until the General and his entourage came back from signing the final release papers in downtown Hanoi. Then, after a ten-minute joint ceremony, they completed the exchange of our heroes from their control to ours.

At that juncture, we were given the OK to begin the process of boarding our silent passengers. The North Vietnamese soldiers immediately stepped forward to help us with the boarding. We also stepped forward immediately toward them and formed a cordon between the armed guards and our waiting passengers. We motioned with head and hand gestures that they should come no closer to our men. They stopped with a puzzled look on their faces, but never tried to cross the line. Somehow, they understood that we were serious and they never challenged us. It was probably just as well. We were flat certain and they got the message:

They had touched our heroes for the last time.

Now it was time to return them to United States soil. In this case, it was to our Recovery C-130 aircraft. Abandoning the Honor Guard in front of the tents, General Ulatowski and Colonel Navas stood on either side of the cargo ramps with other crew members alongside to form another Honor Guard. I was part of three pairs of crewmen who would gently lift a now sacred green box, remove it from the tent and reverently carry it up the ramp of the Recovery aircraft. We were followed by another crewman bearing the rock. The head marker. It was their headstone!

The General called for a "Hand Salute" as we started up the ramp. It was held until he called "Order" as we entered the bay of the C-130. Inside the aircraft, two more crewmen relieved us of our precious cargo and tied them in real coffins. Each coffin had already been tied down. Now closed, it would be draped with an American flag. We would exit through the crew entrance door to recover another hero. This continued until all twelve of our patriots had been recovered and secured in the aircraft. We took our time to insure that all of our fallen heroes were properly cared for. We felt proud knowing that each former Prisoner of War was honored by what we were doing. This was the most precious cargo this aircraft would ever hold.

Our guys were back on American soil in the cargo deck of an American aircraft. After the final hero had been placed on board, been properly secured and draped, we cranked engines and began to make preparations to depart Gia Lam.

As we were getting all four engines churning, the Aircraft Commander contacted the Gia Lam Control Tower to get ready. The Ground Marshals were still in charge and they gave us the signal to start rolling. As they motioned for us to turn, we each got a smile on our faces. We needed something light on this somber occasion.

For some reason, the Ground Control folks were turning us in a direction opposite our arrival. Our prop wash would soon be aimed directly at the now empty tents. We all smiled as we listened on a discreet frequency while our Aircraft Commander contacted the second ship and pointed out the obvious. You could hear the joy in the response. Both planes turned as one and as the prop wash hit the tents, full pitch was applied for just an instant. While we continued our turn, we saw those tents, a bunch of big military hats and quite a few of the smaller former guardians of our fallen comrades flying and/or rolling across the Gia Lam tarmac. Things really went flying! It was a dusty, but a fitting end to our visit. Yep, we had done that one little thing in an act of revenge so our guys could show the "American wave" to their former captors. We reduced pitch and taxied to hold short of runway 02.

Now on the way back to U Tapao, the Recovery aircraft would be the lead aircraft and we would remain on the ground until we were sure that our fallen comrades were well on their way and we were certain that they could make the return to U Tapao without having any problems. As soon as we got the OK from the Recovery aircraft and Gia Lam Tower, we taxied into position and began our takeoff roll for my third and last time down runway zero two, heading home.

After takeoff, we requested and obtained permission for an unrestricted climb. I think they were as happy to be rid of us as we were to get on our way. Turning in a right bank, we began our climb to twenty-eight thousand feet and headed back down the Red River.

Our fallen warriors were in the Recovery aircraft about twenty-two minutes ahead. They had crossed the coastline.

General Ulatowski, still with an open line to the White House, informed President Nixon directly that the recovery of our brave Americans who died in captivity had been performed in a completely honorable and professional manner. President Nixon asked the General to pass on the message "Job well done." I must admit those three words sounded pretty damned good.

The silent passengers continued non-stop to U Tapao Air Base. There they were taken to the General's Joint Casualty Resolution Center. From there, our patriots would go on to Hickam Air Force Base, Hawaii for further identification as necessary.

Now, with your indulgence, another real short story. When I was attending our forty-fifth anniversary of graduation from Officer Candidate School, one of my former classmates came over to me at our dinner table. He said his wife wanted to speak to me. Of course, I wondered what kind of trouble I was in now. It turned out that she just wanted to thank me. Her first husband had been on that first flight. We both cried, holding each other.

HEROES FLOWN HOME

January 31, 2019

They waited for us to arrive
Their souls had gone ahead
The one they carried when alive
Had left when they were dead

But still we came through fog and rain
We came to take them home
They didn't have to wait in vain
Best mission ever flown

From the Hanoi Hilton where they died
Which was empty now for good
Eleven more were waiting too
We'd have taken them if we could

They were waiting in a box so small
It damned near seemed obscene
That they had brutally killed them all
Then put them in boxes of green

We took them from that foreign soil
The soil on which they died
Took them from hell were they had toiled
Our mission flown with pride

We flew them from North Vietnam
To finally top the crest
Far from their death cells all so damned
Our Heroes were at rest

We flew them from that place with pride
Far from their living hell
They flew in peace from where they died
To heaven where their souls dwell

We took them to a place so far
To a place they'd never known
Yes, we took them to a place so far
With God's help, we took them Home!

John E. "Jack" O'Connor
Major, USAF, Retired

CLOSINGS

"Leaving Wreckage in My Wake"

I was sitting around talking with some of my Docent friends at the Military History Center in Broken Arrow just a few days ago about various parts of my career and how, no matter where I was stationed, the particular outfit or squadron in which I was stationed or even school I attended seemed to close while I was there or not too long thereafter.

I began thinking and the more I thought of it, I began to think of the old comic strip character "Joe Btfspik. He was a little character in the now defunct comic strip called "L'il Abner." I still miss those old comic strips and hated seeing them go away. He always went around with a dark cloud permanently hovering over his head and always raining down upon him. Not the luckiest person in the world as I considered myself to be. Joe never recovered from his misfortune. I always came out smelling like a rose or at least a thorny flower!

Even my whining about being Red Lined and thus being passed over for promotion turned out to be one of the best things that ever happened to me. Without that vengeful act, I just don't know where I would be. I wouldn't be among my "brothers" at the Military History Center and that is where I belong!

I was always one to believe that everything happened for a purpose. I just couldn't figure out the purpose until that fateful day in May, or maybe was it June, when I walked into that little museum on Main Street in Broken Arrow. Ya see, if I had been promoted to Lieutenant Colonel, I would have been transferred to another duty station and not only my life would have been changed, but the lives of my entire nuclear family would have been affected. It would be senseless to speculate in how many different ways, but suffice to say, we all would have taken different courses.

And now, back to my closings. I was quite surprised when I was passed over for the first time in 1976, but the second time? Well, it kind of boggled my mind, but I was either too weak or too dumb to follow up on it and challenge it, even though I was the only one in my age group who wasn't selected on the second go around!

I was going to be transferred to Dyess AFB in Abilene Texas. Now, there is a pretty good country and western song about Abilene, but at the time, it was a dry city in a dry county and that didn't bode well for my particular lifestyle.

I also would have been that old passed over Major" in the Navigator Section that just couldn't quite hack the program and couldn't figure out why. I had seen that type before along the way and I did not want to be seen in that light. Ergo, I declined the United States Air Force's kind offer and submitted my retirement papers, thus ending my inglorious career with no goal in life but to stay in Bluff Park, Alabama where I had become comfortable and complacent.

However, if you ever want to get complacency and comfort knocked out of your life, just wake up some morning and see that your take home pay had been reduced by two-thirds! That, my friends, is an attention getter! Ya see, I had not worried about putting anything away for retirement. I knew I was going to stay in the Air Force forever and just didn't give it another thought. Soon, I found myself pounding the pavement looking for a job. I had some pretty lucrative ones lined up with various companies like AT&T, Golden Flake Potato Chips and a few others, but they all fell through for one reason or another, including computerization.

I did do very well selling siding and roofing for a friend, but I really didn't want to do that sort of measuring, etc. in the bad weather elements. "Hmmm," I thought, Maybe I was not cut out to be a civilian. Maybe I should have stayed in the Air Force as that old "passed over Major" after all. At least, I would be drawing a fatter paycheck than I was now. I guess I should have been more studious in preparing for retirement than just having a good time as I rolled along life's merry way!

The reason for losing almost two-thirds of my paycheck is that I lost my flight pay, my housing allowance and my rations allowance.

Beyond that, I was drawing only fifty-five percent of my active duty base pay. I thought about how nice it would be to be an old "passed over Major" drawing full flight pay and all of those other entitlements. Besides, a gold leaf should be worth more than a silver leaf. I never did figure out the logic in that one. However, that horse had left the barn. Now I was a bit like a new babe in the woods. My six years plus as an enlisted man made me old even in chronologic years among my peers though it did help me with my pay and many other ways. I discovered that I could sell.

Now to get back to my original premise. I want to tell you about these "closings" in chronological order so come back with me to the not too thrilling days of yesteryear.

After a very stable enlisted career of over six years, things started to come undone. My flying career and indeed, my commissioning seemed to herald the beginning of a long trail of destruction or closings of squadrons and even Officer Candidate School (OCS) itself. I entered OCS on March 17, 1960. OCS closed exactly three years after I graduated in Class 60C. Class 63C was the last class to graduate. The last few classes produced a few Full Colonels and even some Generals. My class produced one. His name was Colonel Kevin "Mike" Gilroy of Wild Weasel fame.

The Colonel Mike Gilroy Award is given to the top graduate of the Air Force EWO School,

One of the full Colonels from 63C, Colonel Chuck Ulmer and my OCS Classmate Lieutenant Colonel Forrest Bennett, somehow sought me out and apprised me of a bogus writing of my wondrous trip to Hanoi, North Vietnam. I'll be forever grateful for their efforts to seek me out so I could put forth the correct version. The bogus version appeared to be one of my early drafts, but I still have no idea how it escaped my computer.

It was those two gentlemen who set me onto this great military flight website: www.aircrewremembered.com. It is operated by two landlocked Irish Brothers who operate this site out of London, England, and it was they who delivered to the world, the correct version of my mission and a wonderful music video, "Thanks to You" released by Irlene Mandrell honoring all of our veterans. Guess who the old guy is in the video, who had the honor of wearing an old Navy flight jacket once worn by the Mandrel sisters' grandfather. Thanks to you, gentlemen and Irlene!

After OCS, we motored south to my ten-month Navigator School. It was conducted at Harlingen AFB, Harlingen Texas, about sixty miles north of Brownsville, Texas and Matamoras, Mexico. It was from here that I began to be aware of closings. Harlingen AFB closed on the sixth of June 1962, one year after I graduated from the school.

I began the hardest school of my life in June of 1961. I still have scars from Navigator Bombardier (Nav/Bomb) School at Mather AFB, California in Southeast Sacramento. Mather AFB was decommissioned on 30 September 1993. I have no idea when or where they moved the school and I really couldn't care less! California is still there!

Then on to Survival school at Stead AFB which is about twenty miles north of Reno, Nevada. The schooling lasted three weeks total, one of which was a week from hell, in a simulated North Vietnamese Prison Camp. They made it as realistic as they could, short of torture. And, yes, I was water boarded and offered them anything thing they wanted when they got ready to do it to me again. But, no scars, so I didn't and don't consider it torture. I felt fine within seconds after they stopped me from that drowning feeling. The week long survival trek culminating at the prison camp was no jewel either! I left both OCS and Survival School with a twenty-eight inch waist and weighing one hundred twenty-six pounds after going in at a well-trimmed one hundred sixty-five pounds.

Stead AFB closed in 1966. The Survival School moved to Fairchild AFB near Spokane, Washington. Now I was through with over two years of schools and I was going onward to my line-flying career which was going to be so enjoyable, but so exciting and, in retrospect, downright dangerous. Of course, the dangerous part didn't bother any of us while we were flying. We all figured that if we had a rough flight, it would be the last rough one. But, it didn't always work out that way.

My first and arguably the best line outfit was the 48th Military Air Transport Squadron (MATS) at Hickam AFB in the new state of Hawaii, as a new 1st Lieutenant. I had left two and a half years earlier as a Staff Sergeant to attend OCS. This wonderful squadron, the 48th MATS closed on 25 June 1965. I hated to leave Hawaii again, but I had received my choice of assignments to the 28th MATS, later designated as Military Airlift Squadron (MAS) at Hill AFB, Utah.

The closure of the 48th MATS was followed by three and one half years of arguably, (I argue with myself a lot) at least as good, if not better, flying when I settled into my choice of assignments to the 28th MATS at Hill AFB just south of Ogden, Utah. It was the best-kept secret in the Air Force. What a ride! But that story would best be presented in another tome. It is just too good to be included here. Needless to say, everyone was extremely sad when the word came down that again that old saying raised its ugly, head again. The 28th closed in the spring of 1970. I had been called up to Military Airlift Command Headquarters (MAC HQ) to report in January 1970. The idiots wouldn't even let me help close the squadron even though I was the Administrative Officer and knew where the skeletons were hidden. They took me to Scott AFB in St. Clair County, Illinois for nothing!

After two and a half years of the worst assignment of my career, the bad things that needed to end came into play. I'm referring to the end of my assignment at Scott AFB and MAC HQ.

I escaped with Lieutenant Colonel Hoskins who took over as Commanding Officer of the 57th Air Rescue and Recovery Service (ARRS) at Lajes Field in the Azores, a beautiful and quaint fleet of islands about six hundred miles west of Portugal, to whom they owed their allegiance. Another great assignment! Every six weeks, I spent a week in Iceland sharing rescue duties with a crew out of Milden-hall AB in England. Great flying! I was ready to put in for a year's extension when we got blindsided. The 57th closed after I was there only eighteen months. Damn!

Then I received my Isolated Tour (one year away from family in a remote location). My assignment was one of the plums of the isolated tour locations. I spent the next seven months as the Executive Officer (XO) for the 776th Tactical Airlift Squadron (TAS) at Ching Chuan Kang (CCK) AB and lived in nearby Taichung, Taiwan.

They closed CCK because Chairman Mao of China and President Nixon became friendly and Chairman Mao demanded we withdraw all military from Taiwan which also claimed to be China and were one of our strongest allies. Because of an accommodation between their two countries, almost all of the entire CCK entity was moved to Clark AB, The Philippines. The agreed-upon move included the entire 374th Tactical Airlift Wing. Needless to say, they didn't ask me or any of the others stationed there. The 374th Tactical Airlift Wing (TAW) and the 776 Tactical Airlift Squadron (TAS) moved to Clark AB. The other two squadrons moved to Kadena AB, Okinawa which had recently been turned back over to Japanese control. With little warning, the jewel of Southeast Asia assignments, CCK, had been unceremoniously shut down! After five months of living in Angeles City, it was time to go home and on to Birmingham, Alabama. The 776th TAS closed in October of 1975, slightly a year after I had departed. I arrived at Defense Contracting Administrative Service (DCAS) Hayes, a Periodic Depot Maintenance facility in June of 1974. It closed shortly after I retired partly because I blew the whistle on our commander for taking favors from the facility and forcing us to fly unsafe planes in exchange. Hayes Corporation closed in 1978. The replacement company closed some years after.

As for me, I closed my career on June 30, 1978. I am still alive as of this writing, so that chapter is not closed.

It should be noted that in my early years, my two grade schools closed as did the Abbey School, my high school. And now, even the ranch where I grew up is gone!

Jack O'Connor being presented with the Bronze Star with "V" device at MAC HQ (Directorate of Personnel). October, 1968.

JACK AND DAUGHTERS

Pat, Michelle, and Tina

| Barbara Jean
"Bobbie" Avery
& Brenda | Brenda R.
O'Connor
Feb. 18, 1956 -
Oct. 18, 1987 | Barbara Jean
"Bobbie" Avery
Sept 18, 1936 -
Mar 29, 1995 |

POSTSCRIPT

Though my exploits have been many and varied, every aviator with thousands of flying hours, and some with but a few, has experienced episodes of fear, perhaps of the unknown or even the known. Either kind is not an emotion to be anticipated with eagerness, but to be faced, not because we want to, but because it is unavoidable. I know of no sane person who would eagerly go out of his way to feel the sensation of real fear.

Real fear is not to be confused with the nervous anticipation of some daring feat nor with the willful thrusting of one's self on a mind-bending sensation of exhilaration which, while testing the mind or resolution of a mindless or even mindful exercise of bravado or terrifying skill, knows that the final and safe resolution can rationally be anticipated.

Real fear knows no master. Real fear appears instantaneously and can be gone just as quickly, leaving the victim speechless, indeed sometimes without the capability of rational thought or action. Fear is, perhaps, the most overwhelming of any emotion. –

Jack O'Connor
February 28, 2019

"Life or death is truly determined in the blink of an eye."